WORKING
WITH PARENTS
AND INFANTS

WORKING WITH PARENTS AND INFANTS

An Interactional Approach

by
Rose M. Bromwich, Ed.D.
Department of Educational Psychology
California State University, Northridge

with contributions by
Dorothea Burge
and
Ellen Khokha

University Park Press
Baltimore

UNIVERSITY PARK PRESS
International Publishers in Science, Medicine, and Education
233 East Redwood Street
Baltimore, Maryland 21202

Composed by University Park Press, Typesetting Division.
Manufactured in the United States of America by The Maple Press Company.

Library of Congress Cataloging in Publication Data
Bromwich, Rose M.
Working with parents and infants.
Bibliography: p.
Includes index.
1. Infants. 2. Infant psychology. 3. Parent and child.
I. Burge, Dorothea, joint author. II. Khokha, Ellen, joint author. III. Title.
HQ774.B76   306.8'7   80-16141
ISBN 0-8391-1568-7

Contents

Foreword

It is with great pleasure that I write this foreword to Dr. Bromwich's book on one of the most important topics of our time, namely, helping parents and infants in their interaction with each other. As we have learned more about the competence of infants, particularly their capacity for visual, auditory, and tactile interaction with their parents, the importance of parent-infant interaction for the mental and emotional development of infants has become more apparent. Most normal infants and their parents intuitively fall into appropriate interaction processes, each advancing as the infant matures. There are, however, many ways in which this natural system can be disrupted through transient deviations in an infant's development or by a manifest handicap in the infant such as a sensory or motor inadequacy. A social disruption in the life of the family or parent may also interfere with the parents' potential to interact intuitively and normally with their infant. We now feel it is possible to be helpful to parents when there has been a breakdown in the normal interaction between the caregiver and the child through difficulties in either partner or in the mutuality of their interaction. We recognize that many of the details of normal caregiver-infant interaction are still unknown. Nonetheless, understanding the range of styles and modes of parent-infant interaction that lead to normal development, particularly in various cultural situations, is very important in planning intervention. Interventions that are not individualized for each child and family may be more harmful than helpful. Dr. Bromwich has been particularly skillful in her book in taking these variables into consideration in devising her intervention strategies.

There are few people as highly qualified as Rose Bromwich to write on this topic and in such a helpful way to all professionals working with parents and infants. She has had a wide variety of experiences with both normal and handicapped infants and preschool children. These included working with deaf children at the John Tracy Clinic Nursery School, hospitalized children at Yale University School of Nursing, disturbed and autistic children in the Los Angeles Child Guidance Clinic Observation Nursery School, and normal children in child care centers and nursery school programs. In fact, she anticipated the national Head Start programs by organizing a kindergarten enrichment project for children in an impoverished area before the national Head Start program was initiated.

Since 1972 she has been working with infants and toddlers in the Infant Studies Project of the Department of Pediatrics of the University of California at Los Angeles, full-time while on leave from her teaching position as Professor of Early Childhood Education in the Department of Educational Psychology at California State University, Northridge, and subsequently as a continuing consultant to this project. In the Infant Studies Project, intervention programs for both handicapped and normal infants and toddlers were developed within a home and center-based setting. This book is based primarily on these experiences. It is important, however, to emphasize that when Dr. Bromwich came to this program she had a wide range of experiences not only in working with normal and handicapped preschool children, but also in teaching students from a variety of disciplines the concepts of child development and their importance for helpful interactions with children. Throughout my work with Dr. Bromwich, I have always been impressed by her extraordinary intuitive skill in selecting from current research the information and concepts most relevant to clinicians and teachers. She has an unusually lucid way of organizing this subject matter for clinical application. I think the organization of this book and its contents amply illustrate this.

Dr. Bromwich presents very clearly in this well-organized text the importance of working with parents and infants through an interactional approach. I find the organization of the text extremely helpful for the understanding and ultimate application of her approach to intervention with parents and infants. She first presents the rationale for this particular approach and some guidelines for its implementation. This is followed by a discussion of the particular study in which she developed the organization and application of her model. The reader is thus prepared to analyze, with her help, specific cases that illustrate both successes and failures in intervention. Some of the unexpected, helpful understandings that came from the individual cases and also some of the pitfalls encountered in others are provided. Finally, the reader is given a list of the major problems encountered and the procedures used in dealing with these in providing intervention to the families. It is important to note that she deals mainly with problems in the social-affective, cognitive-motivational, and language areas, as they are of primary importance in her intervention program. The emphasis is on supporting the parents in their interactions with their infants. This book will be an important guide and information source for all professionals working with parents and infants.

Arthur H. Parmelee, M.D.
Professor of Pediatrics
Head, Division of Child Development
School of Medicine
University of California, Los Angeles

Preface

The purpose of this book is to introduce an approach to intervention that focuses primarily on the interactions between parents and infants. Research findings show that the quality of parent-infant interaction has a powerful impact on the development of the young child. Although interest in parent-infant interaction is growing rapidly, the aim to enhance the quality of that interaction has yet to be translated into specific goals and ideas for implementation that could be used in programs for parents and infants. This book is an attempt to achieve that task.

The book is meant to be used as a tool for teaching and learning. The reader is told in some detail about a particular process of parent-infant education and intervention, a process that was carefully and painstakingly developed and then used in a program serving infants and parents. However, the text should not be viewed as a "cookbook" approach to intervention or to parent education; in fact, one of the motivations for writing it was to counteract the "how-to-do-it" trend in the complex and rapidly growing field of infant intervention and parent education. Some individuals who enter new fields like parent-infant intervention look for prescriptions that give them "easy" answers and what is often a false sense of security. They would like to believe that all they have to do is to match the problems confronting them with similar problems presented in a book or manual and then apply the prescribed techniques to their cases. The complexity of human behavior defies such easy answers.

We believe strongly that there is no one "right" way for parents to interact with their infants, and no "best" way to help parents to become more competent in parenting. We advocate here the use of the problem-solving process. This implies that parents should gain competence in solving the problems that they encounter with their infants not by getting the "right" solution from the "expert," but by getting the kind of support, information, and encouragement that enables them to discover which solution is best for *them* and *their* infants at a particular time.

The pronoun "we" and the past tense are used deliberately, especially in Chapter 8 which contains specific suggestions for intervention, to encourage the reader to view the material presented as illustrative of how a particular staff in a program with a particular philosophy worked with its families. We make no claim to have developed the "best" strategies or

interventions for all parents and infants or for any one group of professionals working with families. In fact, it is unlikely that a specific set of
interventions or staff responses to a problem, like those listed in Chapter
8, would be applicable in its entirety to any one parent-infant dyad. (The
reader should be aware that most of the sets of interventions listed under
the problems in Chapter 8 were derived from work with several families.)
The ideas for intervention, as presented in Chapter 8, are intended to provide a framework and to establish a mode of intervention that will serve as
a springboard for creative ideas to be tried out with particular parents and
infants.

The book is divided into five parts. Part I introduces the interaction
model. Part II contains a description of the Intervention Program that
was part of the UCLA Infant Studies Project and that formed the matrix
for the development of the interaction model. The Parent Behavior Progression, an assessment tool that was developed and used in the Intervention Program, is also discussed in Part II. Part III presents in varying
detail the 30 cases that were in the Intervention Program. Part IV is a cata-
logue of specific interventions that were applied in response to specific
problems. Part V is used to reflect upon and sum up the intervention experience. More detail is given below about the content of the individual
chapters.

In the first chapter, the parent-infant interaction approach to intervention is defined within the context of three other approaches to intervention that are in wide use. Chapter 2 presents the theoretical framework
and the goals and guidelines of the Intervention Program, which reflect
the philosophy of the intervention model. Chapter 3 contains a description of the population, staffing, and procedures of the Interaction Program in which the interaction model was developed, and it also includes
discussions of assessment for intervention, of videotaping, and of program evaluation. Chapter 4 introduces the Parent Behavior Progression,
a tool that sensitizes staff to parenting behaviors. This assessment instrument has already evoked considerable interest among individuals who
work with parents and infants within a variety of disciplines.

Chapter 5 presents the cases with which intervention successfully
achieved program goals. The cases described in Chapter 6 are those in
which intervention was evaluated as partially successful or unsuccessful
with respect to their goals. The discussion of the less successful cases in
Chapter 6 may be a unique contribution to the literature on intervention.
Although it is generally agreed that one learns at least as much from
failures as from successes, even partial failures are rarely documented and
presented to the public.

Chapter 7 serves as an introduction and guide to Chapter 8. Chapter
8, the longest in the book, contains specific interventions that were used in

response to problems of parents and infants and the interaction between them.

Chapter 9 is used to reflect upon the intervention experience, summing up what we perceived to be major influences on intervention effectiveness and sharing with the reader some clinical observations regarding intervention with parents of handicapped infants. The chapter concludes with a few generalizations derived from our experience.

All of the cases in the Intervention Program, except those in the pilot phase, are discussed in Part III because every case was unique in important aspects relevant to intervention. The cases are grouped in a way that gives proper emphasis to differences as well as to similarities. The inclusion of all the cases, rather than the selection of a few, gives the reader an honest and realistic perspective of the complex situations and circumstances that were encountered in the various families. The separation between the more successful and the less successful cases serves to emphasize the factors and conditions that either helped or hindered the effectiveness of intervention.

In conclusion, this book presents *an* interactional model in some detail. It is referred to in these pages as *the* interactional model because it is the model central to this book. We do not claim, however, to have developed the only model in which parent-infant interaction is a major focus. There are programs for preschool-age children and for infants and parents in various parts of this country in which the improvement of mother-child interaction is an important instrumental goal in fostering the optimal development of the child.

The pages that follow present information drawn from both knowledge and experience. It is hoped that the content will encourage readers who are now working with parents and infants—or who plan to do so in the future—to be creative and resourceful in finding ways of enhancing parent-infant interaction and thus fostering the infant's development.

One final note about style should be called to the reader's attention. When singular pronouns were necessary in our writing in reference to a child or infant, we used the masculine form. This decision should be viewed not as discriminatory or exclusionary, but as an effort to ensure ease of reading and to avoid the repetitive introduction of awkward constructions such as he/she.

The writing of this book has meant much to me as well as to Dorothea Burge and Ellen Khokha, who did the largest portion of the work on Chapter 8 and who helped significantly by reviewing drafts of other chapters and making useful suggestions. The process of writing this book has given us a sense of closure to an experience of several years' duration which taught us much and which we thoroughly enjoyed. Arthur H. Parmelee, M.D., the director of the UCLA Infant Studies Project, gave us the opportunity to have that experience. Much time, effort, and "heart" have been invested in this book. We hope it will be both thought-provoking and of practical value to the reader.

Rose Meyer Bromwich

Acknowledgments

I want to express my special thanks to Arthur H. Parmelee, M.D., for giving me the opportunity to be a part of the UCLA Infant Studies Project. He has been the source of much knowledge, inspiration, support, and encouragement.

All of us who worked with the infants and parents in the Intervention Program owe much to E. Wallie Kass, who started the program and whose superb skill with infants and sensitivity to parents were excellent examples for us. Many of her ideas for intervention were implemented in the Intervention Program and have thus been incorporated into this book.

I also would like to express my appreciation to the other people on the intervention staff who did much of the work with the families in the program and who kept the records on which parts of this book are based: Eleanor Baxter, L. Suzanne Fust, Gloria Ruth, and Armony Share. Special thanks go to Eleanor Baxter and Sue Fust who, with Dorli Burge and Ellen Khokha, helped in the various stages of summarizing and analyzing the information gathered throughout the program.

Last, but not least, I want to express my thanks to my husband, Leo, for bearing with me as I worked throughout weekends and two summers in order to complete the book, and to my two sons, David and Michael, who have shown interest in the progress of the book and have encouraged me in various ways over the last 15 months.

R. M. B.

PART I

PARENT-INFANT INTERVENTION
An Interactional Approach

In Part I, the interaction model for parent and infant intervention is introduced. Chapter 1 compares the interaction model with three other models that are in wide use and discusses their common features. The second half of Chapter 1 introduces aspects of theory and research that contributed to the structuring of the interaction model.

Chapter 2 presents the philosophy and guidelines of the UCLA Infant Studies Project Intervention Program, which follows the interaction model and which stimulated the writing of this book.

The UCLA Infant Studies Project, "Diagnostic and Intervention Studies of High Risk Infants," was supported by NIH-NICHD Contract No. 1-HD-3-2776, and NICHD Grant No. HD-04112, Mental Retardation Research Center, University of California, Los Angeles.

Chapter 1
Introduction to the Parent-Infant Interaction Model for Early Intervention

Early intervention programs, especially those designed for infants from birth to 3 years of age,[1] are rapidly increasing in number. There is great variation among these programs in focus and approach, yet their goals are quite similar. All are aimed at providing the infant with the best possible opportunity for optimal development. Before the Interaction Model, which is central to this book, is defined, three other types of programs which historically precede the interaction model and which currently exist in large numbers across the United States are described. The parent-infant interaction model bears a relationship to aspects of all three models described below.

THE INFANT CURRICULUM MODEL

The infant curriculum model concentrates on the infant and the particular skills that the infant needs as he or she progresses from birth to childhood (usually birth to age 3). The curriculum consists of a predetermined sequence of activities for skill development that is similar to a curriculum for teaching reading to older children. In the case of the infant curriculum, the skills to be taught are infant behaviors in different areas of development.

In the last few years there has been an important modification in the majority of these curriculum-geared programs as a result of overwhelming research evidence regarding the impact of parents on the development of their infants and young children. Evaluation studies of intervention with handicapped infants and with infants in poverty communities have shown that programs that involve parents in the educational process are

---

[1]The labels *infant* and *child* are used interchangeably in this book to refer to the child between birth and approximately 3 years of age.

more effective than those that do not (Bronfenbrenner, 1974; Gordon et al., 1975). Therefore, parents are involved in more programs, but the model has remained basically the same: the infant curriculum still constitutes its core. The staff instructs the parent—most often the mother—in what and how to teach her infant.

This parent-as-teacher model is currently the most common one used with handicapped infants and with infants from low-income families who will later have access to Head Start programs. The model defines the mother (or other person in the major parenting role) as the primary teacher of the infant. The mothering role is thus transformed into the role of teacher of the infant. The mother takes the place of the home teacher and is taught how to, in turn, "teach" her infant sequentially ordered developmental skills. The infant curriculum remains central to the program, whether the infant is taught by the mother or by a member of the program staff.

The staff, with or without the parent's involvement, assesses the development of the infant by using a behavior checklist that is usually derived from standardized infant development tests. Each behavior on the checklist that is to be mastered corresponds with a particular set of suggested activities and materials that are thought to encourage the behavior. The curriculum is sequentially ordered within behavioral areas such as "cognitive," "motor," "language," "self-help," and "socialization."[2] The rationale for curriculum-based infant intervention is that the behavioral sequence on the checklists and the curricular sequences in books or on cards correspond to the natural developmental progression of all infants. Most available curricula were developed by the staff of infant intervention projects that were funded for a model development and demonstration phase and then for an "outreach" phase. During the latter phase, materials were prepared and printed for dissemination to other programs. The materials were designed so that their use would require a minimum of prior knowledge of infant development and minimal experience in working with infants and parents.

A number of questions arise with regard to this model. For example, is it valid to assume that there is a uniform behavioral progression in infant development? Does the model take into account the sharp individual differences among infants and the manner in which their developmental patterns vary? Is the role of the mother-as-teacher advantageous to the

---

[2]These categories are taken from the *Portage Guide to Early Education,* probably the most widely known of the infant curricula. The Portage Project materials are distributed in the form of a color-coded card file. Each color designates a particular behavioral area, e.g., blue activity cards are for the cognitive area, red cards are for the self-help area, etc. (The Portage Project, Cooperative Educational Service Agency 12, 412 East Slifer, Portage, Wisconsin 53901.)

development of the infant, and does it lead to a quality of interaction between mother and infant that lays the foundation for optimal development of the infant? Is the *teaching* model conceptually consistent with what is known about development, especially with Piaget's formulations about sensorimotor development in the first 2 years of life? Does the infant not learn and develop skills by spontaneously "acting upon" things and "interacting with" people in his environment rather than by being "taught" skills? Furthermore, should adults base their interactions with infants on a sequentially ordered checklist or should adult actions be guided, broadly, by a knowledge of general developmental sequence and, more specifically, by reading and responding to an individual infant's behavioral cues? Also, is the parent or teacher likely to be tuned in to the infant's behavior when preoccupied with following a checklist and curriculum sequence that are not adapted to any particular baby? How do the rather precise directions in what is called "prescriptive teaching" affect the sensitivity of the mother to her infant, her responsiveness to him as an emerging personality, her spontaneity, and the emergence of her own style of interacting with her infant?[3] These are all important issues to be considered and questions to be resolved regarding the curriculum-based model of infant intervention.

THE PARENT THERAPY MODEL

The therapeutic model represents quite a different approach and can be called a parent-oriented type of intervention. The parent—not the child— is the target in this model, and the primary methods used are individual or group counseling and psychotherapy. The rationale is that if the primary caregiver of the infant, most often the mother, can begin to recognize and accept some of her negative or ambivalent feelings toward the child, toward herself, and toward others in the family, and can, with various types of guidance, be helped to deal with these feelings and thus cope more effectively with the current stresses in her life, she will be a more competent parent. The assumption is that if these therapeutic efforts are successful, the parent will be able to function effectively in caring for and raising her young child.

The therapeutic approach is followed in most parent programs in mental health centers or psychological clinics, especially when it is the parent who has the major problem. These centers provide services for alcoholic or drug-addicted parents, for parents with a psychiatric history,

---

[3]Throughout the book, *parent* refers to the primary caregiver, whether this person is the father, mother, or other individual taking the major responsibility for the care of the infant. To avoid confusion and for the sake of brevity, *she* refers to the primary caregiver and *he* refers to the infant of either sex.

or for those who are in protective settings for a variety of reasons. Recently, the concern about parents at risk for child abuse has added to the number of parents for whom mental health and child guidance clinics attempt to take some responsibility. In some community agencies that use a predominantly therapeutic approach, a "warm line" is provided, allowing parents under stress to talk to a sympathetic voice over the telephone, as well as introducing parents to existing therapeutic programs in that community.

The therapeutic model may well be the most appropriate one for the parent who cannot cope with her "mothering" role because of emotional stresses or because of internal conflicts that must be resolved before she can be free to attend to her young child. However, it is not clear that all mothers who need help in coping with their infants need this type of program. Some mothers, who do not suffer from severe emotional stress unrelated to the infant but who still need help with their mothering, may profit more by intervention with another emphasis. In addition, even parents who have had psychotherapy may need and benefit from further assistance with their parenting to overcome problems related to the infant or to their lack of knowledge or experience with young children. A feeling of self-confidence and actual competence as a parent are not assured by the absence of personal problems or stresses.

Although therapeutic intervention may be the primary help that many parents need, it is often not sufficient to ensure the kinds of mothering and mother-infant interactions that satisfy either the mother or the developmental needs of the infant. Group or individual counseling or therapy is the necessary first step for many parents. However, it often needs to be followed or be concurrent with a kind of help that deals more directly with what takes place between the mother and her young child.

THE PARENT EDUCATION MODEL

Parent education programs, especially in the form of parent-infant and parent-toddler groups, are rapidly spreading across the United States. They are usually sponsored by agencies like adult education divisions of school districts, community colleges, private nursery schools or other private and public educational institutions in the community. These programs are aimed at fostering greater parental competence and an increased feeling of adequacy on the part of parents. Such groups are springing up in California faster than well-qualified leaders or instructors can be found. The burgeoning of these groups seems to be in response to a demand by predominantly middle-class mothers who feel isolated from other mothers with infants and who are often separated by long distances from their own families. Although many leaders of such groups are not able to deal with serious problems of either infant or parent, the better qualified leaders readily refer families with special needs to appropriate resources in the community.

A variety of approaches can be found within the parent education model. The most common ones are the didactic teaching approach, in which the instructor teaches parents about child development as well as techniques in caring for and managing their infants and toddlers, and the parent discussion group approach, in which parents share their concerns and questions. In both types of groups, parents spend time observing and, in some cases, interacting with their own and other children. In many discussion-oriented programs the emphasis is on supporting the parents' feelings of confidence in themselves and reinforcing the positive parenting behaviors that are observed.

Such parent groups, although flourishing in middle-class neighborhoods, are sadly lacking in poor or even working-class neighborhoods. Some concerned and socially responsible individuals have begun to explore ways of meeting the needs of parents in communities other than middle-class suburbia—needs that are often more extensive and more critical to the welfare of the infant, the parent, and the family. The "Family Focus" centers in Chicago and in Evanston, Illinois are an example of a thoughtful and creative project that makes a serious attempt to meet a broad spectrum of needs of parents and infants in their own communities.[4]

The parent education model serves an important need by helping parents to become more self-confident as well as competent. If this type of educational program were readily available in every sector of the society, it could also be of value by screening for problems of parents and infants and then referring families who need additional help to appropriate community resources. However, there is some question as to whether or not the majority of parent educators who conduct such programs have sufficient training and experience in infant development and counseling to be able to detect problems in infants and parents that require additional help.

THE PARENT-INFANT INTERACTION MODEL

The premise of this book is that the nature and quality of interactions between parent and infant exercise a major influence on the infant's development. Because of the continuing flow of research findings that emphasize the importance of what takes place between parent and infant, and

---

[4]For information about the Family Focus program, write to Bernice Weissboard, Family Focus, 425 Dempster, Evanston, Illinois 60201.

because of the bearing this interaction has on the infant's development, there is much interest in the parent-infant interaction model as an approach that promises to apply in practice what the research suggests. These interactional processes are currently being given insufficient attention in programs that are aimed at fostering optimal infant development, even though their relevance to the long-range development of the child is widely acknowledged.

There are practical reasons for the minimal attention that is given to parent-infant interaction. A program that addresses the needs and problems existing in parent-infant transactional systems must of necessity be more complex than one that focuses on a single element of that system—the parent or the infant. Individual planning for each family has to be attuned to more than the developmental stage of the infant or the psychological needs of the parent. Planning must take into account the·needs of the parent, the dynamics of parent-infant transactions within the context of the family, and the physical and social resources and circumstances in the home. Consequently, such a program cannot simply be centered on a predetermined infant curriculum that is tied to the assessment of the infant's developmental status (the infant curriculum model). Nor can it be exclusively oriented to the parent's feelings (the parent therapy model), because this would lead away from the infant and focus too much on the personal problems of the parent. Finally, because it does entail a direct commitment to the developmental progress of the infant, the interactional or transactional approach cannot be strictly considered as parent education.

Interaction-oriented intervention is tied to both the infant and the parent. It is not the outgrowth of one single discipline, nor is it the application of any of the models described above, although it is linked to all of them. Because the interaction model draws on more than one discipline, the staff's background, experience, and skills must also encompass several disciplines. Those who have the ongoing contact with parent and infant should have knowledge of infant and child development, a high degree of sensitivity to human interaction, and skills in working with parents. Additional expertise may be needed in varying degrees, depending on the particular population of the program.

THEORETICAL BASE OF THE PARENT-INFANT INTERACTION MODEL

Interactions between parent and infant immediately after birth begin a process that has received increasing attention from researchers in infant development. The earliest phase of that process has been called *bonding*. (For reviews of research on bonding and attachment, see Ainsworth, 1973, and Rutter, 1972, 1979.) These early interactions, which are instrumental in developing a "bond" or an emotional tie between parent and infant, become more varied and complex as the infant develops cognitively and socially. Between 6 and 8 months of age, most infants develop the ability to conceive of objects and people as continuing to exist through time—through periods when they are not directly perceived by the infant via the senses. When infants achieve this cognitive milestone of *object permanence* and *person permanence,* they also begin to show evidence of *attachment*—a concept from ethology—by expressing distress upon separation from their parents. (For a theoretical discussion of attachment, see Yarrow, 1972, and Sroufe and Waters, 1977.) The degree of distress, as well as the manner in which it is expressed, depends on circumstances, the infant's temperamental characteristics, and the quality of his attachment to the parent. As infants begin to differentiate between familiar and unfamiliar persons, they will generally show a preference for the familiar person—usually the parent.

Bonding and attachment are theoretical constructs that signify stages in the ongoing interactional process between infants and their primary caregivers. This process is set into motion as the infant gives signals or behavioral cues to the parent who reads and responds to these cues. The parent, in turn, gives signals that the infant gradually learns to read. The reciprocal reading and responding to each other's cues form the core of a complex interactional (or transactional) system between parent and infant. It is within that system that the child develops trust in the human and physical environment. This trust frees him to explore his environment. The child also becomes motivated to develop language as the communications between parent and infant steadily increase in complexity and sophistication.

When early interactions have not resulted in a mutually satisfying relationship, that is, when bonding and attachment have not been established satisfactorily, the subsequent interactions may fail to lead to the kind of relationship and communication system that will enhance the infant's development. It then becomes the role of intervention to examine or to *assess* the nature of the interactive process taking place between parent and infant and to *intervene* to help make their behavior with each other more reciprocal and their interaction more mutually pleasurable.

Both the words *interaction* and *transaction* are used here to denote communication between parent and infant. *Interaction* is more descriptive of behavior and is therefore used in this book to identify the model and to refer to what takes place between parent and infant or any two human beings. *Transaction* is used to indicate the complexity of the system of interaction between parent and infant. *Transaction* emphasizes the multi-faceted effects that infant and parent have on each other as well as the effects that the behavior of each has on his or her own subsequent behavior. For example, the way a mother holds her infant during feeding affects not only the infant's behavior or response, but also her own perception and, consequently, her own behavior toward the infant. Sameroff and Chandler (1975) refer to transactions between infant and caregiver as "the complex of mutual influences that operate between the child and his environment." Bell (1974) defined "the parent-child system" as ". . . a reciprocal relation involving two or more individuals who differ greatly in maturity although not in competence, in terms of ability to affect each other."

The powerful influence that the infant has on the parent's behavior and, thus, indirectly on his own development has been supported repeatedly by research findings during the last few years. For example, Bell (1971) found that an infant or young child initiates approximately 50% of the interactions that occur with adults. Other studies have attributed an even greater percentage of interactions to the infant's initiation. Studies by Brazelton, Koslowski, and Main (1974), by Korner (1974), by Stern (1974), and by Fraiberg (1974) give evidence of the infant's influence on the parent in various research contexts. Studies by Beckwith (1976) and Goldberg (1977) have shown similar results.

The infant's behavior, as it is affected by his own constitutional makeup and temperamental characteristics (Thomas, Chess, and Birch, 1963, 1968; Thomas and Chess, 1977), plays a vital part in what takes place between parent and child. According to Sameroff and Chandler (1975), constitutional variability in children strongly affects the parent's caregiving style. In a summary of research, Clarke-Stewart (1977) wrote that it was difficult to determine whether the mother's or the infant's influence is primary in shaping their interaction. She concluded:

> Overall, the frequency of the child's positive social behavior to the mother (looking, smiling, vocalizing) seems to affect how much time mother and child spend together, and how responsive the mother is to the child's distress. (p. 31)

In an earlier study, Clarke-Stewart (1973) showed that maternal responsiveness was highly correlated with measures of the infant's general competence and motivation.

> [Maternal] responsiveness was related to the child's Bayley mental score, to his speed of processing information, and to his schema development, as well as to language, social, and emotional indices of competence. (p. 71)

Goldberg (1977) identified *the socially competent infant* as

> the predictable, readable, responsive infant (who) has the potential of "capturing" the initially unresponsive parent into cycles of effective interactions by generating parental feelings of efficacy. (p. 174)

The "competent infant" is one who elicits positive responses from the parent. On the other hand, the infant who is socially "not competent," i.e., who is difficult to read, unpredictable, and unresponsive, brings about parental feelings of inadequacy that can result in parental unresponsiveness and behavior that is unfavorable to the infant's development. The parent may withdraw emotionally from or may even neglect or abuse such an infant.

Intervention that focuses on parent-infant interaction has the function of "intervening" in a parent-infant system where the infant does not naturally evoke positive adult responses. Intervention can affect the interaction by modifying the parent's perceptions of the infant's behavior and, consequently, her own behaviors (and sometimes even the infant's cue-giving and responses), thus preventing a downward spiral in their relationship.

The infant's role in the parent-infant system is emphasized here because this role has been given credence only in the last decade. Conventional wisdom, derived from both psychoanalytic theory and learning-reinforcement theory, barely acknowledged the existence of individual differences among newborn infants and left much unsaid regarding the impact of these differences on parenting behavior. The prevailing view has been one-sided in favor of the effect that the infant's environment—at first, primarily in the form of mothering—has in determining the child's personality or "shaping" his behavior. Particular maternal behaviors were thought to be simply the outward manifestations of the parent's personality, or resulting from her own experiences with *her* parents or learned throughout the mother's exposure to her own environment. Little thought was given to the effect of the infant on the mother's behavior. Historically, this emphasis on the power of the environment was a reaction to the earlier opposite view that whatever a child became was predetermined by his genetic endowment and constitutional makeup. Consequently, in the pre-Freudian and pre-Watsonian, as well as the pre-Skinnerian, period, efforts to modify the child's environment were not thought to be worthwhile because the effect of such modifications was considered negligible. Recently, the pendulum has swung to a more central position with the acknowledgment that the infant and the forces in his environment interact in a complex manner in determining his behavior and directing his development.

The fact that the reciprocity of effect within the parent-infant dyad has become more generally accepted does not detract from recognition of the powerful influence that the parent's feelings, attitudes, and behaviors exercise on the behavior and development of her infant. Because the parent, as an adult, has the potential of conscious choice and control of her behavior toward the infant, whereas the infant, by virtue of his immaturity, does not have that measure of control, it is the function of intervention to help the parent make choices in her actions toward the infant that will favor the quality and mutuality of their interactions and, consequently, the optimal development of the infant.

Clarke-Stewart (1973), in her classic longitudinal study of mother-infant interaction in families from low socioeconomic backgrounds, found a factor that she called "optimal maternal care," which she described as:

> ...maternal care which was not only warm, loving and non-rejecting but which was stimulating and enriching visually, verbally and with appropriate materials...and which, as well, was immediately and contingently responsive both to the child's signs of distress and to his social behaviors. (p. 47)

The importance of parent-child interactions around play with objects and the role of play in the infant's development are emphasized in various ways throughout this book. The author's view is in harmony with that of Yarrow et al. (1975), who emphasized the dual role of the mother as direct social stimulus to the infant and as mediator between the infant and "inanimate objects." This emphasis was evident in the preschool home intervention programs, reported on by Levenstein (1970) and Radin (1972), that were designed to enhance the parent-child relationship and to promote the optimal development of the child, largely through play activities. Bronfenbrenner (1974) made the following comments on this approach:

> ...the mother, rather than a stranger-expert, is the primary agent of intervention. The resulting reciprocal interaction between mother and child involves both the cognitive and emotional components that reinforce each other. When this reciprocal interaction takes place in an interpersonal relationship that endures over time (as occurs between mother and child), it leads to the development of a strong emotional attachment, that, in turn, increases the motivation of the young child to attend to and learn from the mother. (p. 460)

Moreover, Bronfenbrenner supports the contention that intervention that emphasizes mother-child interaction around a common activity may produce the greatest effect.

The importance of play-associated parent-infant interaction has been supported by numerous studies, some of which are referred to in Clarke-Stewart's reviews of the literature (1973, 1977) on the influence of interaction on infant development. Commenting on the results of 31 research studies on the social development of the young child (1977), she notes:

> ...the relationship formed in this age period (between 6 and 36 months) between the child and the mother or other primary figure is a central and essen-

tial one in the child's social development. Mutual attachment evolves through their frequent playful, positive and reciprocal interaction. . . . Interaction is not only immediately reciprocal, but the direction of influence is reciprocal over time; first one then the other person influences the behavior of his or her partner. (pp. 31–32)

Studies of attachment indicate that mutually satisfying social interaction motivates the infant to explore his environment and to experiment with objects. This play, in turn, stimulates the parent to provide an interesting environment for the infant. The parent becomes involved in the infant's reaching out and thus the parent functions as mediator between the infant and his environment (Yarrow, Rubenstein, and Pedersen, 1975; Clarke-Stewart, 1977). A similar process occurs with respect to language development. The infant attends to his parent's face when she talks to him, and the infant experiments with sounds, which, in turn, stimulates the parent to respond vocally and verbally. When an infant is motivated to interact physically, socially, and verbally with his environment, he is able to take full advantage of his opportunities for optimal development.

SUMMARY

Research findings have demonstrated the relationship between the quality of parent-infant interaction and the infant's development (Rubinstein, 1967; Ainsworth and Bell, 1974; Beckwith et al., 1976; Beckwith, 1976; Matas, Arend, and Sroufe, 1978; Stevenson and Lamb, 1979). These findings seem to support an interaction model of intervention. Positive and mutually rewarding interactions between parent and infant are likely to lead to the ultimate goal of optimal infant development. However, it appears that simply including the parent in the educational process is not enough. The intervention must be oriented to the parent-infant system— toward supporting and enhancing the complex transactions that take place in that system. The studies referred to here, although they represent only a small portion of the research on parent-infant interaction that has accumulated in recent years, are those that seem to be most relevant to the parent-infant interaction approach.

Chapter 2
Goals and Guidelines of an Intervention Program
The Interaction Model

The proposition that mutually satisfying interactions between parent and infant establish the foundation for optimal development of the infant was basic to the Intervention Program of the UCLA Infant Studies Project. The population served by the program consisted of infants who were considered to be at risk for developmental disabilities and their parents. (See Chapter 3 for more details on the program population.) The relationship between a parent and her high risk infant is sometimes distorted, especially if the infant gives unclear cues and is unresponsive to the parent and if the parent is fearful of abnormalities appearing or developing in the infant. Such circumstances can undermine positive, mutually reinforcing interactions between parent and infant, the absence of which can lead to parenting practices that are not conducive to the infant's optimal development.

The following three principles further define the theoretical framework of the UCLA Intervention Program:

1. Intervention that helps parents enjoy their infants and that strengthens parental sensitivity, responsiveness, and skills creates a parent-child system in which the parent experiences success and the infant progresses to his maximum potential.
2. Infant-parent interaction is a reciprocal process; that is, the behavior of each affects the other's responses in a transactional manner.
3. As mutually satisfying interactions increase and as the parent gains competence in her role, she also gains confidence in herself as the primary agent of change for the infant. Thus, the consequences of a positive parent-child relationship last beyond the duration of intervention to produce long-range results in the child's psychological functioning and overall development.

These principles lead parent-infant intervention toward strengthening and supporting the parent's positive interaction with her infant. The goals

15

and the guidelines that follow were formulated in the belief that the parent is the primary agent of change for the infant and therefore the primary participant in the program.

GOALS

Achievement of the short-term goal—mutually pleasurable parent-infant interaction—is believed to be instrumental to the achievement of the long-term goal—optimal development of the infant. The staff of the UCLA Infant Studies Project Intervention Program tried to work toward these goals by:

Supporting and encouraging parent-infant interactions that
    Are mutually pleasurable and therefore mutually reinforcing
    Are of sufficient quality and quantity to support a reciprocal system of communication
Encouraging and helping parents to
    Gain skill in observing their infants
    Understand that the infant's play is work and that children learn through play
    Be aware of materials and activities that are suitable for infants at each stage of development
    Provide interesting experiences in a variety of settings
    Anticipate the infants' behavior and needs for the immediate as well as for the more distant future (a few weeks or months ahead)
    Be aware that they, the parents, are an important influence on their infants' progress in development
Enabling mothers (or primary caregivers) to
    Gain a sense of adequacy in the mothering role
    View the infants' needs in the context of their own needs and those of the family
    Seek out and take advantage of community resources

Areas of Emphasis in Infant Development

Staff efforts with respect to the infants' development were concentrated in the social-affective, the language, and the cognitive-motivational areas of behavior. Through *social-affective* behavior, the infant communicates interest in or feelings toward another person, consequently influencing his interactions with that person. The mode and manner of his response to the other person's behavior also fall into the social-affective area. The infant's *language* behavior comprises all sounds as well as any attempt to communicate with someone (expressive language), and to try to understand the other person's communication (receptive language).

Cognitive-motivational is a relatively new concept that denotes motivational attributes of play behavior. Motivational aspects of behavior like task orientation, attention span, pleasure in play, pleasure in success, and goal directedness affect the quality of children's cognitive performance and influence their intellectual development. Yarrow et al. (1975) have focused on motivational components of cognitive acts during the first 6 months of life. Some of the motivational variables that they identified in their research were manipulation of novel objects, goal directedness, and problem solving. In a later study, Yarrow and Pedersen (1976) found that the correlation between their "cognitive-motivational cluster" and the Bayley Mental Development Index was as high as .86. The investigators took this outcome to be "...evidence of the centrality of motivation in early development." They were also convinced of "...the pervasiveness of motivational functions and their intrinsic relationship with cognitive development."

> We must conceptualize infant development in terms other than a taxonomy of skills; we must be sensitized to the motivational components of infant abilities. This sensitivity should help in the conceptualizing of infant behavior in more dynamic terms, and ultimately it might lead to more adequate measures of infant functioning. (p. 397)

In addition to cognitive-motivational aspects of play behavior, the Intervention Program staff also encouraged the kinds of cognitive behaviors or skills that Gesell and Amatruda (1954) called "adaptive."

Parents in the Intervention Program were encouraged to interest their infants in activities that would foster motor as well as cognitive development, e.g., using a toy that would challenge the infant in play as well as strengthen his fine motor skills, or providing incentives for the infant to move to a certain place to gain access to enjoyable play materials, or exploring interesting ways to use a piece of equipment that would, at the same time, develop new motor skills. In this manner, motor goals for the infant were linked to cognitive goals and both were incorporated in the cognitive-motivational area of behavior.

Parent Behaviors and Infant Development

The accomplishment of certain goals in the areas of infant development discussed above was tied in the Intervention Program to parenting behaviors, that is, the staff tried to enhance the infants' development by effecting changes in the parents' behavior. Occasionally, a staff member found it necessary to work directly with the infant before the parent and infant could interact in a manner that was rewarding to both. Table 1 shows more specifically how the staff worked to encourage parents' interactive behaviors with their infants. The staff tried to support and build on the

Table 1. Helping the parent to enhance the infant's development

The staff tries...	to help the parent...	...so that the infant will...

Social-Affective Area

	to read accurately the infant's behavioral cues and to be responsive to them, e.g., to respond to the infant's smiles, signs of discomfort or distress, expression of feelings...	give clear cues and, in turn, be responsive to the parent.
	to initiate positive social interactions and social games, and to respond to the infant's playful behavior...	seek (initiate and respond to) social interaction in a manner pleasurable to both infant and parent.
	to show clearly positive affect in social interaction with the infant...	respond to and express affect with pleasurable interaction.
	to give clear cues to the infant that are consistent across gestural, verbal, and other affective channels of communication...	read the parent's cues accurately.

Cognitive-Motivational Area

| | to develop observational skills with respect to the infant's play interests, preferences, and skill level... (This will lead her to stimulate the infant's interest in his environment with appropriate materials and activities.) | play with materials that are satisfying and will focus on an activity and remain involved with it for a significant time interval. |

to find ways of ''tuning in'' to the infant's play and to interact with him in a manner that enhances his play, i.e., that is not intrusive and does not interfere with his goals and spontaneous activity...

be goal-oriented in some of his play; will experiment with materials and use them in a variety of ways; and will seek challenging and increasingly complex activities.

to identify those activities from which the infant gets satisfaction on his own and those for which he needs the adult's participation in order for his play to be satisfying...

enjoy his play and his problem-solving and will play constructively by himself or seek the involvement of the adult with some toys.

Language Area

to acknowledge and to respond to the infant's cooing, babbling, and vocalizing...

continue to experiment with sounds and vocalizations.

to understand the importance of reciprocal communication between infant and adult, so as to motivate her to initiate as well as respond to language...

initiate language communication as well as reciprocate with language.

to become aware of the infant's interest in the human face and voice, so that she will then talk to the infant in a focused manner when he is looking at her face...

attend to the human voice and become increasingly interested in language.

to realize the infant's ability to understand a great deal before he is able to say words... (This will encourage her to talk to the infant long before he is able to say words and to give him satisfying feedback as he makes attempts at language.)

increase his understanding of language (receptive language), and will be motivated to experiment with the use of words.

strengths of the parents and also tried gradually to help them achieve some behaviors not in their repertoire. Although the goals stated in Table 1 were generally applicable to all of the families in the program, the emphasis depended on the particular parent-infant dyad. (The topic of parental behaviors as goals is discussed in Part II, Chapter 4, in connection with the Parent Behavior Progression.)

GUIDELINES

A problem common among intervention programs has been the lack of connection between their avowed aims and their actual practice. In a review of infant intervention programs, Gordon et al. (1975) suggested that program developers carefully examine their own philosophical orientations so as not to select program components or procedures that are inconsistent with their philosophy.

The guidelines that are listed below were formulated to ensure that program philosophy and program practice were consistent in the Intervention Program of the UCLA Infant Studies Project. The practices that these guidelines suggest were central to the intervention process. The guidelines were an important part of staff discussions about working with specific families. Frequent reference to the guidelines helped staff members incorporate them into their own individual styles of interacting with parents. These guidelines are broadly applicable to the process of parent-oriented infant intervention. Part III and Part IV of this book contain more specific suggestions to guide staff in helping parents to achieve mutually reinforcing interactions with their infants and to help staff to deal effectively with particular problems that they might encounter.

The first three guidelines suggest some staff attitudes and practices that tend to encourage the parents' trust and that support open communication between staff members and parents. The other seven guidelines govern intervention practices as staff members interact with parents, helping them to increase their confidence and competence in the parenting role.

1. Enabling Parents to Remain in Control

Parents should be in control of what happens with their infant as well as of their own actions during the intervention sessions. It is especially important that parents have a sense of control when intervention takes place in the home.

When the parent feels that she is in control, she will be more likely to take active responsibility for her infant and less likely to slide into a passive role or to become overly dependent on the staff. The staff should be conscious at all times of whose baby it is and of the fact that they are "guests" in someone else's home. The parent's feeling of control is enhanced when she is able to choose as often as possible the date and time of the sessions. During the first few sessions, until mutual trust is established, it is important that the staff ask for the parent's permission before touching or picking up the baby, or even before giving him toys to play with. Similarly, a staff member should not enter other rooms in the home, like the baby's sleeping area, without first asking for permission or without being invited to do so.

2. Avoiding the "Authority-Layman" Gap

In order to establish and maintain good rapport between staff and parents, open and reciprocal communication should be fostered from the beginning. By engaging in sympathetic *active listening* and by viewing the educational process as a cooperative venture between staff and parents, the staff encourages parents to take an active part in the program.

The staff should be constantly aware that the parent knows the infant best and that only the parent can provide the information needed to make intervention effective. When staff members listen carefully to the parent and show that they value her comments and observations by using them in cooperative planning for the infant, the parent becomes aware of the important part she has in the intervention process. This practice tends to prevent the all too common gap that can exist between "the authority" and "the layman." Otherwise, if the parent perceives the staff as the "infallible authority," she may feel inhibited and unable to express her insecurities about her mothering or her ambivalent feelings toward her infant. At the same time, the parent's dependence on the staff may increase, and, consequently, her feeling of self-confidence may decrease. Another parent may perceive intervention as an intrusive and disruptive element in her life if she perceives the staff as the "authority" telling her what to do with her child.

3. Dealing with Parents' Priorities and Concerns

The extent to which parents are receptive to intervention and feel trust in the staff depends, in large part, on the staff's sensitivity to the parents' primary needs and priorities.

When channels of communication between staff and parent are open, the parent will often reveal her major concerns, whether or not they are related to the infant. If other worries, unrelated to the infant, predominate—sometimes reaching a crisis level—they tend to drown out matters associated with the infant. The staff must be able to walk a fine line between responding to the parent's needs as best they can and, at the same time, assisting the parent to find the resource that can most effectively help her deal with her most immediate problem. The parent will have a difficult time focusing on the infant until she has begun to deal in a satisfactory manner with whatever other problems are of more immediate and pressing concern to her.

4. Building on Parents' Strengths

Recognition and support of parents' strengths, that is, the existing positive behaviors of parents toward their infant, are paramount in intervention that purports to help parents feel and be more competent.

The staff should look for positive parenting behaviors that are already in the parent's repertoire and use these as a foundation for planning intervention content and strategies. Staff should be aware of and start building on the strengths of the parent beginning with the very first contact with the parent. By so doing, the staff will support the parent's self-confidence, will prevent her from feeling threatened, and will encourage her to share her feelings and thoughts and to ask questions. This approach not only shows regard for individual styles of parenting but it also models for the parent how the staff would like the parent, in turn, to act toward the infant, recognizing the infant's positive behaviors—strengths —and building on these.

5. Respecting Parents' Goals for Infant

It is important for the staff to be aware of the goals and priorities that parents have established for their own infant.

The staff should encourage the parent to express, and, if necessary, to clarify her own goals for her infant and to communicate the priorities that she holds with respect to the infant's behaviors and skills. This emphasis enables the parent and the staff to set short-term goals and to work cooperatively toward their achievement. Furthermore, if parenting techniques seem inconsistent with the parent's own goals, or if the parent's priorities appear to be developmentally unrealistic, using this approach makes it easier to discuss these matters openly.

6. Involving Parents in Planning

Parents should participate as much as possible in the planning of activities for their infant.

The more the staff tries to involve the parent in planning and decision making for the infant, the more the parent will find herself involved with the infant and the more positively she will feel toward him. She is likely to gain self-confidence when she sees herself in partnership with the staff for the good of the infant. For example, the parent might suggest the nature of the next intervention session, like a visit to the neighborhood park or a session at the home of the child's grandmother. In home intervention programs the parent should be able to choose the play materials, from among those brought by the staff, that she thinks are best for her child. Having responsibility for such decisions gives the parent an active role; it tends to make her a better observer of her child; and, it gives her additional control in matters concerning the child. The staff is given an opportunity to listen to the parent's reasons for her choices, which may lead to a discussion of the child's interests and skills, resulting in the parent's greater knowledge of her own child.

7. Respecting Individual Styles of Parent-Infant Interaction

The individual style of each parent-infant dyad should be recognized and respected so that intervention can support as well as be in harmony with that style.

The first step in working toward the goal of mutually pleasurable interactions between parent and infant requires the staff, through observation and conversation, to become aware of the parent's style of interaction with her infant, the quality and pattern of the infant's responses, and the kinds of activities that the parent enjoys most and least with her infant in the areas of caregiving, social play, play with toys, language interaction, etc. The staff can then use this information to help the parent find activities that are like those she enjoys, as well as explore new and different kinds of interactions that yield enjoyment for both.

8. Using Reinforcement Is Not Enough

Parents should become aware of their own actions and behaviors that are particularly beneficial to the infant.

The staff should talk quite specifically to the parent about *why* and *how* some of her behaviors and actions are helping her infant so that she can generalize from this information and generate new and related behaviors that serve the same ends. When the parent is given this kind of information, she gains self-confidence and she becomes more independent of the staff. Simply giving social reinforcement to the parent *without providing her with additional information regarding her action* tends to increase her dependence on the staff and decrease the probability that she will generalize effectively from her positive actions.

9. Giving Parents an "Out"

Parents should not feel a sense of failure as a result of a staff suggestion that may not work in a particular family.

Suggestions should be made to the parent in a manner that neither threatens nor excludes the option of her rejecting the suggestion without feeling embarrassed. This can be accomplished by giving the parent a number of alternative ways to deal with a situation and by stressing that, because every parent and infant is unique, suggested methods may or may not work for a particular dyad.

10. Sharing How It Feels to Get No Response

Parents whose babies are unresponsive should not feel that they are the cause of this behavior.

The staff should share with the parent the experience of getting no response from the child, especially in the case of a difficult and generally unresponsive infant. This sharing can lead to a discussion about how infants differ and can stimulate the parent to express some of the frustrations that she is experiencing with her child. Ultimately the parent may be stimulated to "brainstorm" and to work with the staff on how her particular infant might be helped to become more responsive. (The process of helping parents use problem-solving techniques is discussed further in Part IV, Chapter 7.)

SUMMARY

The theoretical framework and goals of the UCLA Infant Studies Project Intervention Program have been delineated. The framework and goals reflect the orientation of the Intervention Program toward both parent and infant and to the interaction between them.

Guidelines were designed to help staff ensure that the practical implementation of the Intervention Program was consistent with the underlying philosophy of the program. These guidelines may assist others to find specific ways to support the positive aspects of the complex and delicate transactions between parent and child and to respect the individuality and uniqueness of each parent-infant dyad.

A number of the guidelines listed in this chapter were included in a more abbreviated form in Chapter 20 of *Infants Born at Risk,* edited by Tiffany M. Field et al., copyright 1979, Spectrum Publications, Inc., New York.

PART II

ASSESSMENT AND INTERVENTION

Chapter 3 contains a description of the Intervention Program of the UCLA Infant Studies Project. An overview of the population served by the Program is presented. The procedures that were developed during the pilot phase of the Program and then implemented in work with 30 families are described. The chapter also includes a discussion of assessment for intervention and brief comments on the use of videotaping and on program evaluation.

Chapter 4 introduces the Parent Behavior Progression, an assessment tool that grew out of the theoretical framework and philosophy of the Intervention Program. Based on the idea that the parent's interactions with the infant influence the infant's development in a major way, this instrument was created to allow professionals to focus on and assess the parent's behavior vis-à-vis the infant. The Parent Behavior Progression was conceptualized and developed for use in programs that consider the quality of the parent's affective and cognitive interaction with the child as having a significant effect on the child's development.

Chapter **3**
The Intervention Program
Population and Procedures

THE UCLA INFANT STUDIES PROJECT

The Intervention Program discussed here was part of a more comprehensive research project entitled "Diagnostic and Intervention Studies of High Risk Infants," usually referred to as the UCLA Infant Studies Project. The term "risk" was used in this project to signify an increased probability of developmental delay or handicap based on biological-developmental assessment during the first 9 months of life. Preterm infants were chosen as the target population for the Infant Studies Project because the incidence of infants at risk for developmental disabilities is higher among preterm infants than it is among full-term infants. "Preterm" is defined here as born at 37 weeks gestational age or earlier (term is 40 weeks) and weighing 2500 g or less.

The Infant Studies Project consisted of two parts: *diagnostic studies* of preterm infants between birth and 2 years of age, and *educational intervention* with high risk preterm infants between the ages of 9 and 24 months.[1] All of the infants in the project were assessed on 14 medical, physiological, and psychological measures between birth and 9 months of age. Infants whose cumulative risk score based on these 14 measures was below a predetermined point were assigned to the high risk group, and one-half of those infants in the high risk group were selected to participate in the educational Intervention Program.

Free medical care was provided for all of the infants by project pediatricians and nurses throughout the infants' first 2 years of life. In addition, project nurses (public health nurses) followed the infants from the hospital newborn intensive care unit into the home, making home visits as needed to give support and help to the parents. A project social worker served as a consultant to the medical and nursing team and, later, to the

---

[1]Age was computed from the *expected* date of birth or term date rather than from the actual date of birth. For example, an infant born 3 months prematurely was not considered to be 2 years of age until 3 months *after* his second birthday.

staff of the Intervention Program. (For a report of the outcomes of the Infant Studies Project diagnostic studies, see Sigman and Parmelee, 1979. See Bromwich and Parmelee, 1979, for a report of the outcomes of the Intervention Program.)

POPULATION OF THE UCLA INTERVENTION PROGRAM

The only common element among the families that constituted the population of the educational Intervention Program was that each had an infant born prematurely who, at 9 months of age, had received a cumulative risk score that classified the infant as being at "high risk." A high risk score was the result of the infant having scored low on at least some of the 14 measures that were used to assess the infant's health and development between birth and 9 months corrected age (age from expected date of birth). Some infants received low scores during the neonatal period and not thereafter.[2] Other infants that scored low in the neonatal period continued to score low on some measures throughout the 9-month period of assessment. Still other infants received average scores on most of the early measures, but showed a decline in scores toward the end of the 9-month period. Conditions causing the low scores varied widely among the infants. Therefore, the infants assigned to the Intervention Program included some handicapped infants, some with deviant behavior, some with mild delays in one or more developmental areas, and some without any observable problems.[3]

Thirty-two families were in the Intervention Program at one time or another. However, two of these families participated in the program for only 6 months. In one case, the family moved to another geographical area, too far away to continue intervention contacts. In the other case, the infant was removed from the home by protective services and the foster parent was not willing to continue in the program. Therefore, the Intervention Program population is considered to be 30 families.

Diversity of Families

The socioeconomic status (SES) of the families was determined by a formula that combined the mother's education with the father's occupation. Eleven families were classified as high SES and 19 as low SES. Additional

---

[2]Even when these particular infants received average or above average scores on assessments made between 4 and 9 months corrected age, severe problems during the perinatal period, reflected in low initial scores, could depress the 9-month cumulative risk scores below the cut-off point for "high risk" designation.

[3]The high risk infants assigned to the intervention cohort were matched in terms of socioeconomic status, racial-ethnic background, sex, and—where possible—severity of handicap or delay with the high risk infants in the non-intervention cohort. Infants in the non-intervention cohort continued to receive support from the medical and nursing team as needed, including home visits by the nurses. (See Bromwich and Parmelee, 1979.)

information related to SES became available as a result of the staff's regular contacts with the families in the program. Of the 19 low SES families, 8 were living in conditions of severe poverty. There were others whose income was low but who had extended family support when needed.

The 30 families represented several racial-ethnic groups: 13 were white and English speaking; 10 were white and Spanish speaking (Mexican-Americans and Mexican nationals); 6 were black; and 1 was oriental.

Ten mothers worked full time throughout the entire intervention period; seven were from low SES families and three were from high SES families. Three mothers—classified as high SES—worked full time for a portion of the intervention period. Three mothers, also classified as high SES, worked on a part-time basis.

Family structure was varied. There were 4 single-parent families (mothers only). The other 26 cases were considered two-parent families, although in 8 of these the father was living in the home only part of the time. In two cases, the infants had been placed with two-parent foster families. Consequently, only 16 of the 30 infants were living consistently with their natural mothers and fathers. Not all of the two-parent families were legally married, but as long as the father and mother were living together, they were considered a two-parent family. The number of children living in a home ranged from one (the project infant) to three, although one of the foster homes had four children most of the time. Half of the families had children in the home in addition to the project infant. All were siblings except in the two foster homes. The age of these children at the beginning of the Intervention Program ranged from 10 months (the twin of one project infant) to 10 years. (In one family, the teen-age half-sister of the infant was not counted as a sibling because she played a major role as caregiver of the infant.)

In a home-based program, it is important to determine which member of the family is the infant's primary caregiver and whether or not there is more than one member of the household who takes major responsibility for the care of the infant. In 25 of the 30 cases in the Intervention Program, the mother was clearly the primary caregiver. In two families, caregiving was fairly equally divided between the two working parents, and in two other families the father took care of the infant while the mother worked full time. In the remaining single-parent family, the grandmother was the primary caregiver during the first few months of the Intervention Program.

Of the 25 mothers who were primary caregivers, 7 were teen-agers. In the three families in which the father or the grandmother cared for the infant, the mothers, who worked full time, were between 35 and 40 years of age. The two fathers who cared for the infants were several years older than their wives. The majority of the parents, however, were in their 20's or early 30's.

Infant Population

There were twice as many male as female infants in the Intervention Program. Two infants (one boy and one girl) had moderate cerebral palsy with retardation. (The female infant's retardation was more severe than the male infant's.) One girl had pronounced gross and fine motor delay of unknown origin, as well as general developmental delay. Two male infants, who appeared normal in the early months, developed autistic-like behaviors—one at the age of 12 months and the other at around 18 months. Six infants appeared to have some developmental delay, primarily in language, as well as a variety of other mild problems at 10 months of age. Seven infants still showed mild problems of one sort or another at 18 months of age or later, but some of these difficulties were only of a temporary nature. The most common mild delay (five infants) was, again, in the language area, and in none of these cases can environmental influences be ruled out as major contributing factors. Eleven infants had no apparent problems in development during the entire 14 months of intervention, although the environments of some of these infants were stressful because of problems in the families.

It is clear from the descriptions above that the Intervention Program was involved with a heterogeneous population of parents and infants. The families showed great diversity with respect to socioeconomic status, racial and ethnic origin, working and non-working mothers, family composition, primary caregivers, age of the primary caregivers, and problems of the infants themselves.

THE INTERVENTION PROGRAM STAFF

Most of the staff of the Intervention Program had backgrounds in child development and early childhood education. All had had experience working with infants or young children and their parents. Some had done part of their graduate study fieldwork in the Intervention Program during its pilot phase.

Staff Development

The competencies and skills that the staff brought with them to the program were expanded by additional preparation for working with high risk infants and their families. Experiences provided during the pilot phase of the program included seminars on infant development given by the Infant Studies Project director and weekly meetings of the entire Infant Studies Project staff, with presentations by guest speakers or with discussions of the work done to date by individual staff members from the diagnostic studies and the educational intervention components of the Infant Studies Project. Staff members entering the Intervention Program during its pilot phase also regularly observed the testing of infants at various ages as it was done by expert examiners. The testing was followed by discussions of the infants' behavior and performance.

Throughout the duration of the Intervention Program, intervention cases were discussed at weekly staff meetings that were attended by the Infant Studies Project director and by the Project's pediatricians, nurses, and social worker. Videotapes of the infant or of the parent-infant interaction under discussion were viewed by the clinical and intervention staff. (Videotaping was done both at the homes of the infants and at the project Center.) Communication between the educational intervention staff and the clinical staff was excellent. Everyone was readily available to everyone else for consultation, and the relationships between all individuals involved were friendly and cordial.

The intervention staff met regularly to discuss intervention procedures as well as individual cases. The primary purpose of these meetings on procedures and specific cases was to engage in group problem solving with regard to obstacles that the staff encountered in attempting to reach intervention goals with particular families. In addition, individual case teams conferred frequently with the Intervention Program director, who also functioned as a regular team member on a few cases throughout the duration of the Intervention Program. The teams consulted with the director before and sometimes after intervention sessions involving the most difficult cases or when crises arose in a number of other cases.

The staff members commented that having an opportunity to share their frustrations as well as their exhilarating moments was invaluable. These meetings enabled the staff to cope with discouraging moments and renewed the motivation to search for the most effective ways of working with individual families. Staff members also noted that the director's interactions with them illustrated the problem-solving approach that the staff was encouraged to take with parents: the director listened, asked provocative questions, supported and built on the individual staff members' strengths, and encouraged the staff to look for viable alternatives in pursuing its goals and to make rationale decisions based on observations and relevant information. (The staff in turn encouraged parents to take this same approach in dealing with their children.) Working together in this manner helped the staff to remain flexible and to respect genuinely the individuality of each parent-infant dyad.

Staffing of Cases

The Intervention Program had a full-time director, in addition to two full-time and three part-time staff members. The two full-time staff members were bilingual in Spanish and English. In addition, two graduate students participated in the Intervention Program as trainees and functioned as second team members on two cases.

Two staff members were assigned initially to each case. This team approach allowed greater objectivity in observations. It also made it easier for staff to comply with the research aspect of the Intervention Program, which required that detailed records of every contact with each of the families be maintained. The team approach also provided for more flexibility in adapting to the needs of individual families. For example, if one team member became ill or went on vacation, continuity with a family was maintained. The lack of interruption of intervention was especially important during periods when a particular family needed frequent contact with staff. Notwithstanding the benefits of the team approach, there were a number of cases that were carried by one staff member only after an initial period with the two-person team. This occurred mostly in cases where the parent had formed a close relationship with one team member and the situation made the other member unnecessary, or in situations where a parent was going through a crisis and the presence of the second staff member seemed to make it more difficult for the parent to speak openly with the one to whom she felt closest. In some instances, one team member dropped out of the case only temporarily; in other instances, one team member withdrew permanently from the case.

The relative roles that the two team members assumed with a particular family depended on a number of factors: 1) the kinds of interaction that developed naturally among staff, parent, and infant during the first few sessions, 2) the relative skills of the staff in relating to a particular infant and parent, and 3) the particular needs that seemed to exist in a specific situation. For example, a parent might, spontaneously, talk more freely with one team member, while the other team member tended to play more with the infant. The teams were made up, as much as possible, of two people from different age brackets, and each team included at least one staff person who also happened to be a parent. Some of the parents participating in the program felt most comfortable with a person closest to their own age. Other parents preferred to communicate with a staff member who was older than themselves. In some families, one staff member might be with the infant's older siblings most of the time, especially when they were of preschool age.

In each parent-infant dyad, the staff assessed the infant's developmental status, the interaction between parent and infant, and the caregiver's parenting attitudes and skills. The issue of assessment for intervention and its relationship to program effectiveness is discussed in the next section.

ASSESSMENT FOR INTERVENTION

Behavioral assessment serves two purposes in intervention programs: 1) to establish the current status of the individual's behavior or performance in specified areas so that an educational or clinical plan can be made that is likely to produce change in the desired direction, and 2) to evaluate the effectiveness of the program by comparing behaviors or performance before the program begins with behaviors or performance after the program has been in effect for a set period of time. The methods and tools of assessment that serve intervention programs best are those that can be used both to help decision making in intervention and to evaluate program effectiveness.

The purpose of assessment as an aid to the intervention process is to obtain information that helps determine the areas of behavior in which changes are desired and the magnitude of change needed to achieve program goals. This kind of information is useful in setting short-term goals for each individual case in the context of broad program goals. The two methods generally used in this type of assessment are observation and testing. Observation yields descriptions of behavior in verbal or codified form; testing yields information about performance in the form of scores and, sometimes, profiles. "Performance" can be defined as specific behavioral responses to standard sets of questions or demands. Data from observations as well as from tests have their uses in an intervention program. The value and limitations of both are discussed below in the context of the Intervention Program of the Infant Studies Project.

Testing as Assessment

The staff of the Intervention Program had access to all of the test data that had been gathered on the infants during their first 9 months of life, as a part of the diagnostic studies component of the Infant Studies Project. Some of these data were useful, but they were not sufficient to give the staff the kind of behavioral information that was needed to make decisions about intervention. However, the test results did inform the staff of the status of the infant's performance in relation to age norms. The most valuable test data were the subscores and total scores on the Gesell Developmental Scales, which were administered at 4 and at 9 months of age. The protocols of these tests were also available so that the staff could see which tasks a particular infant performed and those that he did not perform. The subscores indicated the relative performance of the infant on tasks designated as gross motor, fine motor, adaptive play, language, and personal-social behavior, and they provided a developmental profile of each infant at 4 and at 9 months of age. To summarize, these data showed the areas of the infant's strengths and deficits, the extent to which the infant functioned within the normal range of development for his age, and the relative stability of the infant's performance between the two ages.

While test data give some useful information, they also have certain built-in limitations. First, the degree to which an infant cooperates with the examiner depends on how he feels at the time of testing, and, to some extent, on his stage of development. (Eighteen-month-olds are notorious for their lack of cooperation with the tester.) Second, the typical testing situation is standardized, that is, the examiner structures and directs what is to occur and requests the subject being tested to respond to the materials and questions that are presented to him. The procedures and content are determined by the instructions in the test manual. The primary task of the examiner is to score each performance item as it is observed. This priority prevents the examiner from seeing all that the child does before, during, and after each task is attempted or performed. The data collected by the examiner are usually limited to what the test directs the subject to do. In addition, the tester usually records an overall impression of the child's behavior during testing. The Infant Studies Project was fortunate to have competent examiners who were knowledgeable in infant development. Their comments on the child's overall behavior in the testing situation were particularly valuable because the comments were not restricted to the infant's performance on the test items.

With the current recognition of the impact of social-affective factors on test performance, social-affective scales have been developed that formalize observations and impressions of the child's behavior during the testing session. Such a scale usually consists of a behavioral checklist that is filled out by the tester or by other persons observing the testing sessions, either live or on videotape. Still, this type of assessment is restricted to the child's behavior in the testing situation, and there is no way of determining how a child might behave differently at home or in other, less structured settings, short of observing the child in those settings.

Observation as Assessment

Test data give information regarding the child's functioning in relation to developmental norms. This information is valuable to the staff of intervention programs, but, in order to be most useful in planning intervention—especially in a home program—the staff needs to observe the infant's behavior in his natural home environment, as well as in other settings. Most immediately relevant to the process of intervention are observational data on the infant's spontaneous behavior and the infant's interactions with his everyday human and physical environment. Observations in the home are of benefit to the staff in several respects. The child's behavior in his natural environment is likely to be similar to—although not identical with—that which the parents experience most of the time. Thus, the staff gets a more realistic perspective of what the parents are coping with in the home, of how they respond to the infant's behavior, and of the manner in which the infant relates to and utilizes his human and physical environment. Also, in the home environment—which is less restrictive than a testing situation—an observer is more likely to see the full range of the infant's skills in play, language, and social interaction. In pressure-free situations, the infant's behavior toward others tends to be more varied and different in quality. Furthermore, it has been found that when infants are not under the kind of pressure that is created by the demands and expectations of performance, they are more likely to experiment with new skills (Bromwich, 1977).

> New achievements in both manipulatory activity and language are most likely to occur during spontaneous play—in situations where no demands are made on the infant either by the situation or by a person...in an atmosphere that is not stressful. (p. 79)

In spontaneous play, the infant also shows what is motivating to him. In this type of self-selected activity he can be assessed with regard to cognitive-motivational behaviors like attention span, task orientation, and pleasure in success.

In intervention programs that are geared to infant *and* parent, observations of the infant must be supplemented by observations of the parent interacting with the infant. The need to structure observations of parenting behavior as a preliminary to planning intervention led the Intervention Program staff to develop the Parent Behavior Progression, which is discussed in the next chapter.

Observational data, unlike test data, can be gathered at different times of the day and in different places. Observations can be planned in specific situations, e.g., during the infant's independent play, or while the parent is interacting with the infant in play, or during a caregiving routine such as feeding or dressing the infant. Observations of parent and infant in these situations provide valuable information that should be used in planning intervention for each individual family.

The difference between the *structure of testing* and the *structure of observation* is important to note. In testing or in any standard laboratory exercise, the structure of the situation is predetermined and outside the control of the tester or observer. However, in the realm of "natural" observation, it is the observer who determines what and where to observe, as well as the purpose and the manner of recording the observations. The content of recorded observations should be such that the information can be easily retrieved for the purpose of planning interventions in particular areas of the infant's development or with regard to particular kinds of interactions between parent and infant.

In the past, some scholars thought that observational data were of limited value to research because of their relative subjectivity. Today, however, the great value of natural observations is recognized in developmental research. As long as inter-observer reliability is established on checklists used for recording observations, the "subjectivity" factor causes little concern. The study of mother-infant interaction that was part of the Infant Studies Project is an example of research based on natural home observations (Beckwith et al., 1976). Mother-infant interactions were observed by a two-person research team in the homes of the project babies when the infants were 1 month, 3 months, and 8 months of age.[4] Mother and infant were observed over a period of approximately 1 hour while the infant was awake. In addition to using a time sampling procedure with a checklist, the observers commented on parent and infant behavior in a number of categories. These comments provided the Intervention Program staff with valuable information regarding mother-infant interactions and mothering behaviors at three different times prior to some of these mother-infant dyads becoming part of the Intervention Program population.

DEVELOPMENT OF THE UCLA INTERVENTION PROGRAM

In this section, the pilot phase of the Intervention Program is outlined. The process of case referral to the program is described, followed by a discussion of the assessment, planning, and implementation of intervention with the participating families. The chapter concludes with a brief consideration of program evaluation.

The Pilot Phase

A pilot phase for the purpose of making decisions regarding assessment and intervention procedures and methods of data collection preceded the actual intervention work with the Infant Studies Project population. This period was also used to train staff to work with infants and parents. The 27 infants in the pilot population were referred to the Intervention Program by the UCLA Pediatric Clinic. The problems of these infants were more severe than those of the preterm, high risk project infants. This was to be expected because they were identified in the clinic as manifesting problems with which the parent and infant needed help. Intervention with the infants in the pilot population started when they were between 4 and 9 months old, and all but three of them were followed until they were at least 2 years of age. (Some were followed longer.)

Based on the experience with the pilot cases, some important decisions were made about the process of intervention.

1. It was decided that no written infant curriculum would be developed in the Intervention Program, nor would an existing curriculum sequence be used to plan activities for the infant. The parents' priori-

---

[4]The same research team developed a set of home observations (the Beckwith Home Observation measure) to be made when the infant reached the age of 2 years. These carefully planned and structured natural observations were used as one of the outcome measures of the Infant Studies Project. (See Beckwith et al., 1976.)

ties, attitudes, and skills would play a significant role in determining what activities would be most suitable for parent and infant at any particular time. Thus, structured sequencing of activities for infants was not in harmony with the Intervention Program's philosophy.

2. Play materials, although frequently brought to the homes, had to be used with sensitivity to the parents' perceptions. Materials that were motivating to the infant as well as to the parent were used when they served the current intervention goals with a particular family. However, in some cases the practice of taking toys to the infant was found to distract parent and staff from the primary goals of intervention. The parents' perception of what the Intervention Program could do for their infants and themselves tended to change when toys were not so central to the intervention process, and parents were more likely to ask questions and bring up issues that were not immediately related to play materials and activities.

3. It was soon found that one of the most important tasks of the staff was to become familiar with resources in the communities in which the families lived. Parents often needed help in becoming aware of agencies and places in their neighborhood that could meet many of their needs. Sometimes, during crises in families, direct referrals to appropriate community resources helped the staff in negotiating smooth transitions between the families' participation in the Intervention Program and their involvement in programs in their own communities.

The above are some examples of decisions about intervention procedures that were made during the pilot phase of the Intervention Program. There was a time overlap in the work done with families from the pilot population and that done with families from the Infant Studies Project population. However, by the time the entire staff began to work with the project infants and their families, the general philosophy and the methodological framework of the Intervention Program had been established. Sufficient flexibility was built into the program to allow new ideas to emerge and modifications to be built in when these appeared to improve the quality of the program.

Referral of Cases to the Intervention Program

When a "high risk" infant was assigned to the intervention cohort by the Infant Studies Project research coordinator, the director of the Intervention Program was provided with preliminary information about the infant and the family of the infant. This information was taken into consideration when the two staff members who were to constitute the intervention team for that family were selected. The intervention team then met with the pediatrician-nurse team on the case to get more detailed information that would help the staff in planning how to approach the family.

The pediatrician and nurse introduced the intervention team to the family during the first pediatric clinic appointment following the assignment of the infant to the intervention cohort. Occasionally, the nurse on the case accompanied the intervention team on its first visit to the home, especially if the nurse had a close relationship with the parents. It was felt that this kind of introduction would help the family to accept and to trust the intervention team more quickly. The first home visit by the intervention team, with or without the nurse, took place when the infant was between 9 and 10 months old. When the infant showed no particular problem or had a mild delay that the parents were not aware of, the medical staff was careful to avoid suggesting to the family that it needed help with the child. Instead, the intervention team was introduced as being interested in following the development of infants and as a potential resource for the parents. The development of each infant was, of course, closely followed and documented with written records and videotapes.

The Assessment Phase

The intervention team's sessions with the family during this initial phase of the Intervention Program had two major objectives: 1) to establish rapport with the family, and 2) to gather the information needed to plan the kind of intervention that would best meet the needs of infant and parent. The staff assessed the developmental status of the infant, the nature of the interactions between parent and infant, and the human and physical resources and limitations of the home environment. With respect to the human environment, the team tried to become aware of the stresses and the potential and active support systems within and outside the family that might have an effect on parent-infant transactions. With respect to the physical environment, the team observed both indoors and outdoors the use of space and the materials that were available for the infant.

The staff used three sources for the assessment that led to the planning of intervention for a family: 1) communications with the medical-nursing team who had known the family since the infant's birth, 2) information gathered by the intervention team during its initial contacts with the family, which included information derived from the use of the three assessment tools that are described below, and 3) the diagnostic data that were recorded for all project infants from birth on.

The assessment phase generally consisted of the first three meetings that the intervention staff had with the family—usually two home visits and one session at the project Center—although there was some flexibility in the number and the scheduling of sessions. The intervention team attempted to schedule the first two home visits at different hours so as to get a more complete picture of what took place between parent and infant during various caregiving and play interactions at different times of the day.

The parent who was *not* the primary caregiver was included if at all possible in at least one of the first three sessions. The staff was available for intervention sessions on Saturdays and in the late afternoons or early evenings for the convenience of the families. Throughout the program the staff continued to try to involve all of the family members who were close to the infant in intervention sessions. Evening home visits were arranged occasionally for several families to enable fathers to participate more fully in the program.

The guidelines discussed in Chapter 2 governed the approach used with participating families. They were applied to all contacts between the staff and the parents. In addition, the following suggestions were made to the staff for their first encounters with a family:

1. Keep the conversation and questions on a positive note at the first meeting with the family to build rapport and trust. The questions should be part of the conversational flow so that the session does not have the characteristics of an interview. Hold questions that may need to be asked but that are a little more sensitive until a later session.
2. Begin with questions that the mother might enjoy answering and that, at the same time, will elicit responses that reflect her observational skills and general interest in her infant, e.g., "Which are the baby's favorite toys?" "What do you enjoy doing with your child?"
3. Ask open-ended questions and guard against questions that imply that there is a "right answer" that would indicate "good parenting," e.g., "What is your baby's sleeping pattern?" instead of "Does your baby have a well-established sleeping pattern?"

The second session, also usually in the home, was considered a follow-up of the first session. Again, building trust was emphasized, and an attempt was made to gather additional information that would aid in the planning of intervention. In order to create and preserve good rapport and informality in the staff-parent relationship, the intervention team was careful not to be intrusive. Although the major objective of the second session was still assessment, the staff responded to requests of the parent for help or suggestions. In other words, no sharp line was drawn between the assessment phase and subsequent intervention sessions. In a sense, assessment was a continuous process and an integral part of intervention.

Whenever possible, the third session in the assessment phase was held at the project Center. (Project families received transportation to and from the project Center when needed or requested.) The session began with the taping of a 10-minute parent-infant play interaction episode in a standard setting. (See the discussion of the Play Interaction Measure below.) This taping was followed by an informal discussion with the parent(s). Sometimes a staff member would experiment with presenting various toys to the infant, after first asking the parent(s) for permission to do so. Later, the infant was observed in a play yard and in a large nursery school playroom, when these were available. Some parents felt more at ease voicing certain concerns and questions in these pleasant surroundings and away from the home.

Assessment Instruments   Three instruments were used by the intervention staff to aid in the assessment process:

1. *The Knobloch, Pasamanick, Sherard Developmental Screening Inventory,* an adaptation of the Gesell Infant Test, can be used more informally than a standardized test.[5] It was used to guide the staff's observations of the infant in the developmental areas designated by the Gesell test. The use of the Inventory provided the staff with an opportunity to compare the infant's behavior at 9 months on the Gesell test with his behavior in the same developmental areas at home a few weeks later.

2. *The Parent Behavior Progression* (PBP) was used both for the purpose of diagnostic assessment to help in the planning of intervention and in the evaluation of program effectiveness. This measure is described and discussed in detail in the chapter that follows.

3. *The Play Interaction Measure* (PIM) is an instrument for the assessment of parent-infant interactions in a standardized laboratory setting.[6] Parent and infant were taped in the following situation:

> Parent and child are alone in a small carpeted room for a ten-minute period. The infant is seated in a high chair and the parent is seated in a chair next to the infant. A standard set of toys, suitable for infants between six and thirty months of age, is placed on a platform next to the parent and out of reach of the infant. The parent is asked to give the infant toys to play with, and to interact with the infant as she would at home.

This play session was repeated and taped three more times, at 4-month intervals. Parent and infant behaviors on these tapes were observed by the intervention team and used, in conjunction with

[5]Hilda Knobloch, Benjamin Pasamanick, and Earl S. Sherard, Jr., *A Developmental Screening Inventory: From 4 Weeks to 18 Months.* From the Division of Child Development of the Department of Pediatrics, and the Department of Psychiatry, the Ohio State University College of Medicine, and the Children's Hospital, Columbus, Ohio.

[6]The Play Interaction Measure, developed by R. M. Bromwich and D. Burge, has not been sufficiently refined to permit its dissemination.

other observational data, to assess the status of parent-infant interactions. These observations in the laboratory setting revealed certain qualities as well as problems in particular parent-infant dyads that were not always visible in the home.[7]

The videotapes taken at the project Center were valuable to the staff because they offered a perspective of parent-infant interaction that was different from the one that resulted from the observations in the natural home environment. Whereas the Parent Behavior Progression helped to focus the staff's observations in the home, the taped play sessions gave the staff an opportunity to see the parent-infant dyad in a laboratory situation where no one else was present to interrupt or otherwise to influence the interaction. The use of both measures also gave the staff an opportunity to compare styles of parent-infant interaction across families.

Assessment Summary   The assessment phase concluded with the preparation of a written summary that incorporated relevant data from all available sources, including:

1. Observations of infant and parent-infant interactions during the preceding three or more sessions   (These observations were made in the home, at the project Center and sometimes during the first meeting of staff with parent and infant in the waiting room of the pediatric clinic.)
2. Information from conversations with parents during the first three or four sessions
3. Observations of parent-infant interaction from the 10-minute taped play sessions
4. Assessment of parenting with the use of the Parent Behavior Progression
5. Data from the diagnostic studies phase of the Infant Studies Project, i.e., protocols and tester's comments on the 4- and the 9-month Gesell tests, and notes from the home observations of mother-infant interactions when the infant was 1, 3, and 8 months of age
6. Information from the medical-nursing team

The summary was used as the basis for the formulation of the first set of intervention goals and plans that would span a period of approximately 4 months. The summary covered the strengths and problems in the three major areas that were assessed: the infant's behavior and developmental status, parent-infant interaction and style of parenting, and resources and limitations in the home environment.

---

[7]A scoring system was later developed for the Play Interaction Measure so that the first and last play sessions could be compared to evaluate program effectiveness. The scoring of the play sessions was done by persons outside the Intervention Program, who were not acquainted with the parent-infant dyads shown in the videotapes.

The Process and Content of Intervention

The intervention plans for each case were based on periodic assessment summaries. (See Kass et al., 1976.) The plans were formulated by the intervention team working with a particular family. Summaries and plans, especially those for difficult cases, were reviewed at staff meetings or in individual consultation with the program director. The team periodically reviewed the intervention plan to ensure that current work with the family was consistent with stated goals and suggested activities. The staff on the case added to the goals or changed them whenever continuing observations and additional information suggested the need to do so.

The Intervention Plan   Each intervention plan included: 1) initial *goals* for the subsequent 4-month period, 2) *rationale and considerations,* i.e., information from the assessment that indicated the need for a goal (rationale) and circumstances that should be taken into account as activities were planned and carried out with parent and infant (considerations), 3) a *program of activities* planned to implement the goals, and 4) an *evaluation plan* that listed which behaviors would suggest the effectiveness of the intervention and when to look for them. Table 2 shows three goals taken from an initial intervention plan that was made for one of the families in the Intervention Program.

Each initial plan was reviewed and evaluated as to its effectiveness after 4 months of intervention. A second summary was then written and a new plan was formulated for the subsequent 4 months. The summary was based on: 1) the continuing assessment that had been in process over the 4-month intervention period, 2) the viewing of a new 10-minute play interaction tape, and 3) another assessment of parenting with the Parent Behavior Progression. This cycle was repeated until the termination of the intervention program for each family.

In addition to the 4-month plans, detailed activity plans were made for each intervention session. These were generally in harmony with the 4-month goals and plans. Continuing assessment was, of course, an integral part of every session, and flexibility—which increased with experience—was a consistent characteristic of the work that was done with the families in the program. The staff soon realized that, although the planning of each session previous to the home visit was paramount in a good program, a set of plans might have to give way to immediate concerns or crises in a family that could not be anticipated. Rigid adherence to an intervention plan, even when the parent had participated in making it, would be tantamount to staff insensitivity to what was taking place in the home.

Because the Intervention Program was part of a research project, the staff had to keep precise records on the content and process of interven-

Table 2.   Sample goals from an initial intervention plan

Goals	Rationale and considerations	Program plan	Evaluation plan
To increase social behavior of infant with parents; to increase parents' valuing of infant's social behavior & consequently their responses to it.	Infant's vocalizations are pleasurable to him; minimal eye contact observed between infant and mother; no social games observed or reported with infant. Mother enjoys talking to us.	Respond to and reward infant's vocalizations. Point out that infant is like mother—likes to "talk" too. Discuss with mother the importance of eye contact. In response to mother's questions, provide list of, and bring, suitable records and books. Model social games, nursery rhyme games.	Look for increase in infant's social and affective behavior with parent by second summary time, 4 months hence.
To help parents see importance of infant's language development at this stage, and increase their awareness of the effect of more language interaction on his overall development.	Infant's language subscores have gone down steadily (from 4-month Gesell to 9-month Gesell to 11-month KPS Inventory[a]). Quantity and variety of vocalizations have not increased between visits, nor has receptive language.	Model imitating and responding to infant's sounds. Model verbal games, physical closeness when talking with him, giving him time to respond. Try singing to him. Evoke mother's reaction to infant's responses. Ask mother to "keep track" of his vocalizations and other responses, and to share information with us.	Check infant's vocalizations and receptive language. Look for increase in language reciprocity with mother. Expect mother's spontaneous reports on infant's vocalizations and on what he understands.
To develop third caregiver's skills in play interaction with infant.	Third caregiver is teenager who spends several hours a day caring for infant.	Model presenting toys to infant and interacting with him to increase his interest and attention span.	Look for infant's increased pleasure in play and a longer attention span.

[a]Refers to Developmental Screening Inventory by Knobloch, Pasamanick, and Sherard, an infant development checklist used informally by the staff in the home.

tion with each family. A detailed write-up of every session with the family was prepared, consisting of: the assessment of the infant's behaviors, in which observation of specific behaviors in the Gesell categories was noted; a summary in essay form of the activities and events during the session; an evaluation of the session; and a follow-up plan for the subsequent session, including suggested activities. Thus, the write-up of each home visit or other contact with the family helped in the planning of the next session. (Telephone conversations, except for brief ones for the purpose of scheduling appointments, were also written up.) This detailed record-keeping along with frequent staff discussions of the cases helped to relate the intervention closely to the staff's observations as well as to the questions, concerns, and priorities of the parents.

Process Decisions   Decisions regarding the process of intervention were tied to the philosophical orientation of the program, to the observations of the staff, and to information obtained from the parents and from other individuals inside the Infant Studies Project who were acquainted with the family. For example, the first operational guideline discussed in Chapter 2 stipulates that the parent's sense of control over what transpires in her own home is of extreme importance. The staff supported the parent's sense of control by respecting her priorities and her style, as well as the flow of family life, the routines that were central to the family's functioning, and the family's values and standards of behavior. An illustration of how this guideline affected decisions related to the process of intervention is the manner in which staff might bring toys and materials into the home of a family that placed a high value on neatness. To arrive for a home session with "messy" materials and suggest that they be used in the living room or even to bring a variety of small toys that might clutter up the house would be intrusive and inappropriate. Instead, before introducing materials that would foster the infant's development but that might also be annoying or disturbing to the parent and disruptive to the family's sense of order, the staff first discussed with the parent some ways of keeping a few toys available to the infant in a special place, so that they would not "make a mess" in the house. Once the parent realized that some of these materials were important for the child to have occasionally, she could work out her own way to make them available to him.

The ultimate aim of the program was to have an impact on the infant's development by effecting changes in the parent's attitudes and interactions with the child. Therefore, it was necessary for the parent not only to have a sense of control over what went on in her home, but also to realize the extent to which the decisions she made about herself and her infant influenced her child's behavior and development. The role of the intervention staff was to enable *the parent* to make decisions on how to meet her child's needs based on her own observations, her sensitivity to what the infant was expressing, and her sense of adequacy and competence in the parenting role. In deciding on the most effective approaches to intervention toward the end of meeting this goal, the staff had to balance and keep in perspective not only the value of certain activities for the infant, but also the attitudes of the parent and the risk of negatively affecting the parent-infant relationship or of damaging the rapport between parent and staff.

Range of Content   Although the focus of intervention was on parent-infant interaction, and the aim of intervention was to increase the parent's skill and satisfaction with her infant, the staff often found itself doing many things that, on the surface, seemed unrelated to the infant or to the interaction between parent and infant. When stresses on the primary caregiver-parent were so intense as to interfere with her attention to the infant, the staff tried to help the parent deal with whatever was troubling her. It was clear that the parent could not attend to the infant as long as her concerns about other things took priority over the infant.

Among the things that the staff did and considered an important part of its work with families—even though these activities seemed to be only indirectly related to parent-infant interaction—were assisting working mothers to find and evaluate good child care resources and helping parents to find and assess community resources to resolve the family's financial, legal, or housing problems.

The fact that the intervention staff focused on the infant and parent usually resulted in increasing the parent's involvement with and interest in the infant. However, the extra attention accorded the infant sometimes occurred at the expense of the other child or children in the family. Therefore, the staff intentionally spent a considerable amount of time and effort in helping parents deal with their older children so as to balance the attention paid to the needs of the baby with that given to the needs of the other children. As a matter of policy, the staff brought toys for other children in the family and made a point of not ignoring them, especially if they were under school age. This practice was another example of modeling, that is, the staff emphasized through action rather than words the importance of appropriate interactions and activities with *all* of the children in the family. Moreover, this practice had important long-term benefits for the infant and the parent. It tended to preserve good feelings on the part of the siblings toward the infant and, by helping the parent understand the needs of the older children, it prepared her to be a more competent parent when the baby grew older.[8]

Frequency and Length of Sessions   The frequency of sessions was decided on an individual basis for each family and could vary for the same family, depending on the degree of need of the parent and the infant. The most common interval between sessions was 2 weeks. With several fam-

---

[8]See Part III and Part IV of this work for detailed discussions of both the process and content of intervention with each family in the Intervention Program.

ilies intervention sessions were held weekly for periods ranging from about 6 weeks to 9 or 10 months. In cases in which neither the parent nor the infant needed intensive help or support from the staff, home visits were made approximately once a month.

The length of the intervention session varied as much as the frequency of sessions. Several factors influenced the length of the sessions, including the preference of the parent, either sensed by the staff or made explicit by the parent; the style of the team or staff member; and the intensity of the parent's need at the time. Certain patterns developed with many cases, e.g., the general duration of a session might be 1 hour with one family and close to 2 hours with another. The time of day of the session also varied, although in the early weeks of the program the staff tried to make appointments at different times of the day in order to see the parent and infant in various caregiving routines, such as feeding, outdoor activity, etc.

Use of Videotaping   We experimented with the use of videotapes in a variety of ways in order to:

Offer staff and trainees opportunities to see the range and variety of skills and difficulties of infants and parents in the program

Increase objectivity and precision of observations by staff, e.g., viewing a recent tape of an infant to pinpoint his problem of poor exploratory play behavior with materials so as to refine the intervention planning and activity for that infant

Document changes in the infant's development, especially when cases were reviewed, summarized, and evaluated at 4-month intervals

Offer consultants from various disciplines an opportunity to view the problem with which intervention staff needed their help, e.g., gross motor activities of an infant suspected to have cerebral palsy

Enhance observational skills of parents as staff reviewed tapes of their infant's activities with them

Point out to parents their infant's strengths or the nature of a problem or the infant's progress over time, e.g., showing tapes of an infant taken 3 months apart to demonstrate changes in his interests and skills

Help the parent become more aware of her skills in interaction with her infant, e.g., showing her a section of videotape in which she adjusted a toy to help the infant experience pleasure and success

Involve a second parent, not present during most intervention sessions, by showing parts of taped sessions

Train students and trainees for the work of infant intervention

Evaluation of Intervention

The effectiveness of intervention was evaluated by comparing the intervention group with a non-intervention group on 2-year outcome measures and also by assessing changes in infant and parent behavior and parent-infant interaction in the intervention group only. The outcomes of the comparison study and some of the issues related to the comparison of groups in the Infant Studies Project have been reported and discussed elsewhere (Bromwich and Parmelee, 1979). Evaluating the effectiveness of intervention by assessing changes in behavior, which is more relevant to the contents of this book than are group comparisons, is briefly summarized below.

In any "treatment" program, it is logical to measure those variables that are considered to be critical to the achievement of the program's goals. Because parenting behavior and parent-infant interaction behaviors were the variables considered to be critical to achievement of the ultimate goal of facilitating the child's optimal development, the thrust of the evaluative process was an assessment of those two variables as well as an assessment of infant behavior. The same procedures and instruments were used for formative and for summative evaluation of the Intervention Program. The Parent Behavior Progression, discussed in Chapter 4 and in the Appendices, was used to assess parenting behavior.[9] The Play Interaction Measure (PIM) was used to assess the behavior of parent and infant as they interacted with each other.

Formative vs. Summative Evaluation   In a discussion of methodology, it is fitting to differentiate between formative and summative evaluation. Formative evaluation ". . .involves the collection of appropriate evidence during the construction and trying out of new curriculum in such a way that revisions of the curriculum can be based on this evidence" (Bloom, 1971). It is an ongoing process that leads to the modification of intervention content and procedures in order to increase the likelihood of achieving the intervention goals. In contrast, summative evaluation takes place at the termination of the program in order to determine the program's effectiveness. Summative evaluation is usually determined by means of standardized outcome measures. Both types of evaluation play an important role in shedding light on the effectiveness of intervention as well as on the validity of various evaluation procedures.

The use of outcome measures, like the Bayley, Gesell, Catell, or other infant development scales, to evaluate the effectiveness of intervention has become controversial, especially when these measures are used to assess infant behavior immediately after the termination of an intervention program. It has been argued that when infant behavior is the focus of both the program and its evaluation, the outcomes immediately after the program termination may well show changes in infant behavior in the

---

[9]Bromwich and Parmelee (1979) reported the strong relationship that existed between the PBP and the Beckwith Home Observation measure, which was external to the Intervention Program, and between the PBP and the clinical judgments of staff as to the success or lack of success of intervention in a particular case.

desired direction. However, it has also been found that unless the parents' attitudes, behavior, and interactions with the infant have been affected by intervention, the benefits to the child may be of short duration (Bronfenbrenner, 1974; Brown, 1978). These findings support the idea of supplementing developmental assessments of infants with assessments of parental behavior and parent-infant interaction, since both are likely to have a long-range effect on the child's development.

The use of infant test scores as evidence of program effectiveness, especially when such tests are administered immediately after the treatment is terminated, raises questions for programs whose goals lead to the expectation of a long-term rather than a short-term impact on the infant. Moreover, evaluation studies have shown that immediate and long-term effects are often not the same. Bronfenbrenner (1974) in his review of early intervention programs reported that center-based programs showed greater gains than home programs at the end of the experimental year. However, when the children were tested 3 years later, those who had participated in the home program showed greater gains. Meier (1978) referred to the "emergence of a 'sleeper effect' wherein significant differences are found [between experimental and control groups in early intervention research] at older ages although none were found earlier." Meier further states that "the evidence to date indicates that knowledgeable and skillfull parenting is the most effective and economical means of fostering the optimum development of the child. Active participation by family members is critical to the long-term success of any intervention program." The results of these studies and Meier's conclusions support the idea that home programs that enhance parenting and parent-infant interaction will show greater effects after the lapse of a period of years rather than immediately after the termination of the program. It remains to be seen whether assessments of parenting and parent-infant interaction at the termination of intervention are better than infant test scores as predictors of children's later performance and competence.

To summarize, the assessment of parent and infant behavior and interaction had multiple purposes and functions:

1. to direct and guide the process of intervention with each individual family
2. to carry on a continuing evaluation of the intervention process so as to be able to correct or modify that process when necessary (formative evaluation)
3. to enable examination of the differences between cases and the various factors and conditions, singly and in combination with each other, that appeared to coexist with various degrees of intervention effectiveness

The first two functions of assessment are discussed earlier in this chapter and are alluded to throughout the book. The differences between cases and the relationship of these differences to intervention effectiveness are issues dealt with in Chapters 5 and 6. The examination and sorting of factors that appeared to coexist with effective or ineffective intervention, and that therefore might be related to effectiveness, are briefly summarized in Chapter 9.

Chapter **4**

Focus on Parental Behavior in the Interaction Model
The Parent Behavior Progression

In this chapter the Parent Behavior Progression (PBP) is presented. The PBP, which was developed for use in the UCLA Intervention Program, was a direct outgrowth of the theoretical framework of the interaction model. The instrument became a useful assessment tool for the implementation of the basic principles of that model.

RATIONALE FOR THE PARENT BEHAVIOR PROGRESSION

In any intervention program, what is assessed and the way in which the assessment is done should be consistent with the program's theoretical framework, should facilitate the achievement of program goals, and should give direction to the planning of intervention. In most programs for infants and young children, the primary goal has been to achieve a higher level of child competence, with a frequent emphasis on cognitive development. Consequently, intervention has been oriented toward fostering the child's acquisition of skills so that he would achieve a higher level of competence that would enable him to succeed later in school. In many infant programs, standardized infant scales have been modified with the specific intent of helping intervention staff to develop individualized curriculum exercises and materials to encourage desired behaviors that are identified on those scales. Thus, in most early intervention programs, and especially in those for handicapped infants or for infants at risk for later disabilities because of neonatal problems, the focus of assessment and therefore of intervention has remained the infant's behavior and performance. Although the role of the parent in infant intervention programs has been strengthened, parenting behavior and parent-infant interaction per se are rarely incorporated into the goals or assessment procedures of the programs.

In a model in which satisfying and mutually reinforcing parent-infant interactions are acknowledged to have a major effect on the infant's development, such interactions emerge as a major program objective. Because the desired quality of interaction is most easily achieved by influencing the parent's behavior vis-à-vis the infant, the parent's as well as the infant's behaviors must be assessed. Assessment is defined here as structured observation, usually in relation to predetermined areas of behavior. The Parent Behavior Progression is structured to assess in behavioral terms the parent's interactions with her child and the way in which she responds to the child's developmental needs.

An infant specialist who views the parent's role to be simply that of the "teacher of the infant" may not realize the need to become more aware of the parent's behavior and to have an effect on parenting. The specialist's major focus may be the teaching strategies that the parent should learn to use with her infant. However, as discussed in Chapter 1, there is increasing agreement that instructing the parent to teach the infant specific skills, without considering the interactional process between them, has only a limited long-range effect on the infant's development. When the conditions that enhance parent-infant interaction do not exist, and when, in addition, the parent feels pressured to teach the child certain skills, she may try to engage him in activities that he rejects. The parent can then become frustrated and resentful of the child who is making her feel inadequate in her "parenting role." Similarly, if she thinks that what she has been asked to do with her child is important for his development, she may pressure the child to "perform," but this pressure may make the child respond negatively to her. Such behaviors on the part of the parent and the infant could interfere with, rather than enhance, mutually pleasurable interaction.

Of course an improvement in the interaction between parent and child may occur in any intervention program, regardless of its model, when the staff is naturally sensitive to the need of parent and infant to enjoy activities together; when the infant responds positively to the activities that the parent initiates with him, which, in turn, increases the parent's responsiveness to the infant; and when the parent's awareness that she is doing something important for the infant makes her feel more adequate, thus freeing her to be more sensitive to the infant's behavioral cues. However, in the interaction model, instead of relying on chance, an active and conscious effort is made to enhance and improve the quality of parent-infant interaction. When the thrust of intervention is to effect positive changes in the parents' behavior "as parents, not as teachers" (Lasater et al., 1976), the staff has to increase its awareness of the behaviors that are desirable, i.e., that positively influence the transactional process between parents and infants. The purpose of the Parent Behavior Progression is precisely to increase the staff's focus on parental behavior that enhances satisfying parent-infant interaction as well as the parent's overall competence with the infant.

DESCRIPTION OF THE PARENT BEHAVIOR PROGRESSION

The aim of the Parent Behavior Progression (PBP) is to sensitize the staff of infant programs to the feelings, attitudes, and behaviors of parents and thus to enable the staff to work more effectively toward helping the parents to experience greater enjoyment, satisfaction, and competence in caring for their infants. It is a tool that is designed to help developmental specialists to optimize the child's functioning and development by supporting and enhancing desirable parent behavior.

As an assessment tool, the PBP enables persons working with infants and their parents to increase the productivity of their work with parents. The PBP gives structure to observations of parenting behavior and to parents' reports of their own feelings and activities vis-à-vis the infant. The PBP also organizes staff observations and parent reports by providing a conceptual framework that helps the staff to make sense out of what they see and hear in relation to their intervention goals. The PBP is founded on the principle that when a parent achieves mutually satisfying interaction with her infant and acquires sensitivity and responsiveness to his needs in all developmental areas, she creates an environment in which the infant is able to develop to his fullest potential.

The Progression is divided into six levels. Each level consists of a number of behaviors that are grouped under various subheadings. The first three levels of the Progression have been identified as the affective base, even though they contain cognitive components (Bromwich, 1976). When this base has been established behaviorally, it gives some evidence for the existence of parent-infant attachment. Level IV through level VI behaviors demonstrate that the parent is actively providing opportunities for experiences to promote the growth of her infant. The theoretical framework of the interaction model is reflected in the Progression in the following manner: the parent's enjoyment of her infant (level I) and her sensitivity and responsiveness to his behavioral cues (level II) lead to mutually enjoyable and satisfying interactions (level III). When these conditions exist, they constitute together the foundation for more complex parenting behaviors that are favorable to the infant's development (levels IV, V, and VI). The parent progresses toward greater competence in providing the infant with an environment—play materials as well as opportunities for language and social experiences—that fosters various aspects of his development (level IV). The parent's behaviors become more complex as she cues in to the subtleties of the infant's needs. She progresses in competence as she learns from her own experience and/or from intervention (level V). Gradually she is able to generate independently a variety of activities and opportunities for different types of experiences for the infant. She is able to anticipate the infant's more complex needs in the next stage of development and to view his needs in proper relationship to her own needs and to those of the rest of the family (level VI).

The sequence or "progression" from level to level constitutes a conceptual framework for the development of the kind of parenting that encourages the development of the infant. The PBP conceptualizes what happens in the growing relationship between "healthy" parents and their infants. One must realize, however, that the parents and infants who are most commonly found in intervention programs tend to have the kinds of problems that interfere with the optimal development of the parent-child relationship. Therefore, although the sequence of levels is of value as a point of reference and as a framework for normal development, it is not to be taken as a rigid structure or hierarchy to be followed in sequence in the planning of intervention. The term "progression" is not meant to imply that parents must acquire the behaviors at level I before they can move on to acquire the behaviors at subsequent levels. In fact, experience in intervention programs suggests quite the opposite. For example, when dealing with a mother who, for any number of reasons, does not enjoy her infant (level I) it is usually better to begin intervention by involving her in some play activity with her infant (level IV). When she sees the effects of her efforts with the infant, she becomes more self-confident in her parenting role and usually will take more initiative in trying other activities to which the infant might respond positively. When the parent sees the infant respond to something that *she* has done, she may begin to change her perception of the infant because she sees positive responses that she had not seen previously. The parent finds more things to like about her infant and therefore she begins to "enjoy" him more (level I).

Even though enjoyment of the infant is not easily achieved by parents whose infants are unresponsive and difficult to care for, for a variety of reasons (this includes handicapped infants), some parental enjoyment of the infant has to come about eventually because, in the long run, it constitutes an essential element of positive parent-infant interaction. The more disturbed the parent-infant relationship is— because of the infant's problem, the parent's difficulties, or both—the more difficult it is for the parent spontaneously to enjoy her infant. Instead, enjoyment of the infant is more likely to come about as a by-product of the parent's actions to which the infant gives a pleasurable response. The importance of the mother's enjoyment of suggested activities with her infant—which often leads to her enjoyment of the infant—should not be minimized. The parent and infant will not achieve mutually pleasurable interaction as long as the parent cannot find any pleasure in being with her infant.

LEVELS OF THE PARENT BEHAVIOR PROGRESSION

Level I: The Parent Enjoys Her Infant[1]

Even if this enjoyment is limited to brief periods of the day or only to certain types of interactions, like playing peek-a-boo or bathing the baby, the goal of intervention can be to help the parent find more situations in which she can enjoy interacting with her baby.

At this level, the behaviors listed in the PBP demonstrate that the parent enjoys the infant, that is, she enjoys being in his company, or watching him, or playing with him, etc. Enjoyment by the parent does not need to be reciprocated by the infant at this level. The parent can get pleasure from her baby *on her terms,* without regard to what the baby is experiencing. This is in contrast to level III, where the enjoyment has to be reciprocated by the baby (mutuality).

Level II: The Parent Is a Sensitive Observer of Her Infant, Reads His Behavioral Cues Accurately, and Is Responsive to Them

A parent who enjoys interacting with her infant may do so primarily on her own terms. If she does not observe her infant closely, thus missing cues that indicate his needs, her behavior is unlikely to be satisfying to the infant. Reading behavioral cues is a skill that is readily learned by a parent who already enjoys her baby.

Level II consists of two elements: 1) the parent's reading of the infant's cues, and 2) the parent's responses to those cues. It is possible for the parent to be aware of the meaning of some of the infant's behavior or to read his cues, and still not respond to him. This is, of course, insufficient for a desirable interaction between parent and infant. A consistent pattern of the parent reading cues without responding to them may indicate serious difficulties in parenting and in the parent-infant relationship. On the other hand, the ability to observe and to read behavioral cues accurately is basic to the development of sensitive responsiveness.

Relationship Between Levels I and II   Usually a parent is not an active observer of her infant unless and until she enjoys him at least in some respects (level I), although it is possible for a parent to be an accurate

---

[1]See Appendix A and Appendix B for Form 1 and Form 2 of the Parent Behavior Progression. Both forms are taken from the unpublished manual of the PBP. The various levels in Form 1, which is for parents of infants from birth to 9 months, are numbered i, ii, iii, etc. The same levels in Form 2, which is for parents of infants between 9 and 36 months of age, are numbered I, II, III, etc., so as to distinguish between the two age categories.

observer of her infant even though she does not enjoy him. However, if the parent does not enjoy her infant, it can be expected that her responsiveness will be limited and of a low quality. Enjoyment of the infant (level I) is an important base on which to build observational skills and the reading of behavioral cues (level II).

Level III: The Parent Engages in a Quality of Interaction with Her Infant That Is Mutually Satisfying and That Provides Opportunity for the Development of Attachment

When levels I and II have been established, behaviors at level III are not difficult to attain. As the parent becomes more alert to the baby's cues and responds in a manner that is satisfying to him, the quality of the interaction improves and mutual enjoyment increases. The parent and infant now experience reciprocal, positive feedback in their interactions. At level III, the parent also understands the developmental value of a considerable amount of parent-child interaction during the periods of the child's greatest alertness or—with the increase of mutual enjoyment—she simply spends more time with the child when both can enjoy it most. If the parent works outside the home or is not available to the infant for other reasons, she provides the kind of caregiving that allows the infant to experience continuity of interaction with a significant adult.

At level III not only is the parent aware of the *infant's pleasure* in their interaction with each other, but also she values and enjoys his pleasure. Mutuality of enjoyment and a new level of complexity are evident in their relationship. The parent arranges for some of her time to be spent with her infant, no matter how limited her time might be.

Relationship between Levels II and III   When the parent is able to read and respond to the infant's cues (level II), she is likely to receive positive feedback and thus enhance mutual pleasure (level III).

Level IV: The Parent Demonstrates an Awareness of Materials, Activities, and Experiences Suitable for Her Infant's Current Stage of Development

Behaviors at this level deal concretely with what the parent actually provides for or does with the infant in the areas of play, language, and social interaction. The parent not only knows what toys are most appropriate to the infant's skill level, but also *how to use these materials* in interaction with him. She identifies and plans experiences for the child that are developmentally appropriate and motivating to him, and that are therefore satisfying to him.

Relationship between Levels III and IV   Mutually satisfying interaction (level III) establishes the foundation for a system of communication. Such pleasurable interaction allows the infant to trust, to explore, and to get satisfaction from the physical environment. It motivates him to listen and talk, and it encourages him to seek social experiences with others (level IV).

Level V: The Parent Initiates New Play Activities and Experiences Based on Principles That She Has Internalized from Her Own Experience, or On the Same Principles as Activities Suggested To or Modeled For Her

The parent generalizes from an explanation, suggestion, or observed activity by developing other activities related to the same developmental goal. She reaches this level when she sees that a particular activity is enjoyed by her infant and she understands how it contributes to his developmental progress. Although the parent at this level may not be sufficiently aware of the underlying principles to articulate them, she is nonetheless able to apply them.

The parent develops behaviors at this level as a result of either her own experience in parenting and her encounters with other parents and infants, or her participation in an intervention program. The parent begins to base her parenting behaviors on principles she has learned.

Level VI: The Parent Independently Generates a Wide Range of Developmentally Appropriate Activities and Experiences, Interesting to the Infant, in Familiar and in New Situations, and at New Levels of the Infant's Development

Level VI is characterized by behaviors that tend to establish the basis for continued desirable parenting. Here the parent is able to perceive the infant functioning within the framework of the family and is able to generate a variety of experiences to meet the physical, intellectual, emotional, and social needs of the growing infant. The parent is aware of what to expect next in the infant's development and plans to try to meet his increasingly complex needs. Also built into this level is the ability of the parent to be aware of and to respond to her own personal needs as well as to those of other members of the family.

Levels V and VI consist of more complex behaviors across all areas of parenting. Many parents who have normal and easy-to-care-for infants will develop these behaviors on their own, based on their parenting experience. Other parents will need outside help for a variety of reasons, be it problems of the parent herself, social and environmental circumstances, a difficult and unresponsive baby, or any combinations of these factors.

SELECTION OF INDIVIDUAL PARENT BEHAVIORS

Each of the six levels of the PBP consists of a series of descriptions of behavior that reflect attitudes and feelings of parents as well as patterns of parenting. These descriptions of behavior (henceforth referred to as "behaviors") were empirically derived from the staff's experience with parents in the Intervention Program of the UCLA Infant Studies Project. The six levels comprising the framework of the PBP were conceptualized during the pilot phase of the program. The staff members recorded a large number of parent behaviors that either they had observed on home visits or at the project center, or that parents themselves had reported. The many behaviors thus assembled for each level were condensed into a manageable number and carefully scrutinized to avoid duplication and overlap. They were then grouped into content areas within each of the six levels. Only behaviors that were judged to be identified with positive or desirable parenting were included in the final list. Subsequently, the behaviors, their organization into levels, and their assignment to subgroups within levels were reviewed by a number of professionals outside the UCLA Intervention Program. Changes resulting from this review were incorporated into the Progression.

The quasi-hierarchical progression of the levels suggests an increase in the complexity of behaviors from level I to level VI. Therefore, components of complex behaviors at the higher levels, i.e., levels V and VI, are found at the lower levels. For example, in Form 2, item 13, level IV—"Parent talks to infant about what he sees, hears, feels, and does"—is a component behavior of item 1, level VI—"Parent makes everyday family activities and tasks meaningful for the infant." In such cases, when the same behavior can be recognized at two different levels of the PBP, it should be acknowledged or checked at both levels (see Appendix B).

USES OF THE PARENT BEHAVIOR PROGRESSION

The PBP was primarily intended to serve a clinical function, that is, to help infant specialists to focus on parent-infant interactions as well as to increase their awareness and sensitivity to parenting behaviors. The Progression can be used in a similar manner with students and trainees who are working with infants and parents. In educational and clinical programs, the PBP can serve as a tool that leads staff to support positive behaviors already in the parent's repertoire and to help the parent acquire new behavior patterns that enhance infant-parent interactions and the infant's development.

The PBP also has an evaluative function. The effectiveness of an intervention program can be evaluated by comparing initial assessment data with later data obtained with the PBP. However, it should be noted that certain fluctuations in parental behavior are due, in large part, to particular developmental changes in the behavior of infants and to the manner in which these changes affect their parents. For example, when

the infant between 15 and 18 months developmental age becomes assertive and begins to say *no* to the parent (behavior which is expected at this
age), the parent may go through a period of adapting to the new behavior.
This process of adaptation may affect her behavior toward the infant in a
way that will decrease, at least temporarily, the number of checks that a
parent receives on the PBP. Other fluctuations may be due to any number
of events in the home that either relieve or cause stress in the parent.

CONSIDERATIONS AND CAUTIONS IN THE USE OF THE PBP

There are several important issues and considerations that must be taken
into account by individuals attempting to use the Progression. One question is whether or not the PBP would benefit parents if it were to be
handed to them for their own use.

Not Intended for Use by Parents

The PBP was developed for use by professional staff who work with parents and was not intended to be used by the parents themselves. One might
logically claim that if the parent were handed the instrument, she could
evaluate her own parenting—using the PBP as a criterion—and set out on
her own to work toward achieving the behaviors that she perceives to be
"missing" in her repertoire. Some might even claim that it would be un-
ethical to "withhold" such an instrument from parents. The developers
of the PBP believe the opposite to be true and feel that it would be unethi-
cal and psychologically unsound to give the PBP to parents. Their reasons
are as follows:[2]

1. Parents' Need to Achieve Self-Confidence   One of the aims of the
PBP is to help parents grow more self-confident in their parenting role. It
is widely acknowledged that this self-confidence brings about greater effectiveness in parenting. The infant specialist can use the PBP to identify
the many desirable behaviors that a parent exhibits toward her infant. The
specialist can then find appropriate ways to support these positive behaviors and can explain to the parent specifically how she is fostering the infant's development. If the parent herself were to use the PBP to try to
achieve greater competence, the effect might well be the opposite, that is,
the parent might become less competent because of a reduced feeling of
self-assurance. Reading the behavioral descriptions in the PBP—which
supposedly represent "desirable parenting"—might make the parent feel

---

[2]The section containing the four reasons for not giving the PBP to parents was included
in the second of a series of papers on topics of interest to persons working in projects within
the Handicapped Children's Early Education Program. These papers are distributed by the
Western States Technical Assistance Resource (WESTAR), Seattle, Washington.

more doubtful and more anxious about her competence than she did before. This anxiety could interfere with her viewing the PBP behaviors in their proper perspective, as they relate to the infant's stage of development and to her own mothering style. Her anxiety would also make it difficult for her to keep in mind the fact that *no* parent, no matter how competent, is expected to engage in *all* the many behaviors listed in the PBP, and the fact that not all the behaviors in the PBP are realistic or even desirable goals for any one parent-infant dyad.

2. *Feelings Underlying Behavior*   Many of the behaviors listed in the Progression are simply behavioral expressions of feelings and attitudes that are not established at will, e.g., items 1 through 11 in level I (see both forms of the PBP in the appendix). The PBP was not conceived to be a list of behaviors from which a parent would select the ones that she would try to achieve in order to become a "better" parent. If a parent were to use the PBP in this manner, that is, to identify behaviors that she should practice, it is conceivable that she could exhibit behaviors without having the feelings that usually produce these behaviors spontaneously. (This is especially applicable to the behaviors at level I.) The conscious practice of "behaviors"—like the reporting of pleasure—that were meant to reflect feelings might cover up the way the parent *really* feels toward her infant, or might even result in her expressing the opposite from what she is really feeling. A parent's behavior that is incongruent with her feelings would be confusing to her infant—he would receive contradictory messages from the parent on the feeling and action (or verbal) levels. Although it is, at times, possible to practice intentionally a behavior and to produce gradually the feeling that goes with it, the self-consciousness that would accompany the parent's intentional expression of enjoyment, if it were not actually experienced, might further inhibit her movement toward genuine enjoyment of her child.

3. *Sharing Feelings with the Staff*   One of the valuable aspects of an intervention program is the relationship that usually develops between the parent and the intervention staff. This relationship prevents the parent from feeling so alone in carrying the burden of her infant's problems or her own problems in parenting the infant. The parent is often able to share with the staff her feelings toward the infant and her feelings about herself in the parenting role. However, it is difficult to imagine that a mother who needs to share some of her troubling feelings of inadequacy and ambivalence about her infant would do so if she were given the PBP. Handing this instrument to the parent tacitly conveys the message that the parent should try to achieve the behaviors that it lists. She could perceive being given the PBP as subtle pressure from the staff to show how much she "enjoys" her infant and how positively she interacts with him. This perception of pressure could easily prevent the parent from sharing her

genuine feelings and could cause her to distance herself emotionally from the staff. As she further suppresses her feelings of inadequacy and ambivalence toward her infant, she might experience increased anger toward him. This could result in more negative behavior toward the infant and further emotional withdrawal from him, regardless of the behaviors she might "exhibit" to the staff in order to gain their approval. At the same time, the parent may resent the staff for having placed this additional burden on her.

4. The Infant's Effect on Parenting   Many desirable parenting behaviors can be obstructed by the infant's behaviors. For example, the parent's reading and responding to the infant's cues (level II) is interfered with when the infant gives few cues or gives cues that are difficult to read. Parents find it hard to get pleasure from a passive, unresponsive infant, or even to continue to initiate social, play, or language interactions with him. The staff should be alert to the absence of parental enjoyment or mutually pleasurable interaction (levels I and III) that is caused primarily by the infant's behavior.

Parents with difficult-to-read and unresponsive infants are especially prone to feelings of inadequacy in their parenting role. They often believe that they are the cause of the infant's passivity, and they find it difficult to accept that they are not responsible for every aspect of their child's behavior. Parents of such infants need much support, and this support could be undermined by their being handed the PBP. Parents' own use of the instrument might increase their tendency to feel guilty and to withdraw from their infants as they see the gap between their own interactions with their infants and the kinds of interactions that the PBP suggests.

Parents of infants who are unresponsive and whose cues are difficult to read need to become aware of the part their infants play in discouraging positive and mutually pleasurable interaction. When an infant makes it difficult for the parent to become involved with him, the staff and the parent need to share the problem and pool their efforts and knowledge of the infant in order to cooperatively find ways to successfully engage the parent and infant with each other. This difficult and emotionally stressful task should not be imposed on the parent to deal with on her own; it is too heavy a burden!

Because consideration of the infant's effect on parent-infant interaction could not be built into the Progression, the staff has to be relied upon to be sensitive to the infant's impact on parenting and on the parent's feelings about herself and the infant.

Active Role of Parent in Intervention

It might appear to some that because the parent does not use the Parent Behavior Progression, the parent is put into a "passive" role in the intervention program. On the contrary, the guidelines set forth in Chapter 2 make clear the thinking that the parent should be an active and conscious participant in effecting change, rather than a "passive receiver" of assistance. As is stated in the guidelines, the parent should be in control, should take the initiative as much as possible, should communicate or clarify her priorities for the infant and for herself and her family, and should be strongly supported by the staff in the positive parenting that she exhibits. The intervention staff should be a resource to parents who are self-initiating. In the case of parents who function at first in a more passive manner, the staff should provide the kind of support that will help them gradually grow more independent. At level VI—the highest level of the Progression—the parent shows through her attitudes and behaviors that she is engaging in desirable parenting, independent of the staff. Since this kind of behavior is identified as highly desirable, it can be inferred that the PBP encourages the staff to help parents achieve independence as effectively as possible. A parent who initiates positive interactions with her infant and who, on her own, provides for him the kind of environment that enhances his development is likely to have played an active rather than a passive role in the intervention process.

Use of Behaviors as Goals

Professionals working with the PBP should exercise caution when using the behaviors as intervention goals. First, the behaviors that are included in the PBP do not constitute an exhaustive list of all of the possible, desirable parenting behaviors that could be identified. In addition, some of the behaviors, especially those at level I, are not necessarily the kind of behaviors that one expects to become part of a "good" parenting pattern, that is, they are simply examples of behaviors from which one could infer that the parent is experiencing some enjoyment of her infant, like "Parent spontaneously talks about the things the infant does that please her." Moreover, all of the behaviors in the Progression may not even be desirable in the context of an individual parent-infant dyad. For example, suppose that the mother of an infant who is severely delayed and unresponsive frequently comments in exuberant language about how alert her infant is and about how much she enjoys watching his responsiveness to her. It is unlikely that this behavior would be considered desirable, especially if it is part of an extensive denial system. Similarly, if the parent of such an infant reported that she experiences no pleasure in watching her infant, her demonstration or reporting of pleasure in this activity (item 1, level I) would not become an intervention goal to be pursued actively with this parent. In this particular case, it would be preferable to move to level IV so as to get the mother engaged with the infant in an activity in which the infant might show some minimal positive reaction. The infant's responses gradually might lead to the parent's enjoyment of her infant in a few activities.

These examples are given to emphasize: 1) that specific behaviors of the PBP may or may not be evidence of desirable parenting, depending on the circumstances of the case, and 2) that the absence of particular PBP behaviors may be appropriate or even desirable in a particular case. Only the absence of *many* of the behaviors, especially those at the first four levels of the PBP which represent the more basic caregiving practices, would indicate a need for intervention at one or more levels and might point to specific areas of behavior where intervention could be particularly effective.

Not All Behaviors Expected

It should be clearly understood that *no one parent is expected to show all of the behaviors of the Progression,* no matter how competent he or she might be. Parents differ in style, i.e., two mothers might exhibit different combinations of PBP behaviors and still be considered equally competent. Even if, hypothetically, a particular parent were to practice all of the behaviors listed, it is highly unlikely that the staff would be able to get evidence for every single behavior simply from observing and talking with that parent. It should also be taken into account that some parents are much less communicative about their interactions with their infants than others. Therefore, behaviors may be practiced by a parent but may not be checked on the PBP because the staff has not observed them and the parent has not reported them.

Focus on Positive Behaviors Only

The only behaviors that were selected to be included in the PBP are those that describe desirable attitudes, feelings, and actions. This focus was intentional, so that the behaviors could serve as possible goals of intervention. The omission of undesirable behaviors could be interpreted as a limitation to the use of the PBP by those who feel that noting detrimental behaviors of parents toward their infants is just as important in an intervention program as identifying positive behaviors. However, experience has shown that program staff have little difficulty in becoming aware of undesirable parental behaviors and attitudes, but that staff find it more difficult to become aware of the many strengths that parents show in their interactions with their infants. Staff in the UCLA Intervention Program also found that it is often more effective to add positive behaviors to the parent's repertoire than to try to eliminate undesirable behaviors. When the parent learns that there are alternatives that seem to be more effective than her customary way of dealing with her infant in a particular situation, these alternatives frequently become incorporated into her pattern of parenting and gradually replace the undesirable behaviors.

Parents' Expressions of Negative Feelings

The developers of the Parent Behavior Progression recognize that the parent's ability to express her negative feelings about her infant—sometimes even directly to him—is an important part of a healthy relationship between parent and child, even though such behaviors were not included in the PBP. Healthy parent-infant interaction involves the parent *reading* the infant's cues as well as the parent *giving* cues that are clear enough for the infant to read. A parent who is unable to express some anger verbally and facially when she feels it gives mixed messages to the infant that confuse him and interfere with his emotional development, which includes adaptation to the reality of people's responses to his actions. Furthermore, many parents, especially those with difficult or deviant babies, may need help before they are able to express to other adults some of their disappointments and frustrations with their infants. (Legitimate expressions of anger exclude, of course, psychological or physical abuse or neglect.)

Cultural and Individual Differences

The PBP behaviors do not necessarily reflect the mores and childrearing practices of a number of cultures or sub-cultures with whom this instrument might be used. It is important for staff to become familiar with the cultural influences on the childrearing patterns of the parents in their programs. This knowledge would provide the staff with some basis for making judgments about which behaviors could be expected in a particular family or about which behaviors can be realistically viewed as intervention goals. However, caution should be exercised not to overgeneralize about cultural mores in relation to individual families. The importance of staff sensitivity to individual styles and patterns of interactions within a particular family cannot be overestimated when working with parents and infants, whatever their cultural milieu.

Using the PBP with Parents of Handicapped Infants

Many parents of handicapped infants or infants with atypical behavior tend to be under great emotional stress, especially within several months after they become aware of their children's problems. Infant specialists working with such families should guard against being intrusive—emotionally or physically—in their eagerness to help. It may be unrealistic to expect many behaviors from the first three levels of the Progression, especially during periods of intense stress. In such cases, it is usually more productive to focus on behaviors at level IV, which deal more specifically with things that the parent can *do with and for* the infant. It may be best to find out first what type of contact the parent enjoys the most—or minds the least—with her infant and then to help her expand her effectiveness and sense of adequacy in these areas, instead of moving into areas where the parent may feel uncomfortable. Intervention that allows the parent to set her own direction and pace in her interactions with her handicapped infant is most likely to lead ultimately to mutually satisfying transactions between parent and child.

Many parents have ambivalent feelings about their handicapped young children. The parents can become overwhelmed with problems with which anyone would find it difficult to cope. The behavioral manifestations of such ambivalent feelings are varied. They can include overprotective behavior, excessive physical or verbal expression of affection, or withdrawal from the infant. When ambivalent feelings are reflected in exaggeratedly affectionate or solicitous behavior, it is better for staff not to support or reinforce such behavior if it seems incongruent with apparent feelings. When such behavior is acknowledged in a fairly neutral manner by staff who are not clinically experienced or qualified to deal psychotherapeutically with the underlying feelings, it may help the parent to deal with or even to express her feelings sooner.

Another type of situation comes to mind in which the Intervention Program staff was careful not to encourage behavior that ordinarily would be considered desirable. In the pilot program, the staff chose not to encourage the mother of a severely retarded infant to hold him closer to her body for his greater comfort. Holding this well-cared-for baby at a slight distance from herself seemed to be this mother's way of protecting herself from getting too emotionally involved with an infant that she might not be able to keep in her home.

The above examples are discussed here in order to make it clear that some PBP behaviors could be counterproductive to the overall goals of intervention, depending upon the circumstances of a particular case. It is the responsibility of the staff to make the delicate and difficult decisions as to the best use of the Parent Behavior Progression in any given case.

Family Crises

Although the Progression does not specifically assist staff in noting acute crises and the resulting stresses that impinge on a parent or family from time to time, sudden changes in parenting behaviors that may signal a sudden increase in stress can be detected with the PBP. When a parent is going through a crisis—whether or not it is related to the infant—the most immediate goal of intervention should, of course, be to help relieve some of the stress by whatever direct assistance or referral the parent may need. Helping the parent cope with the immediate crisis is also likely to be the most effective way to bring the parent's attention back to her infant as soon as possible.

Balancing Needs within the Family

A natural effect of infant intervention is that the parent pays more attention to the infant. However, in some cases the increased focus on the infant is accompanied by a decrease in the attention accorded other family members, which sometimes can border on neglect. It is the responsibility of an intervention staff to try to support the parent in maintaining a balance in her response to the needs of *every* family member. (This parental behavior is described in Form 1 as item 4, level VI and in Form 2 as item 7, level VI.) It is equally important for the staff to encourage the parent to consider her own needs and to attend to them. The staff's expression of concern regarding the parent's own needs communicates to the parent that someone thinks of her and cares about her. Moreover, with respect to the parent-infant relationship, it is essential that the parent pursue some of her own personal interests so that she does not become resentful of her child for being the cause of her deprivations.

PBP Requires Sensitive Decision Making

Because of the complexity of parenting and parent-infant interactions as well as the delicate nature of assessing parenting, great sensitivity is required on the part of those who use instruments such as the Parent Behavior Progression. Users of the PBP have to make keen judgments based on their experience in working with parents and their knowledge of child and infant development. The person using the PBP has to be able to determine for each individual family which behaviors can and should be aimed for in the course of an intervention program. Staff who work with a family on a continuing basis will be able to make the best use of the instrument.

In conclusion, the best justification for using the Parent Behavior Progression is that it serves as a means of sensitizing intervention staff to the feelings, attitudes, and behaviors of parents toward the end of better enabling the staff to help parents achieve greater enjoyment, satisfaction, and competence with their infants.

INTERVENTION
IN ACTION
Case Discussions

In part III the thirty cases that were assigned to the UCLA Intervention Program are presented. Cases that were evaluated as "successful" in reaching intervention goals are discussed in Chapter 5. Cases that were considered to have been only partially successful or unsuccessful in attaining intervention goals are presented in Chapter 6.

Most of the case discussions in both chapters begin with a brief description of the family and events in the home. Information regarding the infant is then given. The case discussion concludes with a summary of the intervention that was provided.

Chapter 5
Cases with Successful Intervention

This chapter contains descriptions of cases for which intervention was judged to have been effective, i.e., in which the program goals were largely achieved. Staff judgment was one of the ways by which intervention effectiveness was evaluated. Staff members were asked to rate the intervention for each of their cases as being either "successful," "partially successful," or "unsuccessful," and then to elaborate on the rating with statements providing the rationale for the evaluation. Some examples of those statements, taken from a number of different cases, are as follows:

+ *Statements* (refer to achieved goals)

Mother makes appropriate choices of activities for her infant.

Mother became confident in her parenting role.

Mother learned to communicate her own needs and found ways of satisfying at least some of them.

Father made good use of intervention staff to help him cope with the child's deviant behavior.

Mother is less intrusive, overstimulating, and infantilizing—allows more autonomy to her infant.

− *Statements* (refer to unachieved goals)

Mother still fails to anticipate child's behavior enough to provide adequately for his physical safety.

Mother gives little thought to continuity of caregiving.

Baby's needs continue to be a low priority—overshadowed by demands made on a single working mother with low income and with three children.

Mother's compulsive talking prevents her from listening and contingently responding to the infant's language.

Intervention was unable to help mother have more consistently pleasurable interactions with her infant.

The staff judgments, given specific force by statements such as the above, were found to be positively related to scores obtained from the

Parent Behavior Progression (used only with the Intervention Program population) and from the Beckwith Home Observations (a measure used with all of the UCLA Project cases). This correlation—especially with the latter measure, which was external to the Intervention Program—makes a strong case for the validity of the staff's judgments.

Families with which intervention was judged to be successful varied widely as to socio-economic status, racial-ethnic background, home environment, and the nature of problems of both infants and parents. The 16 cases discussed in this chapter have been divided into three groups. The first group contains six cases in which either the infant or the parent(s) had minor or temporary problems. Everyone involved was highly responsive to intervention and progressed satisfactorily with minimal assistance. These cases were classified as "low time/effort cases." The second group contains eight families with a variety of serious problems. The predominant problems were either in the infant, in the parent, in the parent-sibling relationship, or in the environment. The third group contains two very complex cases in which the infants' problems were compounded by various other stresses unrelated to the infant.

It should be remembered that the intervention staff began to see the families after the infants' cumulative risk scores had been computed subsequent to their 9-month testing. Therefore, the infants were all between 9 and 10 months corrected age when they were referred to the Intervention Program. Intervention began at about 10 months and continued with each family until the infant reached 2 years corrected age, unless otherwise indicated in the case discussion.

The cases in Chapter 5 and Chapter 6 are presented in the following manner.[1] First, the *family* is described: who the family members are, who is in the home all the time, who is employed outside the home, and the SES and racial-ethnic make-up of the family. The background of the parents, the support system available to them, and recent events in the life of the family are referred to when they appear to have significantly affected family dynamics and the infant's environment.

Information is then given about the *infant,* including gestational age and any medical and developmental problems that occurred during the first weeks or months of life. Medical and anthropometric data at birth are not included in order to avoid placing undue emphasis on facts that, in most cases, had relatively little relevance to parent-oriented intervention that began when the infant was 10 months of age.

Finally, the particular course that *intervention* took is discussed in relation to the sequence of events in the family and to the changes that oc-

---

[1]The descriptions of cases *a* through *f* are quite brief and do not entirely conform to the indicated format. These six cases are dealt with more as a group than are the other cases presented in Part III.

curred with respect to the infant, the parent, and parent-infant interaction. The length of this section varies greatly from case to case. Some cases are discussed in greater detail than are others so as to enable the reader to gain an understanding of the complex factors that were involved in the dynamics of individual families and in an intervention process that extended over a period of 14 months or more.

FAMILIES WITH MINOR OR TEMPORARY PROBLEMS

The cases in this group had the following characteristics:

1. Four of the six infants had serious neonatal problems
2. All six infants had minimal problems by age 10 months and by age 2 all were functioning at age level or above
3. All six children were responsive and were enjoyed by their parents by the end of the intervention program
4. The mothers in each case were receptive to help and profited a great deal from relatively infrequent contact with the intervention staff
5. All were intact nuclear families in which the mother was the primary caregiver of the infant

The families differed with respect to SES and racial-ethnic background. Two families were low SES and hispanic. Although relatively poor, both families were stable. One of these two families had twin infants, both of whom were in the program. Both fathers had low-paid but steady employment. The three other families were high SES—one black, one mixed hispanic and white, and the third, white.*

Case *a*

In the first of the two low SES hispanic families, the infant's problems began at delivery. He was quite ill for several weeks after birth and, although he was only 3 weeks preterm, there was concern regarding his survival. His early problems were described as a weak suck, hypertonia, heart murmur, and "difficult to soothe." He had frequent illnesses for the first 8 months of his life. At 9 months, however, all his medical difficulties disappeared.

Publisher's Note: In the Southwest United States, where a large portion of the population is hispanic, the word "anglo" is often used to designate the racial background of individuals who are white but not hispanic or American Indian (now sometimes called *Native American*). Although the author originally used the word "anglo," "white" has been substituted because of its more widely accepted usage. In the remainder of the book, hispanic is used to designate Spanish-speaking backgrounds and "white" is used for those who are neither black nor hispanic. Other racial groups that are represented less frequently in these pages are identified with more precision, i.e., Korean and American Indian.

From the beginning, the infant's young mother was remarkably sensitive to the needs of her difficult baby. She was receptive to help from the medical-nursing team during the infant's first 9 months and later from the intervention staff. As the infant became more responsive, the interactions between infant and mother became more mutually pleasurable. The difficult young infant grew into a charming and responsive toddler who was functioning at age level or above in all developmental areas by 18 months of age, after some initial delay in fine motor and language development.

The thrust of intervention in this case was to support the mother's sensitive responsiveness to her infant, to model for her some language and play interaction with the infant, and to give evidence to both parents of the infant's rapid progress by showing them videotapes taken over a period of time. The infant's motivation to play was increased by the provision of materials with which he could experience success. Play with these materials helped to increase the infant's fine motor skills. By age 18 months, the infant was developing satisfactorily and the parents enjoyed their child and felt secure in their parenting. Intervention visits were made only once a month during the last 6 months of the program for the purpose of monitoring the progress of parents and child.

Cases *b* and *c*

The second of the two low SES hispanic families had a pair of twins, a boy and a girl. They were born 5 weeks preterm but did not have the kind of traumatic beginning that the other infants in this group had. Still, their cumulative risk scores at 9 months categorized them as "high risk." By 10 months of age, both were slow to warm up to anyone outside the immediate family. The female infant was quite passive and her male twin was slightly delayed in gross motor development. Neither infant initiated much vocalization. The twins had an older sister, who was 2 years older than they. The older sister tended to overpower the twins, but their very competent mother was able to control the situation when she was made aware of it. The mother stayed home to care for all three children, although the family barely made ends meet financially. She responded quickly to modeling and suggestions by the staff. She was able to generalize easily and soon generated a variety of experiences for the infants to enhance all areas of their development. Both father and mother were eager to do everything they could to ensure that their children "would do well in school."

Although both infants were at first somewhat delayed in adaptive play and in language, they were functioning well within the normal range by 20 months. Around that time, the frequency of home visits was decreased to once a month, again because of diminished need by parents with a high level of competence.

Case *d*

The fourth infant in this group was born 9 weeks preterm to an upwardly mobile black couple (high SES). The female infant was one of a pair of twins—the other twin died at birth. For several months, there was concern about the project infant's survival. The parents considered their baby to be vulnerable and kept her in bed with them for several months for fear that she might die during the night. However, by 9 months of age, the infant was a well-developed, healthy, delightful little girl who commanded everyone's admiration and attention. The mother had positive and mutually pleasurable interactions with her attractive and responsive daughter up to about 20 months of age. At this point, the mother experienced some difficulties in dealing with the child as she began to show a strong will and some assertiveness which the mother interpreted as aggressive behavior. The father's role with the infant as well as with the mother appeared to be somewhat inconsistent. At times he seemed to be quite interested in the infant and supportive of the mother, while at other times, he seemed remote and uninvolved.

The mother, although taking full advantage of the play materials that the staff provided, was somewhat less responsive to modeling than were the other mothers in this group of cases. Both parents viewed their child as a "superbaby" and may not have felt much need for help until the mother began to have problems in setting limits for her. The infant was very social and made good progress in all areas of development. Gradually, the mother and child were able to adapt to each other's temperament.

Home visits were scheduled about once a month after the child reached 12 months—at least until the last few weeks of the program. The infant was doing well and the parents did not seem to seek, want, or need much help. The contacts became more frequent as the child approached 2 years of age. During the last 2 to 3 months of the program, the staff helped the mother to cope more effectively with the child's assertiveness and helped her to find a suitable group program for the child in the community. The staff agreed with the parents that this mature, independent, physically large and strong child would profit from a group experience earlier than some other children her age.

Case *e*

The fifth infant in this group was a little girl born at only 25 weeks gestational age, weighing 2 pounds. Everyone was greatly concerned about the child's survival. The family's private pediatrician had warned the parents about the uncertain prognosis for this infant, even if she should manage to survive. The mother's reaction to this warning was to be somewhat overprotective. However, with the reassurance of the pediatric-nursing team at UCLA during the infant's first few months of life, and subsequently with that of the intervention team, the mother was able to relax and realize that her baby was healthy and was progressing normally.

At the time intervention began with this middle-class family (hispanic father and white mother), the father was finishing his professional studies. Toward the end of the 14-month intervention period, he began to practice his profession, which entailed the family moving to a different city in California, at a considerable distance from Los Angeles. In spite of this distance, the team continued its contact with the family, although home visits were made less frequently.

The infant became one of the most delightful and responsive infants in the program. Interactions between parents and infant were pleasurable and satisfying. The child's developmental test scores at 2 years of age were in the superior range—the highest of any child in the program. Mention is made here of the high scores only to support the position that low birth weight combined with low gestational age—although putting the infant at risk for survival—do not necessarily result in delayed development or in deviant behavior.

The work of the intervention staff was satisfying with this family, as it was with the others in this group, because of the receptiveness of the parent and the rapid progress made by parent and infant. The kind of help that the team provided for this family consisted mainly of reassurance regarding the normal progress of the infant, support for the excellent quality of parenting and parent-infant interaction that was observed, and, toward the termination of the program, some emotional support for the mother when she became pregnant again and was somewhat anxious during the first few months of her pregnancy.

Case *f*

In the last case of this group, the mother was seriously ill before the birth of the infant at 35 weeks gestational age. She was told that future pregnancies would be hazardous. The pediatrician was concerned about the infant's health and development, but only for a couple of months. The mother did not seem to share that concern and once she was well again she took him out to show him off to family and friends. He was the first child in this white family and his parents and his grandparents apparently enjoyed him. The mother had support from her parents and she shared babysitting arrangements with other women in the apartment house where the family lived. The infant showed satisfactory progress in all areas of development.

The intervention staff had no particular concern in this case, except for the mother's extreme eagerness to do everything she could to ensure that the child would be a high achiever in school. The staff helped her to become more relaxed about his future performance so that she could enjoy him more fully and be more sensitive to his cues. When the infant was 17 months old, the mother felt compelled to go back to work to pay back the large debt incurred as the result of expenses connected with her extended hospitalization after giving birth. Yet, she did not want to leave the child. Her conflicting feelings about going to work produced temporary stress in her relationship with the child and she became tense in her interactions with him. Gradually, she was able to accept her dual role, she became more relaxed with her child, and the quality of interaction took an upward turn. At the termination of intervention, the infant scored above average on developmental tests and the mother received high ratings on the PBP.

The five families in the group just discussed had several things in common that contributed to effective intervention. First, the infant was a high priority compared with other matters. The staff felt that this particular factor was critical for successful intervention with every case in the program. Second, these families were eager for help and were responsive to the program's approach. The parents profited from modeling, they acted readily upon suggestions, and they were able to incorporate new behaviors into their natural patterns of parenting. Third, none of the mothers needed much help in the area of affective interaction with their infants when the intervention staff first met these families. Bonding and early interaction between mothers and infants was, of course, supported by the medical-nursing team in the first few months of the infant's life, especially in cases where infants and mothers were separated for a period after birth. The five mothers' initial profile on the Parent Behavior Progression showed enjoyment of the infant, fairly accurate reading of the infant's biological and affective cues, and mutuality in interaction with the infant—either from the start of the program or soon after (levels I, II, and III of the PBP—see Appendix B). Therefore, the staff was able to concentrate on the language and play area of the infant's behavior. All but one of the six infants needed some help and support in these areas.

The intervention approach followed in the program seemed to be effective with the six infants discussed above. The staff helped to make the parents aware of their skills and the parents responded well to the support that the staff gave them for their responsiveness to their infants and their strengths in parenting. They all were able to generalize from the staff's modeling and from their own successes. They were able—even with very limited financial means—to provide environments that were conducive to the optimum development of their infants.

Four of the five families discussed in this first group experienced a great deal of stress due to traumatic experiences related to the birth or to the survival of mother or infant. Nonetheless, the parents sustained their high level of motivation to be competent parents. It may be that the combination of early concern about the infant, stability of family, acceptance and enjoyment of the parenting role, and eagerness to help the infant develop optimally made these families especially receptive to intervention. (All of the infants except the twins were first-borns.) Minimal time spent with these families led to rapid achievement of intervention goals: self-confidence as parents, mutually pleasurable interaction with their infants, and generally competent parenting.

FAMILIES WITH DOMINANT PROBLEMS IN ONE AREA

The cases described here all had problems of a serious nature in one of the following areas: in the infant's development, in the mother's attitude toward her role, in the parent-sibling relationship, or in the home environment. The two team members assigned to each case independently judged the intervention to have been successful. An analysis of these cases seemed to indicate that when problems tended to be concentrated in one area rather than to be spread across several areas, intervention was more likely to be successful.

Locus of Problem: The Infant

In the two cases that follow, the infant's problem was of major concern to the staff and the parents. The first case involved an infant who appeared to function well within the normal range in every respect up to about 11 months of age, but whose behavior became increasingly deviant between 12 and 18 months. Intervention was very active with the mother-infant dyad and frequent staff conferences and consultations took place with regard to the case. The infant in the second case was mildly retarded and had cerebral palsy. The mother's intense concerns about this child were expressed in her overprotectiveness and overstimulation of him.

Case M   The infant was the first-born of a black couple. The father was American by birth and the mother had been born and raised in a middle-class family in a country in West Africa. The mother's teenage sister lived in the home and became increasingly involved in the care of the infant. The father, although apparently quite active with the infant, was not often at home during the intervention home visits which were made—at the request of the mother—in the late afternoon when the mother had just returned from work. The mother was employed full time throughout the 14 months of the program, and during her working hours, the infant was cared for by a daycare provider outside the home.

A number of Mrs. M's childrearing practices differed from those most common in the United States. For example, the infant was not allowed to mouth objects. He was started on solid foods much later than is common practice in the United States, and he was not encouraged by his mother toward greater independence. Finger foods were unfamiliar to the mother and no value was put on the child's beginning to feed himself when he seemed ready. Also, feeding was not considered to be a social time for mother and infant. Furthermore, the mother did not allow the child to be outdoors for fear that he might hurt himself.[2]

The infant's pattern of development was an unusual one. He was born at 35 weeks gestational age without serious medical complications. At 10 months of age, when the intervention team first saw him, his strength seemed to be his sociability and the level of his language development. The only peculiar quality about him from the outset was his uncommon fascination with television. At 13 months, he stopped vocalizing and interacting with people. The team became concerned about the infant's hearing when he stopped responding to his name and to other sounds around him. His hearing was tested and found to be normal. By age 14 months, it was extremely difficult to make eye contact with him. He began to produce a low, groan-like monotone—a sound that sometimes continued for several minutes and that had a self-stimulating quality. At about 17 months, the team observed that his adaptive play often deteriorated into repetitive turning of objects in his hands. He also began to spin objects. He often reached for people's arms or hands, as tools or extensions of his own hands, without making eye contact or without even looking toward the person connected to that hand. Occasionally he would be successful in an activity with a toy, but he would not be able to repeat his success. He also became increasingly resistant to being held, and he was in constant motion.

At first the parents did not realize that the infant's behavior was becoming deviant. For instance, the mother stated that she thought his long, self-stimulating sounds were normal vocalizations for his age. But when the infant's babbling stopped, she became quite anxious. As a result of the infant's lack of responsiveness, the mother found it difficult to initiate interactions with him.

The team assured the mother that she was not responsible for the unexpected changes in the infant's behavior and tried to help her work with the infant in ways that held the most promise for guiding his development in the direction of more normal behavior. Once the mother became active in carrying out some of the specific plans that were made cooperatively

---

[2]It is unclear how much Mrs. M's childrearing patterns reflected those of her native country and how much her mothering reflected her personal attitudes. According to conversations with Mrs. M, it appeared that a greater protectiveness of the infant is more common in her native country—primarily with respect to the ingesting of unhealthy substances (dirt or germs)—and that thought is given much later than in the United States to the infant's movement toward autonomy.

with the intervention staff, her anxiety diminished. As the child began to respond to her efforts to engage him in eye contact and social interaction (at around 18 months), she again began to initiate more interaction with him. At the time, it was difficult to convince the mother that the more basic problem was not the language delay but his problems in interacting with people. Only when the infant had become more social again was the mother able to talk about how upsetting his lack of social responsiveness had been.

At 19 months, the infant started again to produce some language sounds—*ba ba* and *da da*—and to experiment with voice intonation. The unusual monotone still occurred, but it became shorter and less frequent. At 20 months, the child occasionally made eye contact with adults and sometimes engaged in social games with parents and staff. At about 22 months, he repeated verbalizations like *bye bye,* although he did not seem to understand their meaning. Two weeks later, he looked for approval from his parents for the first time and showed some satisfaction in his own success in play. The quality of his adaptive play remained inconsistent, but he was able to solve some problems when he could focus long enough to pursue a goal. By age 24 months, the child was quite social again, but he still produced few vocalizations spontaneously. (He said *Mama* with awareness of meaning.) The monotone had stopped, but it reappeared occasionally when he was either bored or upset. His play continued to be inconsistent in quality. This inconsistency characterized most of his behavior during that period.

The staff was not aware of any dramatic events in the infant's environment that might have traumatized him sufficiently to cause this deterioration in behavior between 12 and 18 months. No changes occurred in the family, and the only stressful event in the mother's life appeared to be the changes in her child's behavior. The team member who worked with the parent and infant throughout the period of their participation in the program had excellent rapport with the mother from the beginning, and communication between them remained open and active for the entire intervention period. (This staff member was also from a non-English-speaking country and had had to make an adjustment to an unfamiliar culture. This common experience added to the good rapport.)

There was a potentially significant "unknown" in this case: the infant's environment in the home of the daytime caregiver and the nature of that individual's interactions with the infant. The mother showed no concerns about this daycare provider situation at any time. She had requested the team not to visit the daycare provider—she claimed to have lost a previous daycare provider as a result of a visit by "people from the University." She did not want to take any more chances of losing another caregiver who seemed adequate to her and who lived in her immediate neighborhood. The same person took care of the child throughout the intervention period—during the deterioration of the infant's behavior and then, later, during his developmental progress in a positive direction.

Interventions with this mother-infant dyad were primarily of three kinds. First, support was given to the mother to help her through a difficult period with the infant. The staff member communicated to the mother her own frustrations and failures in getting the infant to respond to her or to materials that she presented to him. This helped the mother realize that the infant's unresponsiveness and unusual behavioral patterns were not due to her "incompetence," as she feared. Second, the staff member and the mother cooperatively explored ways to motivate the infant to make eye contact with them; to respond affectively to their efforts; to use materials in a less perseverative and affectless manner; and to gain greater enjoyment from social, language, and play activities. This cooperative effort was possible because of the mutual trust and open communication that existed between the mother and the intervention team. Third, the staff stimulated and reinforced the mother's positive efforts with her infant and alerted her to any progress in the infant's behavior, no matter how minute. The staff saw the mother's skills increase rapidly, as she was steadily reinforced by the infant's gradual increase in responsiveness. This intervention approach was very successful with Mrs. M.[3]

The team maintained contact with this family even after the child turned 2. The staff member who had been on case M from the beginning continued to see the mother and child as long as it seemed necessary to give the mother the help and support she needed with the difficult child. The trust that the mother felt toward this staff member transferred smoothly to a relatively new team member when the mother needed immediate help in relation to a school placement while the other staff member was on vacation.

Intervention was evaluated as successful both because of the mother's responsiveness to the staff—evidenced by her many questions and by the quality and nature of her efforts with her infant—and because of observations demonstrating increasingly normal and positive mother-infant interactions. Furthermore, the mother gradually accepted the fact that her child was "different" and that she was not to blame for his deviant behavior. As a result of her trust in the staff and her ability to profit from the help that was given to her, she became an accurate observer of her child's behavior. She gained not only from modeling by the staff as the latter explored ways of motivating the child to interact affectively, but also from frequent discussions in which she raised questions and shared her observations and, at times, her anxiety. She was able to incorporate

---

[3]Interventions used in relation to specific problems will be discussed in more detail in Chapter 8.

much new behavior into her mothering style and to generalize from what she observed and experienced.

The gradual increase in mutual pleasure in the interactions between mother and child became quite visible to the staff. This change was probably due to the mother's persistent efforts with the child and her increased confidence in her own competence as a parent as she began to see progress in the child. According to the mother's own report, her steady efforts were strengthened by the solid support she felt from the team.

As would be expected, there was quite a delay before the positive changes in the infant's behavior that had been observed in the home situation affected the infant's test performance. Although he scored low, in the educable retarded range, on developmental tests at age 2, he was recently reported to have scored at the low end of the normal range at age 4. The examiner's report indicated that his behavior did not appear deviant. He was also doing quite well in a child care center in his community.

One can speculate in this case that intervention prevented complete deterioration of mother-infant interaction as a result of an extremely difficult and unrewarding child. Intervention support enabled the mother to continue initiating interactions with him, despite the child's unresponsiveness and autistic-like behavior. The developments in this case support the proposition that changes in parent behaviors and in parent-infant interactions constitute a potent force in the development of the child. However, the effects of these changes on the child are gradual and are not demonstrable in test performance until after a considerable time has elapsed.

This case, although a particularly difficult one because of the infant's gradually deteriorating behavior, constitutes an example of effective intervention in the following manner: The staff's interactions with the mother appeared to reduce the mother's anxiety sufficiently to enable her to become actively involved in "interventions" with the infant. The continuous support by the staff and the gradual response of the infant to the mother's efforts raised the mother's confidence in her own skills as well as her expectations. This change, in turn, made the mother increasingly open to change in response to the infant's more normal behavior.

Case O   The infant was the youngest of three children in a stable, low SES, Spanish-speaking family. The mother was in the home and cared for the children. Home visits were made in the late afternoon to allow the father to be present. There appeared to be no particular financial stress in spite of the family's low income. The mother and infant received much support from members of the extended family who lived nearby.

The infant was a very high priority with his mother. The staff felt at times that priority was given to the infant at the expense of the mother's relationship with the middle child, an 8-year-old girl. The mother's strong commitment to doing whatever she could for her handicapped infant was clear from the outset. Although it took the mother 2 hours to travel to UCLA, she came to the Center for alternate intervention sessions. (These trips were made because she and, later, her oldest son and the infant had medical problems for which they were seen at the UCLA Medical Center. The intervention sessions at the project Center were scheduled on the same days to coordinate with the medical appointments.)

The infant, 5½ weeks preterm, was the mother's third live birth out of seven pregnancies. He had respiratory complications, CNS abnormalities (mild spasticity), and serious eye problems. At age 4 months, and then again at 9 months, his developmental scores indicated mild retardation. When first seen by the intervention staff, he was delayed in all areas of development, with the least delay in the personal-social area. Although he made considerable progress in gross motor functioning, some spasticity persisted in his arms, hands, and legs. Fine motor problems interfered with his play, although his right hand was less tight than the left one. An eye examination at 12 months indicated that he was very farsighted and cross-eyed. He was fitted with glasses and was seen regularly at the UCLA Eye Clinic. Although his adaptive play improved considerably after he began to wear glasses, he continued to have some problems with visual processing. The child's expressive language lagged far behind his performance in the other developmental areas, but his receptive language improved more rapidly.

The parents gave a great deal of time, energy, and attention to the infant, and members of the extended family further supplemented the affection and social stimulation that he received from his immediate family. The mother's attention to him was reinforced by his responsiveness and positive affect. Unfortunately, the intensity of her activities with him did not allow her to be sensitive to some of his more subtle cues, nor did it encourage his development of autonomy. The staff felt that the mother tended to overstimulate the infant, especially in the form of continuous verbal bombardment. It should be noted that intensity in a mother's interaction with a handicapped child is not at all uncommon. It may result from anxiety about the child's condition and fear of what the future may hold in store for him, combined with an eagerness to "overcome" the handicap by sheer intensity of effort.

In case O, the short-term goals of intervention were to help the mother: 1) reduce the level of her anxiety, 2) tune in to the infant's cues and be responsive to them, 3) moderate the intensity of her activity and involvement with this child, and 4) anticipate the next stage of his development in different areas and therefore be able to plan for his immediate future. The mother was given much reassurance and specific information regarding the infant's progress, as well as strong support for those of her behaviors that were beneficial to his development. More appropriate verbal interactions with the infant were modeled for the mother, and alternate ways of presenting toys to him without directing his play were modeled and discussed.

The mother became more sensitive to the infant's subtle cues and more attuned to his behavior. She found it most difficult to modulate her verbal interaction with him—to stop her "verbal bombardment." After considerable discussion about language development and repeated modeling of language interaction with the infant by the staff, some improvement in the mother's language interaction with him was observed. She became conscious of having to pause long enough in her communications to him to give him a chance to respond vocally to her.

As the mother became more competent in enhancing the infant's developmental progress, another problem—only indirectly related to the infant—intensified. The mother was giving her 8-year-old daughter little positive attention and she became increasingly impatient and irritated with the daughter over minor incidents. The relationship between them seemed to be deteriorating. The staff, aware that a common effect of infant intervention is the parents' decreased attention to other children in the family, attempted to counteract this situation by involving the girl in conversations and activities as much as possible. The staff also discussed with the mother and grandmother the common problem of siblings of handicapped children feeling neglected. The team tried to model positive interaction with the girl by showing interest in her and appreciation of her qualities and abilities. The mother's relationship with her daughter improved, although it was not as positive at the time the program terminated as the staff would have wished. The team's efforts with regard to the mother's relationship with her daughter were less effective than their interventions with the mother regarding the infant.

Intervention was successful in relieving the mother's anxiety about her infant by helping her to see the progress that he was making. Mrs. O was able to incorporate many new behaviors into her mothering pattern that were beneficial to the infant's development. With much help and support from the team, the mother was finally able to allow the infant some autonomy, especially when he began to walk—albeit poorly—around age 2. The mother was also helped to develop more realistic expectations of her handicapped child. She gained sufficient knowledge of child development and the conditions that enhance it to enable her to make a wise choice regarding a special program for the child beyond age 2, even though the program she chose was not the one closest to their home. The mother demonstrated a growing independence from the staff, combined with the ability to ask for their help when she really needed it, even after the child had turned 2 years of age.

In this case, the minimal changes in infant test scores did not provide the evidence for the success of the program with the family. However, the effectiveness of intervention was demonstrated by the positive changes in the mother's interactions with the infant (reflected in the PBP profiles); the rise in the infant's motivation in language, social interaction, and play; the infant's improvement in task orientation and increased pleasure in success; and his steady progress in receptive language, gross motor development, and quality of play (recorded observations).

Locus of Problem: The Mother

The two cases that follow were similar in that both mothers had ambivalent feelings toward their infants, although probably for different reasons. The mothers' affective interactions with their infants were considered to be the primary problem. In both cases, the infants were male, born into intact middle-class families. The mothers were professional women and knew little about infants and their development.

Mrs. H's ambivalence toward her infant seemed to be due primarily to her isolation and her conflict regarding her role. Although she, unlike Mrs. E, chose to stay home with her baby (first-born), her consequent isolation apparently caused her to have resentments and ambivalent feelings toward the infant. On the other hand, Mrs. E's conflicting feelings toward her infant (second-born) seemed to be related primarily to her fears about his possible abnormality.

Infant H did not cause the staff any concern from the start. He was developing normally, his cues were clear and easy to read, and he was an active, responsive baby. The infant in case E, however, did present some problems that made mutually reinforcing interactions more difficult to achieve between mother and infant.

Case H   The family, a middle-class Korean couple, had recently immigrated to the United States. Mrs. H had finished college in Korea and had been engaged in a profession there. Her husband was still attending graduate school in Los Angeles and he worked in the evenings. Mrs. H's command of English was poor and she felt lonely and isolated. She did not make social contact with other Korean families in her community, partly because she felt emotionally torn between being part of the Korean culture and wanting very much to become part of the American culture. Because Mr. H was away from home so much of the time, the mother had to take care of the baby almost completely by herself. In a sense, she felt trapped, which aggravated her feeling of isolation.

The mother went through a succession of depressions. The most serious one occurred when the infant was 14 months old. She felt extremely lonely and ambivalent between wanting to be a "perfect mother" and continuing to pursue her career. While depressed, she sewed almost compulsively to take her mind off other things. (Periodically Mrs. H did sewing at home for which she was paid on a piecework basis.)

The infant was born shortly after the parents' arrival in the United States. Although born 11 weeks preterm, there were no serious concerns regarding his survival or normalcy. The "high risk" classification was due mostly to low scores on some physiological and psychological measures at term and 3 months.[4] His developmental scores were well within the normal range by 9 months of age. However, at 9 months his profile on the Gesell test showed a sharp contrast between a low fine motor and a very high gross motor score.

When the intervention staff first saw the infant, he was doing quite well. Around age 18 months, there was some concern about his short attention span and the parents commented on his lack of speech. At the start, a team of two staff members visited the home. Communication was difficult because of the mother's poor command of English. When a team member asked a friend of hers, a Korean woman, to accompany her on a home visit to act as interpreter, some misunderstandings were cleared up and communication improved. After that visit, the mother felt more comfortable telling the staff when she did not understand what someone was saying. When there were indications that the mother could communicate more easily with one person than with two, one team member visited the home by herself every other visit. Later, the second team member dropped out of the case altogether.

Intervention increasingly took the form of providing an opportunity for the mother to converse informally with the staff member (who was also a recent immigrant). Mrs. H was able to talk with her about the problems she was experiencing. She shared her feelings—her anxieties about being an "outsider" (foreigner), her ambivalence about her mothering role, and her confusion regarding the different modes of childrearing in the Korean and American cultures.

The team had serious concerns about the interaction between the mother and the infant almost from the beginning. His high activity level, quite normal for a robust child with outstanding gross motor ability, bothered her. She was also irritated with his inability to occupy himself for periods of 2 to 3 hours while she was sewing. She was not aware that such behavior could not be expected from an infant so young. The mother had many concerns about her child and about her mothering skills. She felt she knew nothing about what to expect from him as he progressed in age, and she was quite open to child development information when she was not depressed. She was afraid that the child would become "clingy"

---

[4]"At term" signifies the expected date of birth.

and unable to separate, "like Korean children." She wanted her child to become "independent like American children."

The mother sought the staff's help on how to handle separation with the infant. Ways of achieving separation without trauma to the child—gradually getting him used to a new environment and new people—were discussed with her. Although she seemed to understand the suggestions made to her, she dropped him off at a babysitter's home without preparation only a short time after this discussion. The child became very upset and subsequently the mother decided that he was not ready to separate from her. This decision was made despite the staff's offering to help her work through separation so that it would not be so difficult for him.

Much of the time, Mrs. H felt that she was unable to manage her child. She complained that she could not control him and that he was breaking their radio and television set. The team helped her realize that she was giving him mixed messages—saying "no" and laughing at the same time. Alternate methods of dealing with him were suggested and were modeled for her. She was able to utilize this new understanding, but a couple of months later a new problem of management arose. The child began to have tantrums in public—in grocery stores and other places. Mrs. H would become frustrated and very angry at the child. As she related what set off the tantrums and exactly how she tried to handle them, she began to realize that she could not use the same methods of discipline in public places that worked at home because she felt embarrassed and closely scrutinized as a foreigner. In public it was important to her that her child be a "well-behaved Oriental child." Eventually she resolved the problem by not exposing the child to situations she knew were difficult for him and for her.

When the child was approaching 2 years of age, the maternal grandmother arrived from Korea and she helped Mrs. H with the care of the child. This was a welcome event for the mother. As she felt the child to be less of a burden to her, she was able to enjoy him more. His greater verbal understanding also helped her in dealing more satisfactorily with him.

Intervention was judged to be successful because the staff was able to give this mother emotional support when she needed it and direct help in dealing more effectively with her child. As the mother's needs were being met, she was able to meet the child's needs more competently. Mrs. H asked many questions and was able to utilize information and suggestions effectively. She had no difficulty in generalizing both from modeling and from discussions—in fact, she was very imaginative and resourceful in applying her increased understanding to help her child develop skills in language and play. She was particularly skillful in motivating him in play and lengthening his attention span once she learned to read and respond to his cues and become aware of his play interests. Once she realized how competent she was and how she helped him increase his satisfaction in play, she particularly enjoyed her interaction with him in this area.

Mrs. H made good use of new knowledge in all areas to help her understand and cope with the child's changing behavior, especially when he went through stages that were difficult for her. As she felt more competent as parent and understood his behavior better, she was able to enjoy him much more in general and their interaction became mutually more pleasurable. Toward the end, she even confessed that her child had become a good companion to her.

Case E   The E's were an intact middle-class family, consisting of the parents, a 5-year-old girl, and the male project infant. The father was energetic, active, and talkative, whereas the mother, although very articulate, seemed reserved and controlled. Both were professionals and both worked full time. The mother resumed work when the baby was 1 month old. Daytime care, outside the home, was provided by an older woman who also cared for other children. The staff observed that this woman's interaction with the infant was limited to physical care.

The parents talked openly about their lack of knowledge about infants and their relative lack of interest in children in infancy. Both were anxious to prevent the 5-year-old from becoming jealous of the baby and consequently they lavished attention on her. The staff observed that this was sometimes done at the expense of the infant. The parents, especially the mother, seemed to ignore the infant much of the time for fear that the other child's jealous feelings might otherwise be aroused. At least, this was the rationale given to the team.

Both the male infant, born 2 months preterm, and his mother were in critical condition after delivery. The parents were told that the baby might have brain damage and that his development would have to be watched carefully for indications of deviations or delay. (This warning was given by a private physician before the infant was transferred to the UCLA Medical Center Newborn Intensive Care Unit.) At 10 months of age, the infant was a picture book baby—rosy, pudgy, with an appealing smile— but he was often passive and inclined to watch activity around him rather than to engage in it himself. His developmental pattern was quite uneven. He was somewhat delayed in gross motor development—he sat at 11 months and walked at 19 months. Once he began walking, he moved very carefully and somewhat stiffly, but he seldom fell down. Both his fine motor and adaptive ability were superior. At 18 months, he spontaneously performed tasks in adaptive play at the 30-month level—he was able to work puzzles intended for 3-year-olds. His expressive language was slow in developing, although his verbal understanding was advanced. He answered complex questions with grunts and gestures, yet, by age 2, he had a speaking vocabulary of less than 20 words. Given the cognitive potential he displayed with materials and by his receptive language, the staff speculated either that he was withholding language for emotional reasons or that he might have a neurologically based problem in expressive language.

Some peculiarities were observed in the infant's affect. From the beginning of intervention, he seemed to change rather abruptly from smiling to crying. Later on, the same sudden switches could be seen from smiling to a completely sober expression, almost as if he were putting on a mask and taking it off again. Yet, when he showed pleasure by smiling, he was extremely appealing. The team noticed that in the presence of a relative who was especially fond of him, he was more active, demanding, and socially responsive.

From the first home visit on, it was striking how infrequently Mrs. E paid attention to the infant. Many intervention sessions went by without the mother once smiling or talking to him or touching him. The first rather dramatic instance of the mother's ignoring of her baby occurred during a home visit when the mother returned from work after the team had arrived. As the mother entered the living room (the father was already home), she greeted everyone warmly, paid special attention to her 5-year-old, and ignored the infant who was sitting in the middle of the room on the floor. During later visits, the infant would sometimes crawl over to his mother and try to involve her in his play. More often than not, his attempts failed. Once or twice, he managed to get her attention only to have it diverted suddenly by a loud call of "Mommy" from the 5-year-old across the room.

Based on observations and conversations with the parents, the staff believed that the mother's fear of the child's possible abnormality, exacerbated by his delay in motor and language development, was a major factor that interfered with the development of a close and affectionate relationship between herself and her infant. The father initiated interactions more frequently than the mother—mainly roughhousing or getting the child to do "tricks," but the child remained passive to many of the father's attempts to interact with him. He seemed to keep an eye on his mother as if waiting for *her* attention. (Some of these behaviors were recorded on tape and viewed several times before the above interpretations were made.) On several occasions, during intervention sessions, the child voiced distress by mild fussing, but although the mother commented on it, she did not respond to his signals. The parents enjoyed discussions of child development and of current events but it was difficult for them to focus on or to talk about *their* infant.

The intervention team found that the parents knew little about their infant. They were unaware of what he could or could not do or what his interests were. They seemed to value some of the very behaviors of the infant that concerned the staff most: he was independent, he made few demands, and he rarely asked for attention. The parents told the staff with great pride that the infant was a "born observer" and that he showed no interest in being involved in the activity that he was watching. When the staff would inject the idea that observing all the time might not be sufficient activity for an infant his age, the parents would find a way to dispense with the comment either with humor or by changing the subject.

The staff's two major concerns in this case were the quality of attachment and interaction between mother and infant and the uneven developmental pattern of the infant. As this baby began to show advanced skills in fine motor development and adaptive play and as he progressed toward walking, the primary concern about the infant was in the affective area. Because he was advanced in fine motor development and because he showed a lag in expressive but not in receptive language, the staff thought that the language delay might be due to emotional factors and to the limited number and quality of adult-infant interactions. Therefore, the major thrust of intervention was to help the parents perceive this infant's affective needs and to see the urgency for more interactions between mother and infant. (Even though the infant did not openly demand these interactions, he gave many subtle cues that he wanted them.) The staff tried to encourage and support more expression of affect on the part of both mother and infant. Interactions with the *mother* were stressed in this case because the infant was giving signals that he was seeking more responsiveness in that relationship. The absence of warm and mutually reinforcing interactions between mother and infant was salient in this otherwise rather congenial middle-class family.

It was difficult to judge the extent to which the infant's behavior contributed to the interactional problems. On the one hand, he was a handsome and sensitive child with an attractive smile who could be quite responsive and social when he chose to be. On the other hand, he seemed very passive at times, with an almost mask-like expression, flashing smiles off and on. Just as there was an unevenness in his development, so too his behavior seemed uneven and sometimes difficult to anticipate. The staff had few clues regarding his behavior in early infancy because the parents revealed little of what he was like then.

The major intervention goal—that of developing a closer, more affectionate, and pleasurable relationship between mother and infant—was pursued in a number of ways. First, when the infant began to show special strengths in fine motor coordination, adaptive play, and receptive language—which indicated the probability of normal or even superior abilities—the staff pointed out these skills to the parents and discussed with them their significance with respect to the overall functioning of the child.

Since it seemed so difficult for the parents to focus on the infant's activities in the home, a special session was set up in the project Center playroom during which the parents had no alternative but to observe the infant's play and to acknowledge his abilities. However, it took a relatively long time until they finally allowed themselves to accept the staff's interpretations of these skills and consequently to recognize that their infant was of at least normal intelligence. As noted earlier, the parents' resistance to focusing on the infant during intervention sessions and to discussing the infant's behavior with the staff may have been due, in part, to the mother's resistance to becoming emotionally attached to this infant while he was still suspect—at least in the mother's eyes—of being brain-damaged.

Second, the staff explored ways of making interactions between mother and infant more mutually enjoyable. There were times when the team could comment positively on the mother's interactive behavior, when she elicited positive affect from the child. As the pleasurable response of the infant was acknowledged by a team member, a glimpse of pride and pleasure was observed in the mother. In further efforts to make mother-infant interactions more pleasurable, the team tried to elicit more expression of affect from the infant both in his play and in social interactions. Since he gave repeated signals that he wanted more of his mother's attention, it was hoped that if he could show more affect, he would be able to engage his mother in activities with him that would be more mutually enjoyable. It was anticipated that as the mother saw his expressions of pleasure and his positive social qualities, she would be encouraged to interact with him more because she would find the experience more satisfying. Although the infant was quite responsive to the staff most of the time, he took some time to warm up to them at almost every session. (Sessions were held regularly, every other week.) Moreover, there were times when he was passive and sometimes even rejecting of the staff's attempts to engage him in play. His socially difficult behaviors were discussed with the parents, and the staff's experience of feeling rejected by the infant was also shared with them. The team's acknowledgment of their occasionally unrewarding experiences with the infant was considered important because it had the effect of relieving the parents' feelings of inadequacy. They could see that *the infant* may have contributed to their own unsuccessful attempts to interact with him.

Third, the team tried to help the parents get a better understanding of the needs of their infant and of what they could expect from him at his developmental level. Discussion about development met with least resistance as long as it stayed general. As soon as the conversation turned to their infant and his behavior, one or the other parent tried to bring it back to more general issues.

Early in the program, the team visited the infant at the home of the daycare provider and subsequently raised questions with the parents regarding the very limited opportunities that the infant had to participate in activities with others, or even to play with materials that were appropriate for his skill level and that were of interest to him. The daycare provider kept him in a playpen with animal toys in which he showed no interest. Thus, passivity was almost forced upon him as he found that watching others was the only possible "contact" he could have with the other people in the room (an elderly daycare provider and much older children). The parents responded by bringing toys to the daycare home, but the team was asked not to visit the infant there again.

The parents acted and spoke most of the time as if they were not at all concerned about their infant. There were a few sessions, however, during which they were able to speak more freely about their earlier fears of brain damage. Yet, such sessions were followed by others during which the parents persisted in discussing topics that were irrelevant to the infant. The staff perceived these attempts to keep the discussion on subjects of general interest to be a combination of avoidance of facing and dealing with their feelings and concerns about the infant, and genuine enjoyment in having intellectual conversations with the staff.

The mother was best able to share her worries—past and present—during a session when she found herself alone with the team member who had been interacting primarily with the parents. She expressed her worries about his lack of language and, for the first time, wanted to discuss ways of helping him to develop language. She was able to listen to the staff member talk about the infant's need to interact with his parents even if he did not actively seek out or initiate this interaction. In the course of this discussion, the staff member explained and the mother seemed to understand the relationship between the affective communication that occurs during that interaction and the infant's resulting desire to communicate verbally.

Following this conversation between the mother and the one team member, steady improvement was seen in the mother-infant interaction. The mother was more joyful when with the infant and more attentive to him and both seemed to experience pleasure in the other's company. It was the beginning of summer, and both parents were able to spend more time with their children. The mother's relationship with the infant and the infant's affective and language development showed progress. Unfortunately, however, the unevenness of the infant's mood was paralleled by an unevenness in the mother's interactions with the infant and in her responsiveness to the staff.

In the last few months of the program, the staff tried to build on the positive events that had followed the session with the mother alone. The idea of having one team member meet more frequently with only the mother and the infant was introduced delicately to the parents, but it was adroitly and politely rejected. It was as if the mother needed the protection of her husband—with his enjoyment of general conversation—and her 5-year-old daughter to keep herself from talking about her own feelings and concerns. Throughout the intervention program, it was clear that the mother did not realize that she might have profited from some therapeutic help. Her frequent, spontaneous assertion that she had no problems with this child or with anything else made it difficult for the staff to suggest further help for her.

There were a few weeks in the last quarter of the intervention period when the mother seemed to be closing the door to meaningful communication with the intervention team and, at the same time, seemed to be withdrawing a little more once again from her infant. This created some doubts regarding the effectiveness of intervention in this case. Fortunately, this period was followed by some important breakthroughs in the form of significant changes in both mother and infant in interaction with each other. The mother became more sensitive to the infant's cues and his cues, in turn, became easier to read. The infant also expressed more satisfaction with the attention the mother was giving him and became more responsive to her. These were indications that a gradual adaptation was taking place between a very bright and sensitive child and his mother, who had somehow missed out on the early bonding with him and who may have been fearful, for a long time, that he might be brain damaged.

Several conditions made this case a particularly difficult one. The mother appeared to rationalize her lack of involvement with the child. Both parents often alluded to their lack of interest in infants. They also talked about the infant's independence—that he didn't need or want anyone to interact or play with him. They seemed to ignore the child's more subtle cues that indicated his desire for his mother. They further rationalized their inattention to the infant by convincing themselves that they were treating their children as individuals—some children needed attention and some did not. The parents seemed surprised at the staff's suggestion that the infant might benefit from a "special time" every day with each parent, like they had with their 5-year-old. They thought that a child of 18 months was too young to profit from this kind of experience.

The team working with this complex case consulted regularly with the director of the Intervention Program. There was also much brainstorming with all of the staff members on how best to proceed at various times with this family. The UCLA Project social worker, functioning as a consultant, was asked to participate a few times in these deliberations. Videotapes were reviewed often and strategies were discussed following these viewings. (The parents had no objection to the occasional videotaping in the home. In fact, they appeared to enjoy it.) The roles of the two team members became quite distinct. One would play with the infant, while the other would talk with the parents. Both parents were present during most of the sessions.

In conclusion, the major problem in this case was the mother's difficulty in developing an affectionate and mutually pleasurable relationship with her male infant. This may have been due partly to her fear of abnormality and partly to some of the characteristics of the infant—he did not demand attention and he was rather uneven in his responsiveness. Most probably, he was not an easy infant for his mother because of his complexity, his sensitivity, and, sometimes, his very subtle and unclear cues. If these parents had not received steady support and help from the intervention staff, the relationship between mother and infant might have grown cooler and resulted in a withdrawn or even depressed child. The opposite occurred in this case. The mother and infant drew closer together, they became more affectionate with each other, and mutual pleasure in their interactions gradually increased. Although intervention sometimes seemed to move one step back for every two steps forward, the goals for this case were finally achieved as a result of great sensitivity, perseverance, and considerable thought and effort on the part of the staff.[5]

Locus of Problem: Parent-Sibling Relations

The intervention staff always took some responsibility for keeping siblings of the project infants occupied during home visits, especially when those siblings were under 5 or 6 years of age. This was done so as to communicate to the parents the importance of giving attention to the other children in the family so that the focus on the infant would not be at the expense of the psychological welfare of other children. Moreover, in some families, it was necessary to have the siblings involved in some activity simply to allow the parent to be able to focus on the infant and to converse with a staff member. Whenever siblings were expected to be home during intervention sessions, the staff brought toys that were appropriate for them. The team member not involved with the parent and infant often played with one or more of the children in the home. That was the extent to which the staff was involved with the siblings in most of the families.

However, there were two cases in which the parents' primary concern was the older sibling. In both cases, the mother's preoccupation with her difficulties with the other child took her attention away from the infant, and in both cases, that other child was a preschool-aged boy, the only sibling of a male infant. Both were high SES, white families.

---

[5]When this child was seen again at about 5 years of age for evaluation, the relationship between parents and child seemed to be warm and positive, and the child tested in the superior range.

Case W   Mother W's major concern was her poor relationship with her first-born, who was 20 months older than the project infant. When this case was referred to the Intervention Program, the nurse informed the staff that the mother was depressed. Mrs. W, in her early 30's, soon shared with the older of the two intervention team members (this person remained on the case throughout the 14-month intervention period) her conflicting feelings about her mothering role and her intermittent resentment of her husband's prolonged absences on business trips. She felt inadequate with the older child, who was not yet 3 years old, and she was very concerned about his jealousy of the baby. At first, her preoccupation with her feelings of guilt toward the older child and her concern about his emotional development made it impossible for her to give much attention to the infant, with whom she experienced no problems. Her conversations with the team centered around her problems with the older child, and sometimes she aired her anger about being left so much of the time with the entire responsibility for both children. She worked 2 nights per week in a nearby hospital for her own satisfaction, and she provided appropriate child care in her home during those hours.

The infant, born at 29 weeks gestational age, had some difficulties in the perinatal period. However, he seemed to be a normal, healthy baby by age 10 months. His fine motor development remained somewhat delayed for a period, but not enough to seriously interfere with his play. At 10 months of age, he showed much interest in materials and was already persistent in goal-directed tasks. He appeared to be easy-going and calm, and a little more interested in objects than in people. By 17 months, he had become very demanding, negative, and quite irritable. He had recurring ear infections and underwent minor surgical procedures related to his ear problem. For about 3 months, the mother had a difficult time with this frequently ill and irritable baby, but at around 20 months of age, his health problems subsided and he progressed well developmentally, especially in the areas of language and representational play.

The intervention staff tried to do the following in this case: 1) to respond to the mother's needs to be listened to as she expressed some of her feelings of inadequacy and ambivalence, 2) to help her resolve some of her problems in her relationship with her older child, and 3) to enable her to expand her mothering skills with the infant beyond physical care after having been relieved of some of her overriding anxiety regarding her older son. The staff was successful with all three of these tasks. The mother was able to utilize the emotional support provided by the staff and some of their specific suggestions on how to deal more effectively with the older child. She was helped to see that the older child's jealousy was a normal reaction and to realize that it is difficult to satisfy fully two young children and to prevent entirely feelings of jealousy.

The staff discussed with the mother the need for the older child to experience firm limits to prevent him from hurting the baby, both for his own sake and for the baby's safety. The staff also discussed the older child's need to have his "special time" alone with the mother and to have satisfying social contacts beyond the immediate family. When the child turned 3, the benefits that he might gain from attending a neighborhood nursery school were discussed with the parent. The staff helped the mother to identify important criteria for selecting a good program, and they assisted her in finding such a program in her community. The boy's positive reactions to the school experience further eased the tension between him and his mother and dissipated much of the mother's anxiety about him. The mother was now ready to focus more on the infant.

The staff's efforts to help the mother perceive the infant's needs as extending beyond physical care were also largely successful. Discussion and modeling with interpretation were used to help her appreciate the kind of play environment that would be supportive to the infant's interests and development. While observing the infant's play with the mother, the staff pointed out to her how the infant's attention span lengthened and how his play became more complex when he was provided a flat surface on which to use some of the materials, and when his toys were separated from those of the older child and reduced in number, leaving only a few in which he showed particular interest at that time. As a result of modeling and discussion, the mother was able to allow the child increased autonomy. The mother became more relaxed about both children and "less controlling." Her verbal interactions with the infant improved as soon as she was able to relax enough to spend more time with him. Her natural style was to be very verbal and she soon engaged in the kind of language with him that was responsive to his vocalizations as well as interesting and informative for him. The infant's responsiveness to her language enhanced mutuality in their interaction (a mutuality which had not always been present), and the mother reported getting more pleasure from being with her infant.

The aspects of the mother's behavior least influenced by intervention had to do with her general style of interaction with the infant, especially in play. The absence of humor and playfulness in her style made it difficult for her to enjoy "playing with" the infant in a relaxed manner.

The mother's ratings on the PBP went up considerably in the areas of reading and responding to the infant's cues and in providing an environment favorable to his play and language development. Her interactions with him became somewhat less directive as well as more affectionate, but they were not of the quality the staff had hoped for. The infant became increasingly competent in all areas of development, which was reflected in his high test scores at age 2.

A review of the intervention process and outcomes in case W makes it clear that the team could not have influenced the mother-infant interaction before it dealt with the mother's feelings of guilt and inadequacy in relation to her older child. The one staff member who worked on the case throughout the entire intervention period recommended personal counseling to the mother. Although the mother temporarily showed interest in obtaining this additional kind of help, she did not follow through on the recommendation. Nevertheless, the emotional support and the very specific help that she received in finding more effective ways of dealing with her 3-year-old allowed her to gain a greater sense of confidence in herself as mother. This new feeling of adequacy freed her to focus on the infant, and subsequently, with the help of the staff, she was able to meet more of the infant's language, play, and social needs.

Case D   The project infant was the second male child in family D. Both children in this family had problems at birth due to RH incompatibility. The project infant required resuscitation and blood transfusions in order to survive. Upon the physician's advice, the mother, having had considerable problems with both pregnancies and births, underwent voluntary sterilization after the second birth. This was a difficult decision for this young and religious couple to make. (Both husband and wife were from large families.) Unfortunately, the physical proximity of the mother's own parents and many of her siblings was stressful rather than supportive for her. Their disapproval of the sterilization did not help her relationship with them.

Mrs. D was also disturbed by her husband's lack of understanding of their 4-year-old son and by the harsh punishments he administered to this child for bedwetting. In addition to these stresses, which affected the quality of her mothering, she also felt ambivalent about her role and she experienced some conflict in deciding whether to work or to stay home with her children. She chose to stay home until the baby was 20 months old. At that time she went to work full time. Three months later, the family moved away from the mother's many relatives, and next door to one of her sisters with whom she was able to share babysitting arrangements.

The father, who was working and going to college, spent little time with the children. His wife, already feeling overburdened, sensed no support from him—he was either not home or too tired to be of help to her or even to listen to her troubles. When he stopped attending college and when some of the financial stress on the family eased, tension in the home was reduced.

The infant, born 6 weeks preterm, almost died at birth, but he was doing well by 10 months of age. His development proceeded uneventfully until age 18 months, when sleeping problems appeared. Shortly after that, he developed asthma. He showed considerable independence and resourcefulness in his play, although his language was slightly delayed and remained so until age 2.

At the time the Intervention Program began with this family, neither parent was worried about the baby's survival or normalcy. As in the preceding case, the mother's competence in parenting was confined to the physical care of the infant. She had little awareness of the social and cognitive needs of either of the children, and she provided little in the way of stimulation that was appropriate for their respective developmental levels. Interestingly, the infant, who was independent and self-confident, was able to find things to engage his interest, whereas the 4-year-old, who was a very sensitive child, was by his own admission bored ("nothing to do") and unhappy at home.

The parents' major concern was the 4-year-old's enuresis. The father's intolerance of this condition and his harsh punishment of the child for his poor bladder control were a source of major conflict between the parents. Later, when the infant developed sleeping problems and then asthma (both problems kept the family awake at night) the father's tendency was again to administer physical punishment, this time to the younger child.

One of the highlights of the intervention program with family D was a carefully planned 3-hour evening home visit in which both parents participated. The problems of the older child were discussed openly, after he had gone to sleep, and some acceptable ways of dealing with him and his problem were suggested. (The 4-year-old had been checked for possible physiological causes of the enuresis, but none were found.) As a result of this session, the father appeared to understand better that punishing the child for wetting would increase his tension and therefore aggravate the problem. According to the mother's report, the open discussion of issues that bothered both parents also improved the parents' ability to communicate more honestly with each other about such matters. Furthermore, the staff, by insisting that the evening session be scheduled after both children were in bed for the night, communicated to the parents that it was better to discuss such issues when the children were not present. The parents seemed unaware that children as young as theirs would understand what was said or be affected by being present when they were being talked about.

Intervention with family D was judged to be largely successful. The staff's rapport with the parents was excellent from the start. This almost instant trusting relationship may have come about, in part, because the mother had developed great confidence in the UCLA medical staff, dating back to the birth of the infant. (It was the pediatrician from that staff who referred the family to the Intervention Program.) The mother gradually gained self-confidence and consequently found it easier to make rational decisions regarding herself and her two children. The parents were able to discuss more openly the issues about which they disagreed, especially the handling of the 4-year-old boy. They also were able to see the potential benefits to this child of attending a good half-day nursery school program. Following discussions with the staff, the child was enrolled in a neighborhood group program. The parents could see how much happier he seemed after he started attending the nursery school and how much he had needed this social and cognitive stimulation, which was missing at home.

Once the situation with the sibling had improved, the mother was able to turn her attention to the infant. Although she showed much interest in play activities with the infant that were modeled for her, she did not follow through with many of the activities that she appeared to value. Fortunately, the infant was highly self-motivated, task oriented, and persistent, and he was able to satisfy his needs independently in the area of play. The more relaxed emotional climate in the home and the mother's less ambivalent and more affectionate relationship with both children enabled the infant to pursue his interests without hesitation.

In case D intervention took a path that was in many ways similar to that in case W. The mothers in both cases were ambivalent about the mothering role and expressed some anger toward their husbands, although for different reasons. Mrs. D experienced the additional stress of criticism from her parents and siblings. In both cases, the staff listened to the mothers' expressions of their feelings of inadequacy, their ambivalence toward the mothering role, and their resentment about their husband's role in parenting. Lending emotional support to the mother as well as giving specific help regarding the problem that preoccupied both families—the behavior of the older sibling—became the first intervention priority. The parents could begin to focus on their interactions with the infant only after considerable emotional support and help with the older boy had been given. The staff expected that modeling and discussing with the parents alternate ways of dealing with the older child would generalize to their interactions with the infant by effecting changes in parenting attitudes and behavior. In addition to needing help to cope with the older child, both mothers also needed to increase their competence in meeting some of the developmental needs of the infant.

In both cases, the infants, who had had perinatal problems of a serious nature, developed normally. Also in both cases, the infants scored in the superior range on the 2-year developmental tests. The mothers' relatively low level of involvement with the infants, at least until the last few months of intervention, would not have led us to predict the infants' high scores by age 2. It may be that these two infants were naturally endowed with positive temperamental qualities and above-average cognitive potential. The gains made by the parents, i.e., the greater sense of adequacy and greater competence in dealing with their children, are expected to have ongoing positive effects on the development of the infant and the older child in both families.

Locus of Problem: Environment

In the two cases that follow, the overriding problem was poverty and its effects. Both mothers were poor and single, and both had little education. The limitations of space and resources, the mother's appropriate concern with the day-to-day survival of the family, and the mother's worries about an older child were common to both cases. Family KC, with two young children, and family CH, with three children more spread out in age, lived in very small apartments in fairly dismal surroundings. In spite of these circumstances, intervention achieved considerable success with both cases.

Case KC   Mrs. KC, a black woman in her early twenties, had only recently left a rural community in the Deep South. She had come to California in order to start a new life for herself, leaving behind a husband who had frequently beaten her. The project infant, her second child, was born almost 2 months prematurely and only 8 months after her first child (who was born in the South).

The mother, separated from her whole family, was able to develop a fairly close relationship with some of the other women living in the same apartment house. She seemed to have strength and inner resources, and she was spirited and outgoing. She valued her role as mother and did not consider going to work as long as her children were so young. In addition to her two children, both still infants, she took care of one and sometimes two or even three other children. She showed considerable presence of mind and resourcefulness in caring for her own and the neighbor's children. For example, when she could no longer tolerate all the noise and fighting in a tiny indoor space, she would take all the children on a bus ride—they would ride "anywhere." On the bus the children were busy looking out the window or at the people and the mother could recover from all the "chaos and confusion." (Mrs. KC did this often while the Los Angeles buses offered 10-cent rides for any distance to encourage their use. Unfortunately this fare did not continue for more than a few months.)

When the intervention staff first saw this family, the mother was particularly worried about the project infant's sibling, who was only 18 months old. She showed more concern for this male child, despite the younger infant's greater medical problems. She could not understand or accept his dependence and rather passive behavior, and it was difficult for her to keep in mind that although he was the "older one," he was still only 18 months old.

The project infant was born at 30 weeks gestational age. Her neo-natal problems contributed most to her high risk score. She also showed a considerable drop in the Gesell score between 4 and 9 months of age. There is a tendency to attribute this type of decline in scores during the first 9 months of life to inadequate mothering and to insufficient nutrition. Yet, the public health nurse associated with this case since the infant's birth had reported that the mother gave good physical and loving care to both children. The infant was found to function generally at a very low activity level, and a blood test revealed severe anemia. There was fear of sickle cell anemia, but further tests proved this fear to be unwarranted. After the administration of iron, she became an active, healthy little girl.

The infant's adaptive play skills were very limited at 10 months of age. As she progressed, with the help of intervention, she rapidly increased in the number of play schemas and the complexity of her skills. Yet she appeared to be easily distracted from her play in the rather chaotic home environment. By 18 months, she was capable of goal-directed play when her environment was less distracting.[6] She developed most rapidly in the social-affective area and she became quite assertive and "willful," as her mother called it. While the mother gave the appearance of complaining about this "mean little girl," she was actually quite pleased and proud of these qualities in her. It seemed as if she had recognized some of her own spirit, determination, and strength in her young daughter. By 24 months of age, the project infant's play and language were well within the normal range. Her developmental test scores were between 11 and 20 points higher at age 2 than they had been at 9 months.

It was easy to establish rapport with the able and energetic young mother. Her relationship was equally positive with both team members, allowing them to keep their roles flexible and interchangeable during the intervention sessions. One staff member would talk to the mother or work with the infant and mother while the other would occupy herself with at least one and often several other children in the home.

At first, Mrs. KC wanted some specific help and needed much reassurance regarding the older child. He was progressing normally, although he was more mild-tempered and more passive than either mother or daughter, and he was very dependent on the mother. The fact that her dealings with him encouraged his dependence further was gradually made clear to the mother through discussion and by modeling alternate ways of meeting his needs.

The mother was a caring person and she met the children's physical needs. However, there was much that she needed to change in her interactions with her children if they were to have the maximum opportunity to become competent in all areas of development. She initially disre-

---

[6]See Chapter 3 for a description of the playroom sessions at the project Center.

garded the infant's tempo. Her interactions with the infant tended to be intrusive, not allowing her the autonomy that she was increasingly demanding. She did not give the infant sufficient time to complete activities that she had begun. The mother also had expectations of both children in social behavior that were unrealistic for their levels of development. Her language with them was quite directive (mostly commands), as is commonly found in parents with limited educational background.

In case KC, as in the case that follows, the staff felt that intervention should not be limited to home visits. Adding two adults to the already overcrowded, small apartment did not make the atmosphere conducive to good communication. Furthermore, the staff intended to separate the mother and the infant from other children who might be present for at least part of the intervention session in order to concentrate on the mother-infant interaction. This was, at best, difficult to manage in the home. Apart from the logistical problems, the infant's distractibility required a reduction of stimuli in her environment. She had shown the ability to engage in goal-directed play, but she was easily distracted by noises and visual stimuli extraneous to her activity. Early in the program, the staff suggested that the family come occasionally to the project Center. The mother's response to this suggestion made it obvious that she welcomed opportunities to get away from her little apartment as long as transportation was provided. Also, in this case, as in a few of the others, the staff was sensitive to a certain degree of embarrassment experienced by the mother in the home because of the very crowded quarters.

The staff's objectives were: 1) to support the mother in her mothering role, to which she gave high priority; 2) to help her appreciate the role of play in the cognitive development of the infant so that she could provide the infant with opportunities to explore and experiment with materials instead of interfering with her play; 3) to provide a setting for the infant in which she could experience success in reaching her goals in play without the interference of too many distracting stimuli; 4) to help the mother gain greater awareness of the individual characteristics, the differing strengths, and the special needs of her two children; and 5) to help the mother become more aware of and responsive to behavioral cues of the infant, especially in the areas of play and language.

The first goal was easily achieved in the context of conversations with the mother, during which much support was given her by way of positive comments about her skills as a parent. The mother gradually found more and more good things to say about both her children, and she showed a certain pride in them and in her ability to manage with such limited resources. Efforts to achieve the remaining goals took the following approach: one team member and the mother observed while the other team member played with the infant. The staff member with the mother interpreted to her what the child was doing, pointing out to her the many things the child could do when she was provided with interesting materials, not necessarily just "toys." The team member working with the infant modeled ways of interacting with her during play that enhanced her enjoyment without being intrusive. The mother began to appreciate the satisfaction and pleasure the infant was getting from achieving a goal that she set for herself. The play materials that the staff made available to both children were important contributions to effective intervention in this case.

The sessions at the project Center (a little less than half of all the intervention sessions) served two ends. First, they gave the mother a chance to concentrate on the infant's activities in a setting where household and child care responsibilities did not interfere. Second, these sessions not only allowed the infant to play with materials that were motivating to her, but also, they gave her an opportunity to experience satisfaction in play without the interruptions that occur in a distracting environment. The infant appeared to get pleasure from this type of play, and gradually her play increased in complexity. As a result of this experience at the project Center, she was able to use her natural assertiveness to protect her activities even when the environment (including her mother's intrusiveness) threatened to interfere.

Mrs. KC gained a greater understanding of the particular strengths and weaknesses of her two children. The infant's increasingly clear cues became almost impossible to ignore. Nevertheless, because the mother's dominant and somewhat authoritarian style was difficult to alter, the goal of helping her to allow both her children greater autonomy was only partially achieved. Yet, the infant's assertiveness was seen by the staff as a healthy adaptation by the infant to a strong-willed mother who sometimes seemed overpowering to her young children. Fortunately the mother showed some pride in her little girl's strength of will and persistence regarding some of her demands, but this quality in both mother and child also led to some "clashes" between them, as would be expected between two strong-willed persons.

The team predicted that there would continue to be conflicts between mother and daughter, but the staff had relatively little concern about this because the mother had a deep love for her child and she had gained a greater appreciation of her daughter's qualities as a result of the intervention.

There was much discussion of this case among the staff. The predominant feelings were that the strength and willpower of this mother were a blessing to her because it made her able to survive, first by having the courage to leave her abusive husband, and then by being able to manage psychologically, socially, and financially in strange and new surroundings with two very young children. The staff felt that the little girl, possessing some of her mother's strengths, would "make it" in this world. However, the staff was concerned that the boy, who was less assertive and outgoing and less independent, might have increasing difficulty, being surrounded with a dominant mother and a sister who would soon be able to "outwit" him in many respects. The staff tried to encourage the mother to look for a Head Start program in her neighborhood when her son would be old enough to be enrolled.

It was reassuring and gratifying to receive a phone call from this mother just a few weeks before the time of this writing. She asked for some help in finding a preschool program for both her children. Her financial situation remained the same and, not having a car, she had to find a program close enough to her home so that she could walk to it with her children. It was good to know that Mrs. KC was finally following up on the staff's earlier suggestion to place the children, especially the boy, in a group program. The staff member whom the mother phoned had some difficulty in locating a program within walking distance, but a suitable program was finally found after numerous phone calls were made to various Head Start agencies. (These details are given to call attention to the frequent lack of coordination of services that makes it difficult for parents to locate programs that are theoretically available to them.)

Case CH   The project infant in case CH was the youngest of three girls in a single-parent, Spanish-speaking family. Mrs. CH, a handsome woman in her late thirties, lived in a one-room apartment with her own mother, her 9- and her 10-year-old daughters, and the infant. The mother worked nights on a job she had held for 7 years. When intervention began, the grandmother was the infant's primary caregiver. When the infant was 14 months old, the grandmother moved in with another daughter whose 2-year-old child needed daytime care. For a short period following the grandmother's move, the three children in family CH were left alone during the night while the mother was at work. The 10-year-old was responsible for the infant and the middle child. The mother's only opportunity to sleep was in the morning after returning home from work. Therefore, whenever possible, the baby was left in her crib during part of the morning.

The mother, aware of the risks of leaving the infant alone with the two older children, began to take the infant to the grandmother before she went to work at night. (Aside from her concern over leaving the three children alone at night, the mother was aware of her middle child's emotional instability.) This arrangement also became untenable for everyone involved. Next, the mother tried to let the infant live with the grandmother during the work week, at the home of the infant's aunt and 2-year-old cousin, and then return home with her over the week-end. This situation continued for a while, until the grandmother became ill. Then a young relative of the mother moved in with family CH so that the children would not be alone at home during the night while the mother was at work. This arrangement allowed the family to move to a little roomier apartment because the relative shared in the expenses. However, the mother had to resume the daytime care of her infant while still working at night.

When the infant was 19 months old, the mother took a bus trip to Mexico City to obtain her American citizenship papers. She was unsuccessful this first trip, but during a second trip, made 4 months later, she finally achieved her aim. These trips, besides being emotionally upsetting for the whole family, were an additional financial strain on a family with a borderline subsistence income. In spite of these hardships, the mother was a warm and caring person. She became concerned about her infant, especially after the grandmother moved out of the home, and she welcomed the help that intervention was able to provide.

The infant, born 1 month preterm, had had no serious problems after birth. She was classified as high risk due to her relatively low scores on two physiological measures that were taken within a month after birth. When the staff first saw the infant at 10 months of age, she was functioning well in all areas of development, with only a slight delay in expressive language. It was noted that she was advanced in adaptive play and in fine motor development. Although she scored lowest in language on the 9-month Gesell test, she engaged in a normal amount of vocalizing. She continued to function well in all developmental areas up to 14 months of age. Her behavior took a sharp turn for the worse after her grandmother moved away. Shortly after that, the staff also heard that the 9-year-old sister, the middle child in the family, had physically threatened, frightened, and possibly abused her at a time when there was no adult in the home. The infant developed problems in several areas. Her language dropped out altogether—she communicated only with grunts and gestures—and she showed little affect. A little later, when she was spending the workweek with her grandmother and her 2-year-old cousin, she became aggressive with the cousin and increasingly unmanageable. At the same time, she became very fearful of everything and everyone unfamiliar to her.

The staff decided to work directly with the infant in this case in addition to working with the parent. The mother, as she became concerned about the changes in her infant, was pleased when the team offered to bring the family to the Center once a week to try to reverse the negative spiral that the infant's behavior was showing. There were several reasons for moving the sessions to the project Center. First, the crowded conditions in the small, overpopulated apartment were not conducive to effective parent-infant intervention. Second, the staff felt that it would be a positive experience for mother and infant (and sometimes for the older children) to get away from their rather oppressive quarters. Third, experience with other families had shown that the mother is often able to focus more readily on the infant when she is away from a chaotic home situation where constant demands are made on her. Fourth, and most importantly, this child needed to build a trusting relationship with a person outside the family—in this case, a project staff member—so that she could be helped to overcome some of her anxieties and the block in her language. The sessions with the infant were carefully planned by the team in consultation with the Intervention Program director, who was experienced in therapeutic work with young children, to help the infant overcome some of her specific fears and to lower her general level of anxiety so as to enable her to use language again.

The staff decided to take on the task of driving the mother and child to and from the Center, instead of sending a driver to transport them (as was usually done with families who needed transportation). Because children are often quite relaxed while riding in a car, it was felt that the car ride could be used to advantage. This 20-minute drive between the family's home and the Center subsequently proved to be a good use of intervention time.

By the time these weekly sessions at the project Center began, the infant had developed an elaborate system of communication using grunts and gestures to manipulate her environment. She showed a strong need to be completely in control, and when she was not in control, she became either fearful or passively resistant. The infant displayed fear of riding the elevator at the Center, of an animal puppet, of airplane and car noises, and even of trees swaying in the breeze.

During the course of several weekly play sessions in the nursery school playroom, where there was ample space and where no other children were present, the infant's behavior gradually changed. She showed fewer fear reactions, greater freedom of exploration of space and materials, less passive behavior, more testing of adults, and a gradual emergence of expressive language. She began to move and act with less constraint. Throughout these play sessions, the mother sat in a corner of the big playroom to help the infant feel secure in an unfamiliar environment. In addition, the mother had an opportunity to observe her child without interruption—a situation that could not have been easily replicated in the home.

After each indoor session, everyone went to the play yard where the mother and one team member were able to talk while the other team member remained with the infant. No conversations with the mother took place in the playroom so as to avoid disturbing this highly sensitive and silent child. The mother was made aware that it was not a good idea to talk about the child in her presence. Also, the mother's silent observation with the staff member by her side gave her a chance to "take in" some of what was happening with her child, without the intrusion of adult interpretation.

By the end of the intervention program, the child was noticeably less fearful than she had been a few months earlier. Her expressive language increased rapidly. The initial step toward her return to the use of verbal language was rather dramatic. Her first vocal utterances occurred in the car on the way home from the Center after almost 2 months of weekly sessions. During playful interactions initiated by one of the team members, the infant imitated her language. A few weeks later there was another exhilarating moment for the staff, this time in the play yard. The infant put her arms up and spontaneously waved them slowly in the air, imitating the trees swaying in the wind that had frightened her a few weeks earlier. The infant's behavior became less fearful, more verbal, and less controlling of others. She also became less aggressive with her cousin, according to the mother's report. In the last few weeks of the program, she demonstrated considerable skill in adaptive play and imagination in symbolic play. Her 2-year developmental scores were within the normal range and, interestingly, her score on receptive language at 24 months was particularly high. This performance corroborated our judgment that she understood a great deal, although she was still somewhat shy in responding to verbal requests and slightly delayed in her expressive language (both behaviors depressed her developmental test scores at age 2).

The mother valued the sessions with the infant so much that while she was in Mexico the second time, she asked if we could pick up her infant with the older sister so that the infant would not miss her session at the Center. The mother became much more aware of the infant's subtle cues and generally more responsive to the infant. She was astounded to find how much this child was expressing in dramatic play and, in the process of these observations, she discovered the value of play for her child.

Mrs. CH knew that some of the events in her family had had a negative effect on the infant, but she felt powerless to change certain conditions brought about by poverty and her "illegal alien" status. The staff was able to refer her to the proper sources that helped make her second trip to Mexico City successful. Achieving her aim of becoming an American citizen gave her more security and lessened her feeling of powerlessness. The opportunity to discuss with the staff some of the things that were happening at home helped her to explore alternatives open to her in making decisions, especially regarding her children.

Intervention with this case was evaluated as successful. This judgment was based on: 1) the increased confidence that the mother had in herself as a result of the support that she received from the staff, 2) the staff's success in helping this vulnerable child to deal with feelings and overcome behaviors that might have developed into serious problems without intervention, and 3) the mother's increased awareness of her child's needs and sensitivities.

The two women described in this section had great inner strength. They were able to bear enormous responsibilities, to cope with incredible stresses, and to survive physically and psychologically. They were able to grow as parents and get greater enjoyment from their children with the help of intervention. Yet the staff realized the limitations to the help that this type of intervention program can offer to families whose daily lives are fraught with stresses that many individuals don't experience in a life-time—families whose major obstacles to a stable and decent life are the by-products of poverty.

INFANTS' PROBLEMS COMPOUNDED BY OTHER PROBLEMS

In the two cases that follow, it was difficult to decide whether the problems of the infant, the parent, or the environment were the weightiest. Both infants had problems from birth on, some of which were still in evidence at age 2. Both had mild neurological abnormalities that influenced their behavior and social interactions with their caregivers. They also suffered various environmental stresses, which probably aggravated their problems. The two infants were at risk for developmental disabilities in childhood because of: 1) their mild problems, which showed up early and persisted beyond the first year of life, and 2) stresses on the caregiver that could affect the care of the infant.

Case *RO*

At the beginning of intervention, family RO consisted of a teenage mother, a slightly older father, and the project infant. Mrs. RO was the oldest of four children from a closely knit, middle-class family. She was the only one of the children in her family who did not have academic interests or ambitions. She did not go on from high school to college, but instead, she married a man whose education had also ended with high school. She was proud of having a child, and she felt that motherhood gave her status vis-à-vis her parents, her younger siblings, and her friends.

When the infant was 16 months old, the parents separated. The mother and infant moved into a small apartment not far from her parents' home. The father visited the infant frequently, in fact, almost daily when he was not working (which was for extended periods). These visits made him very much a part of the infant's environment.

Mrs. RO wanted to find a job right after the separation, but her parents convinced her to stay home until her baby girl was a little older. The mother's parents were quite supportive of her and the infant throughout the intervention period. They offered every kind of support, including financial help, to enable the mother to stay home with the infant. The mother did not work outside the home until the child was 21 months old. The grandparents and even the infant's great-grandmother became involved with the intervention program. (When the mother started working, the great-grandmother cared for the infant in the grandparents' home.)

Mrs. RO basically enjoyed her child from the start. When she became aware of the infant's difficulties, she was concerned and she welcomed the help that the intervention staff was able to offer. A little later, her separation from her husband and events preceding the divorce were quite upsetting to her. The staff was drawn into a role of providing emotional support and an opportunity for the mother to talk about her feelings while she was going through a stressful period.

The infant weighed under 3 pounds at birth, even though she was only 1 month preterm. The newborn medical examination revealed hypoglycemia with abnormal reflexes in the extremities. (The mother had had toxemia and hypertension during pregnancy.) There was concern regarding possible brain damage and dwarfism. The profile on the 4-month Gesell test showed very low performance in the fine motor area and in adaptive play (sub-scores were in the fifties). At 9 months, the infant was doing better in all areas, although still scoring in the low normal range. At 15 months, she still showed fine motor problems, including an uncontrolled, explosive release, as well as awkwardness in movement and a lag in expressive language. The child became increasingly active motorically, but without sufficient judgment of what she could physically manage. This lack of judgment was interpreted as a lack of body awareness.

Although the infant seemed to be persistent in goal-directed play at 15 months, she became increasingly distractible after 18 months. This change occurred simultaneously with a change in mood, from happy and outgoing to whiney and unhappy. Her high activity level became more apparent as she developed great motor agility, especially in climbing. This was in contrast to the continued lag in fine motor coordination. She was observed to have occasional slight tremors in her arms and hands.

The infant presented a mixed picture developmentally and behaviorally. She progressed rapidly in the gross motor area and in her representational play. Yet, she became more difficult to manage because of her high activity level and increasing distractibility. Although she had eye contact with adults some of the time, she seemed more interested in objects than in people. Her lag in fine motor functioning interfered with certain types of play and may have contributed to her distractibility.

In case RO, it was especially useful to have two staff members working with mother and infant. The intervention team consisted of two women a generation apart; the younger member was only a couple of years older than the mother. The rapport between the team and the mother was good from the start. The older team member spent most of her time talking with the mother and the younger one worked primarily with the infant.

During the first few months after birth, the mother was quite worried (as was the pediatrician) about this tiny infant who grew so slowly. However, by the time the infant was 10 months old, there was less concern about her size and weight. The mother showed much pleasure and pride in her child, even though the child had no hair before 1 year of age and was not consistently responsive to the mother or to other adults. The mother responded contingently to the infant's biological cues but knew little about what to expect from her in behavior, especially in the area of play. Mrs. RO was responsive to modeling and suggestions regarding the choice of toys and ways of presenting them to the child.

The mother's generally controlling manner became more evident as the infant grew more active. As she became more difficult to handle due to her high activity level and distractibility, the mother grew more tense and more controlling. Moreover, Mrs. RO's almost continuous flow of speech interfered with her attention to the infant's vocalizations; she largely ignored the child's utterances. It was not until the last few weeks of the intervention program, when the infant was close to 2 years of age, that a dramatic positive change was observed in the mother-infant interaction and the mother's competence as parent.

In case RO, intervention had to be flexible to follow the course of events with respect to changes both in the infant and the parent. As the situation demanded, the staff's efforts shifted from a major focus on mother-infant interaction, to support of the mother during personal stress resulting from the marital crisis, to the infant as she showed increased problems and became more difficult to manage. In the last few months of the program, the staff was compelled to attend to all three of these areas as they became more and more closely interrelated. During the last third of the program, the frequency of home visits and phone contacts increased. As the child became more difficult to handle, the staff was concerned about how the mother, already under stress, would be able to cope with this high risk infant and what would happen to the quality of the mother-child interaction.

The last few months of the program were clearly the most critical period in case RO. In spite of all the problems confronting this mother-infant dyad toward the end of the program, intervention was successful in all the areas in which attempts were made to effect change. After a period of very little progress, positive changes in both infant and mother were seen during the last 6 weeks of the program. The mother became more relaxed, she was able to deal more effectively with the infant, and she began to enjoy the infant more again as the infant's behavior became more appropriate. The infant still showed some deviance, especially in the critical area of eye contact, which occurred intermittently and was difficult to anticipate. However, the mother was able to accept her child and to make sincere efforts to help her. Mrs. RO became somewhat less controlling, she interacted with her child much more appropriately in the language area (she was able to stop talking and listen to her daughter more), she became skilled in selecting play materials for the child, and she was responsive to her in play.

A conversation that occurred late in the program indicates how much the mother valued the help she received. In one of the last sessions, the mother told one of the staff members that there was a child living on her street who had many problems, and she mentioned that the mother was at her wit's end with him. She added, "I wish that woman could get the help that you have given me with my child!"

Some of the intervention approaches described in the guidelines in Chapter 2 were highly effective in case RO. For example, when the staff shared with the mother that they were having difficulty getting her child to focus on an activity for more than a few seconds, the mother expressed tremendous relief that she was not the only one having this difficulty. She also responded with great satisfaction whenever the staff called her attention to things that she was doing well with her child and she was eager to understand how her actions were helping the infant. Once, when the mother complained about having no control over her child, the staff pointed out to her that the child, who rode a tricycle by 22 months, obeyed her mother consistently after she had been told that she could only ride to the end of the building. The staff also gave credit to the mother for her sensitivity to the child's needs and interests when they observed that she had given her a paint brush with water while the mother was doing some painting in the yard.

The salient feature of this case was that the infant's problems increased during the last 6 to 8 months of the program. It would be easy to conclude that the mother's emotional stress resulting from the marital crisis made the child worse. Yet, at least some of the child's problems might have taken a turn for the worse regardless of the mother's emotional state. The staff, who had continuing contact with this mother-infant dyad, saw how the increasingly deviant and difficult behaviors of the infant depressed the mother and strongly contributed to her stress. The staff felt that there was negative impact in *both* directions during critical periods for the child and the mother. Fortunately, Mrs. RO had the strength and family resources that enabled her, with the help from the intervention team, to improve her interaction with her infant rather than allowing it to deteriorate further.

The staff was pleased to find out recently that the mother and child were doing quite well. The child's behavior had improved considerably (she was observed briefly in a child care center). The mother seemed satisfied and her life was more stable. She continued to communicate her positive feelings toward the staff by making several brief and unannounced social calls to the project Center after the termination of intervention.

Case RO demonstrates in a powerful manner how important flexibility can be in an intervention program. The staff felt that intervention with this family would have been a failure if there had not been continuing sensitivity to the state of the mother and the infant, and staff flexibility in the process of intervention. In order for the staff to be able to adapt to the changing needs of the parent and infant, they had to be aware of the events that took place and their effects on mother and infant. A too narrow intervention focus on the infant's problems or on therapy only for the mother would probably not have resulted in effective intervention in this case.

Case *ML*

In this case the intervention staff actually worked with two families. The infant was cared for by foster parents until she was 20 months of age. At 20 months, the infant was adopted and the staff continued working with the infant and her adoptive parents. Case ML was of special interest to the staff from the start because of the nature of the infant's problems and the possibility that she might be moved to an adoptive home while still in the Intervention Program. The infant's problems and the changes in her behavior are traced here from birth to the termination of intervention. This case is described in greater detail than the others in the Intervention Program because it is thought to be a prototype of an infant biologically at risk for later problems in which the quality of parenting becomes a major factor in the outcome, at least until the child begins school (where additional pressures influence development). The outcomes in this case seem to corroborate the hypothesis that the environment has the potential of "minimizing or maximizing" early developmental difficulties (Sameroff and Chandler, 1975). The phenomenal progress of this infant between 21 and 26 months of age seemed to be due, in large part, to the dramatic changes in mothering, which were strongly supported and enhanced by intervention.

Infant ML, a white female, was born 5 weeks prematurely to a heroin-addicted woman in her early twenties. The infant entered the

UCLA hospital at age 12 hours with seizures, for which she was given phenobarbital. She was also treated for gonococcal conjunctivitis in one eye, and 6 weeks later she was readmitted to the hospital for treatment for the same infection in the other eye. During her second hospitalization she was also observed to be jittery, but a neurological check did not show any abnormality. She was given phenobarbital again to control her jitteriness but she became increasingly irritable and had difficulty sleeping. The drug was tapered off gradually until she was without medication 2 months later. Shortly after that, between 5 and 6 months of age, she began to have periodic "screaming spells," which lasted anywhere from 15 minutes to 4 hours (according to the foster mother). During these spells (one was witnessed by her project pediatrician) she became stiff, red-faced, and tremulous, and she could not be calmed or comforted. She did not sleep more than 2 or 3 hours at a time before about 9 months of age.

In spite of all these problems, her development seemed to progress normally, and at 10 months of age she was an active and sociable baby. Nevertheless, she was considered ineligible for adoption until it could be determined whether or not there was any neurological damage. When the case was referred to the Intervention Program, the social worker from the Department of Public Social Services reported that the foster mother was threatening that she would not continue to care for the infant unless something could be done to stop her screaming spells. The Program director was asked to take the major responsibility for this case and was urged to provide sufficient support and help to the foster mother so that she would be willing to continue caring for the infant until adoption was possible.

The foster family consisted of a middle-aged couple and their youngest child, a son who was still attending high school (two daughters in their twenties were not living at home). The foster mother was also caring for another infant with problems. This second infant was 3 months younger than the project infant. The foster mother seemed to enjoy taking care of babies and, although she had had many newborns in foster care that were adopted soon after birth, she said that she liked to care for high risk infants because she felt competent with them, saw them as more of a challenge, and could keep them longer.

The foster mother had traditional patterns of childrearing. She was responsive to the infant's biological needs, e.g., she was eager to provide wholesome food for the infants in her care, so she cooked for the infants rather than buying baby foods. However, her language interactions with the infants were limited and she had little interest in their play. The playpen was cluttered with stuffed animals, but with very little else to manipulate. The infants were kept in the playpen in the living room much of the time. With some encouragement from the intervention team, the foster mother began to allow them to play on the living room carpet more of the time.

When the staff first came to the home, the project infant was alert and very friendly. She was large for her age and physically quite active, but she showed little body awareness or motor planning. She would crawl into and over objects and people's legs without realizing what she was doing. She made no attempt to avoid obstacles in her path. She seemed to see small objects after they had been removed from a surface. For example, she attempted to "pick up" a small cookie crumb from a wooden surface when it was no longer there. When she was about 14 months old, she repeatedly attempted to grasp objects represented in the pictures of a baby book.

Close observations of the infant's activities revealed that, although her goal-directed behavior was well developed, she did not have the necessary eye-hand coordination to allow her to achieve her goals in play. She dealt with this inability to satisfy her goals by immediately giving up when she could not accomplish what she intended. She attempted a great deal in manipulative play, but she would abandon an activity when she did not experience immediate success and move on to a new one. She thus gave the impression of having a short attention span.

The staff was puzzled by her low affect. Although she was very social, she seldom smiled and she had not been seen to laugh. When the foster mother was questioned about this lack of affective expression, she volunteered that the infant smiled and laughed when "roughhousing" with her teenage son or with her husband. During the following home visit, the foster father demonstrated how the infant laughed in a pursuit game that ended in vigorous physical play.

Another behavior of the infant was of concern to the staff. She would be playing with a toy when suddenly, without any apparent provocation, she would stop her activity, put her thumb in her mouth, and begin to rock in what appeared to be a self-stimulating manner. This behavior lasted about 15 to 20 seconds. Then she would resume her play as if nothing had happened. This interruption of play with a sudden withdrawal into self-stimulating behavior was seen again later in another form in the adoptive home—the same sudden interruption of play by momentary but intense masturbation on the floor.

The foster mother had revealed in one of the early intervention sessions that the infant "rocked herself to sleep every night." She later told the staff that the infant would rock so hard that the crib would be propelled from one end of the room to the other, eventually banging into the wall. To prevent this from happening and to dampen the noise, the foster mother padded the legs and both ends of the crib. Upon further inquiry, the staff learned that the foster mother absolutely refused to enter the infant's room after having put her to bed for the night. She was convinced that if she went back into her room, the infant would not go to sleep for hours. She was unshakable in her stand on this matter. This undesirable aspect of her caregiving may have been the consequence of the infant's severe sleeping problem in the early months, before intervention began.

The team had no difficulty in establishing rapport with the foster mother. The following pattern of intervention was established and seemed to work well in this home: the staff first attended to both infants and then conversed with the foster mother. In this manner, the infants, eager for attention, were satisfied, and the foster mother was helped to focus more on details of the project infant's activities and behavior. She became more interested in the infant, and she seemed to give more thought to the infant's social needs. It seemed to the staff that the regular bi-weekly home visits became an important part of the foster mother's life. She was also able to share with the older team member some of her serious personal problems and worries which, at times, made her tense and anxious.

Gradually, the foster mother gave both infants more of her attention and more floor freedom and play space indoors. She became a better observer of the project infant's play and she provided more developmentally appropriate materials for her. Less progress was made with the foster mother in her play interaction with the infant. It was not part of her style of caregiving to *play with* the infant in an informal and non-directive manner. Either the foster mother was uninvolved in her play or else she directed the infant to do a particular task in an effort to "teach" her something. The child would then be asked to "show" what she could do at the subsequent home visit. The foster mother's typical style of interaction with the infant, aside from caretaking tasks, was to engage her in a kind of social game (without objects) that would make the infant laugh. It was difficult to alter the mother's style of language interaction with the infant.[7]

The foster mother seemed quite sure of herself in the area of biological care and she was extremely resistant to any suggestions in that area. For example, when the infant developed a severe diaper rash that would not subside, the project pediatrician advised the foster mother to use a particular medication and, most importantly, to change the infant's diapers just before the parents went to sleep for the night. The foster mother refused to abandon her own unsuccessful method of treatment of the rash (which made the condition worse according to the pediatrician) and she would not follow the pediatrician's prescription and advice. The

[7]The staff found generally that it was difficult to alter parents' language interactions with their infants or young children. See Chapter 9 for more detail.

infant became very fussy and whiney from her discomfort, and, as the rash worsened, the mother finally had to let the infant go without diapers for periods during the day because she could see how raw the skin had become. The rash lasted for 7 weeks. This is an example of the foster mother's inflexibility in areas of physical caretaking, in spite of the fact that she was quite attached to this infant and later had great difficulty in letting her go on to the adoptive home. One of the obstacles in effecting change in the foster mother was her extreme eagerness to be perceived as an excellent caregiver. Regardless of the number of positive comments that were made to her about her care of the infants, she was still apt to interpret suggestions as criticism.

During the last 3 months of the infant's residence in the foster home, the foster mother's anxiety about matters unrelated to the infant increased. In the middle of this rise in tension, the mother went on a short trip (the second trip within a month) to attend a funeral, leaving the two foster infants in the care of her daughter and a friend. The project infant was very upset upon the foster mother's return from this second trip and she remained so for several weeks. The foster mother had rejected the staff's offer to visit the infant while she was gone. The daughter, not in good mental and physical health at that time, told her mother that the infant had cried almost constantly during the 4 days while she was gone. It was also during the mother's second trip that the infant contracted the rather severe rash referred to above. The staff was never able to obtain a clear picture of what occurred during the foster mother's absence.

For a few weeks after the foster mother returned from her second trip, the infant would not let her out of her sight and she became fussy and whiney. The mother complained about her clinging and was disturbed by her behavior. At times when she was upset about the infant, or about other things, she would share her concerns with the staff via lengthy telephone conversations. At these times, the team followed up the telephone call with a home visit as soon as possible. Usually, when the team arrived at the home and inquired how things were going, the mother would respond that everything was well—almost as if the earlier telephone conversation had never taken place.

Fortunately, the last month of the infant's stay in the foster home was a positive time for both mother and infant. The other foster child had left the home to be adopted and the foster mother was able to enjoy being just with the project infant. The infant's rash finally cleared, she became less clinging, and, on the whole, she was more relaxed and happier.

In addition to enhancing infant-caregiver interaction and increasing the foster mother's competence in parenting, intervention goals were to effect changes in the infant by working directly with her—especially in language and play, areas in which the foster mother seemed to be difficult to influence. In this case it seemed particularly worthwhile to work directly with the infant because she was expected to leave the foster home soon after she was considered eligible for adoption. It was anticipated that the intervention team working with this child would be the only people with whom she was familiar who would continue to see her in her adoptive home. Therefore, the relationship between the child and the staff could help to ease for her the transition from one home to the other. (The anticipated adoptive parents were to be asked by the social worker to continue with the Intervention Program if at all possible.)

The team worked directly with the infant in a variety of ways. In order to help her become more persistent in pursuing her goals in play, materials were provided with which she could experience success. For example, she had tried but had been unable to put large wooden pegs into a pegboard with four holes. Another pegboard was given to her with only one peg that fit very loosely in its hole. She was able to put this peg into the hole, and, for the first time, her face lit up, and she looked up and smiled with an air of great satisfaction. Three other pegs were handed to her, one at a time, and she painstakingly inserted them into their holes. The toy was left in the home for her over a 2-week period. At the start of the next home visit, she immediately produced the toy and proudly showed her success with all four pegs. The original peg toy, with which she had failed previously, was re-introduced, and when she was finally able to insert those pegs in their holes, she again expressed pleasure. This description of the infant's use of the pegboard demonstrates that she was conscious of her goal but that her eye-hand coordination prevented her from achieving her goals with ease; she had to be helped to work gradually toward reaching *her* goal. This newly experienced enjoyment of success in play was an important step forward for this infant. She was now motivated to explore and experiment with a variety of objects, and she quickly developed greater persistence because she had more confidence in what she could do. There was, unfortunately, very little follow-up by the foster mother to expand her opportunities for success with materials.

The staff also tried to involve the infant in language interaction and to increase her interest in pictures and books. The foster mother's response to modeling in this area was minimal, but it was felt that if the infant became more interested in language and therefore "talked" more to the foster mother, the latter might be drawn into more verbal interaction with the infant. Greater interest in language would also help her to engage her future adoptive parents in verbal interaction with her.

The transition between the foster home and the adoptive home was a rather sudden one. The social worker from the Department of Public Social Services (Department of Adoptions) called to inform the staff that the adoption had taken place. She was new on the case and knew little about this 20-month-old infant and even less about the Intervention Program. She had not spoken to the adoptive mother since the infant had been moved, 6 days previously. Upon hearing details about the Program, she promised to call the adoptive parents to tell them about the services that the Intervention Program had to offer. The parents would call back if they decided to participate in the Program and when they felt ready to do so. Twenty minutes after the staff's conversation with the social worker, the adoptive mother called. She was eager to meet the team, and an appointment was made for the following week—2 weeks after the infant's move into their home. She said that she was looking forward to seeing and talking with people whom the child knew well and who were acquainted with the child.

In this first telephone conversation, the adoptive mother mentioned that she was surprised how well the child was doing and she asked whether there might be problems later on. Toward the end of the conversation, she revealed that she and her husband had changed the infant's first name. She said that she had made a point of asking the social worker from the Department of Adoptions about this and that she had been told that it was all right to change a child's name up to 2 years of age. On the advice of that social worker, they had combined the child's new and her old name for a couple of days, but after that, the old name had been dropped out. She further reported that the child had said her old name once or twice since, more or less to herself, and she asked if that was anything to be concerned about. It was suggested that it might be a good idea to keep the two names combined a little longer—maybe for a week or two—and then to drop out the old name gradually; otherwise, the child might be confused. During the course of the conversation, it became quite clear that calling her new child by a name of her own choosing was extremely important to the adoptive mother. Consistent with this action was her refusal to maintain personal contact with the foster mother, beyond a few phone calls to find out more about the child's routines. On the basis of this first communication with the adoptive mother (hereafter referred to as "mother"), it was anticipated that the mother would have no difficulty in talking openly and asking questions about anything that concerned her about the infant. It was obvious that she wanted the staff to be of help to her in becoming a competent mother and that the child was a high priority in her life.

The new parents, who were in their late forties, had no other children, and they had not had much previous contact with young children. It was revealed later that they had gone to the Department of Adoptions 4 years earlier and that they had been told in an indirect way that, because of their age, they would not be able to adopt a young child. Four years later, with a new social worker in charge, they were suddenly "young enough" for an infant. They were so happy to be able at last to have a child that they agreed to take infant ML in spite of her early history of problems. Although these parents' knowledge about young children was limited, it soon became apparent that both husband and wife were open to learning as much as they could. They were eager to be good parents to their much-wanted child.

The mother greeted the team cordially on the first home visit, and in spite of her reserved and, at first, somewhat guarded manner, it was clear that she was glad and relieved to see people who knew this child and to whom she felt she could talk freely. She immediately brought up problems related to the infant's sleeping. She was reassured that these were not new problems "caused" by the change of home (she voiced fear that that was the cause), but that they were probably aggravated temporarily by the transition. On this first and on subsequent visits, the team observed that the mother was not allowing herself to respond spontaneously to the infant for fear that this might encourage "bad habits" in the child. She seemed eager to "train" her to be the kind of child whom they would want in their family and with whom they would want to share their apparently happy home.

Mrs. ML shared some of her experiences related to the infant that she found to be confusing and somewhat upsetting. For example, she revealed a conversation she had had with the social worker from the Department of Adoptions that had bothered her. When she told the social worker that the infant had "slapped her in the face" while she was changing her diapers, the social worker said that this was the child's way of expressing hostility about having a new mother. Mrs. ML was not well versed in the psychodynamics of interaction, and this statement had preoccupied her. She was told by the intervention staff that sometimes the actions of young children are overinterpreted by people who do not know a particular child. Much later in the intervention program, the mother talked about what her feelings had been when people in her neighborhood had asked her whose child this was. She related that her answer at first had been that this child had come to live with them. (She explained that that was how she felt about the infant at first.) She had felt guilty at that time for not being able to say that this was her and her husband's child and that they had adopted her. She further related that a couple of weeks later, when a similar situation arose, she had felt that the child really *was* their own and that she could say so. She expressed how proud she had felt when she was able to say with conviction that the child was theirs and that she was part of the family. The author, who had the most contact with Mrs. ML, was particularly touched by her sharing these feelings, which provided glimpses of Mrs. ML's honesty with herself and with others. The author gained a deep respect for Mrs. ML as she saw how this mother was coping with her own feelings.

The intervention goals were first and foremost to foster mutually enjoyable interactions between the infant and her new parents. The two most pervasive problems that the staff encountered in this home were the mother's lack of knowledge of what to expect from a 20-month-old infant, and her somewhat rigid approach in areas of training and discipline. Mrs. ML's eagerness to train the child well from the start apparently prevented her from comforting her when she cried after being put to bed at night, for fear that this would reinforce the crying. She was encouraged to respond to the child's crying as it felt most comfortable for her, and her natural tendency to go to the child and calm her was supported. The staff believed that the mother's greater spontaneity would help the bonding that was taking place between herself and the infant and that needed to be strengthened. The staff emphasized to the mother how important it was for this child to develop trust in her parents and to know that they would be available to her in moments of stress.

There was no question that the child had problems that made parenting difficult, e.g., her sleeping problems of long standing and the sudden disruptions of her play (first by rocking with thumbsucking, later by intense masturbating). On the other hand, she was quite adaptable to new people and situations and to demands made of her, as long as these demands did not cause serious conflicts or anxiety in her.

Mrs. ML seemed particularly anxious to toilet train the child and to teach her to play alone in her own room. The mother hoped and expected to meet with success in these two areas with the help of the intervention staff. The mother's eagerness to succeed with toilet training seemed to interfere with her potential for being alert to the infant's cues. The infant, feeling pressured, became very tense and resistant. Again, Mrs. ML was able to discuss her concerns. The team explored with her what might be causing the child to resist so adamantly "going to the potty." After discussing alternatives with her and weighing these, the mother was able to decide on the best way for her to deal with this issue, which was to pay little attention to toilet training for a while until she and the child could be more relaxed in this area.

Six weeks after the adoption, Mrs. ML voiced surprise that the child wanted constant attention from her; she wondered whether that might be because she had received too much attention from the foster mother. The new mother was told that in the foster home, the child was used to being in the same room with the foster mother—usually in the living room or in the kitchen—but that she had not received much undivided attention from the foster mother. The child's current need for attention was further discussed with Mrs. ML. It was noted that the infant was receiving much undivided attention from her new mother, which was important for her in her new home, and that she might continue to demand much attention until she overcame her remaining anxiety about the change of home and parents.

The staff further discussed with the mother that it was not realistic to expect the child at this age to play alone in her room, that needing and wanting to be near her mother at 21 months of age was normal, and that satisfying that demand would not impede her development of independence later—in fact, quite to the contrary. It was explained to the mother that it would help the child develop healthy autonomy if her emotional needs, so intense during this period, were met adequately. The staff did explore with her how she could help the child to become more autonomous in her play while in the mother's presence. A plan was cooperatively developed with the mother to lengthen the periods of the child's independent play in a secure setting. (For further details, see Chapter 8: social-affective area, problem 2.)

An inability to play alone, constant demands for attention, difficulty in going to sleep at night, and periodic intense masturbation (with sudden onset, at times) were the child's most persistent problems and also those which the mother found most burdensome. As a result of much discussion and cooperative planning with the mother, the child gradually was able to play longer by herself. At the same time, the mother gave up her unrealistic expectations of having the child play alone in her room. Gradually, with the support of the staff, the mother was able to help the child feel more relaxed in these problem areas instead of adding to the child's anxiety with her own. Bedtime improved as the mother was able to soothe the child by giving her a warm bath, reading to her softly in a quiet atmosphere in her own room, rocking her gently, and then patting her for a few minutes after putting her in her crib. (The infant had discontinued her violent bed-rocking.) This gradual calming also helped the child get over her intense masturbation at bedtime. When it diminished at bedtime, it almost completely disappeared in the daytime during play activities (the mother had to be reassured that masturbating was not at all uncommon at this age as a way of self-soothing).

The issues discussed above are related to the problems that the infant still presented at 20 months of age and to the difficulties these problems created for the mother in dealing with this new child in her home. The team was able to provide for the mother the kind of help and guidance that gave her a better understanding both of her child and of what was important in supporting her child's development and adjustment to her new home. The mother learned quickly to use a rational problem-solving approach based on sensitivity to cues and skilled observation. She became increasingly able to make wise decisions for the infant and for herself which showed sensitivity to the infant as well as consideration of her own and her husband's needs.

The intervention efforts to enhance the infant's language development and the quality of her play met with dramatic success. Both parents
enjoyed playing and talking with the child. The mother was eager for any
help that could make language and play interaction between herself and
the infant more rewarding for both. The modeling and suggestions that
were provided were utilized intelligently. The mother quickly became alert
to the infant's skills in these areas and was able to generalize easily and
imaginatively from modeling and information in building on the child's
strengths. The mother's motivation, intelligence, and special interest in
language and music were advantageous to the child's progress. Moreover,
both parents' enjoyment of reading made it easier to interest their daughter in books. The mother was quite receptive to information regarding the
developmental sequence in children's evolving interests—talking about
pictures that related to the child's immediate experience and then reading
books together with simple story lines. She learned to select pictures and
books that were meaningful to the child and that made the experience of
"reading together" enjoyable for both.

The child's progress in language in the adoptive home was phenomenal. The team was impressed by her new achievements that were evident at
successive home visits. When she left the foster home at 20 months of age,
she was saying a few words. By 23 months she was speaking in 2-, 3-, and
sometimes 4-word sentences with appropriate voice modulation. A couple
of weeks later, she was observed conversing with her mother about people
not present in the room, while at the same time playing with a peg bus in a
relaxed manner. The mother understood all that the child said and enriched the verbal interaction by answering the child's questions and adding new statements filled with information to which the child could respond again.

The reciprocity and mutual enjoyment that were evident in language
interactions between mother and infant appeared to be instrumental in ce-
menting the warm relationship that was developing between the two. It
seemed to ease the occasionally tense moments that occurred between the
mother and her new daughter. Their pleasure in language as well as in
music appeared to help mother and child to express positive affect more
openly, which, in turn, increased mutual pleasure.

The child also made rapid progress in cognitive skills expressed in
play. She took great pleasure in being able to do puzzles and was successful with rather complex formboard-type toys. Probably her most important gain in this area was that she was finally able to enjoy her successes
with toys without expecting applause every time she mastered a task (a
habit that had been formed in the foster home). Her developmental score
rose by 28 points between 18 and 24 months of age.

With this family it was evident that the combination of support and information helped the mother to deal more effectively with her child. The following is an example of how well the mother utilized information. Toward the beginning of intervention, when the infant was saying very few words, the mother was disturbed that the infant had said a word or two spontaneously but was not willing to say them when they should have been used—such as "milk." The mother wondered whether she should withhold milk (and other things) from the child until she would say the word for it. She wondered especially about words that she had heard the child say spontaneously in play or to herself. First, much support was given to the mother for the kinds of language interactions that she engaged in with her daughter, that produced such an increase of interest in language on the part of the child. Then, it was explained to her that many words appear in children's spontaneous language (where words are sometimes played with and experimented with like toys) and in play before they are solidly established in the infant's repertoire, and can be retrieved at will when the situation demands. It was discussed with her that the expectation of a word by an adult who is important to the child puts a certain amount of stress on the child, and therefore new words that are still tenuous in the child's vocabulary often are not available to the child on the adult's demand. The mother was interested in this information and was able to utilize it. The result was that she no longer pressured the child for language. Subsequently, the child's language progressed rapidly and language interaction remained enjoyable and pressure-free for child and mother.

Before concluding the discussion of this case, something must be said about the adoptive father. The team, who saw him twice, found him to be a warm and responsive person who enjoyed his new role. During an early intervention session, the team came in the evening to show parts of some videotapes that had been taken of the infant when she was younger and still in the foster home and which the parents had requested to see. The father asked many questions about the child when she was younger. The questions and his way of talking about the child showed his genuine interest in her. The mother reported, and the team saw, how joyful father and child were with each other. The father seemed to be warm, accepting, and relaxed with her from the start.

The second time the staff saw the father in the home, the mother was having a difficult time in coping with the child. She was quite tense and had called for this home visit at a time when her husband could be present. A conversation between Mr. ML and a staff member revealed how supportive and helpful he was to his wife. He seemed to understand the stress that his wife was experiencing in learning to adapt first of all to a new life in which a child was constantly intruding upon her privacy, and second, to learn to cope with a child who still presented some problems that would not be easy to cope with for any mother. It was apparent that the father was a powerful force in the lives of both his wife and new child as these two had the difficult task of learning to live closely and intensely together.

The conditions in this case were favorable to effective parent-infant intervention. The following circumstances all helped to make intervention highly successful: the high priority of the child with both parents; the absence of financial worries or other outside pressures; the father's uncomplicated, warm relationship with the child and supportiveness of his wife; the mother's realization that she needed help with her new child; the mother's trust in the staff and the good rapport that was established quickly; and, last but not least, the mother's strong motivation to be a competent parent.

Chapter 6
Cases with Partially Successful or Unsuccessful Intervention

This chapter contains the description of cases in which intervention either failed to achieve altogether or achieved only in part the major Intervention Program goals. Information about such cases highlights many factors that have a bearing on the course of intervention. An effort has been made to identify some of the obstacles to effective intervention that were encountered. The discussion of these less successful cases may alert others to areas that have to be carefully considered in order to avoid misdirected efforts and to bring about more effective intervention.

In a number of the cases discussed below, several problems—often unrelated to the infant—coexisted, causing considerable stress to the parent and, consequently, having a negative effect on parent-infant interaction. Such cases were difficult to work with, especially when the major problems of a family were unrelated to the infant or to parenting, and yet were so severe that they almost totally absorbed the mental and emotional (and sometimes even physical) energy of the parents. Because intervention efforts oriented to enhance the parent-infant interaction were not likely to get much response from such a family, efforts were often redirected to help the parents deal first with their primary problems. However, some of these problems were not easily overcome or solved.

Intervention was judged to have been "partially successful" in nine and "unsuccessful" in five of the fourteen cases presented in this chapter. The staff judgment of "partially successful" signified that some of the important goals of the cases were achieved, but that some were not achieved. "Unsuccessful" signified that the major intervention goals were not achieved to the staff's satisfaction.

In an attempt to parallel the organization of the previous chapter as much as possible, the two cases that are discussed first are those with which intervention contacts were infrequent. However, in these two cases, contrary to the six cases discussed in the first section of Chapter 5, the infrequency of home visits was probably an error in staff judgment. The second section contains six cases in which there were multiple problems that persisted, although the infants did not appear to be a significant cause of these problems. The third section contains two cases in which the parents were overprotective of their infant, who was likely to remain the sole child in the family. The fourth section includes cases like those in the last part of Chapter 5, in which the infants' serious problems were compounded by the problems of the parents and the circumstances of the families.

FAMILIES RECEIVING DISCONTINUOUS INTERVENTION

The two cases in this category were seen regularly during the first few months of the program. After this initial period of uninterrupted intervention (approximately bi-weekly for case F and monthly for case K), the frequency and regularity of home visits diminished in both cases as the staff became involved in a rapidly increasing number of cases that seemed to need much more attention. During the middle period of the intervention program for both these cases, the continuity of home visits was interrupted for two or more months because of problems in making appointments. (Family F had no telephone for several months. In family K, the mother did not return phone calls from the staff several times and she was also hospitalized for a period of time.) The outcome in both cases suggests that more consistent visits, at least once a month, might have prevented the problems that developed in the last few months of the program.

Case F

Family F was a young hispanic couple who lived in a one-room apartment converted from a store. From the start, the mother seemed disturbed by the father's controlling manner both of the infant and of her. A little later, the mother revealed that she had been beaten rather severely several times, although she stressed that her husband had not beaten or hurt the baby in any way. There was a brief separation (the mother, with the baby, left her husband temporarily), but after the reunion the marital problems appeared to have been resolved (according to the mother's report). The intervention team gave the support to the mother that she needed during this stressful period.

The mother was 19 when the infant was born at 35 weeks gestational age. The infant's only remaining problem by 10 months of age seemed to be a mild delay in language: he vocalized very little. The mother, young and inexperienced, welcomed the team's visits and responded well to modeling in both the play and language areas. The father was the oldest of eight children, he had raised several of his siblings in Mexico, and he had some definite ideas on childrearing. He was authoritarian and he proudly demonstrated his "control" over the child's behavior. The home visits were made most of the time when the father could be present. The modeling and discussions with both parents appeared to be effective in increasing the inexperienced mother's skills and in softening the "tough" attitude of the father toward his child.

Intervention was considered to be effective during the first 7 months. Except for the initial marital crisis, which was severe but of short duration, no serious problems had been seen in this case. The mother had become more confident in her parenting role and she was enjoying her infant. She had demonstrated her ability to expand on suggestions made to her and to generalize from the modeling of the staff with the infant. She had increased her skills in selecting and presenting play materials to the infant and she was engaging in appropriate language interaction with him. In spite of these early gains, a deterioration of mother-infant interaction was noted when the infant was about 20 months old. After not having seen the family for over 2 months, the staff observed that the mother had become detached, depressed, and punitive toward the child. She found it difficult to deal with his new negative behavior and she did not allow him to express negative feelings in any manner. The change in the mother's state and in her behavior toward the child may have been due, at least in part, to her new pregnancy and her concern about her own health.

A combination of factors probably contributed to the team's inability to effect necessary changes in the parent's dealings with her child in the last few months of the program. First, the excellent rapport that had existed between the team and the parents seemed difficult to reestablish after a long interval of no contact, which came at a time when the mother was in a depressed state. Second, only one member of the original team assigned to this case continued with the family (the other staff person moved to another geographical area). Third, the mother seemed detached and showed little interest in the child and his activities.

Several home visits were made in the last few weeks of the program, when the staff became aware of the negative turn the case had taken. Another experienced staff member was substituted for the one who had left the program. The team discussed with the mother some ways in which she could have some time to herself, but the mother showed little interest in any of the suggested possibilities. Her response to intervention during this period was much more passive than it had been earlier. She continued to share some of her worries, mostly about her own health, but she did not actively participate in problem-solving about how she could make the situation easier for herself and how she might deal more effectively with the negative behaviors of the child. (Because of a change in his working hours, the father did not participate in these later sessions.) The child's language delay had also become more pronounced, but the mother showed no concern regarding his silence. She no longer appeared to profit from the staff's modeling of language interactions with the child, nor did she follow through on specific suggestions made to her on how she could enhance the child's language.

The conjecture made is that the physical and emotional state of the mother was solely responsible for the deteriorating mother-infant interaction and the increased delay in the child's language. However, if the staff had been more persistent in its efforts to continue seeing this family regularly in order to monitor infant development and parent-infant interaction and to maintain a close relationship with the parents, the problems that developed might have been less severe. Unfortunately, there had been no warning of the negative turn in the mother-infant relationship. Furthermore, the family had moved some distance from the project Center. Nevertheless, the staff learned from this case (and from the one that follows) that some ongoing contact with families is vital, especially during the second year of the child's life, in order to be able to monitor progress and to detect changes toward a negative direction as soon as they occur.

Case K

Mr. and Mrs. K both came from large families and both received support from their own parents and siblings. There was evidence of all the advantages of a closely knit extended black family. The mother began to work full time when the infant was 1 month old (corrected age) and continued to do so throughout the first 2 years of the child's life.

The infant, born at 30 weeks gestational age, had respiratory problems after birth as well as other physiological and medical problems. By age 9 months, he was functioning within the normal range in all areas of development, although his language scores were the lowest. His behavior at home appeared to be strikingly different from his behavior at the project Center or in any other unfamiliar place. He was active in the gross motor area and in his play in the home, and the parents—especially his father, who seemed to dominate in the home—valued and encouraged his independence. At the project Center, the child was passive and somewhat fearful at first, and he generally displayed the behavior of a "slow-to-warm-up" child.

From the start, the relationship between the intervention team and the family was cordial. The parents saw the child as functioning normally (as did the staff), and they saw no particular need for help from the staff. This relative lack of interest in intervention continued and was probably the major cause for the infrequency of home visits made after the initial 3 to 4 months. In addition, there were problems in making appointments because of the irregular working hours of the mother and the wish of both parents to be present during intervention sessions. Also, the parents infrequently returned the team's telephone calls after the first 6 months of their participation in the program.

The team did not express sharp concerns about the interruption in the process of intervention with this family because everything seemed to be going well with infant and parents. The team did note in the first few months that neither the father nor the mother showed much interest in the child's play or play materials. (They paid polite attention to the staff's modeling of play interactions with the infant and to the staff's requests that they observe the child's use of the materials that were left for him.) Neither parent seemed to talk much with the child, but both parents took great pride in his gross motor exploits.

During the last half of the intervention program with this family, visits were infrequent and irregular. There was an interruption of contact lasting several months—the period when calls were not returned. (The staff found out later that the mother had been hospitalized for an acute health problem.) In summary, there were several factors that interfered with the continuity of intervention in this case. First, the relationship between the parents and the team remained at a superficial level throughout the 14-month intervention period. Second, the child appeared to be doing well and the parents were not eager for frequent home visits. Third, the staff's awareness that there were no unusual stresses in the family and that support was available from the extended family made regular contacts with parents and child seem less than urgent. Fourth, the travel time (1 ½ hours) required for home visits to this family may have appeared to take away from time that could be spent with families that seemed to need more help and that were more appreciative of the time spent with them. It also must be assumed that the level of staff interest and involvement in a case is not at all a negligible factor in the effectiveness of intervention. In this case, all the above circumstances may have contributed to low staff involvement with this family. Nonetheless, the staff was dismayed to find that the infant's developmental test scores at age 2 had dropped into the low-normal range.

Cases F and K constitute two of the five cases that were evaluated as unsuccessful with respect to intervention because either the infant's functioning or the parent-infant interaction or both had not progressed in a positive manner during the family's participation in the Intervention Program.

The failure of the staff to provide continuity of intervention in these two cases requires further comment. The policy with cases in which parents and children seemed to be doing well was to make home visits at least once a month to "monitor" the progress of the family. These infrequent visits would occur mostly in the middle period of a case—never at the beginning and rarely toward the termination of a case. Because of the difficulties in making contact with families F and K, the policy of monthly monitoring was not maintained. Furthermore, it is obvious that the staff's rapport with these two families (especially with family K throughout the intervention period and with family F toward the end of intervention) was not of the same quality as the rapport established with the great majority of families in the Intervention Program. Neither the staff nor the parents were particularly motivated to spend much energy or effort toward maintaining regular contact. Moreover, intervention with case K was initiated at a time when all staff members had a number of cases that seemed to require more attention.

Upon retrospective evaluation of intervention with these two cases, the infants and parents in both cases probably could have profited from much more help than was assumed necessary by the teams assigned to these cases. Both infants did rather poorly (low-normal DQ) on the 2-year developmental tests and both these preterm infants evidently needed more motivation in language and in play than they were getting in their homes. Moreover, the affective interaction between mother and infant deteriorated in one of the two cases during the last half of the program.

The staff learned an important lesson from these two cases: It is vitally important to keep uninterrupted and regular contact and to maintain open communication with all families with high risk infants for whom a staff takes responsibility. Sometimes appearances can be misleading. Furthermore, things can change rapidly in a family with a young infant, especially when that infant is a preterm first-born (the infants in cases F and K were both first-born males). A review of all the cases in the Intervention Program made it clear that all the families, without exception, needed the support that the staff was able to provide, for at least some portion of the 14-month intervention period. Some families, of course, needed much more than the staff or the program could offer, as was the case with most of the families discussed in the remainder of this chapter.

MULTIPLE PROBLEMS IN THE FAMILY

Two groups of cases have been subsumed under the above heading: 1) families suffering from poverty and disorganization, and 2) teenage mothers with problems. There is some overlap between these two sub-categories, e.g., cases Z and N could go in either group. The parents in both sub-categories have in common the fact that they experienced external stresses as well as stresses from within themselves and from their families. The first of the two sub-categories consists of families in which the external pressures seemed to play a large part in causing disorganization and instability. In the second group, the status and the relative immaturity of teenagers in this society constitute stresses in themselves, which are exacerbated by the responsibility of caring for a young child. Other problems from within and outside the family added to the problems that these teenagers already had in raising their infants. The high risk status of all six preterm infants discussed here was caused by problems that occurred early in their lives. The forced separation of mother and infant after birth that these perinatal problems required (hospitalization of infant immediately after birth) added to the vulnerability of the relationship between the teenager and her infant (all six infants were males).

Low-Income "Disorganized" Families

The common characteristic of the two families described here was poverty compounded by disorganization. In both cases external pressures contributed significantly to family disorganization and instability. Both families were hispanic.

Case L   This case was one in which poverty, combined with the family's "undocumented worker" status (a term currently applied to Mexican nationals who have not legally immigrated into the United States) made the family vulnerable to external pressures and powerless to control its own destiny. Family L consisted of a young father (age 19), a mother 5 years older, and the prematurely born infant. Both parents worked whenever they could find employment. Their lives were quite unstable because the mother or father was either looking for work or working for short periods on a particular job. The unsteady employment of these two people, who had few marketable skills, made it necessary for them to move frequently from one place to another. As long as they were employed, they could afford to rent an apartment of their own. When they did not earn sufficiently to pay rent, they would move in temporarily with friends or relatives. When the infant was 14 months old, the father, discouraged by his lack of full-time employment, went to Mexico; the mother and infant moved in with the mother's aunt and uncle who lived in a small one-bedroom apartment. This aunt was the major source of emotional support for the mother, who suffered considerably from the instability of the kind of life she and her husband and child were forced to lead. The aunt also cared for the infant part of the time while the mother was working.

Shortly after the father returned from Mexico, the father and mother (who were working at the same location) were deported to Mexico from their place of work. Several days later, the infant was taken to Mexico by an acquaintance and "delivered" to his parents. The family returned to the United States about 7 weeks later. Again, unemployment of both parents forced the family to move in with relatives. The crowded conditions—living with a family that included two small children—was extremely stressful to the mother. Her own child's aggressiveness to one of the other children, a behavior that she could not tolerate or cope with, made the situation worse for the mother.

These life circumstances would have created difficulties for any new mother, but especially so for Mrs. L, who appeared to be emotionally vulnerable. Moreover, she had had a difficult pregnancy that had been complicated by hypertension and convulsions. From the start of the intervention program, the mother seemed tired and lethargic much of the time. The staff noted that her attention to her infant as well as to adults had an "off-again-on-again" quality, that is, she seemed unable to stay long with the reality of the moment. She seemed to love and value the baby, but she seldom initiated interaction with him. She seemed to be waiting for him to involve her.

The infant, born only 4 weeks preterm, had some neurological problems at 10 months of age, including convulsions, although he had had no serious difficulties surrounding his birth. He suffered temporary weakness in connection with the convulsions around the time that the family was referred to the Intervention Program. When the staff first saw him, his fine motor coordination was poor. He was highly distractible, but he seemed to be responsive to adult encouragement. His problems increased in magnitude and in number after the parents' deportation, which separated him from his parents for several days. While in Mexico, he contracted dysentery that resulted in dehydration for which he had to be hospitalized. This entailed his second separation from his parents, in the context of a completely new environment. When the family returned to the United States, the mother contacted the team immediately. The child had contracted two skin diseases in Mexico and had regressed developmentally (he was 17 months old at that time). The mother complained that he had become irritable, excessively demanding, and aggressive with other children. Furthermore, when his mother went back to work a couple of months later, he could not tolerate being separated from her. His low-average developmental score at 9 months had dropped further by 24 months. Delays were seen especially in adaptive play and in language.

Mrs. L could perhaps have dealt adequately with normal problems of childrearing in a more stable environment and with a certain amount of support, but in this case, each of the traumatic events aggravated the child's problems, increased the difficulties in mother-infant interaction, and lessened the mother's ability to deal effectively with her child. The father was quite relaxed with the child and initiated much more interaction with him than the mother, but unfortunately his presence in the home was inconsistent (for brief periods he worked on two jobs at the same time).

The parents welcomed home visits of the staff and were always cooperative in making and keeping appointments. Intervention contacts with the mother were characterized as friendly and cordial—the mother was very eager to have the team come to see her and the infant (both staff members spoke Spanish).

The staff questioned the mother's ability to focus on aspects of the child's development that were not directly related to his physical health and development, even during less stressful periods. The child's great-aunt, one of the caregivers while the mother was working, appeared to profit more from intervention than did the mother. For a short time when this aunt was the child's primary daytime caregiver, his play and his language environment were a little more stimulating. When working with the mother, the staff's goals—increased mother-infant interaction and appropriate motivation of the infant in play and language—were often diverted by the more immediate needs of the mother.

In this problem-ridden case, some positive changes in parenting behavior were observed in the first few months, before the traumatic events connected with the deportation occurred, but most of these newly acquired parenting behaviors were not maintained through the stressful periods. The parents became aware of the kinds of materials the infant could enjoy; this was evidenced by their choice of Christmas toys and by the household materials that were provided for him. The mother also talked more to the child, interpreting to him the sights and sounds that he was experiencing (observed during car rides). She also provided increasingly appropriate pictures and books for him to look at. However, the staff was unsuccessful in helping the mother prepare the child for the many changes in home environments and caregivers that he had to undergo. It was especially difficult for the mother to help reduce the child's anxiety about changes because the changes were so stressful to the mother herself. While the mother's aunt cared for the child, she was able to involve him in the kind of interaction and play that increased his concentration and afforded him the experience of pleasure in his successes. As the child became older, the mother seemed drained emotionally and physically much of the time. Her state made it especially difficult for her to deal effectively with the increasing demands of a toddler who had also undergone considerable stress.

The failure of intervention to produce major changes that persisted in the parent-infant interactions and the quality of parenting was judged to be due primarily to the serious and pervasive social, economic, and legal problems that overwhelmed this young family and that put tremendous stress on a mother who probably was not a vigorous, emotionally stable, or resourceful person. The drop in the mother's ratings on the

Parent Behavior Progression paralleled the drop in the infant's developmental scores; both reflected the low level of parental effectiveness at the termination of the program. The positive effects of intervention were manifested by the infant and the mother at the time of the 16-month staff summary. Shortly after that, the most traumatic period began for this family with the deportation. The effects of subsequent events on mother and infant interfered markedly with the further achievement of major intervention goals. The continued home visits no doubt gave the mother needed emotional support. To some extent, the home visits ameliorated the tense parent-infant interaction, but not sufficiently to produce perceptible changes in parenting or in the child's functioning during this stressful time.

Case A This was another case in which poverty had a disorganizing effect on the family. The mother, although not lacking in intelligence, strength, and vitality, was single with three children to support. She had to work full time, which entailed the need for babysitters. The mother also had realistic fears of losing her job and of exposing her two young daughters (ages 5½ and 7) to the environment of a crime-ridden neighborhood. Although vigorous (a word appearing over and over again in the case summary), the mother was impetuous in her actions and disorganized in her life with her children. The already chaotic home environment became intolerable even to the mother when relatives moved in with them. She took the children on a trip to Mexico to get away from this situation. In addition, she had to face surgery for her middle child. She finally felt it necessary to find an apartment in a safer neighborhood where she could allow the girls to venture outside of the house. She received help from the community aide employed by the Infant Studies Project in finding an apartment in a safer neighborhood.

The infant, born 6 weeks preterm, appeared to be without problems by 10 months of age. His problems at the time of his birth and immediately after birth accounted for his categorization as "high risk." He was an active infant, which pleased his equally active mother. His strengths were a generally positive affect, vigorous play, clear cues as to his preferences, and a strong social response. His expressive language lagged behind the other developmental areas.

During the first half of the intervention period, the infant developed goal directedness and persistence in his play with developmentally appropriate materials that the staff provided for him. He was not easily distractible and was seen using problem-solving skills with more complex toys. The mother enjoyed her infant—she said one day, in passing, that he was the most pleasurable thing in her life. Nevertheless, it was difficult for the staff to help this mother focus long enough on the infant's behavior to enable her to become more sensitive to his cues. Her high level of activity and many concerns did not allow her to become aware of the kinds of language interactions and play environment that the infant needed to encourage his optimal development. Throughout the intervention period, there was good rapport between the staff (first two, then one staff member), but the staff became increasingly discouraged about the mother's parenting behaviors and the environment that she provided for the infant.

After the first few months, the staff worked as much with the daycare provider and with the older children in the family as with the mother. Unfortunately, the staff had to deal with a succession of six daycare providers, some more adequate than others. Most of them had other young children to care for in their own homes. Because of the many caregivers, intervention could not have an appreciable long-term effect on the infant, although the staff worked with one after the other. (Occasionally the staff would become involved in helping a daycare provider with problems of her own.)

By the termination of intervention, the lag in the infant's expressive language had increased. His earlier initiative in a variety of activities was somewhat diminished and his assertiveness seemed subdued at times. Fortunately, he was still able to assert himself sufficiently with the mother to force her to pay attention to him when he really needed her. In that sense, he showed his adaptability to her temperament. The mother, burdened with responsibilities and worries, found it difficult to tune in to her youngest child's more subtle cues and needs. She continued to be vocal but non-contingent to his language and insensitive to his tempo and play needs. Her perception of him as a healthy and vigorous boy did not help her sensitivity. On the one hand, the mother's continued positive feelings toward her youngest child, and, on the other hand, her unresponsiveness and relative lack of parental competence were reflected in the contrasting ratings on the Parent Behavior Progression (high on level I and low on the other levels).

When the infant approached 2 years of age, the mother showed some minor concern about his lack of language, but, in spite of repeated staff efforts to help her become more verbally contingent to his vocalizations and to his interests, little change was seen in the mother. She did learn to respect the child's need to play with materials at his skill level. She was able to provide greater safety for him, especially in the car (she began to use the infant car seat that the staff provided for her), and in one of the daycare situations (after the staff had reported to her that the infant was being left alone in the house while the daycare provider escorted the other children to school). The staff was also able to help the older sibling to take some responsibility for the infant's safety in the home.

Comments The infant's development was not a high priority in either of these two families. In case A, the mother did not have any serious concern about her healthy infant's development. In case L, there was intermittent worry, first with regard to the infant's convulsions and subsequent weakness at 10 months, and then about his illness and hospitalization in Mexico. However, these concerns were temporary and were overshadowed by more pervasive and severe problems. Infant A, although he became less assertive and persistent and received lower scores at age 2 than at 9 months, weathered the stormy home life fairly well. Infant L, less sturdy at the outset in a number of ways, probably suffered more from the environmental stresses (which were also more serious in his case) to which he was subjected.

In both cases, the conditions of poverty and the stresses that go with it helped to precipitate the other problems with which these families had to cope. (The insecure alien status and the deportation of Mr. and Mrs. L caused much additional distress to mother and infant in that case.) The parents liked their children—both mothers showed occasional affection toward them as well as pride in them. But they did not see their infants as being in need of any kind of special attention. These burdened women, who engaged in erratic and inconsistent parenting, did not realize that in the kind of environment to which their infants were exposed they were not likely to grow into "competent" children without specific kinds of adult attention. In both cases, consistent and competent daycare for the infants would have helped to relieve some of the stress that had a negative effect on parent-infant interaction and on the quality of parenting.

Teenage Mothers with Problems

The four cases that follow resemble the previous two in some respects but not in others. Although these families were also poor and classified as low SES, their major problems did not seem to be related to poverty and other environmental circumstances to the same degree as in the two previous cases. Three of the four couples had marital problems—two couples were separated for periods varying in length during their 14 months in the Intervention Program. Three of the infants were very small preterm babies—one of them had heart surgery after birth, followed by 6 weeks of hospitalization.

In these four families, as in the two in the previous section, the infants, in spite of their early problems, did not have high priority with their mothers or fathers at the time intervention began. By that time, the parents were not especially concerned about their survival or normal development, or at least they did not show concern. All were male infants; three of them were first children. The low priority of the infant appeared to be related to the youth and immaturity of the mothers, whose own childhood and adolescent needs seemed unsatisfied, and to the mothers' insecurity regarding the future with respect to their own lives. Furthermore, in two of the families, the fathers had serious problems that had a distinctly negative effect on their infants. All these circumstances apparently contributed to the low priority of the infant, and this, in turn, made effective parent-infant intervention more difficult to achieve.

The first case discussed below is the one that could most easily fit into either group of cases under the heading "Multiple Problems in the Family." Mrs. Z is the only one of the teenage mothers for whom the preterm infant was not the first-born child.

Case Z   Mrs. Z was 19 years old when the infant was born, 4 weeks preterm. He was her second child, although there were three children in the home, all of them male. The oldest, age 4, was her husband's son from a former marriage. The parents were white, with little education, and they were struggling financially to make ends meet. Continuous financial stress, a strong desire for upward mobility, and frequent moving from home to home (three moves in 14 months) put additional burdens on this young family of five.

The project infant appeared to have no particular problems by 10 months of age. In spite of an emotionally and physically unstable environment, the infant continued to function well in all developmental areas. He was able to maintain average developmental test scores from 9 months to 2 years of age. The genuine affection that his mother felt for him and that she showed him occasionally may have sustained him sufficiently to cope in this emotionally turbulent home.

Mrs. Z's behavior was erratic, and her interactions with the infant alternated between physical affection and punitiveness. However, her interactions became more punitive as the infant grew older and more independent. Nevertheless, this young mother showed considerable resourcefulness, common sense, and appropriate concern for the care of her children during periods when she appeared to be calm and more stable. During these periods, which became less and less frequent as time went on, she was receptive to intervention and she showed interest in learning about the kinds of experiences that would foster her children's development. Most of the time, however, she felt harassed by her husband's demands and dissatisfactions and overburdened with the care of three young children. She reported that her husband criticized her continuously and that he showed no appreciation for her efforts as a homemaker and mother of three young children. She felt inadequate and depressed much of the time and found it difficult to cope with everyday living.

Not surprisingly, this 19-year-old mother often felt that she had to get away from her home, sometimes for 2 or 3 days at a time. Although in general she showed concern regarding the care of the children in her absence, during these "flights" from home, her own needs became uppermost in her mind, and she gave little thought to the care of her children. She would leave them with a teenage acquaintance who, by her own description, knew nothing about children and took poor care of them. This babysitter was observed by the staff to be oblivious to the children's needs or demands. In contrast, Mrs. Z quit her full-time job early in the program because she could not rely on her babysitter (another woman) to give proper care to her children.

In spite of the uneven quality of care that the children received, from their mother as well as from others, the mother talked proudly about her two babies and she expressed reluctance to see them grow up so fast. As soon as the infant started to walk and to become more self-sufficient, the mother was observed yelling at him, slapping him more frequently, and expressing less affection to him. Physical roughness, harsh language, and much yelling seemed to be part of this mother's style, not only with her children but also with her own mother (witnessed by staff). Yet, her behavior toward the children did not have the characteristics of child abuse. It seemed more characteristic of an immature teenager who, under considerable stress, tended to vacillate between extremes of behavior. Although she was able to show affection toward her own two children (but apparently not toward her stepchild), they had little warning of shifts in her mood and her responses to their behavior.

In the first few months of the family's participation in the Intervention Program, Mrs. Z was able to accept some support from the staff, and at times she seemed to feel better about herself. This greater sense of adequacy was immediately reflected in her more positive attitude toward all three children. But the positive effects of intervention were only intermittent as the mother continued to have periods during which she felt angry or depressed. During those times she reverted to her negative parenting behavior. Even though there were moments when she was warm and positive with her children, her behavior was often impulsive, inconsistent, and punitive.

Mrs. Z's commitment to the Intervention Program was tenuous. From the very beginning, she frequently canceled appointments or was not at home when the team arrived, even when the appointment had been confirmed by mail or by telephone the previous day. (Most of the time there was no telephone in the home; the staff mailed reminders that would arrive a day or two before the planned and agreed-upon home visit.) The mother's attitude toward the staff fluctuated, as did her behavior toward her children; both seemed to depend on her emotional state. After a series of intervention sessions, uneven in quality, the mother discontinued all contacts with the program by consistently being away from her home when the team arrived at the appointed time. (The infant was 18 months old at this time.) Finally, she failed to return to the staff a pre-addressed, stamped card on which she was to indicate by a checkmark whether or not she wanted to continue in the program.

The following conditions may have influenced the course of intervention in case Z. First, because the mother was aware that the infant had no developmental problems, she may have questioned the justification for the home visits. Second, the father was neither involved in the program nor did he support the mother in any way. Third, the mother felt overburdened and depressed much of the time, and in this frame of mind she may not have been able to face the idea of having two more people in her home. Yet, there were times when the mother seemed to welcome the opportunity to talk with a sensitive person who listened sympathetically to her and who helped her with some problems that she was experiencing with her children. (One team member usually played with the three children while the other talked with the mother.)

It was difficult to understand why Mrs. Z cut herself off from what appeared to be her only source of emotional support at that time. This isolated young mother of three young children, with no support from her husband, certainly needed someone to talk to whom she could trust. As mentioned above, the staff did see considerable changes in her behavior toward her children early in the program. These behavioral changes, more specifically with the infant, were reflected on the Parent Behavior Progression: her ratings rose on levels I through V between the first and second assessments. Yet this mother dropped out of the program at a time when she appeared to be making good use of it.

Case Z was the only one in which the family discontinued its participation in the program, though in a passive manner. This unique experience with case Z caused the staff to reflect upon the intervention process with this family. It was concluded that little could have been done to alter the course of parent-infant intervention in this case. Still, one incident that might have made it more difficult for this mother to continue seeing the team warrants discussion. The last home visit was longer than usual (over 2 hours). During this visit the mother aired some of her negative feelings about her marriage and the anger that she felt toward her husband for all his criticism and lack of support. She may have felt guilty or uncomfortable about having expressed these negative feelings; and subsequently, the anticipation of facing again the people to whom she expressed these feelings, which had been bottled up for so long, may have been more than she could tolerate. It is often difficult to gauge at what point a parent's pouring out of feelings becomes psychologically too risky for her and leads her to cut off contact with her empathic "listener" (outside of clearly defined psychotherapy, which is structured to encourage the expression of feelings). One of the intervention goals was to gain the confidence of the mother sufficiently to refer her for personal counseling or to refer both parents for marital counseling. The mother broke off contact before this could occur, but it was anticipated that this type of referral would have been very difficult to achieve because the mother's thinking was not along the lines of needing, much less, seeking outside help for herself or for her marriage.

Intervention intended to enhance parent-infant interaction could not help this family solve its most serious problems, which were marital and financial. The staff was also unable to help the mother get some relief from caring for three young children from morning to night, day in and day out. They explored the possibilities of babysitting arrangements with the mother so that she could get away some of the time, but she showed no interest—she seemed to cling to the idea that the children were her responsibility, and apparently her husband reinforced that way of thinking.

Case R   The project infant was the first child of this young white couple. Mr. and Mrs. R lived in a one-room furnished apartment in an apartment house that did not allow children. When the intervention staff first met this family, both parents were working at night, in low-paying jobs, and the baby was taken to a close relative for the night. This arrangement lasted for a few weeks, until the father lost his job after having had an accident in which he incurred a head injury. The father began to be the nighttime caregiver of the infant. The injury exacerbated a condition, brought on previously by heavy drinking, which caused the father to have episodes of violent behavior. As a result of reports of such an episode, protective services insisted that the mother shift her work schedule to daytime so that the father would not have the care of the infant during the night. The same relative who earlier had cared for the baby at night now became his daytime caregiver. When the infant was 18 months old, the father was reported to have physically abused the infant. This time, protective services removed the infant from his parents, and the court placed him in foster care for 1 year with a close relative who lived over 100 miles away from the parents.

The infant was born 2 months preterm with a heart defect that required surgery soon after birth. During the 6 weeks of the infant's hospitalization after surgery, the parents visited him only two or three times. A few days after the infant was released from the hospital, Mrs. R's mother died. When the intervention team first saw the infant at 9½ months of age, he was small; he looked "sickly," with somewhat protruding eyes; and he had a hoarse and weak cry. He was not an appealing baby but he was functioning at age level in all but the gross motor area.

When the staff began making home visits, they noticed two rather unusual caregiving practices: the infant slept on blankets on the carpet near the wall heater because there was no crib, and the mother put several diapers on the infant—presumably so that she would not have to change diapers so often—making the infant's movements difficult and awkward. The parents subtly conveyed the message that they wanted the staff to "keep their distance" from the infant and from them. The mother's manner of talking about the infant and her stance during caregiving activities seemed to communicate: "I know it all and I don't want any help." Therefore, the team's first goal was to establish a relationship of trust with the parents, both of whom participated most of the time in intervention sessions.

The intervention team consisted of a staff person in her late forties and a young woman close to the parents' age (the mother was 19 and the father, 23). Mrs. R, who had recently lost her own mother, formed a close relationship with the older of the two team members. Conversations during home visits became more relaxed and, after the first few sessions, the parents asked the staff to plan longer visits so that they could have more time to "chat." Both parents seemed to value the warm social contact with the intervention team, and they often led the conversation away from the infant.

Parent-infant interaction problems were numerous. For example, the mother was attempting to "train" and discipline her infant early in his life. This attitude resulted in an excessive and unreasonable number of "don'ts" for the baby and extreme restrictiveness of spontaneous activity and exploration. The mother's rigid ideas regarding "early training" were compounded by a punitive manner of discipline. Through discussion and modeling (the staff played with the infant and interpreted his play behavior to the parents), the staff tried to point out how the continuous stream of rather threatening "no's" that the infant was hearing limited the experience necessary for his mental, emotional, and physical development.

The father became quite interested in the infant's development, and he began to play appropriately with him, appearing to enjoy this kind of interaction with his child. It should be noted that the father's interaction with this male infant was more relaxed, less restrictive, and less punitive than the mother's interaction with him. Apparently, it was only during his episodes of uncontrollable behavior (brought about by drinking combined with the effect of the head injury) that he became physically dangerous to the infant.

The staff also saw growing evidence of mutual pleasure in play interactions between mother and infant. The mother was becoming quite skilled in selecting play materials and presenting them to the infant in a stimulating manner. Her language with him increased considerably and became developmentally more appropriate. While some changes in play and language interaction took place between parent and infant as a result of intervention, the staff was not able to effect changes in a more basic area of caregiving. The mother continued to be insensitive to the infant's distress, to react negatively to much of the infant's normal exploratory behavior, and to be punitive with him when he violated the many unnecessary restrictions. Furthermore, the mother could not tolerate any expression of negative feelings by the infant: she interpreted these as the infant's rejection of her. At 16 months of age, the infant was observed to respond apprehensively even to mild indications of the mother's disapproval of his behavior, as noted in the description of a videotape, below.

During the last 2 months before the removal of the infant from the home, the older team member proceeded alone with this case because of the excellent rapport that existed between herself and the mother. When the father spent several weeks in a hospital in a detoxification program, this staff member met with the mother and the infant. In spite of the relaxed atmosphere during the sessions, the mother was not able to express any negative or even ambivalent feelings toward the infant, or earlier concerns that she might have had regarding his survival. She came closest when she stated on two separate occasions that her own mother (who had died shortly after the infant was released from the hospital) had been hesitant to get emotionally involved with the infant in case he might not live. This may have been a projection of her own fears regarding the baby's survival or continued vulnerability to severe illness.

At 18 months of age, when the infant was placed in foster care with a close relative who had young children of her own, intervention continued with the infant and his temporary caregiver as well as with the parents. Before proceeding with monthly home visits to the foster home, the natural parents were consulted and asked if they would approve of the staff's continued work with the infant in the relative's home. The parents favored this idea, showing again that they trusted the intervention staff (the original team of two made visits to the infant and foster mother while the older member continued seeing the parents). Fortunately, the foster mother and the natural mother were on good terms, which made the infant's placement a little less traumatic for the parents and the staff's visits to the foster home more acceptable to them.

The warm and caring foster mother was responsive to the staff's modeling of play and language interactions with the infant, as well as to specific suggestions. The infant received excellent care in his temporary home and he was exposed to a more secure and a richer environment than the one in his parents' home. By age 2, his fearfulness, his exaggerated eagerness to please, and his oversensitivity to negative reactions had all diminished considerably. After having spent over 6 months in the foster home, the infant functioned well affectively and cognitively; he performed well within the average range on developmental scales at age 2, receiving higher scores than at 18 months. He appeared to be a reasonably happy and relaxed child.

In spite of the infant's separation from his own parents during a developmental stage when such separation is considered harmful to affective development, the infant appeared to be in a better emotional state in the foster home 6 months after the separation than he had been before the separation. Greater emotional stability, a higher quality of physical and affective care, and a more positive environment may have outweighed the negative factors of separation from his parents at a vulnerable age. The extreme apprehensiveness about adult disapproval that had been observed when the infant had been with his parents was not seen in the infant's interactions with his foster mother.

The startling oversensitivity of the infant to his mother's subtlest cues of disapproval merits further discussion. An episode that was recorded on videotape exemplifies this behavior:

> The infant (16 months old) puts the protruding end of a plastic pop-bead in his mouth and takes it out again quickly; at the same time he gives his mother an anxious look and shakes his head in a questioning manner, awaiting her response. The mother reacts with a similar shake of her head accompanied by a soft "no." He acknowledged her response with another slow (and sad) shake of his head.[1]

The infant, aware that he was not allowed to mouth objects, was checking with his mother to see if this rule included the nipple-like part of the bead, which was so perfect for mouthing. His mother's response, although mild, confirmed what he had feared, although he apparently anticipated her response.

This oversensitivity to negative reactions, which is painful to observe in an infant this young and one who was certainly not precocious in other ways, may develop in children who are restricted from spontaneous activity in a punitive manner. One can imagine how hesitant even a young infant would be of exploring and experimenting with new objects or schemas if he had to guard himself at all cost against parental disapproval for reasons of self-protection. Although this kind of behavior may look like precocious affective development, it could be a sign that the child has been dealt with in a punitive or even abusive manner.

On the same videotape of mother-infant interaction, a second episode is noteworthy because it shows another, although quite different expression by the infant that may indicate a fragile parent-infant relationship. The episode demonstrates how hard this infant worked to get his mother to respond positively to him: he tries to engage her in pleasurable activity with him, he succeeds, and he then maintains her positive involvement.

> The mother bounces a ball to the infant on the high chair tray in front of him. He bounces it back toward the mother who is sitting beside him. He laughs

---

[1]This excerpt is from an assessment of parent-infant interaction that was taken with the Play Interaction Measure (PIM). See Chapter 3 for a discussion of the PIM.

excitedly; the mother, without change in her bland expression, rolls it back to the infant; the infant rolls it back to her—his laughter becomes more excited and exuberant as he continues to look at the mother. He does this until the mother begins to smile, look at him, and almost affectionately (without touching him) tilt her head; she finally smiles *with* him and returns the ball again. He continues his infectious laughter and ball play as long as the mother reacts positively.

One rarely sees a young infant work so hard to get his mother involved in his play and then try to maintain this pleasurable interaction. In this case, the infant used all the charms he could muster (attachment behaviors) to get his mother to respond affectionately and pleasurably to him. This behavior may be another facet of the infant's oversensitivity to the responses of his mother; it demonstrates the energy that he expended to try to bond the mother to him in a positive manner.

Many factors, biological and environmental, influenced what took place between the parents and the infant in this family. The premature birth of a biologically defective infant; surgery during the neonatal period with uncertainty regarding his survival; 6 weeks of hospitalization of the infant after the surgery; the death of the teenage mother's mother only a few days after the infant was brought home from the hospital; the father's head injury, which weakened his control over his behavior that was already affected by an addiction: the cumulative effect of these crises would foreshadow trouble even in a stable, middle-class, financially secure family. A case like this one shows what tremendous stresses sometimes coexist with the birth and the first few weeks of life of a baby. It also is an example of the kinds of complex circumstances an infant intervention program can face in its efforts to support positive parent-infant interactions.

Case Q   When Mrs. Q and her infant began their participation in the Intervention Program, she had just gone through a difficult divorce. When the infant was 15 months old, the divorced father moved back into the home. Mrs. Q was a white teenager from a middle-class family. She married early and had only a high school education, as did her husband. She worked for the entire 14 months of the program, and the infant was cared for in two successive family daycare homes which the mother had carefully selected.

The infant, born at 30 weeks gestational age and weighing only 1180 g, was among the smaller infants in the Infant Studies Project. Still, he made good progress during the first year of life. As his 9-month performance on the Gesell test indicated, he was a capable infant whose language became superior at 15 months of age. The mother first took great pride in him and expressed only positive memories of her early weeks with him. As long as the infant remained in the stage of complete dependency, she felt adequate and satisfied in the mothering role. But when the infant began to assert himself as an independent being, the mother felt the need for complete control. She seemed to have the misconception that disciplinary training starting in infancy with frequent and harsh punishment of "undesirable behavior" was the way to bring up a child. The interactions between mother and child became strained and suffered additional stress when the father moved into the home again.

Although there was no evidence of physical abuse, there were indications that the father was punitive with the child, both physically and verbally. His teasing of the infant bordered on sadism, and, by the time the child was 2 years old, the father appeared to have involved the mother in rather cruel games of teasing and confusing the child until he would cry. (It was revealed after the program had terminated that the father's strange behavior may have been associated with a serious illness.) The mother enjoyed the child as long as she could control him completely, but she became frustrated and punitive as he grew older, more active, and more assertive and independent. She was unwilling to alter her disciplinary techniques of slapping and yelling at the child. Her expectations of this active and verbal child became more and more unrealistic. Even though she modeled for him physically and verbally aggressive behavior, she expected him to be well-behaved, quiet, and able to occupy himself for long periods of time, even at 15 months. Both parents' restrictive and punitive treatment seemed to be reflected increasingly in changes in the child, from friendly social behavior to withdrawal from others, from gentle to aggressive behavior, and from abundant expressive language to greater hesitance in talking.

During the first half of the intervention period, the communication between the team and the mother was open and productive. In the beginning, the mother responded positively to intervention—she enjoyed the sessions with the staff, who adapted to her work schedule, and she seemed to profit from modeling and discussions. The staff began to see more appropriate language and play interactions between mother and infant. Yet, in the area of discipline, the team was not successful in changing the mother's punitive reactions to an active child's age-appropriate behavior. (The mother's punitive reactions were later reinforced by the father.) The staff also failed to help the mother to be more realistic about the child's need for a safe physical environment.

When the father began to play a more active and prominent role in the intervention sessions and in the life of the child, the effectiveness of intervention further diminished. It appeared that the increasing tension between the parents, the apparent subservience of the mother to the father, and the father's modeling of extreme punitiveness—reinforcing the mother's tendency in that direction—seriously damaged the mother-child interaction. Even the open relationship between the intervention team and the mother deteriorated toward the end of the program. An intense effort was made during the last couple of sessions to help the mother realize what was happening to her and to her child (the social worker, who was a consultant to the Infant Studies Project, was involved in this effort) and to try to refer her to resources that could offer psychological help to her and possibly to her husband. These efforts were unsuccessful.

Although the staff judged the child's intelligence to be superior, it was predicted that at 24 months he would not cooperate sufficiently with the tester to have his performance reflect his ability. He performed in the average range at age 2 even though his language was decidedly above age level. Without knowing the case, the tester reported that the child's language ability seemed to be much higher than the test performance reflected. A year later, it was reported that the child scored in the low-normal range.

This case was depressing to the staff as they could see the gradual deterioration of this charming, friendly, verbal, and intelligent child without being able to prevent it. The events and outcomes in case Q seem to give support to the relationship between the quality of parent-child transactions and the psychological health and development of the child. They also demonstrate the importance of focusing on the parent behaviors and parent-infant interactions and the necessity of incorporating these in the goals of infant intervention. In retrospect (assuming that the family would have allowed themselves to be referred or would have referred themselves) a more psychotherapeutically oriented intervention for the mother and father would probably have been more effective in this case in which the father's behavior, bordering on the pathological, had a powerful negative effect on the interactional dynamics in the family.

Case N   The problems that existed in the mother-infant interactions in this case may be fairly common in families with teenage parents. When the infant was born, the mother was 17 years of age. She herself was small and almost child-like in appearance. The father was 19. Both had hispanic backgrounds, but they spoke English (the mother spoke no Spanish) and appeared to have little identification with the Mexican-American culture. They lived together in a common-law marriage, except for 2 months during which they were separated. The young mother lacked self-confidence and she felt inadequate in all areas of her life. It was difficult for her to make decisions either for herself or for her child. She vacillated between wanting to work and wanting to stay home with the infant. During the 14 months of the intervention program, she did work for short periods, but she stayed home most of the time and received welfare support.

The infant, born 6 weeks preterm, weighed less than 1750 g at birth. His rate of growth and weight gain was slow. It was reported from the 1-month home observation (external to the intervention program) that the mother propped the baby's bottle in his crib and that she let him "cry hard" before responding to him. During that 1-hour observation while the baby was awake, it was also noted that the mother did not hold the infant or make frequent eye contact with him. The intervention staff's observations in the early weeks of the intervention program were that the mother seemed to like the infant, show some pride in him, and enjoy his company, but that her caregiving and overall parenting were less than satisfactory. The infant vocalized infrequently, he exhibited a high activity level and an inability to sustain attention in play, and he gave unclear cues regarding his likes and dislikes. There was relatively little interaction between mother and child.

The mother's lack of self-confidence and her preoccupation with her own problems in relation to her life and immediate future made it difficult for her to give much thought to her child. She was not able to focus long enough on the infant to make realistic judgments regarding his needs. Consequently, she welcomed his independence and let him fare for himself most of the time. From the moment that he was mobile, the staff worried about the mother's lack of appropriate provisions for the child's physical safety. Yet, she did not seem to reject him, nor did she show any behavior resembling abuse or even punitiveness. She apparently considered her young child to be quite capable and she may have felt that he was better able to care for himself than she was able to care for him. He was advanced in the gross motor area even at 10 months of age. The child's high level of motor skills, his early walking, and his ability to occupy himself may have led this inexperienced young mother to attribute more general competence to him than he could possibly have had at his age, including making judgments regarding his own safety.

The mother had a need to talk about herself and her problems not only in coping as a mother but also in facing the many incidents and decisions that seemed to flood her everyday life. She seemed to move from one crisis to another, and, in fact, managed to create additional crises for herself—she had a strong compassion for sick or injured animals and she was continuously taking care of several of these in her small apartment. Some of the sick animals were health hazards for the infant. The staff felt that her caring for these animals in insufficient space reflected a strong need to feel competent and that this need may have been easier to satisfy by caring for helpless and completely dependent animals than by parenting a child who was growing increasingly autonomous and whom she saw as more able to care for himself than he really was.

Intervention goals were first to enhance the mother's self-confidence so that she could better face the many decisions she had to make for herself and for her child. (The mother was easily influenced and confused by contradictory advice about childrearing that she received from family and neighbors.) The second goal was to help the mother to focus more on her infant so that she would get more interested in him and consequently make him a higher priority in her life. Third, intervention attempted to foster the mother's awareness of the child's survival needs, such as providing a safe and nurturing environment, and to increase her sensitivity to his cues and developmental needs, especially in the areas of social interaction and language.

Intervention had its successes and its failures in this case. The continuous, if insufficient, support that the staff provided for this mother may have made the difference between serious neglect of the infant and the mother's willingness to consider at least some of the needs of her young child in her struggle to cope with everyday life. Intervention was also effective to the extent that the mother came to enjoy her child more due to the staff's focus on him. However, her responses did not become significantly more contingent to his cues. Although the mother showed interest in the intervention sessions, she seemed unable to increase her language interactions with her infant, and his language showed a delay throughout the 14 months of intervention. Moreover, in spite of repeated staff efforts, using a variety of approaches, the mother's awareness of the child's safety needs increased only minimally. On the side of success, intervention was effective in helping the mother realize the importance of stable caregiving for her infant. She made an effort to provide a stable and competent caregiver while she was working. (The infant had previously been taken care of by six different people within a short period of time.) The mother was also better able to prepare the child for transitions in caregiving when those could be anticipated. Toward the end of the program, the staff involved the mother in exploring a number of community resources that would provide a stable situation favorable to the child's well-being and development, so that she could go back to work, which she intended to do.

An interesting contrast between home and laboratory observations was revealed in case N. Spontaneous mother-infant interactions were infrequent in the home, as observed by the intervention staff and by the external home observations at 8 and 24 months. The mother showed very little responsiveness to the child's cues in the home. On the other hand, the observations and scores on the Play Interaction Measure (PIM), repeated every 4 months in a laboratory setting, revealed increasingly warm, mutually pleasurable, and contingent interactions between mother and infant. During these 10-minute periods, the mother had no choice but to be with her child. The difference in quality of interaction between the laboratory setting, where infant and mother were forced to remain in the same space (child in high-chair, mother in chair next to child), and the home setting, where mother and child were free to walk away from each other, led the staff to the following conclusion: the capacity of the mother and infant to interact pleasurably and contingently with each other when the setting forced them to be together showed that their relationship had developed into a positive one with warmth and mutuality. The contrast in quality of interaction observed in the home and the laboratory setting may signify that it is important to observe mothers and infants interacting in a variety of situations.

Intervention probably enhanced the quality of the mother-infant relationship which, in turn, produced certain changes in the child—he gave clearer cues, expressed more affect and was more responsive to others. He was also able to move away from his mother and play independently and constructively by himself. At 24 months of age, the Home Observation team (external to the Intervention Program) observed this child initiate friendly contact with unfamiliar persons and engage in fairly complex and sustained play while away from his mother. It should be mentioned that the father and the infant appeared to have a warm and relaxed relationship, although it is not clear how much time the father spent with the infant. The mother, although she felt she should get a job for financial reasons, chose to stay home most of the time (working only intermittently) until the child was close to 2 years of age. On one occasion, she was not willing to send the child to his grandmother, who lived in a neighboring state, because she said she would miss him too much. Yet, the infrequency of the mother's sustained social and verbal interactions with the child is seen as a factor which may have impeded his progress in language and left him with a language delay (in receptive and expressive language) at age 2.

In reflecting upon case N, it seemed to the staff that a center-based program might have been more advantageous for this family—a program in which the infant could have had a rich environment at least part of the time, and in which the mother could have spent time with the child. She might have profited from observing her child with a staff member and from interacting with him in the playroom with modeling and encouragement from the staff. This experience would have taken her away, at least briefly, from her preoccupation with a myriad of problems and might have brought her closer to her child. She could also have spent some time away from the child, talking with other parents and sharing her concerns with them. In a center setting she would have had easier access to personal counseling which, toward the end of the program, she finally realized she needed.

Comments

A review and reevaluation of intervention in the preceding six cases (not including cases F and K), reveal no great faults in intervention approach, content, or methodology. The major obstacles to successful intervention seemed to have been intrinsic to the cases themselves. Two factors, which were identified as contributing importantly to effective intervention, were absent in all these cases: high priority of the infant and parental concern about the infant. The infants were not a high priority in the problem-ridden lives of these six families and, for the most part, the parents did not have serious concerns regarding the development of their infants. Even from the perspective of outsiders, such as the staff, the six families had burdens to carry and stresses in their lives that outweighed the relatively minor problems that their infants had. The staff was aware of the primary needs of these families and knew that until their immediate life crises could be overcome or at least ameliorated, the parents would not be able to focus adequately on their infants or on the quality of their parenting. The staff spent much time with most of these families, with the exception of family Q, exploring community resources of the kind that they needed the most and that they needed most immediately.

Nevertheless, the emphasis of a program determines its boundaries to some extent. The primary intent of the Intervention Program, as defined by its philosophy and goals, was to enhance pleasurable parent-infant interaction and to help parents acquire skills that would both support that interaction and foster the optimum development of the infant. The particular problems of the families in the six preceding cases required the staff to adapt their immediate goals and interventions to the primary problems of the families. Most of these problems were not directly related to the infants, but they nonetheless interfered with the parents' attention to their infants. Because of the nature of the Intervention Program, the design of the larger research project, and the background of the staff, there were limitations in what could be done to alleviate the primary concerns and stresses of the parents. Considering their areas of greatest need, these families might have gained most from broadly conceived social services such as high quality infant and child care facilities, vocational training programs, and personal and marriage counseling.

If these parents had been able to attend constructively to their high-priority needs by using appropriate resources, assuming that these had been available, they might have been better able to take maximum advantage of the offerings of the Intervention Program. This speculation points to the advantages of a comprehensive network of community services in which one could pinpoint what would be most helpful to a family at any particular time.

The following question is pertinent here: Even if these families had had easy access to the services they required, would they have made use of them? The question brings up an important social issue. As long as child care and vocational training are conceived by society as "services for the poor'' (as free health care is still viewed by many), many individuals—including some of the parents in the Intervention Program, who did not think of themselves as part of the "underclass" of society—would not avail themselves of such programs. On the other hand, if, for example, quality day care were to be considered an essential public service, like public schools, parks, and libraries, to which everyone has access regardless of ability to pay, a very different attitude would prevail.

OVERPROTECTIVE PARENTS

The two cases discussed here had the following in common: 1) the infant was the first born and was likely to remain the only child; 2) the infant was a high priority in the parents' lives; 3) the parents appeared to have limited ability in following through with and generalizing from suggestions made by the team; and 4) the mother was employed full time.

Case V

The infant was the first child of a 40-year-old mother and a father in his early fifties. Although poor, this white couple was stable and managed to live within its financial means. The mother worked in an unskilled job that she had held for 15 years. The father was employed intermittently up to the time the infant was 16 months old. At that time, without a job once again, he decided to stop looking for employment and stay home to take care of the infant. He remained the infant's primary caregiver for the duration of the program. The relationship between the parents seemed stable, and they were both delighted with the child who had come along late in their lives. Still, their expectations of the infant, especially those of the father, were unrealistic. Neither parent had had experience with or knew much about young children.

The infant, born at 34 weeks gestational age, had no serious neonatal problems. His relatively low language and personal-social sub-scores on the 9-month Gesell scale were consistent with his language and social behavior as observed by the staff. Although an attractive child, he did not readily elicit social responses from others, and his receptive and expressive language showed some delay. His special strength was in adaptive play, although the materials made available to him by his parents were few and, for the most part, developmentally inappropriate.

Most home visits were made in the daytime when the father was home with the infant. At the mother's request, the team also maintained communication with her. She wanted to be involved in the program, but she did not want to have all the home visits scheduled in the evening. However, a few home visits were made in the evening for the purpose of showing and discussing with both parents the videotapes of the infant that had been taken during previous daytime visits. In addition, after each daytime session, the mother asked for a telephone report from the team.

The kinds of intervention strategies used with Mr. and Mrs. V were those quite commonly used with inexperienced parents who had little knowledge of infant development. It was observed that the parents had no idea that an infant needed anything other than being cared for physically. Consequently, they did not provide an environment that stimulated either play or language. To help the parents tune in to the infant's play behavior, the team left certain play materials in the home. The parents were asked to observe how the infant used these materials and to share their observations with the staff during the subsequent home visit. The parents' observations usually initiated discussion of the child's play style and play needs. Much modeling was used: one team member played with the infant or talked with him, and one or the other team member interpreted what was happening between team member and infant. The response of the infant, rather than the reasons behind the staff's actions, was more often the focus of interpretation. Sometimes the infant's response was highlighted by "talking for the infant," when the infant was too young to verbalize on his own. The team helped the parents determine what were developmentally appropriate materials, how one could tell what the infant was interested in, how one could arrange the environment to make it more stimulating for the infant, and finally, how the adult could present materials and elaborate on the infant's play to make the activity more exciting and challenging for the infant.

In the language area, the staff modeled responding to the infant's vocalizations, talking to the infant about what he was doing or seeing, and accentuating the names of objects and action words in the flow of conversation with the child. For example, the staff would say, "You want to *go up!*" if the child stretched his arms out to be picked up; or "Yes, that's a *spoon,* you want a *spoon!*" This infant, as many other infants, was quite interested in action words because he was involved in the action himself.

The team provided the kinds of materials for the infant that supported his interests and matched his skills so that he could achieve his goals. The staff members modeled for the parents how to engage the infant with materials to help him toward a longer attention span and greater persistence. They also modeled how to engage the infant in problem-solving with materials that were at a level of complexity that was challenging to him, but that would still allow him to achieve his goals and experience pleasure in his successes. With the staff's help, the infant was able to learn to make order out of the chaos of toys that usually surrounded him at home, and thus he was able to make progress in adaptive play. In the language area, in which the infant's progress was more directly dependent on his language environment in the home, his progress was slower and he continued to have a delay in both receptive and expressive language.

There were successful as well as unsuccessful outcomes with this family. The parents were better able to focus on the immediate future of the child, rather than engaging in distant fantasies about his adult life. The mother, whose language had been inappropriate, became somewhat more contingent to the child's language. She more frequently interacted verbally with him during play, but she did so in a stilted fashion, mostly by labeling rather than saying words in the context of phrases or sentences. Both parents were able to observe and report on the infant's play behaviors and to anticipate, in a limited way, the next stage of development. The parents were generally resourceful in providing certain opportunities for their child, e.g., they took him for frequent bicycle rides to show him interesting sights in the neighborhood. (They did not own a car.)

On the other hand, they were less able to make good use of modeling and suggestions regarding language interaction with the infant and provision for a more orderly and organized environment for the child's play activities. Moreover, the father was not able to change significantly his ideas about age-appropriate behavior for the child in areas of social interaction and autonomy. The team tried to effect change in his methods of discipline by helping him to evaluate the child's behavior in various situations and by offering alternate methods of limit-setting and discipline. The team discussed with both parents the value of play and the connection between play and later school achievement. The parents were also helped to be more realistic about their child's ability to play harmoniously with other children once they stopped interfering in every minor squabble that occurred between their child and others. The team discussed with the parents the long-range effects of parental overprotection and how such parental behavior could interfere with the child's social adaptation to his peers. None of these staff efforts were entirely successful. Both parents found it quite difficult to change some of their ways in attempting to adapt to the more subtle needs of a very young child. Nonetheless, their love and affection for their child remained intact and probably did much to enhance his development in the social-affective area and to give him a sense of security in the midst of a stable relationship pattern and home environment.

Case C

In this family, the Spanish-speaking mother and father were young and poor. Although they were not legally married, their relationship seemed more stable than that of a number of the legally married couples in the Intervention Program. The mother worked as a cleaning woman, but she would only go to homes where she could bring her baby girl.

There was great concern for the mother's health and survival during the latter stages of her pregnancy. The infant was delivered by C-section 2 months prematurely because of the mother's medical complications. She was told that, for her own protection, she should not have any more children. The infant experienced no serious medical problems.

The staff was concerned that this mother, who took her child with her everywhere she went, was too dependent on the infant. Although she seemed to get some emotional relief from talking to the team about her concerns regarding the infant and about her personal and financial worries, her inability to leave the child with someone else continued. Later, the mother experienced considerable emotional stress, resulting in physical symptoms, in connection with some legal problems. Even after the formal termination of the program with this family, the mother continued to ask for help to enable her to deal with some rather unpleasant legal difficulties. (Help was provided, mostly through referral to appropriate community resources.)

The team felt effective primarily in influencing Mrs. C to improve the infant's play environment. She was able to choose more developmentally appropriate toys for the child and to value toys other than stuffed animals. She also became more accurate in reporting on the child's language, and she came to recognize the value of the infant's representational play. Nevertheless, the mother continued to be overprotective of her child, which may have made her less sensitive to some of her infant's cues, e.g., the mother was needlessly worried that the infant was not eating enough and she was unable to respond to the infant's unwillingness to continue eating when she was satiated. During one home visit Mrs. C was observed "stuffing" food into the child's mouth at age 22 months, but this little girl seemed to be able to adapt to her mother's excessive feeding. The child got out of her chair, walked to the bathroom, and spit a big mouthful of food into the toilet while the mother was talking to someone.

The following observations and comments apply both to family V and family C above. The two families were overprotective of their infants. In family V, the child came along in the parents' middle years and meant a great deal to both. In family C, the child was to be the only child of a young mother who had almost died during her pregnancy. In family V, the parents' overprotectiveness had some social consequences: the parents made a few "enemies" in their neighborhood because they repeatedly came to the rescue when their child was playing with other children.

In the area of greatest concern of both families—that the child get sufficient nourishment—the staff was able to be of some assistance, especially with family V, by reassuring the parents that the child was growing properly and gaining sufficient weight, and by giving some specific suggestions. For example, infant V had been given jello water several times a day and consequently was not hungry at mealtime. The suggestion that a more appropriate drink be given between meals was taken and this problem was alleviated.

If one were to speculate what might have been ideal intervention for these two families, early home intervention followed by a combined home and center-based program would come to mind. Beyond approximately 18 months of age, both of these children would probably have gained much from a group program where they would have been exposed to more adequate stimulation than they were receiving in their homes. The parents might have been able to profit from interaction with other parents and from staff-guided observations of their children in a group. Such observations might have helped these parents gain a more realistic perception of their children's social and adaptive competence.

Toward the termination of the program, in our efforts to help parents become independent, we spent much time with families like C and V to lead them to explore community resources where the children could have opportunities to interact with experienced teachers and other children in high quality group programs.

INFANT'S SERIOUS PROBLEMS
COMPOUNDED BY PARENTS' PROBLEMS

The primary problems in the cases described in the preceding sections of this chapter were related to the family as a whole or to one or both parents. The infants were neither handicapped nor did they have other serious problems beyond 9 months of age. In the cases that follow, the infants as well as the parents had serious problems: the infants exhibited physical handicaps, developmental delays, deviant behavior, or a combination of two or more of these disabilities.

Parents' Preoccupation with Infant's Motor Problems

Gross motor behavior like sitting up and walking are the most widely valued developmental milestones in infants. When these motor achievements do not occur at the expected age, most parents become worried because they tend to view these milestones as indices of normal development. In some infants, relatively slow gross motor development coexists with delays in other areas, but in many infants it does not indicate generalized retardation.

Families J and T, although vastly different in almost every other respect, both had infants with gross motor problems. In both cases, the mothers focused on the motor handicap almost exclusively and did not recognize the infants' delays in the language, cognitive, and social areas.

Case J   Infant J was placed in a white foster home when her mother died soon after childbirth. The foster parents had two children of their own and, most of the time, two other foster children in addition to the project infant. Mrs. J was the primary caregiver, although her husband seemed to be supportive of her both personally and in her role of mother and foster mother. She was energetic, hard working, and assertive and she seemed quite sure of herself.

The infant's natural parents were American Indian. She was born 6 weeks preterm, and she was one of only three infants in the Intervention Program who scored under 85 D.Q. (developmental quotient) on the 4-month Gesell scales. At about 12 months of age, the infant was put into a heavy cast from her hips to her feet, following surgery for hip displegia. She was also diagnosed to have mild to moderate cerebral palsy and she appeared to be developmentally delayed in all areas. The cast, followed by splints, created extra problems of physical care of the infant and made it more difficult to keep her comfortable and happy. The foster mother took these challenges well and seemed to grow fonder of this little girl as she became more difficult to care for. Mrs. J's reluctance to attend to other aspects of the infant's developmental problems persisted until the infant's cast and splint were removed and she could become involved in an intensive physical therapy program in her community.

The infant's retardation became more manifest as she grew older. Her developmental scores dropped between 4 and 9 months of age and again between 9 and 24 months. However, the foster mother's preoccupation with the infant's motor problem made her unable to accept suggestions for fostering the infant's personal-social, language, and play skills. Mrs. J spent much time and energy in caring for the handicapped infant, especially while she was in the cast. Additional stress was put on the mother by a succession of other foster children who presented a variety of problems. Mrs. J seemed to seek and welcome challenges and heavy responsibilities and, most of the time, she became saddled with more problems than she, or anyone else, could comfortably handle. For a period, her responsibilities included the care of an older foster child who had serious psychiatric problems. She was quite concerned about him and tried very hard to help him, but she finally had to let him go because he could not be trusted around the younger children. During the last few weeks of the program, Mrs. J took on a new foster child in addition to her own two children and the project infant, and shortly after that, she was ready to take the twin of the new foster child, even though she had just found out that she was pregnant again. These self-imposed stresses made the foster mother even more tense and "hyperactive" than she appeared naturally to be. Her apparent need to take on more than she could comfortably handle may have prevented her from being tuned in to the infant's more subtle language, social, and play needs. However, it became increasingly clear that the foster mother had a strong emotional investment in and a genuine commitment to this child in spite of all her problems. The family adopted the child sometime after the termination of the Intervention Program.

The team's assistance in providing equipment to allow the infant maximum movement and locomotion and in providing information regarding physical therapy programs in her community was well received by the foster mother. She also welcomed the team's acknowledgment and support of her resourcefulness in giving the infant excellent physical care and in helping her to be reasonably comfortable through her siege with the cast and the splint. When discussion or modeling dealt with the relationship between motor functions and other behaviors such as language, self-help, and play in the total development of the child, e.g., showing her how important it was for the infant to be in positions in which she could move her arms and hands freely in order to manipulate objects, the team's modeling was not responded to and the suggestions fell on deaf ears. The foster mother's strong resistance to attending to the needs of the infant other than physical ones was perceived as a combination of rigidity and a negative attitude toward any idea that she did not originate herself. The team finally was able to effect some change in the foster mother's language interaction with the infant during the last few weeks of the program, by acknowledging and reinforcing behavior on her part that stimulated the infant's language or that was contingent to the infant's vocalization.

In case J, the staff encountered several obstacles to effective intervention that were related to the foster mother's attitudes and characteristics: 1) the foster mother's negative attitude toward anything connected with UCLA, due to a prior experience that she allegedly had had; 2) her preoccupation with the physical and gross motor problems of the infant, which precluded her consideration of problems in other developmental areas; 3) her inclination toward "doing" and need for constant activity, which made it difficult for her to sit back long enough to tune in to the infant's subtler cues and needs; and 4) her tremendous need for recognition, which sometimes led her to interpret ideas or suggestions by the staff as criticism.

Case T   Case T was an intact, Spanish-speaking family with two children in addition to the project infant. The family lived in an immaculate, well-furnished apartment in a public housing unit. The mother appeared to have little energy and initiative and seemed unable to cope with her task of taking care of three children, the oldest of whom was 6. She had no control over the two older children, and their excessive demands interfered with the mother's attention to the infant. The mother seemed to cope with stress by being passive and apathetic and by turning to her compulsive housekeeping. The father was aware of the mother's lack of self-confidence and low coping ability, and he took an active part in the care of the children when he returned from work in the mid-afternoon. This situation unfortunately did not last beyond 3 or 4 months because he took on a second job when the infant was about 16 months old.

The infant, born 4 weeks preterm, moved very little. She seemed passive, that is, she did not initiate her own activity, was slow in her responses, and gave diffuse and unclear cues. At about 16 months, her cues became easier to read, she became more responsive, and she showed more affect in her social interactions. However, her developmental scores remained in the borderline normal range throughout the 14 months of the program. It is worth noting that both siblings appeared to function at approximately the same level: borderline normal or mildly retarded. Although the infant's motor delay was not severe, seeming rather to be part of her overall developmental delay, the mother was preoccupied with her motor functioning and paid little attention to her lack of motivation, her unresponsiveness, and her low level of language and cognitive functioning.

The mother did not respond to modeling or even to direct suggestions and demonstrations by the team. Yet, she was quite friendly and welcomed the team to her home. Weekly visits were made to this family during the major portion of the 14-month period because the staff felt that increased exposure of the mother to the staff's interaction with the infant, the staff's involvement of the father, and their direct work with the infant might all have a positive effect on the mother-infant interaction and consequently on the infant's development. The father showed greater ability than the mother to comprehend and to respond to ideas and suggestions, and he therefore played an important role in the intervention process. The staff's visits were planned to take place in the late afternoon on alternate weeks so that the father could be present.

The infant made considerable progress in language, in initiating activities, and in expression of affect in social interaction and in play. Her progress was attributed to the father's responsiveness to intervention as well as to the staff's direct involvement with the infant. Although the mother did not initiate any more interaction with the infant than before, more mutually pleasurable interaction occurred because the infant's behavior was easier to read and it elicited more responses from the mother. When the father began to work longer hours and could not continue to be as involved in the intervention program, the infant's progress seemed to slow down.

Intervention in this case was considered to be partially effective. The staff was least successful in helping the mother to grow more self-confident and competent as a parent. Intervention succeeded, however, in effecting some positive changes in the infant, both directly and through the father. The effect that the changes in the infant had on the mother probably produced the most positive impact on their interaction and on the mother's competence in meeting the infant's needs.

Although cases J and T involved mothers who were preoccupied with their infants' gross motor development, the factors that interfered most with intervention were quite different in the two families. In case J, the staff's attempts to make the foster mother more aware of the infant's strengths—like her interest in toys, the ease with which she could be motivated to play with objects, her focused attention to the face of adults when they were talking to her—made no impression on Mrs. J. She was unresponsive to the idea of building on the infant's strengths at the same time that she was working with her in the most obvious area of deficit. Mrs. J, active, energetic, and strongly committed to the infant, could have done much to enhance this infant's language and cognitive development if she could have shifted at least some of her attention away from the infant's motor and physical problems to her play and language behavior a little earlier in the program. In case T, although the mother's preoccupation with the infant's motor delay interfered with her attention to other developmental needs, it was probably the mother's general ineptness in parenting, her low self-confidence, and, most of all, her passivity that were the greatest obstacles to effective intervention.

Mother's Role Ambivalence

Only one case is discussed under this heading. Mothers in other cases also showed role ambivalence (e.g., cases N, Q, and W above) but not with the intensity of the mother in case G.

Case G Family G consisted of a middle-class black couple, both in their mid-twenties, with two children: a 6-year-old boy and the male project infant. The father had just completed his professional studies and was in the process of building a private practice. The mother had finished college and was aspiring to a professional career. In order to maintain the standard of living this couple desired, both parents had to work. Their 6-year-old son attended a private day school. The mother began to work full time when the infant was 11 months old.

The infant, born 4 weeks preterm, was a beautiful child who functioned normally and who was quite social up to 16 months of age. (He scored especially high on gross motor and social behavior at 9 months.) At about 16 months, he began to regress in all developmental areas and to withdraw socially. He experienced three changes in daytime caregivers during the 14-month program. At age 19 months, the infant was put into a family daycare home that was not able to meet his needs because there were too many other children present and because of the relatively insensitive daycare provider. Although the mother previously had shown great sensitivity to the infant's need for a warm, responsive, and stimulating daycare environment, this time she did not look for a better daycare alter-native in spite of encouragement from the team.

The problems in this family seemed to increase in magnitude when the infant was about 20 months old. The infant's regression that was first observed at 16 months of age continued. Furthermore, there were indica-tions that in the relationship between the father and the mother, a kind of distancing was taking place between a "very busy" man and a dissatisfied woman. Mrs. G shared with one of the staff members that her feelings of sharp ambivalence between her professional aspirations and her role of wife and mother. She wanted to pursue her career goals, but, at the same time, she felt guilty about being so unavailable to her young children. The deterioration of the infant's behavior appeared to aggravate the mother's confusion and guilt.

When the staff became aware of the mother's state of mind, the team member who had built a close and trusting relationship with the mother continued the case by herself and the other team member dropped out. This one-to-one relationship with a young woman who was in a situation somewhat similar to her own (the staff member had one child and was pregnant with her second one) made it possible for the mother to talk freely about her feelings of guilt and confusion as well as her dissatisfac-tion. The staff member tried to help the mother understand that she, the mother, had not "caused" the deterioration in the infant's behavior. She also tried to encourage the mother to get some professional help from a counselor or psychotherapist to get her over her state of confusion and emotional upset.

So many things seemed to deteriorate at the same time that it was im-possible to determine which came first—the infant's change in behavior or the mother's emotional upheaval aggravated by the infant's regression. It is probable that the infant's deteriorating behavior was stressful to the mother who, in turn, became increasingly disturbed and therefore less able to meet the child's mounting needs.

The evaluation of the interaction between both parents and the infant was positive until the infant was 16 months old. Both parents had increased their responsiveness to the infant, they were skilled in their lan-guage and play interaction with him, and mutually pleasurable interac-tions were observed between parents and the infant. All this began to change when the infant was 16 months of age. At 24 months, the infant's social, cognitive, and language behavior was below age level. The most dramatic change, and the one that was most worrisome to the staff, was his sudden avoidance of eye contact with his parents as well as with famil-iar and unfamiliar adults. His 24-month scores fell over 10 points below his 9-month score.

At 24 months, there was also objective evidence that the mother expended tremendous effort in the home to make the infant more responsive to her. The 24 month external Home Observation measure of interactive behavior yielded an extremely high "mothering score," indicating the mother's frequent and intense efforts to interact with the infant. She seemed to be trying hard to counteract the infant's withdrawal and regression in social behavior. The attempt on the mother's part to reverse the infant's withdrawal behavior was simultaneous with her increased sensitivity to the needs of both her children. Her comments indicated her awareness of subtle changes and emerging positive behaviors on the part of the infant. Although the mother was not responsive to referrals for therapeutic help for herself, she did talk about changing her job to relieve some of the stress on her.

It would be easy to attribute the infant's deteriorating behavior to the worsening relationship between the parents and to the feelings of ambivalence of the mother about her roles. Yet, almost everyone associated with this case who saw the infant between 10 and 24 months felt that the changes in him were, at least in part, of an organic nature and were not "caused" by his environment. The seeds of the infant's problems may have been present earlier, although they were not detected. One thing is quite clear in this case as in other similar ones: when parents see their children regress and their behavior become deviant, especially when there is no *known* neurological cause, they blame themselves for the change in the infant. This situation puts tremendous stress on the parents. The emotional environment in family G's home probably contributed to the changes in the child, but it is quite possible that the deterioration of the child's behavior was also a "causal factor" in the increased tension and emotional problems of the parents. In a conversation with one of the team members, several months after the termination of intervention, Mrs. G reported how pleased she was that her infant was talking and behaving more normally again.

MULTIPLE STRESSES IN FAMILY

Case P

Although many families in the Intervention Program had to cope with stress from various sources, case P is an extreme in that respect. Infant P was the second baby born to this middle-aged black couple. Their first infant, born less than 2 years before, had died of crib death. The father and mother had both been married previously, and they had several grown children from their former marriages. The youngest of these was a

16-year-old girl who was still living in the home. Another of the mother's grown children had died in an accident not long before the birth of the project infant.

The mother was in poor physical health after the infant's birth and went into a depression which lasted for over a year. She stayed home during that time but gave only minimal care to the infant because of her poor physical and emotional state. When the infant was 16 months old, the father had a heart attack. He had to stop working and his activities in the home were restricted. The mother, who did not want to go back to work outside the home, had to do so to support the family. Consequently, her husband and her 16-year-old daughter became the infant's primary caregivers.

The infant was 27 weeks gestational age at birth and weighed about 1000 g. He had respiratory problems at birth which persisted throughout the first year of life. During that entire period, the pediatric staff at UCLA was concerned about his survival. Although the infant tested within the normal range at 9 months, the intervention team detected some signs of delayed development at 11 months in the adaptive play and language areas. The infant's play was repetitious, unimaginative, and infrequently goal-directed. Although active physically, he seemed to be passive in interactions with adults and did not show pleasure in his play. His attention span was brief unless someone made an effort to keep him involved in a play activity or interaction. He became gradually more responsive to the staff members as they participated in his play. With the introduction of social interaction into his play, he began to initiate more goal-directed activities and showed more pleasure with his successes. He began to smile not only socially but when he discovered that he had been successful in reaching his play goal (22 months).

From the start, the mother worried about his health and showed little interest in the infant's language and play. When the infant was 1 year old, the mother was ready, in fact eager, to share some of her concerns and feelings with the older of the two team members. She was still depressed at this time, and she received brief psychiatric help through referral by the project pediatrician. The mother emerged from her lengthy depression when the infant was about 15 months old. Shortly after that, when the mother began to work full time, the staff tried to direct some of the intervention efforts to the father and sister who were the infant's primary caregivers. After several incidents, the staff came to realize that, although the mother was not a major caregiver of the infant even when she was home, she nonetheless directed the household and needed to be in complete control. This included her having control of the care of the infant. She did not want the staff to become directly involved with either the infant's father or half-sister even though they cared for the infant. The situation was resolved in the following manner: one team member interacted with the infant, and the other one talked primarily to the mother. When the father or sister were present, the staff included them in activities or conversation as much as possible. The team also made sure not to arrive at the home before the mother had returned from work.

The mother was not entirely at ease about the care of the child in their home. She thought that her husband was too permissive and that he lacked control over the child. Therefore, she arranged for her daughter to take care of the child as much as possible. The mother was also concerned about her husband's health and wanted to make sure that he did not strain himself by lifting the child or by playing with him too actively. A few months later, she rejected the idea of having the child attend a playgroup a few mornings a week because she thought that the father would feel useless at home if he did not have the child to look after.

During the first 10 months of intervention, family P was not asked to come to the project Center every 4 months for the assessment sessions, as were most families, to avoid putting an extra burden on the family. The mother's poor health, the father's illness, the mother's long working hours, and the distance between the home and the Center caused the staff's protective attitude. The family did not have the choice of coming or not coming to the Center since they were not informed about the alternatives. When the infant was 20 months old, the parents were asked if they would like to come to the Center for the next intervention session, instead of having the team come to their home. The question was put to the parents because the staff had become increasingly aware of the mother's difficulty in focusing on the infant during home visits, as well as the mother's "slow-to-warm-up" quality when she was in her home. The mother seemed delighted to have the opportunity to bring the child to the Center after 5:00 p.m., in spite of her long day and the distance they would have to travel. (Mr. and Mrs. P insisted on driving their own car rather than being picked up by a UCLA driver.)

It was observed that the mother showed much more interest in the infant's activities and behavior in the Center than she did at home. When the family was given the option to come to the Center for intervention sessions as often as they cared to, the mother eagerly accepted this alternative to home visits. During the Center sessions, which usually included the father and sometimes the sister too, the mother began to observe the infant's behavior, asked thoughtful questions, and became lively and quite responsive to modeling and interpretations of the child's behavior. Her need to assert that she knew how to raise her child lessened, and she became much more open and receptive to intervention. The mother may also have found it easier to communicate with someone who was closer to her own age, and who had also raised children (see next page).

The last 4 months marked the period of intervention that had the most positive impact. The mother was in a much better psychological state, and the conditions of intervention at the Center made the mother more comfortable and relaxed. The case was judged to be partially successful. Although the mother became much more involved with the infant during the sessions and was able to be more responsive to him, there was little evidence that this changed behavior carried over into the home on the part of the mother, father, or sister. Minimal change in their behavior was observed in two home visits in the last 2 months of the program.

In this case, intervention at the project Center was clearly more effective than home intervention in the early months of the program. In the home, the mother appeared to be either unable or unwilling to focus on the child during the staff's visits. The work with the sister and father had little effect because of the mother's close control over their care of the child. The mother may have viewed the home visits as a form of intrusion, although there was no evidence of that during the first few months of the program. The least effective period of intervention was shortly after the mother began to work full-time. In the last few months of the program when intervention sessions for this family began to take place at the project Center, another staff member who was older than the mother and who had not been to the home while the mother was depressed was able to establish good rapport with her. One might speculate that after the mother had overcome her depression, she no longer wanted contact with those who had been witness to her depressed state in the home. Furthermore, some parents may feel freer to communicate with program staff when they are not also in the role of "host" or "hostess" to the home visitors.

Some of the staff's direct work with the infant resulted in important changes in the infant's behavior. The following changes occurred during the last 3 months of the program. While one team member worked with the infant, the other team member discussed with the mother what was taking place, i.e., interpreted the infant's behavior and the staff's actions. The infant's social response to the team member progressed from fear and passive acceptance to active enjoyment. The infant was more sociable and more enjoyable to be with, and consequently, he evoked more positive responses from the adult. With increased success in his play, his interest in materials widened, his adaptive and fine motor skills improved rapidly, he expressed enjoyment more clearly and more often, and he was better able to handle his frustrations when he could not succeed in a task.

It is the author's judgment that unless positive changes in the infant can be supported by changed interactive behaviors on the part of the parents or other adults in the infant's environment, the success of intervention must be considered only partial and probably not of a lasting nature.

When only the infant changes and not the parent, long-term effects can be achieved only if the new behaviors of the infant trigger more desirable adult responses, which in turn support and enhance the new behaviors of the infant. The staff was not able to say with any assurance that the positive changes in the infant's behavior in case P elicited more attention and a different kind of interaction from the adults closest to him. There continued to be many concerns in that family that were not related to the infant. Although the mother's interest in the infant seemed to have increased, there was no evidence that her interaction with him had changed.

The staff learned several valuable lessons from its work with this family. First, it is important to know not only who is the primary caregiver of the infant, but also who is "in charge" of the household, that is, who is the decision maker. The primary caregiver of the infant is not always the person who makes the decisions related to day-to-day caregiving tasks. If such is the case, the person in charge (in family P the decision maker was definitely the mother) must be involved in a primary way in the intervention process. Second, program participants should not be "protected" (for what might be interpreted as being in their own best interest) from making their own choices among alternatives that exist for them. Mrs. P, who enjoyed her visits to the project Center and who gained much from them, would have missed this opportunity if she had not eventually been given a choice. Intervention might have been more effective in this case if the choice had been given earlier. Third, it is important to be aware of the hardships and stresses that impinge on families. This knowledge makes it easier for the staff to understand parents' behaviors that are related to these stresses or concerns, but that may not always foster the infant's development. It makes it possible for the staff to empathize with the parents and to find the best possible ways to help them and the infant without imposing additional stress on the parents.

In this chapter, all of the cases that are discussed show certain conditions, factors, and situations in families that constitute obstacles to effective parent-infant intervention. In most of the 14 cases described here, intervention was judged to have had some positive effects. But, in spite of those positive effects, the staff could not overlook the fact that many of the intervention goals set for these families were not met. Some might say that the staff's judgment of its successes and failures was too harsh. On the other hand, the author feels that the best way to understand and improve intervention effectiveness is to be self-critical and to lay out the problems and mistakes that may have been made rather than to gloss over these and indulge in self-praise that is not always deserved.

PART IV

WORKING
WITH PARENTS
Specific Interventions

Part IV introduces a set of specific problems in parenting or parent-infant interaction. Each problem statement is followed by the modes of intervention and the specific staff responses that were believed to be effective in the UCLA Intervention Program.

Chapter 7 serves, in a sense, as a manual for Chapter 8, "Problems and the Response of Intervention." It contains the operational meanings of terms and concepts that are used. Therefore, it is suggested that the reader take a look at the organization and general content of Chapter 8 before reading Chapter 7.

Chapter 8 groups the problems and interventions into five separate sections, each of which begins with a list of the problems that follow.

Chapter **7**
Intervention
Concepts and Terminology

This part of the book describes how the interaction model was applied to day-to-day work with parents and infants. It demonstrates the kinds of problems that were identified in the Intervention Program and how these problems were responded to by the staff using the interaction model as a frame of reference. It illustrates how intervention was carried out with the immediate intent of helping the parent to gain confidence, to find interaction with her infant more rewarding, and to develop more competence in parenting.

The scope of the problems and interventions that are discussed in Chapter 8 is limited both with respect to the problems and to the interventions in response to each of the problems. No attempt has been made to assemble all of the problems that can arise in parents' interactions with their infants (with or without special needs) or to include all of the possible interventions that might be suitable in response to any one of the problems listed. The focus here is on the problems that were found in more than one case and on the interventions that were effective with the families in the Intervention Program.

The population of the Intervention Program was heterogeneous, consisting of approximately 60 families.[1] The families had a wide range of difficulties, some of which were not directly related to the infants (see Chapters, 3, 5, and 6). The only common characteristic among these families was the age range of their infants: when the pilot population is included, the infants' ages ranged from 4 to 27 months. In spite of the limited age range of the infants in the Intervention Program, many (though by no means all) of the problems and interventions contained in Chapter 8 are applicable to families with older and younger children.

The type and severity of the infants' problems varied greatly. (There were more infants in the pilot group who had serious problems and handicaps than there were in the preterm infant population of the Infant Studies Project.) Yet, a review of the interventions with all the families in-

---

[1]This number includes the families in the pilot population and a few other families who were in the program for a short period of time.

dicates that many of their problems are shared by most parents of infants. There are additional problems, however, that only parents of especially difficult or handicapped infants have to face. With this in mind, at the end of the intervention sections for certain problems, material has been added that relates to particular populations of children, which are identified by age or by the nature of the problem.

Those who are working with parents and children, regardless of the nature of the problem, are dealing with complex transactional systems. Individual decisions on how to approach each issue with each parent-infant dyad have to be made on the basis of sensitive observations, knowledge of child development, and a sympathetic understanding of the particular parent and child and the stresses in their environment. Therefore, the specific interventions that are most appropriate for a given parent-infant dyad are bound to differ from case to case—no "all-purpose solutions" are possible.

The interventions appearing in Chapter 8 should be regarded as a resource, representing a few from among many alternative ways of responding to specific problems with the goal of enhancing positive parenting and mutually satisfying parent-infant interactions. The ideas and suggestions that are presented are meant to stimulate the reader to generate additional and alternate ideas with regard to helping parents. Neither written materials nor expert advice, whether oral or written, can take the place of the sensitivity of a staff member to each individual parent and child.

The remainder of this chapter presents the kind of information that a manual accompanying a curriculum would contain to help the reader to use the material in the most productive manner, beginning with the definition of terms used in Chapter 8.

USE OF TERMS

Child and Infant

Many of the problems and interventions presented in Chapter 8 apply to parents of infants of a fairly wide age range. Therefore, it was difficult to decide whether to use the word "child" or "infant." It was decided to use "infant" when referring to the age range up to about 18 months and to use "child" when referring either to children over 18 months or when the intervention is applicable more widely to parents of children in their first 3 years of life.

Age of Child

When the age of the child or infant is referred to, it signifies the approximate developmental age at which the child is functioning. The difference between chronological age and developmental age is especially important to note in the case of the delayed or severely retarded child because the parents of that child need to be helped to view that child and to deal with him at the level (or developmental age) at which he is functioning, rather than in terms of his chronological age. In cases where the child functions at very different levels in different developmental areas—for example, a child whose play behavior (cognitive-motivational area) is quite advanced but who has a moderate to severe language delay—the parents need to be alerted to these differences so that they can provide appropriately for the child's developmental needs in all areas.

Parent

All the interventions directed to an adult have been addressed to "the parent" because the parent was the primary caregiver of the infant in almost all of the cases in the Intervention Program. Nonetheless, the use of this term leaves out the staff's interactions with other family members, like the grandmother, grandfather, aunt, and siblings, and with other daycare providers. The word "parent" is meant to represent all those individuals who were involved at one time or another with the infant's care and with whom the intervention staff interacted.

IDENTIFICATION OF PROBLEMS

We hesitated, at first, to link interventions to problems because we feared that this might de-emphasize the importance of building on the parents' and the infants' strengths.[2] Still, stating problems as points of departure for describing interventions seemed to be an effective way of presenting the work that was done with parents and infants. The problems listed in Chapter 8 (numbered and divided into five areas or categories) were derived from the work of the Intervention Program in the following manner. After the termination of each case, the intervention process was analyzed and summarized in a number of ways by using both the detailed notes that were kept on every contact with infant and parent and the long-term and short-term goals and plans that were recorded for every case. One way that was used to summarize information about a case was to identify the problems and to record the interventions used in response to the problems, in addition to noting the outcomes. This information was written down on charts that were several pages in length for each case. The problems listed in Chapter 8 were condensed from a much larger number of problems that had been gathered from all the cases.

---

[2]As noted in the Preface, the pronoun "we" and the past tense are used deliberately throughout Chapter 7 and Chapter 8 to encourage the reader to view the material presented as illustrative of how a particular staff in a specific program with a particular philosophy actually worked with its families. The material is not meant to be regarded either as exhaustive or all-inclusive of the problems and interventions that could be relevant to work with parents and infants.

The problems in Chapter 8 are stated from the perspective of persons who work primarily with the parents because they see the parents as the most powerful agents of change for their young children. Stating the problems from that perspective is consistent with the interaction model that focuses on the parents' interactions with their infants. The staff's responses to the problems—the interventions—were meant to help the parents to deal more effectively with their children in order to enhance their development and, at the same time, to increase mutual pleasure in parent-infant interaction.

CLASSIFICATION OF PROBLEMS

The problems have been grouped in five categories. Four are tied to areas of infant development: the social-affective, cognitive-motivational (or play), language, and motor areas. The fifth category contains common problems of caregiving, e.g., feeding, sleeping, safety, and other parenting issues such as problems of the working mother and of the mother who feels isolated in her home. The first four categories, tied to child development, are presented in an order that reflects the theoretical framework of the Intervention Program, in much the same way that the Parent Behavior Progression reflects this framework.

The *social-affective* area of parent-infant interaction is the matrix in which parent-infant bonding and attachment occur. When the infant feels secure in his attachment to the parent, he is able to distance himself sufficiently from the parent to seek objects and activities of interest to him in the physical world around him. In this safe environment, the infant is motivated to explore unfamiliar things and to engage in play that fosters intellectual development (the *cognitive-motivational* area). What occurs between parent and infant in the social-affective area thus has considerable bearing on the quality of the infant's motivation for exploration and play—the kinds of activities that affect cognitive development. The parent further influences the infant's development in the cognitive-motivational area by the kind of play environment she provides for him and by the way she responds to his play.

The early interactions between the parent and the young infant—reciprocal eye contact, touching, and smiling—also establish the foundation for the communication system between them that gradually grows in complexity. *Language* between parent and infant is based on the wish to communicate, which, in turn, grows from feelings of affection and mutual pleasure. Thus, reciprocal language communication develops from mutually rewarding social interaction. As this interaction becomes more complex, it needs the kind of elaboration that verbal language provides. When social-affective interaction is positive—mutually rewarding to parent and infant—language interaction soon follows.

When there is little or no language flowing between parent and infant, social-affective interaction like eye contact, smiling, and physical contact should be assessed first, because it is basic to language interaction. When social-affective interaction is mutually pleasurable, problems in language interaction may occur when the parent is not sufficiently aware of the infant's vocal attempts at communication. In some cases, the infant does not vocalize or respond to the parent's language for reasons that lie within the infant.

The most common problems of the Infant Studies Project infants in the *motor* area were mild delays in gross and fine motor development and a low level of motor activity, which was sometimes related to lack of motivation for movement.[3] Play always involves fine motor and often gross motor activity, especially for the infant. When an infant is not sufficiently active to encourage motor development, one can help the parent find ways of motivating the infant to engage in the appropriate motor activities by connecting these activities with play interests. Thus, there is an overlap between the cognitive-motivational and the motor categories of problems. The problems that are classified as motor are the ones that deal primarily with parents' attitudes and anxieties regarding the timing of the gross motor milestones of their infants and those regarding the infants' motor delays and handicaps.

Most of the problem statements begin with the word "parent." This reflects the staff's focus on the parent's perceptions of the infant, the parent's interactions with the infant in various contexts, aspects of caregiving, and the parent's frustrations as a parent. Problems are stated in terms of the child when difficult or deviant behavior or a handicapping condition noticeably interfered with parenting and mutually pleasurable parent-infant interaction.

MODES OF INTERVENTION AND STAFF ACTIVITIES

The *modes of intervention* are the statements listed under each problem, like: "We *listened* empathetically as the parent...," "We *discussed* with the parent...," "We *asked* the parent...," etc. The wording of the modes of intervention reflects the philosophy of the Intervention Program by stressing the need to listen carefully to the parent, the importance of acknowledging and building on the parents' strengths, and the value of cooperative problem solving.

Not all the modes of intervention appear under every problem because different modes were applicable to different problems. Further-

---

[3] We have not included the more specific interventions that children with severe neuromotor handicaps might need, because these fall into the more specialized area of physical and occupational therapy. Nevertheless, we feel that our parent-oriented approach to children's problems can be helpful in these cases.

more, the sequence of the intervention modes in Chapter 8 represents only in a general way the order in which these were used with a particular family during intervention sessions and, to some extent, over time. The specific staff responses to a problem, which are listed under each mode, and the sequence of intervention modes may represent the staff's efforts with a particular parent and infant that extended over a period of weeks, or they may represent the sum of what was done with several families during one or more sessions. Yet, with respect to the modes of intervention, we could not convey the exact sequence followed in each individual case. For example, in case 1, the staff may have listened to the parent before doing any modeling with the infant, whereas in case 2, a parent may have had difficulty in talking about her experiences or feelings related to a particular problem, and therefore, *listening empathetically* to the parent was not the mode of intervention used first. Similarly, asking some parents certain questions might stimulate them to share their experiences and frustrations, whereas this mode of intervention might not have been appropriate in the first few sessions with a parent who was particularly sensitive or reticent or who felt easily threatened. Still, there were many intervention sessions during which the staff first *listened empathetically* to the parent, then *asked* some questions, and subsequently *discussed* certain issues with her—issues that she raised or that the staff felt needed to be broached. Discussions or conversations with the parent were, of course, associated with observations, with modeling, with listening empathetically, and with the other modes of intervention at various times. In other words, discussions with parents were scattered throughout the sessions with the majority of families, as were positive comments about what the parent was doing.

The Problem-Solving Process

The staff practiced, modeled, encouraged, and engaged jointly with the parent in the problem-solving process whenever the situation allowed it. Problem solving does not appear separately as a mode of intervention in Chapter 8 because the process affects and is a part of several different modes of intervention. It includes *observing* with the parent, *asking* questions of the parent, trying out or *experimenting* with the infant, *discussing* with the parent what alternatives might be worth trying, and *encouraging* the parent to follow through and check what worked best. By their own actions and through discussions with the parents, the staff stressed the value of the problem-solving process: gathering information before acting (observing and asking questions); exploring and experimenting with various possibilities, e.g., with different materials to interest the infant or with new methods of dealing with the infant's undesirable behavior; making decisions about what seemed best for parent and infant; and finally, evaluating whether the problem had been solved in a satisfactory manner or whether more needed to be done.

Selection of Interventions

The choice of particular staff responses to a problem was guided by the overall philosophy and the long-term goals of the Intervention Program. Sometimes it would have been deceptively simple to find an immediate solution to a parent's problem. For example, a parent complained that her child made constant demands for her attention and seemed bored all the time. An easy response would have been for the staff simply to provide new and interesting toys for the child. This might have solved the problem for the moment, but it would not have helped the parent to deal with a similar problem in the future. Moreover, that type of response did not deal with the parent's expression of resentment of her child's "unreasonable" demands for attention, although this feeling might have had a negative effect on the parent-child relationship.

An alternate set of staff responses and actions, which involves the problem-solving process and which is geared to the long-range goals of parental competence and positive parent-child interaction, might have been the following. First, the staff observed with the parent how the child played with materials and discussed with her the concepts and skills he was exhibiting. Then, either the staff person or the parent experimented with a variety of materials and the parent chose the ones she thought interested the child most. The parent was observing the child for a purpose and, in so doing, was practicing a new skill that she would be able to use in the future to make her own decisions about what was motivating to her child. As a result of being given toys that interested him, the child was better able to occupy himself and the parent found that she had more time to herself. A common product of observing and talking about her child's play was the parent's greater interest in his activities and her more positive involvement with him. In order to deal with the parent's resentment of the child's "excessive" demands for attention, it was important to listen to the parent's expression of frustration and to empathize with her before being able to effect any change in her interaction with the child. It was also useful to discuss with the parent the common needs of young children for frequent adult attention.

An individual working with a particular family is involved in a continuous decision-making process regarding strategies and specific interventions that seem most appropriate at any particular time in order to best meet the needs of parent and child. Yet, the following staff behaviors are helpful in response to almost any problem: *listening and observing carefully; helping the parent become an interested and accurate observer of her child; noting and commenting positively on the parent's and the child's strengths; and being conscious of the parent's priorities and the child's needs.*

Overlaps and Interrelationships

In order to present the various problems and staff responses to the problems in a logical structure, we stated problems as distinct from each other, even when they were interrelated in a particular infant-parent dyad. For example, an inexperienced parent knew neither how to meet the child's play needs nor what to expect in terms of his social-affective development; or, a highly active parent with a slow-moving, passive child did not enjoy either verbal or play interaction with him and showed impatience with his motor activities. In practice, when a number of related problems were perceived in a particular family, they were dealt with either simultaneously or according to the parent's needs or priorities. Sometimes, the area in which the parent and child were most likely to enjoy doing something together was attended to first, e.g., play or a gross motor activity.

The reader will detect similar staff responses across several problems because one particular response was often effective with more than one problem. For example, modeling for the parent how to respond to her infant's vocalizations was an effective intervention when the problem was the parent's inattention to the infant's normal vocalizations, or the infant's lack of responsiveness to his parent, or the infant's primitive or infrequent utterances. We decided that it would be better to let the same or similar staff responses appear under several problems than to reduce the number of problems by further condensing them.

Added Interventions for Particular Populations

Parents of handicapped children have the same problems that other parents have, *plus* many others directly or indirectly connected with the handicap. We tried to respond to the needs of professionals who work with special populations of parents and infants in the following manner. When a particular set of interventions (or staff responses) listed under a problem did not fully meet the needs of parents with a particular kind of child, a second section was added to the first set of interventions. The added section is introduced with a sub-heading, e.g., "In cases where the infant was severely delayed, we also....," and additional interventions follow. These added sections deal mostly with infants with specific handicaps, with infants with difficult behavior, and sometimes with older "toddlers" (when the first set of interventions seemed to be limited to the parent of a younger infant).

MODES OF INTERVENTION:
MEANINGS AND IMPLICATIONS FOR PRACTICE

In the remainder of this chapter, the modes of intervention that appear in Chapter 8 are operationally defined, and their role in implementing the Intervention Program principles and guidelines is discussed. The modes, like the problems, are stated in the past tense to remind the reader that the content of Chapter 8 represents the methodology that was effective in the UCLA Intervention Program. Each mode begins with the word "we" because the three persons (D. Burge, E. Khokha, and the author) who collaborated in the writing of Chapter 8 worked directly with the families in the Intervention Program.

1. We *Listened Empathetically*...

Our approach to intervention required that we first listen to the parent carefully, that we acknowledge her feelings, that we be empathic with her by trying to see things from her perspective, and that we try to understand her perceptions of her child and of herself as parent in the context of the family. By first listening carefully to the parent while she talked about her child, her interaction with him, and her feelings related to parenting, we conveyed to her that what she said, did, and felt was important to us and vital to the intervention process.

When we listened empathetically, we communicated to the parent that we valued hearing her talk about what was preoccupying her and that we tried to hear what she had to say in a non-judgmental manner, i.e., that we accepted her regardless of the feelings she might express. We helped her realize that most parents occasionally feel frustrated, ambivalent, or angry. Our acceptance and the parents' realization of the universality of their feelings often provided them considerable relief. At times, when a parent was only hinting at some of her feelings of frustration, we tried to help her express them more openly by making statements such as: "It must have felt pretty frustrating to have him continue screaming after you picked him up and tried to cuddle him," or "I know from my own experience and from other parents that this is a very difficult and frustrating stage to go through with a child."

However, we were careful not to encourage the parent to talk about issues and feelings before she indicated in some manner that she wanted to talk about them. If a parent is "pushed" into expressing feelings that she is not ready to share or even to articulate to herself (assuming that she even has these feelings), she might regret having talked about them, she might feel exposed and resentful and guilty, and she might tend to withdraw from the relationship with the person to whom she aired these feelings. This kind of interaction can result in the parent's loss of trust in the staff member.

We were also careful not to become involved in highly personal matters that were unrelated to the child or to the parent in the parenting role. When a parent seemed to be disturbed, to be in a marital crisis, or to be in need of talking about deeply personal matters, we tried to help her realize the limits of our skills, i.e., that we were not therapists. However, at the same time, we tried to encourage her to talk about these matters with someone who would be best qualified to be of help to her. We made referrals to the appropriate professionals or agencies whenever this seemed indicated. The process of referral itself can be a slow, difficult, and sensitive process in which one has to maintain the trust of the parent whom one is referring.

2.   We *Observed*...

Helping the parent to become a sensitive observer of her child was one of the goals that we tried to achieve early in the intervention process. The parent had to have observational skills in order to be able to read her infant's cues and to be able to respond to them. We shared with the parent what we noticed or "observed" about the child's play, language, social, and motor behavior, and we often asked the parent to observe the child's activities with toys that we left in the home. The parent anticipated that we would ask her to select from among the toys we brought those that she wanted to keep for a while. This motivated her to observe the infant's play with toys. The parent soon learned not only to become aware of his interests and skills, but also to tell us why she thought a particular object would interest her child at this time. Many parents would tell us with great interest (at first upon our request and then spontaneously) how their children used play materials during the periods between home visits. In those cases, we felt that the parents' observations paid off, not only by increasing their interest and skills in providing appropriate environments and materials for their children, but also by raising the quality and frequency of their involvement with their children.

"*Observing* with the parent" also applied to language behavior and therefore included "listening" to the child's language. The kinds of comments that accompanied our observations of the child's play, language, affective cues, social responses, and motor behavior called the parent's attention to the details of behavior that revealed important developmental changes in the child, no matter how small. Observing *with the parent* meant that parent and staff shared with each other what each had observed. The discussions that ensued from the observations were motivating to the parent to continue to observe, and they gave her additional ideas about what was important to look for in order to help her interact more pleasurably and effectively with her child. Observations and the accompanying discussions also made the parents more interested in investing more time and energy in providing the kinds of play opportunities that the child seemed ready for.

When the child had serious problems, it was important for us to keep informed regarding the parent's perceptions of her child's behavior. We had to take fully into account where the *parent* was in her view of the child as well as what *we* were observing, in deciding how to discuss her child's behavior with her. We tried to help her see those behaviors that would aid her in interacting more effectively with him, thus easing her job as a parent. *When* we felt it would be helpful to the parent, we encouraged her to get closer to the reality of the child's behavior through *her* observations, rather than by telling her what we observed. In this manner, we could have greater assurance that when she allowed herself to see, for example, how distractible the child was, she would be more ready to accept talking constructively about how to help him than if we had simply told her "the fact" that he was distractible.

3.   We *Commented Positively*. . .

Parents need to know what their strengths are so that they can both build on them and, at the same time, gain self-confidence. We commented on behavior that showed that the parent was in tune with the infant and was meeting his needs, e.g., "Your expressive face makes it fascinating for the baby to watch you," or "He appreciates when you let him tell you when he is finished." Many parents take for granted many of their parenting skills. They do not value them and they seem surprised and pleased when someone calls their attention to these skills. We feel that it is useful to the parent to know why her actions are beneficial to the child and in what way a particular action or her general style helps her child. These clarifications not only help her to value her own skills and help to reinforce her skills, but also they ultimately lead her to be able to generalize her skills to other areas of interaction in which she might be less successful initially. Simple reinforcement, i.e., telling the parent that she is doing "a good job" without explaining how she is helping her child, does not readily lead to generalization or to independent parental competence. (See guideline 8 in Chapter 2.)

The staff focused on the parent's concrete observable behavior rather than on global qualities of parenting, e.g., "The way in which you accentuate important words in your language with him makes it easy for him to understand you." When a parent took the initiative in dealing with a new issue and decided on her own plan of action, we commented on it and thus supported her new independence in decision making with respect to her child.

We commented positively on the child's behavior to help the parent appreciate his skills or to help her recognize progress, especially in areas of concern. When a child was especially difficult to deal with, we tried to talk with the parent about the positive aspects of his behavior so that she would not become discouraged by all the problems the child presented. There were times, however, when a parent's feelings were so negative or when she was so depressed that she was not able to tolerate hearing anything positive being said about her child. When this happened, it was better for the staff to empathize with her and at times to share with her *their* experience of becoming frustrated with the child.

In cases where there were many problems in parent-infant interaction, it was particularly important to let the parent know what she was doing well and how this was benefiting her child, even if initially her skills were few. Positive comments also helped to build rapport and trust between parents and staff. We only praised behavior of either the parent or the child when we genuinely felt it to be positive or to represent progress, no matter how minimal. To have done otherwise would have impeded open and honest communication between parents and staff.

4.   We *Discussed*...

This mode was the most pervasive one in the intervention process. It occurred either separately from or was a part of one of the other modes. It included a variety of staff responses that took place in the course of informal conversation with the parent, such as following up on observations or modeling, giving information, eliciting or suggesting alternatives to ineffective interactions between parent and child, responding to the parent's questions, and interesting the parent in trying a variety of new activities with her child.

Discussion with the parent was often an integral part of other intervention modes, such as *observing* with the parent and *modeling.* The modes—*listened empathetically, commented positively, asked,* and *encouraged* the parent—represent in themselves a kind of discussion. We separated out these modes from "*discussed* with the parent" in order to give them particular emphasis with specific problems.

Much of what is listed under "we *discussed*..." in Chapter 8 represents only excerpts from our informal conversations with the parents. These statements had to be restricted to the essence of the informational content communicated to the parent in the course of extended informal discussions.

Discussion often served the purpose of helping the parent to recognize and to understand better what was happening between her and her child and how her child's behavior related to the sequence of child development (e.g., "Many children in this age range drop things from the high-chair or out of the playpen as a form of experimentation and play"). It was helpful for the parent to see the larger context for the child's behavior and realize that some behavior that she experienced as a problem was simply part of a normal phase of development.

We usually conveyed child development information by centering on the observations of the child's current behavior and relating the discussion of development to those observations. The developmental information communicated to the parent often helped her to respond more effectively to the child or anticipate the next stage and the behaviors that it was likely to bring, e.g., "K is beginning to sound as if he were talking. We call that 'jargon' and, even though you may not recognize familiar words, it will help his language development if you acknowledge his 'talking' and try to respond to it meaningfully. Pretty soon you will hear him try to say single words."

In the course of discussion, we tried to be aware of the parent's priorities and individual style. When talking about the infant's behaviors, we tried first to elicit the parent's perceptions of the child's behavior in the area under discussion before making our comments. In the *discussion* mode, as in others, we made a consistent effort to support enjoyable interactions between parent and child and to enhance the parent's self-confidence and competence in parenting. The belief in the cooperative problem-solving approach governed the manner in which we discussed observations, alternative ways of dealing with the child, and specific concerns that the parent expressed.

When direct suggestions were made, they were offered as one or two from among many possible methods, solutions, or options. Moreover, we mentioned that some parents had found that this or that method was effective with their children, but that every parent and child is different and that this method may or may not work for her and her child. This way of presenting suggestions did not pressure the parent into doing something that she might be uncomfortable with or that she might not find successful. The approach prevented her from feeling guilty for not following through with a suggestion or from experiencing a sense of failure if what she had tried did not work.

5. We *Asked*...

Most of the time, we asked the parent questions to which she either could provide the answer immediately or could easily secure it within a short time. We rarely asked the parent to engage in an activity with her child in front of us after we had demonstrated it for her. Demonstration was used infrequently as a mode of intervention because we did not want the parent to perceive the staff as her "instructors," just as we did not want her to separate *her* "instructing" or "teaching" the child from her more inclusive function of parenting.

The parents were asked many questions informally in the course of conversation or *discussion*. Nonetheless, "we *asked* the parent" was identified as a separate mode of intervention in order to emphasize certain kinds of questions in relation to particular problems. On the other hand, the staff's responses to the parents' questions were not listed as a separate mode of intervention, but were included under the heading "we *discussed*."

The parent was asked to share with us many things she knew about her child that we did not know and that we needed to know. This type of inquiry, which implied that the staff saw the parent as the person who knew the child best, often raised the parent's self-esteem and, at the same time, helped to establish rapport with the parent. The parents' communications about their observations, experiences, concerns, and priorities were essential to the process of effective intervention and helped to establish it as a cooperative venture between parent and staff.

We sometimes asked a parent to make specified observations of her child's play, language, social behavior, etc. This activity helped her to focus on a particular area of the child's behavior. We found that asking the parent specific questions about her child's behavior could give the staff valuable information not only about the child and the parent-child relationship, but also about the parent's observational skills and degree of understanding of her child's behavior at his stage of development. The information gathered from the parent's observations and the staff's questions was used to build on the parent's strengths and to enhance her sensitivity and skills in particular areas.

Sometimes we were able to build on a parent's strengths by asking her to describe her successful handling of the child in one situation and then exploring with her how she could adapt this method to another situation in which she was having difficulties with the child. For example, we asked a working mother how she went about calming her child so successfully when he was fussy on week-ends, and we discussed with her how she might adapt that method to his crying when both she and the child were tired at night during the week.

We often responded to a parent's expression of concern by asking specific questions as a first step in the cooperative problem-solving process, e.g., "What situations seem to precipitate the child's tantrums?" Moreover, when a particular issue was of concern to us, we might ask the parent the kinds of questions that would stimulate her thinking about that issue, e.g., "How has M reacted to the change in babysitters?"

6. We *Modeled*...

Modeling, as used here, denotes acting or behaving in a particular manner with the expectation that the observer (the parent) might imitate at least some of these actions and behaviors. If the behavior is repeated several times in a specific context and if the parent has reason to view the modeled behavior as desirable, she will try out this behavior. If it fits into her style, she will gradually incorporate it into her own behavioral pattern.

Our intent in modeling an activity was usually to highlight for the parent some particular way of interacting with the infant that evoked his interest and that was beneficial to him in a particular area of development. Modeling often meant engaging the infant in social, play, language, or motor activity that the parent might want to try with the infant herself because she would expect it to be enjoyable for herself and for the infant. Modeling also exposed the parent to ways of dealing with the infant in areas in which the parent had difficulties with him. As the parent watched the interaction, she was able to see how the infant responded, and she could decide whether what she was witnessing would be worthwhile for her to try.

Through modeling, we were able to stress the value of experimenting with activities and different kinds of interactions with the infant. In the course of modeling, we had the opportunity to show the parent that it was all right to try something with the child and fail to get the desired response. When the parent saw that we did not always succeed with the infant but that we were able to learn from our failure and go on to trying something else, she often gained courage to experiment with new ways of dealing with a frustrating situation or with new kinds of activities. Modeling could help the parent feel safe to experiment in a number of areas and to try alternative ways when the "old" ways were not getting the desired response. Modeling also helped her to realize that, when she failed, she could try other ways until she found something that "worked."

Not all modeling was planned ahead of time. Spontaneous, playful interaction with the child often had the most potent effect as a model of behavior. A natural flow of interaction, with give-and-take by adult and child, sensitivity to the child's cues, and enjoyment of the interaction by both, was modeled spontaneously as much as possible. Often, modeling meant simply to engage in a positive interaction with the infant (or even with a sibling) in a manner that might capture the attention and interest of the parent present in the room. In modeling, as distinguished from demonstration, there was no expectation set for the parent to replicate with the infant what the staff was "demonstrating." The parent could feel free to incorporate into her repertoire of activities or interactions with the child whatever met her need, whatever appealed to her, and whatever fit into her style; she could ignore the rest. As the staff became better acquainted with the parent, they would try to model activities with the child in which they could anticipate the parent's interest.

Usually the staff tried either during or immediately after the modeled activity to talk to the parent about what was happening. The staff would explain what they were attempting to do with the child and why, or they would comment on the child's response to the activity, e.g., "She is really interested in having me tell her about the pictures—it is so nice how she points at them and then looks at me, expecting me to talk to her about them," or "The way she is turning her head away, I think she is telling me she has had enough of this toy." The first statement serves the double purpose of commenting positively about the child's behavior and giving the parent information about what adult response the child's behavior calls for.

The manner in which interpretations of the child's behavior were made depended on the style of the individual making it and on the nature of the communication that existed between that individual and the parent. The kind of behavior or activity that was being modeled also influenced the type of interpretation. For example, the modeling of language interactions called for delayed interpretation of what occurred, whereas in play interactions the interpretation could be concurrent with the activity.

Occasionally the staff modeled for a parent without talking to her at the same time. This became the mode with two young mothers who seemed to get more involved in observing or participating with staff and infant when they were not being talked to at the same time. Also, in cases where the infant was about 15 to 18 months or older, it was usually better to talk to the parent *after* the interaction with the child because having a conversation with the parent during the activity interfered with the interaction that was being modeled. Delaying the interpretation was also a way of modeling that it is important to give the child undivided attention when engaged with him in a language or play activity. A two-member team made it possible for one person to interpret for the parent what was happening between the child and the other team member without disturbing the interaction.

The decision to talk to the parent during the activity, afterwards, or not at all depended more on the staff's perception of the parent, and what she would profit from most, than on the nature of the problem. The more structured "demonstration," in which the staff showed the parent how to do a particular activity with the child and then requested the parent to imitate the actions, was not included as a mode of intervention in Chapter 8 because it was used infrequently.

Modeling was usually not used with certain caregiving activities such as feeding, putting the child to bed, or setting or enforcing limits, except in situations where the parent specifically asked the staff to get directly involved in such tasks. In most cases, however, the staff did not want to be intrusive in these more intimate interactions that were often emotionally charged for both parent and child. Problems in these areas were dealt with by a combination of other intervention modes which involved verbal exchanges with the parent.

It should be noted that modeling can be intrusive in any area of behavior or interaction in a home-based program if it is used before the parent is ready to accept the staff's becoming directly engaged with the child or if the staff is not sensitive to particular reservations on the part of the parents. This issue does not present itself to the same extent in a center-based program where the child is *brought* to the teacher and where the "teacher" is *expected* to become engaged in activities with the child. In our home-based program, the staff often had to balance the value of modeling against the danger of intrusiveness and possible interference with the parent's sense of control in her own home. Consequently, we modeled sooner and more frequently in some homes than in others. Our sensitivity to the parent's feelings and needs was in itself an example of modeling for the parent the kind of sensitivity that we hoped she would show toward her children.

7.   We *Experimented...*

The mode of *experimenting* consisted of working directly with the child to try out a variety of ways of interacting with him in different behavioral areas. Although experimenting with activities with the child, especially in the areas of play and language, often took place as part of *modeling,* it was treated as a separate mode of intervention in order to stress its special importance and application in relation to certain problems.

Experimentation sometimes was used by the staff to get to know a child better and to find effective ways of capturing the child's interest. Experimenting with activities with the child also served to stress to the parent that there were many alternative ways of getting a particular child to attend to or become involved in a particular activity. The parent could see that there were many failures that paved the way to successes in getting a desired response from the child. This often encouraged the parent to try new things with her child without feeling a personal sense of failure.

Experimenting was a necessary step in intervention with difficult children. This mode of intervention was used with children whose behavior created special problems in parent-infant interaction. Before the parent could be helped to interact successfully with her child, the staff had to find ways of getting the child to respond in a manner that would be reinforcing to the parent. To tell a parent that a particular activity would produce the desired behavior on the part of the child and then to discover that this was not the case could be a painful experience to a parent, leading to more "failure."

In certain cases it was important to show the parent that the child's behavior made interaction difficult not only for the parent but also for the staff. The parent could observe the staff's lack of success with the child, and this could relieve the parent's feeling of guilt that she might have caused the child's unusual behavior. When the parent observed the staff's failure, she could more easily accept the idea that the child's behavior might be due to something within the child himself.

Nonetheless, the staff had to be very sensitive to parents' feelings and current perceptions of their children so that they would know how to respond to the parents' comments and questions. For example, one parent whose child's behavior was deviant was not ready to be faced with the fact that the staff also was having a difficult time with her child. She was going through the stage of denial and refused to recognize that there was anything "different" about her child's behavior.

8. We *Encouraged*. . .

We introduced this mode of intervention, as we did in the case of the mode "We *asked*. . . ," in order to stress a particular kind of "discussion" with the parent. *Encouraging* the parent usually appears in Chapter 8 as one of the last intervention modes under a problem because it was used most often to help the parent to follow up on what had been *discussed* or *modeled* earlier. Encouragement was used frequently with parents who had shown interest in some activity or interaction with their children, that was discussed or modeled earlier, but who did not continue with the activity or interaction, even though it had appeared to be successful at first. For example, a parent saw that her language-delayed child vocalized while looking at pictures or books with her. When the parent did not follow through with this activity, she was encouraged to sit down with her child at least 5 minutes a day to look at the books that were left by the staff.

Also, when a parent took little initiative in solving a problem that she was experiencing with her child, and when she responded neither to discussion (problem solving) nor to modeling, we *encouraged* her to deal with the child's behavior in a particular way, e.g., "You might find it easier to. . ." or "He might be more responsive if you. . . ." Moreover, when the safety of the infant or other children was endangered, the parent was *encouraged* repeatedly to take direct action to remedy the situation.

In cases where the parent lacked self-confidence and asked us what she should do or how she should handle various situations, we tried to minimize direct suggestions, and instead we tried to help the parent to learn the problem-solving process, beginning with observations of the child. This approach held the greatest promise in leading the parent toward making decisions independently and relying less on the "advice" of others. With parents who lacked self-confidence, the intervention mode of *commenting positively* on their strengths was especially important.

Finally, some parents needed frequent encouragement to take care of their own personal needs when they became over-involved with their infants.

CONCLUSION: SELECTING THE MOST APPROPRIATE MODE

Parents differed in the way in which they responded to various modes of intervention. Some parents seemed to profit most from modeling and seemed particularly to enjoy watching the staff interact with their children. Others preferred interacting with their children in our presence, gaining confidence from our positive comments about what they were doing with their children. Still others seemed to gain most from discussing with the staff the many questions and issues that presented themselves in the course of parenting. Yet, discussion proved to be a relatively unproductive intervention mode with some parents. Clearly, only the staff working with a particular family can best decide which modes or intervention are likely to be most useful in meeting the needs of a given parent, child, and family.

Chapter 8
Problems and the Response of Intervention

PROBLEMS IN THE SOCIAL-AFFECTIVE AREA

1. The parent did not know how to help the child cope with separation.
2. The parent found it difficult to cope with the child's demands for attention.
3. The parent found it difficult to cope with the child who had particular temperamental characteristics.
4. The parent was concerned that the infant was slow to trust people outside the immediate family.
5. The parent did not find it enjoyable to interact with the infant because the infant did not express pleasure.
6. The parent found it difficult to deal with the child's temper tantrums.
7. The parent was anxious and upset about the child's masturbation.
8. The parent had difficulty handling the child's fears after a traumatic event.
9. The parent was upset because the child would not share his toys with other children.
10. The parent was concerned about the child's aggressiveness toward other children and was uncertain about how to deal with it.
11. The parent was uncertain about how to help the child adjust to the arrival of the new baby.
12. The child's excessive persistence made it difficult for the parent to participate in his play or to increase the variety of his experience.
13. The parent was not aware that the child needed help in adjusting to a new caregiving situation.
14. The parent did not respond to the infant's signals of distress (did not give comfort even after lengthy crying and/or when he hurt himself).
15. The parent did not set any limits for the child.

16 The parent had no control over the child (was unsuccessful in enforcing limits).

17 The parent was punitive in disciplining the child (yelled, threatened, slapped, took toys away).

18 The parent did not allow the child to make choices or to have control over any aspect of his daily life.

19 The parent discussed the child's problems, or expressed annoyance about him, in his presence.

20 The parent of a child with a handicap or a delay in language and/or motor development was not able to focus or capitalize on his strengths.

21 The child avoided eye contact as well as physical contact with parents and other adults.

22 The parent of a child with a visible handicap or deformity avoided taking him to public places.

23 The child's deviant, autistic-like behavior was difficult for the parent to tolerate.

PROBLEM 1:   The parent did not know how to help the child cope with separation.

We *listened empathetically* as the parent

...talked about how irritated she felt when the child clung to her whenever she was about to leave the house.

...expressed how helpless she felt leaving her child when he was crying.

...said that she thought the child would not get upset if he did not actually see her leave.

...described how she "sneaked" out the door because she could not bear to hear him cry.

...said that she did not go out at night before the child was asleep because she did not think he could handle the separation.

...told us that the more careful she was about letting the child know she was leaving and giving him a chance to say good-bye, the more upset he seemed to become.

We *discussed* with the parent

...how repeated short separations help to prepare the child for longer ones.

...that first staying with friends and relatives with whom the child is familiar will help him adjust later to other caregivers.

...how helpful it might be to have the child become familiar with the new caregiver while the parent is present.

...that it helps the child to realize that the parent "likes" the new caregiver as he sees them talk with each other in a friendly manner.

...that after the child has enjoyed playing with the new caregiver once or twice in the parent's presence, he may find it easier to accept and even like her.

...that children show more anxiety and stress about separation during certain stages of development (between 8 and 20 months, developmental age).

...that it is usually easier for the child to physically "move away" from the parent than to be "left" by the parent.

...that the parent's leaving may be easier for the child if he can develop a routine for saying good-bye, e.g., waving at the window, handing the mother her purse, driving around the block with the parent, etc.

...that it might be easier for the child to handle the separation if the caregiver is helped to accept the child's feelings upon the parent's leaving, e.g., "Yes, I know you are angry and unhappy that Mommy is going out...."

...that it might help the child to be told when the parent will be back in terms of a sequence of routine events that he is familiar with, e.g., "Mommy will be back after you eat your lunch, take your nap, and

play for a while and she will be home in time to bathe you and put you
to bed tonight.''

...that some young children handle separations more easily if they remain in familiar surroundings or if they can hold on to something
belonging to the parent and some favorite toy when away from home.

...that not only most young children but also most parents find separation a difficult process.

...that it is common for both young children and parents to feel anxious
about the first few separations and that these feelings are indications
of the strength of their mutual attachment.

...that children often cry when the parent returns because it is safer to express their feelings to the parent than to less familiar people.

*In cases where separation had occurred suddenly and the child responded
by clinging and excessive demands for attention...*

We also *discussed* with the parent

...that children need much affection and reassurance after upsetting experiences such as sudden separation.

...that the child's clinging would probably decrease sooner if he could
get the parent's undivided attention a few times during the day *before*
he demanded it.

...how important it is to handle necessary separations sensitively after a
traumatic separation.

...that it takes some children longer than others to overcome the effects
of traumatic events such as sudden and unexpected separation.

We also *commented positively*

...when the parent reassured the child and was affectionate with him.

...when the parent spoke soothingly to the child at those times when she
was not able to hold him or sit with him.

...when the parent reported that she rearranged her schedule so that she
could spend a little more time with the child while he needed her more.

**PROBLEM 2:   The parent found it difficult to cope with the child's
demands for attention.**

We *listened empathetically* as the parent

...talked about how drained she felt because of the child's constant
demands for attention.

...said that she did not want to be with her child all the time.

...expressed resentment about giving so much of her time and of herself
to her child.

...talked about how she needed to be alone and away from the child some of the time.

...expressed concern that her child would never learn to occupy himself.

...talked about how badly she felt because she had no time and energy left for other family members.

...told how difficult it was to get anything done because she was constantly being interrupted by her child's demand for attention.

We *asked* the parent

...whether the child seemed to demand more attention under particular circumstances or in some situations, e.g., when parent was busy doing something specific, like talking on the phone, conversing with her husband or a friend, or when the child was tired or hungry at particular times of the day.

...what kinds of things the child seemed to want when he asked for attention.

...whether the child demanded short or long periods of attention and whether there was a pattern in that respect.

...whether the child was able to occupy himself for brief periods and what he was most likely to be doing when he could play by himself.

...whether she had seen changes in how much attention the child demanded during the past few months.

We *discussed* with the parent

...that most parents express similar frustrations in coping with the demands of their young children.

...ways to make time for herself away from her child.

...that many parents find that they feel better about taking time for themselves if they have given their child undivided attention for some periods of the day.

...that many young children need frequent short periods of adult attention.

...that her willingness to give the child a certain amount of needed attention now was helping him be secure enough to be independent later on.

...that short periods of independent play in the presence of the parent were a first step toward autonomy.

...how some parents find that the child is more likely to play by himself if the parent sits down or stays in the same room with him (to work or do other things).

...that some parents find that their child is content longer if the parent occasionally talks or sings to him as she is working.

...that children differ as to how early they are able to play by themselves for more than a few minutes at a time.

...that some children go through phases of being able to occupy themselves independently, then demanding the parent's presence for a
period (of weeks), and eventually becoming more independent again
in an emotionally safe environment.

...that stress, even if temporary (especially incidents involving separation from the parent), tends to decrease for a period of time the child's
ability to play independently.

...ways of keeping the child occupied during times when the parent cannot give him her full attention, e.g., putting him in the high chair near
her with some toys or finger foods while she is cooking.

...which toys the child can use productively by himself and with which he
needs help.

...that some children may demand less attention if they can watch or
play with an older child.

We *commented positively*

...on the parent's ability to judge when the child really needed her attention.

...on the parent's willingness to be with the child when he seemed to need
her.

...on ways the parent found to help the child play by himself with satisfaction when she was busy, e.g., when she gave him special toys while
on the phone.

We *modeled*

...activities that the parent and child might enjoy together.

...presenting toys to the child and getting him sufficiently involved with
them so that he could play independently for a while.

We *encouraged* the parent

...to explore ways to rearrange her schedule so that she could get important work done when the child was least likely to interrupt her, e.g., at
nap time, after he had eaten, or early in the morning.

...to take the child on outings so she would feel less "housebound" and
so the child would focus his attention on things that interested him
rather than wanting her attention.

...to investigate programs for very young children and their parents in
the community (parent-infant programs at the YWCA, public school
adult education, playgrounds, etc.) so that she could get out of the
house with him and have a chance to be with other parents.

...to ask her husband or a babysitter or relative to watch the child when
she needed to have time for herself.

...to arrange to get out of the house occasionally and pursue her own interests.

In cases where the child was 18 months or older...

We *also discussed* with the parent

...how she might observe and experiment to determine with what activities the child would show the longest attention span.

...that children functioning at this developmental age can learn to spend time playing independently.

...that children learn to play by themselves very gradually.

...that it may help to give the child special toys for the times he is expected to occupy himself when the parent is busy.

...how she might approach the issue in small steps:

1. Engage the child with a toy that motivates him and with which he can experience success, and then let him continue playing with it on his own while the parent remains in the room.

2. Set expectations for the child that he will play independently for a short period in the parent's presence while she is busy doing something else.

3. Gradually lengthen periods during which the child plays by himself in the parent's presence.

4. Leave the room for short periods, with the door open, as the child is playing, and tell him in a calm and casual manner that she is in the _____ room and will come back in a little while.

5. Gradually increase the periods of absence from the room and reassure the child verbally from the other room.

...that for some children it may be easiest first to establish a routine: the child is expected to play on his own at the same time every day in the parent's presence while she is occupied with the same activity (for children who have particular difficulties in playing by themselves).

...that a fairly short attention span, frequent frustrations with toys, and a need to check with the caregiver frequently are typical of many children in the toddler stage, and that children of this age cannot be expected to be happy on their own for very long periods.

We *commented positively*

...when the parent told the child in a calm and firm manner that she was busy and could not play with him just then, after getting him started with an activity.

...when the parent praised the child for having played so happily on his own.

We *modeled*

...complimenting the child on the quality of his play when on his own, e.g., "You pulled all the pop beads apart *by yourself* and put them all in the basket! You can do so many things so well all by yourself!!"

PROBLEM 3:   The parent found it difficult to cope with the child who had particular temperamental characteristics.

We *listened empathetically* as the parent

...talked about how difficult it was to live with this child day in and day out.

...said how angry she felt when she tried to do something new or interesting with the child and he reacted negatively.

...talked about how the child's intense reactions restricted the family's social life and activities.

We *asked* the parent

...which behaviors or situations she found particularly difficult to deal with.

...to describe the child's behavior in a frequently occurring situation.

...whether she had found that she could often anticipate particularly difficult behavior, and if so, how.

We *commented positively*

...on the child's strengths and positive attributes.

...on the parent's efforts to take into consideration the child's behavioral style and adapt to it to a reasonable extent.

...when the parent managed to consider her own tolerance level and needs as well as the needs of the child.

We *discussed* with the parent

...that children appear to be born with different temperamental traits or behavioral tendencies, and that children with a combination of certain traits are particularly difficult to live with.

...that the child's temperament is not necessarily that of the parent and that their adjustment to each other may take time.

...the book by S. Chess, A. Thomas, and H. G. Birch, *Your Child is a Person* (Viking Press, 1965), in which the authors discuss behaviors of children with different temperaments, and how this book might help the parent deal with her particular child.

In cases where the child had difficulty accepting anything new (food, people, routines)...

We also *discussed* with the parent

...that some children just take longer to accept unfamiliar people, places, and experiences.

...that the child's initial negative reaction to a new experience did not mean that he would never enjoy it.

...that the child may need repeated brief exposure to new things and people before he would be able to accept them.

...that it was important to continue to expose the child to new experiences, in a safe situation, even if he rejected them at first.

...that children sometimes find it easier to accept something new when it is introduced in a familiar and secure context or when it is presented with something they like, e.g., introducing a new food with a favorite food.

...that once the parent could see the pattern of initial upset and gradual acceptance of the new by the child, she might find it easier to stay calm and confident in the face of the child's initial negative reaction.

...that it helps to talk with the child about a new experience ahead of time.

...that many parents find that new experiences are easier to accept for some children if they are exposed to them while with another child (friend or sibling).

...that the parent's physical closeness and her acceptance of his slow tempo of approaching the unfamiliar will give him the security to gradually accept it.

We *commented* positively

...when the parent reported holding the child's hand when going with him to the house of a friend unfamiliar to the child, and allowing him to stay close to her until he was ready to move away from her on his own.

In cases where the child was very intense and persistent...

We also *discussed* with the parent

...that persistence, although sometimes difficult to handle now, could be a positive trait that would later help the child in pursuing goals.

...that it is important to let the child know that much of the time his wish to complete an activity is respected.

...the need to help the child balance intense interest in one kind of activity with his need for diverse experiences.

...that the parent needs to determine at what times it was necessary for the child to interrupt his activity, e.g., mealtime, bedtime, etc.

...that the child needs help to adapt gradually to reasonable demands that he stop one activity and start another so that he will be able to tolerate transitions between activities later in school.

...that the child may accept interruptions of his play more easily if he is warned ahead of time in concrete terms, e.g., "After you finish this puzzle it will be time to clean up, wash your hands, and eat lunch."

...that some children find it easier to accept being interrupted in their play when the adult acknowledges their feelings of frustration while at the same time telling him that he is expected to stop, e.g., "I know it makes you angry that you can't go on playing with the blocks, but we simply have to go now."

...how some children will "hear" the parent better when she comes close to the child, touches him, or makes eye contact with him.

We *commented positively*

...when the parent followed through once the child had been prepared for a change or transition.

...when the parent talked about providing the child with many opportunities to play for a prolonged time without interruption while, at the same time, she felt confident in helping him stop an activity when it was necessary.

We *modeled*

...getting the child's attention and interesting him in another activity when he had been persisting in frustrating and unproductive play.

...verbalizing the child's feelings while, at the same time, helping him physically (gently) to move away from a place or an activity, e.g., "I know you want to keep on swinging, but it is time to go inside now."

In cases where the child had a slow speed of response...

We also *observed* with the parent

...the slowness of the child's response to a toy or to another child, but how, nevertheless, the child could become very involved and interested if given plenty of time.

We *discussed* with the parent

...that it may be less frustrating for the parent to allow the child to do things very slowly on his own if the parent could plan ahead of time that it was going to take a long time, e.g., have the child start his meal before everyone else.

...how easy it is to do everything for a child with such a slow tempo, but that he too needs to learn to become independent.

...that slow tempo is sometimes misinterpreted as low mental ability, especially by those whose tempo is much faster.

...how the parent needs to interpret the child's behavior to others so that the child's tempo can be understood and his needs more easily met.

(See also Problem 5 in the cognitive-motivational area.)

In cases where the child was passive . . .

We also *discussed* with the parent

. . . that some children are demanding and ask for what they need (and sometimes more) while others are quiet and seem content with very little.

. . . how the quiet, "good" child, who is undemanding, may be harder to parent and may be more of a challenge because the parent must initiate most interactions and must decide what the child needs.

. . . that requiring the child to make simple choices (between two alternatives at first) gives him the experience of asserting his wishes and of demanding what he needs.

. . . that it was a special challenge to provide stimulating activities and experiences for the undemanding child.

. . . that the child needed opportunities to play with the parent without interruptions from others because playing with the parent would be motivating to him and would help him to feel important to the parent.

We *modeled*

. . . letting the child control play interactions, e.g., "Where do you want me to put the doll, here or there?"

. . . verbalizing what the child was expressing through his behavior, e.g., "I want to play with Mommy *now!*" or "No, don't take it, it's mine."

. . . protecting the child's activity from interference by offering the sibling another toy.

In cases where the child had a very high activity level . . .

We also *listened empathetically* as the parent

. . . told how exhausted she felt living with the child who was on the move constantly.

. . . expressed worry that the child might be "hyperactive."

. . . talked about never knowing when he had had enough activity because he simply never "stopped."

We *discussed* with the parent

. . . that some children are by nature more active than others.

. . . that most parents who have children with a high activity level find it rather exhausting.

. . . that parents with very active children need frequent periods to be away from them.

. . . that many very active children provoke negative reactions in adults because the adults feel they cannot control them.

. . . that she may be able to channel some of that exuberant activity by providing the child with opportunities for challenging gross motor activity, e.g., provide large boxes, toddler slide, large pillows, bean bags to throw.

. . . that the child's high activity level may be easier to tolerate outdoors and to try to provide as much outside playtime as feasible.

. . . that she may need to clarify in her own mind what limits he needs, because active children tend to test limits more than less active ones.

. . . that providing the active child with a safe home environment is a real challenge because he is likely to explore and experiment more widely than other children.

. . . that both parent and infant might benefit from establishing early in his life a daily period when he stays in the play pen with special toys reserved for this time and, when he is older, a similar period when he plays quietly in a particular place in the house.

. . . that a very active child is likely to have mishaps (breaking and spilling things) that are usually unintentional and that are a function of moving a lot before having acquired much fine motor and gross motor control.

. . . how she might help the infant learn to enjoy quiet activities by sitting down with him, holding him on her lap while playing, singing or looking at pictures with him.

. . . that some active children are easily overstimulated, that they need to alternate between active and quiet periods, and that they may need calm and gentle help from an adult to quiet down at first.

. . . that although very active infants sometimes resist being comforted or held, they need physical affection and will usually be responsive to gentle comforting even after brief resistance.

We *encouraged* the parent

. . . to observe carefully at what times of the day the child is most likely to accept "quiet" time with the parent.

. . . to observe all the things her child is able to do.

. . . to have her pediatrician evaluate the child if she is concerned about his activity level.

We *commented positively*

. . . on the parent's observational skills and her appreciation of the child's abilities.

. . . when the parent talked about taking time to calm the child after a period of vigorous activity even when he initially resisted.

. . . when the parent reported that she took some time for herself on a regular basis.

PROBLEM 4: **The parent was concerned that the infant was slow to trust people outside the immediate family.**

We *listened empathetically* as the parent

...talked about how disappointed she was because she had always hoped to have a friendly, outgoing child.

...talked about how embarrassed and frustrated she felt when the infant clung to her when he met new people.

...described being criticized by her relatives who thought the infant acted the way he did because she had spoiled and overprotected him.

We *observed* with the parent

...how the infant needed to observe for a while before he could get involved with a new person.

...how the infant seemed to become even more clinging when someone encouraged him to be involved with others before he was ready.

...how the infant did gradually warm up to new people when he was not pressured and was allowed to take the initiative in approaching new people.

We *discussed* with the parent

...that many parents express similar concerns, particularly around this stage of development (last quarter of first year).

...that many infants who have been friendly and outgoing suddenly become wary and that this is confusing to parents and relatives.

...that "stranger anxiety" is a normal stage of development and indicates the infant's increased ability to discriminate between familiar and unfamiliar persons.

...that many parents feel "inadequate" and as if they had done something wrong when they see their infant needing time to trust an unfamiliar person.

...that there are many adults who take a long time before they become comfortable with unfamiliar people, but that once they feel comfortable they are very warm and friendly.

...that some children need more time than others to accept a new person.

...that it may help the infant to sense that the parent "trusts" this person and to hear the parent express confidence that the infant will also trust the person after a while.

...that the infant may need repeated exposure to a new person before he is able to establish a relationship.

...that repeatedly seeing and hearing the parent interact comfortably with the new person may help the infant to relax.

...that the infant is likely to accept a new person more readily if he is not pressured to be in contact with or reach out to the person before he is ready.

...that the infant may accept new people more readily if the parent allows him to stay close to her when he first meets them.

...that natural curiosity entices most infants to move toward the new person or thing when they feel safe and unpressured.

...how some parents find it helps them to be patient with the infant if they explain his behavior to the visitor.

...that sometimes visitors who are not around children a lot may frighten them inadvertently by approaching them too quickly.

...our own initial experience with the infant when we first tried to interact with him before he was ready: how he drew back, giving us the cue to wait until he was ready to interact with us.

We *modeled*

...allowing the infant to take his time to interact with us.

...the following sequence with the infant:
1. We offered him a toy by placing it within his reach instead of handing it directly to him.
2. We let him play with the toy near his parent or in her lap.
3. We talked intermittently to the infant, from a distance.
4. We interacted with the infant from a distance by playing hiding games (peek-a-boo) with him and singing to him.
5. We offered a toy directly to him.
6. We waited for the infant to reach out to us before touching him or picking him up.

PROBLEM 5:   The parent did not find it enjoyable to interact with the infant because the infant did not express pleasure.

We *listened empathetically* as the parent

...said that her baby was not much fun.

...talked about how hard it was to play with the infant when he did not show pleasure.

...talked about how sad it made her feel that the infant did not seem to enjoy her company.

...said that she never knew what toys he liked because he did not smile or react in any overt way.

We *asked* the parent

...whether the infant showed preferences for certain people and how he did this.

...how the infant indicated that he did not like something.

...what activities they did together that the child seemed to become involved with and therefore probably enjoyed.

We *experimented*

...with activities that might elicit the infant's smile or laughter, e.g., talking animatedly or vigorous tactile or motor stimulation, or with activities that might stimulate his interest and positive response, even if mild, e.g., cause-and-effect toys, puppets.

We *observed* with the parent

...the concepts and skills the infant was exhibiting in his play with objects, and we talked about what skills the parent might expect next.

...the ways in which the infant showed interest in activities, and we said that his interest in itself was an important response.

...how the infant seemed to show satisfaction and enjoyment in his play when he was experiencing success.

We *discussed* with the parent

...how some children are just naturally more sober than others and give very subtle cues of enjoyment.

...our own difficulty in getting the infant to express pleasure.

...that the infant wanted her to interact with him even though his cues and responses were minimal.

...how interactions with the infant would tend to make him gradually more socially responsive.

...that some infants are more expressive when interacting with older children than with adults.

We *commented positively*

...on the ways the infant showed the parent that she was important to him, e.g., he cried when she left, he clung to her in the presence of strangers.

...on her frequent efforts to interact with the infant even though she received little social response.

...when the parent reported experimenting with ways to get the infant to smile.

...when the parent began to read the infant's subtle cues of enjoyment and to respond to them.

...when the parent was successful in getting the infant to express pleasure overtly to her.

...on the gradual increase of the infant's expression of pleasure over time.

We *modeled*

...motivating the infant to look at and respond to us, by nodding, shaking our heads, making faces, producing funny sounds.

...using a mirror, playing peek-a-boo, putting on funny hats, to elicit smiles or laughter.

...talking and smiling with vigorous tactile stimulation.

...activities we thought the parent and infant would enjoy together, e.g., nursery rhymes with gestures, blowing bubbles, water play.

...engaging the infant in vigorous activity, e.g., bouncing, "dancing," to get him more animated.

...responding with dramatic facial and verbal affect when the infant showed even minimal positive affect.

...providing toys that the infant would enjoy more with an adult's participation.

...responding with strong positive affect when the infant was successful with a toy.

...verbalizing for the infant what he seemed to be expressing behaviorally, e.g., "I liked that toy, Mommy," or "I did it all by myself," or "That feels so good!"

PROBLEM 6:   The parent found it difficult to deal with the child's temper tantrums.

We *listened empathetically* as the parent

...talked about the difficulties and frustrations of dealing with a young child.

...told us how angry she felt when the child had a tantrum.

...expressed worry that the child would never grow out of this stage.

...described how awful she felt when the child had a temper tantrum in public.

We *asked* the parent

...if she had noticed what kinds of situations seemed to set off temper tantrums.

...whether his tantrums were more frequent and more intense during certain times of the day.

...what happened when the child had a tantrum.

...about the ways in which she had dealt with the child's tantrums and which seemed to be most effective.

We *discussed* with the parent

...that most parents express similar feelings and find this to be a difficult time in their relationship with their child.

...the normalcy of a toddler's negativism and that the intensity and frequency of it were a passing phase.

...how assertiveness, which is part of the tantrum, indicates that the child is establishing himself as a separate person.

...that many young children use their bodies to show their anger and frustration before they are able to express their feelings verbally.

...that temper tantrums are hard to deal and live with but that they are a step in the child's learning to cope with negative feelings.

...that many parents find that some confrontations can be avoided by recognizing that toddlers want to do things by themselves and in their own way, e.g., "I guess you want to brush your hair all by yourself."

...that ways can usually be found to avoid some situations that provoke tantrums, especially at certain times of the day when the parent's and the child's tolerance level is low, e.g., late afternoon when both are tired.

...that giving the child simple choices when possible may head off some explosions, e.g., "Do you want to wear this shirt or that shirt?"

...how she could decide which limits can be flexible and which cannot be, like safety issues versus less critical issues, e.g., staying in the car seat while riding in the car and not playing in the street might be inflexible, whereas wearing shoes on a warm day, playing with water, or eating another cookie might be flexible.

...that when children know clearly what their limits are and when these limits are enforced, tantrums will tend to decrease because having a tantrum is a child's way of testing limits.

...that as the child grows in self-control, his tantrums will gradually diminish.

...that some children have a much more difficult time than others in learning and practicing self-control and that such children are more trying for their parents because the children need more help and the parents need more patience and support from family and friends.

...that it helps the child if the parent can accept the child's feelings but, at the same time, let him know that his behavior is not acceptable, e.g., "I know you are angry at me, but I will not let you kick me," or "I can see that you don't want to get dressed, but you cannot go outside without clothes when it is chilly."

...that some infants and toddlers get over their tantrums faster when they are distracted by something interesting to do, e.g., "I know you are upset, but why don't we play ball together?"

...that some children escalate their tantrums to such a pitch that they become frightened of being out of control and need adult reassurance to calm down again. (In extreme cases, this may include *gentle* physical restraint.)

...how parents, knowing their children and themselves best, must be the judges of what works best for both of them (parent and child). Some parents find that temper tantrums are shorter and less intense when the child does not have an audience; others find that the child calms down faster when the parent stays in the room with him.

We *commented positively*

. . . when the parent reported not losing her temper as often when the child had a tantrum.

. . . when the parent was able to handle a tantrum calmly or when she ignored a tantrum (when the latter seemed appropriate).

. . . when the parent said she had learned not to always give in when the child tried to use a tantrum to get his way.

PROBLEM 7:   The parent was anxious and upset about the child's masturbation.

We *listened empathetically* as the parent

. . . expressed her discomfort and concern about the child's masturbation.

. . . told us that she was afraid the child would hurt himself physically and emotionally.

. . . talked about how the child became upset and masturbated even more when she tried to stop him or punished him for it.

We *discussed* with the parent

. . . that masturbation in young children is a normal part of exploration of their own bodies.

. . . that many young children masturbate at bedtime to soothe themselves.

. . . that young children will not hurt themselves unless they try to put objects in their genitals, but that that happens rarely.

. . . that some children masturbate when they are upset or bored.

. . . that masturbation usually begins in the second year of life, with boys and girls, and often continues through the preschool years.

. . . the importance of dealing casually and calmly with the child when he is masturbating so that he does not feel that he is "being bad."

. . . that there is no need for concern except: 1) when the child feels anxious or guilty about it, or 2) when the child masturbates excessively and unpredictably during the daytime, to the point where it interferes with his activities. Then, masturbation would be viewed as a symptom of a problem, usually of an emotional nature.

. . . that an increase in masturbation may occur when the child is under tension, just as other ways of seeking comfort may increase, such as thumbsucking, clinging to parent, crying.

We *commented positively*

. . . on her attitude and the calm and natural manner in which she dealt with the child's masturbation.

In cases where the child masturbated excessively...

We also *encouraged* the parent

...to observe in what situation and at what times the child masturbated most.

...to note whether the child seemed to masturbate to calm himself when he was upset or when he was tired or sleepy.

...to engage the child in activities of interest to him if boredom generally tended to lead to masturbation.

...to engage in a mutually enjoyable and quiet activity that involved close physical contact with the child, just prior to stressful events or times like bedtime, e.g., looking at books together or singing while holding the child, etc.

...to provide objects, like a favorite blanket or a soft cuddly toy, which the child could hold to comfort himself.

We *discussed* with the parent

...that much warm, physical contact with the parent may lessen the child's need to seek comfort from his own body.

PROBLEM 8:   The parent had difficulty handling the child's fears after a traumatic event.

We *listened empathetically* as the parent

...talked about how the child's behavior was very difficult for her to live with.

...expressed how inadequate she felt in trying to help the child to overcome his fears.

...talked about her anger and frustration about the child's over-reaction to certain things and events.

We *asked* the parent

...what kinds of situations tended to produce fear in the child.

...whether the fears the child exhibited were new or if he had always shown slight fears in the same areas in which he was so very fearful now.

...whether the child tended to have strong or intense reactions to events.

...how she handled the child when he was fearful and what his responses were.

...if she found that some of her methods were more effective than others.

We *discussed* with the parent

...that most children need time to overcome fears.

...that with some help the child would gradually learn to trust his environment again.

...that after a traumatic event it was natural for children to generalize their fear to other objects or situations of which they had not previously been afraid.

...that many parents find that if the adults around the child are supportive, the child will overcome his fears in a reasonable time.

...that the child needs to be exposed very gradually to what he fears while a trusted adult holds him or is in physical contact with him.

...that reassurance from closeness to or physical contact with the parent helps him overcome his fears.

...that showing impatience or forcing the child into feared situations often worsens the fears.

...that children's fears often persist for longer periods if the family members make fun of their fearfulness.

...the need for the parent to accept the child with his fear, and, at the same time, to help him deal with it in a supportive, calm, and reassuring manner, e.g., "I know that you feel afraid (of the elevator). Come, I will hold your hand—it won't hurt you."

...a way to expose the child gradually to potentially upsetting situations, e.g., when the child was afraid of animals after a dog had jumped up on him:

1. Show the child a picture of a dog and talk about it.
2. Show the child the dog from a distance while holding his hand and talking to the child.
3. Play with the dog while the child watches from afar.
4. Encourage the child to give the parent food for the dog.
5. Model patting the dog when the child is close.
6. Hold the dog and encourage the child to pat it if he wants to.
7. Hold the dog so it will not move suddenly, and encourage the child to feed it.

We *modeled*

...accepting the child's feelings and also expressing confidence that he would soon get over his fear, e.g., "Yes, that is scary for you, but soon you won't be afraid of it any more."

...talking to the child in a calm and reassuring manner when he showed fear.

...handling the feared object or animal ourselves and verbalizing to the child about what we were doing, without suggesting that he handle it.

We *commented positively*

...when the parent accepted the child's feelings of fear and reassured him rather than making fun of him.

...when the parent reported that the child was beginning to react less intensely to situations that had produced fear only a short while ago.

PROBLEM 9: **The parent was upset because the child would not share his toys with other children.**

We *listened empathetically* as the parent

...expressed her concern about having a "selfish" child.

...talked about how embarrassed she felt when her child did not share, even when another child was his visitor.

We *discussed* with the parent

...how saying *no* and *mine* is a normal and expected behavior during the second year of life and that the child was not being "naughty."

...that as the child begins to see himself as a separate person and establishes his identity, he begins to assert his power as an individual: saying *no* and *mine* is an important part of that process.

...that the unwillingness to share was a common behavior up to about age 3, though some children are able to share earlier.

...that a child who does not want to share at age 2 will not necessarily be a selfish adult.

...that some children learn to share more readily after their right to dispose over *their* things has been supported by the parent, e.g., "Yes, this is your toy, and you don't have to share it if you don't want to."

...that sharing a new or favorite toy at an early age is particularly difficult, and that sometimes children are more willing to share something after having had the chance to consider it their own for a while.

...that some parents find that letting the child choose which new or favorite toys to put away before other children visit creates a more congenial play atmosphere.

...that sharing can be easier for some children if they have a choice in what to share.

...that making a child feel he will be protected from losing a toy until he is finished playing with it may make it easier for him to relinquish it.

...that reassuring her child that she will not let the other child take the toy home with him might make him more relaxed and willing to share.

...that large equipment for gross motor play is more conducive to sharing than small toys before age 2 or 3.

...that in outdoor play, ownership and "territory" are usually much less of an issue than in indoor play.

PROBLEM 10:   The parent was concerned about the child's aggressiveness toward other children and was uncertain about how to deal with it.

We *listened empathetically* as the parent

. . .expressed how embarrassed she felt when her child hit or bit another child.
. . .talked about how shocked she was to see her child hurt another child.

We *discussed* with the parent

. . .that the infant usually does not understand that he is hurting the other child when he kicks, hits, or pushes and that he usually does not intentionally hurt the other child.
. . .that sometimes hitting or pushing is part of the infant's experimenting with how to get reactions from other children.
. . .that infants often do not know how to approach their peers in an "acceptable" manner, but express their interest in them by pulling their hair, pushing or hitting them, or snatching a toy away from them.
. . .that children need lots of social experience to learn how to interact with each other.
. . .that the child learns gradually that he cannot always have a toy the instant he wants it.
. . .that the child needs the adult's help in learning to delay gratification.
. . .that conflicts between children before they are able to share can be decreased by providing more than one toy of a kind.
. . .that gross motor activities using age-appropriate equipment often help children to learn to play alongside each other and to interact with each other.
. . .that most young children are aggressive or assertive about protecting their territory or toys, but that this is a passing stage.

We *modeled* (in situations with other children)

. . .touching the child gently and talking about it, e.g., "This is the way it feels to be touched gently."
. . .showing the child how to touch another child gently by guiding his hand.
. . .staying close to the child and redirecting rough approaches to other children before they got upset.
. . .talking to the child about his interest in the other child, e.g., "Yes, I know you like Johnny but you can't sit on top of him."
. . .talking softly to the child about how he was hurting the other child, e.g., "When you pinch like that, you hurt Johnny."
. . .holding the child and talking to him reassuringly when he has to wait for a toy that he wants.

In cases where the child was older...

We also *discussed* with the parent

... that it is not easy for the child to handle conflicts verbally, and that he learns to do this gradually with much adult modeling and help.
... that the child sometimes gets overwhelmed by his emotions and forgets about less physical ways of handling conflicts.
... that it is important for the child to learn gradually that words can help him to settle conflicts.
... that the child often needs the adult's help in learning to control himself.
... that adult modeling of how to use language to resolve conflict encourages the child to do the same.
... that watching a lot of aggression on TV has been found to encourage children's aggressive behavior.

We also *modeled* (in situations with other children)

... accepting the child's feelings and yet letting him know that his behavior was not acceptable, e.g., "I know you are angry at him but I cannot let you kick him!"
... redirecting the child to an acceptable way of expressing his feeling, e.g., hitting a block, a pile of clay, a punching bag, etc.
... encouraging the child to use words to express his feelings, e.g., "Tell him you don't want to play with him now," or "Tell him you would like to play with this toy too."
... removing the child gently from the group for a short time if he needs time to calm down, e.g., "Why don't you go outdoors and run or ride a tricycle for a while."
... staying with the child if he is so excited that he needs the adult's help to calm down.
... encouraging the child to think of alternative ways of reaching his goal.

PROBLEM 11: The parent was uncertain about how to help the child adjust to the arrival of the new baby.

We *listened empathetically* as the parent

... expressed worry that the child would feel displaced by the new baby.
... shared her fear about not being able to cope with a newborn and a toddler who would be upset and difficult to handle.

We *asked* the parent

... what she anticipated to be the areas of greatest difficulty with the child.

...whether she had thought about how she might help the child adjust to the baby and, at the same time, make things easier for her.

...whether she had already told the child about the baby and, if so, what she had said to him.

We *discussed* with the parent

....why it was important to let the child know about the baby ahead of time and how she might talk to him about this.

...that there was no need to introduce the subject of the new baby very early during the pregnancy because the toddler's sense of time is different from the adult's.

...that the child might be helped to recognize the reality of the expected baby by being allowed to feel the fetus kicking in the mother's abdomen, if she felt comfortable letting him do that.

...that preparing the child for the baby's arrival would certainly help him, but that he might still be a little more difficult to handle while he was making the adjustment.

...that the child should know a little ahead of time (how long ahead depends on the child's age) that his mother would be going to the hospital for a few days.

...how it might help the child to be familiar and comfortable with the person who would be taking care of him while the mother was in the hospital.

...that, if the child were not to stay in his own home during his mother's stay in the hospital, it would help him to have some of his favorite toys, blanket, etc., and some objects belonging to his mother that he could "keep" for her until she returns.

...that if he were not to stay in his own home during the mother's hospitalization, it would be important for him to be familiar with the home in which he would be staying and the bed in which he would be sleeping.

...that the separation from the mother might be less traumatic if he could talk to her on the telephone.

...how some children express disappointment when they first see the baby because, "He is so little and won't be able to play with me."

...that it may help the child to be given a new toy that is interesting to him on the day the mother and baby come home.

...that if the child is ready to sleep in a bed a few weeks before the baby is born, this might help to prevent his feeling displaced when the baby sleeps in the crib.

...that the mother should not be surprised if the child suggests returning the baby to the hospital after a few days.

...that many children enjoy a baby doll with which they can act out both affection and aggression.

...that allowing the child to express the normal feelings of anger and jealousy about the new baby may help him to feel accepted, less upset, and, therefore, easier to deal with.

...that the child may enjoy being allowed to help with the baby, e.g., bring diapers, clothes, but that this should not be expected of him if he shows reluctance.

...that it is safer not to leave the child with the baby without supervision because the child may try to pick up the baby or try to play with him in an inappropriate way.

...how important it is for the mother to spend special times with the child every day while the baby is sleeping.

...how the child often enjoys hearing about all the things he can do that the baby cannot do.

...that the child might enjoy special outings with his father or other family members or friends.

...how it helps the child to hear positive comments on his behavior, although he may show less desirable behavior than usual.

...that parents of a new baby often tend to expect too much from the other child, forgetting that he is very young too.

...that the child might experiment with acting like a baby again in some specific ways, e.g., wanting to drink from a bottle, wear diapers again, start wetting again if he was already toilet trained, but that this would be a passing stage if the parent, anticipating it, can deal with it calmly.

...that some children react more intensely to the new baby than others, and that this may be due in large part to differences in children's temperaments.

...the kind of help and support she would need from her husband, family, and friends during the first few weeks back at home.

PROBLEM 12:   **The child's excessive persistence made it difficult for the parent to participate in his play or to increase the variety of his experiences. ("Excessive" indicates here that the behavior is not desirable and *may* be symptomatic of a problem because of its intensity.)**

We *listened empathetically* as the parent

...described how hurt she felt when her child rejected her attempts to play with him.

...expressed frustration over the child's "stubbornness" and lack of interest in having an adult interact with him in play.

...described how irritated she felt when she tried to talk to the child about what he was doing and he would not pay any attention to her.

...related how it exasperated her when he became furious with a toy which frustrated him but would not let her help him with it.

...talked about how difficult it was for her when the child cried and had a tantrum whenever she had to interrupt him in an activity even after he had been with it for a long time.

...described the difficulties that the child's excessive persistence (not only in play) was causing in family activities such as mealtimes, outings, etc.

...talked about how hard it was to take the child anywhere, e.g., "He screams when I try to take him out of the car; he wants to keep on riding."

We *asked* the parent

...which situations or objects seemed to produce the child's excessive persistence.

...about situations or times in which she was able to help the child change activities.

...what methods she had tried to help the child move on to other activities and which had been successful.

We *experimented*

...with ways of participating in the child's activities that he found acceptable or even interesting, e.g., talking dramatically about what he was doing or combining a new toy with the one he had to make his play more interesting.

...with play activities that might encourage the child to interact with an adult, e.g., handing the child blocks one by one, or playing next to the child with the same toy the child had and doing interesting things with it.

We *discussed* with the parent

...how we could understand her problem with the child because he also made it difficult for us to interact with him in play.

...that the child's ignoring her when she tried to initiate interactions did not necessarily mean that he did not want to interact with her at all, but that it took him a long time to "shift gears."

...that she might have to be "persistent" herself in trying to initiate interactions with him.

...that it might be wise to find situations in which he was most open to interactions with others, e.g., mealtimes, bathing, diapering.

...that it might work better to interact with him in play before he got too involved with a toy.

...that even though the child did not seem to "need" her while he was playing, it would be a good idea for him to find out that it can also be fun to have others occasionally involved in his play.

...how at first a gross motor activity might be the easiest one in which to become involved with him.

...the value of having the next activity ready when she had to interrupt the child's activity.

We *commented positively*

...when the parent found ways of moving the child on to a new activity without upsetting him.

...as she described her attempts to continue taking the child out of the house even though his behavior often embarrassed her.

We *modeled*

...helping the child change from perseverative play to another activity by engaging him in vigorous motor play during the transition, e.g., help the child take giant steps to other part of the room or pick the child up and play a "one, two, three" tossing game with him.

...playing alongside the child without making an effort to interact with him at first, to see if he would become interested.

...offering the child another toy that he could incorporate in his play, e.g., give him a truck as he is playing with blocks.

...talking to the child about what he is doing without trying to direct him.

...showing some persistence in efforts to get the child to attend to an adult at times that seem opportune, e.g., when he is looking around.

...preparing the next activity so that the child would have something to focus on immediately after he had to give up a toy.

We *encouraged* the parent

...to continue her efforts to find ways of helping the child accept and even enjoy interaction with her during some activities.

...to share with us her experiences in her future efforts with him.

...to continue to expose the child to some unfamiliar activities and experiences even if he first reacted negatively.

PROBLEM 13: The parent was not aware that the child needed help in adjusting to a new caregiving situation.

We *listened empathetically* as the parent

...described how the infant screamed when she left him with the new daycare provider.

...talked about how embarrassed she had been about the infant's behavior because she had wanted him to be particularly "good" the first time in the daycare home so that he would be welcome there.

...talked about her fear that the new caregiver would not be willing to care for the infant if he continued to "act up" and cry.

We *discussed* with the parent

...that it might help the infant to get to know the new caregiver in a social setting first, e.g., parent and caregiver having coffee together or meeting her in the park.

...that young children can usually accept and trust a new person sooner if they can become familiar with her while the parent is there.

...that it might help the infant to be able to explore the new home in the presence of his parent.

...that allowing the infant to take his favorite toy, blanket, and possibly something belonging to the parent with him to the family daycare home might make him feel more secure.

...that it is a good idea to familiarize the caregiver with the infant's routine at home, e.g., usual nap time, routine for getting the child to go to sleep, mealtimes, favorite foods, etc.

...that it might help the caregiver to meet the infant's needs if the parent familiarized her with how the child indicates his wants and needs, how he expressed frustration, boredom, and fatigue, what his special likes and dislikes are.

...that it might be easier for the infant to adjust to a new caregiver if the parent and caregiver could establish some consistency in certain care-taking practices at home and in the daycare situation.

...that the infant might adjust more easily if he were left in the new environment for only an hour or so the first time.

...how adjustment to a new caregiver takes time and that the parent should not expect the infant to accept the new situation immediately.

...that the infant may trust the new caregiver sooner if the caregiver is aware of how the parent comforts the infant when he is irritable or upset, e.g., giving him his pacifier, his blanket, rocking him, taking him for a walk.

...that it might help the child to be allowed to express his feelings about the new caregiving situation and to be told that the parent understands how he feels.

...that it might help the child to be told ahead of time where he would be staying while the mother is at work.

...that it is helpful to children to be told in concrete terms when the parent will be back, e.g., "After you take a nap, then have a snack, and play for a little while, Mommy will be back."

...that eventually the child will adapt and accept going with the parent to the family daycare home.

...that some day, he may have such a good time with the other children that she will have a difficult time getting him to return home with her!

PROBLEM 14:   The parent did not respond to the infant's signal of distress (did not give comfort even after lengthy crying and/or when he hurt himself).[1]

We *observed*

...carefully to see whether the parent's unresponsiveness was a general pattern or whether the failure to respond to the infant was confined to one area, such as crying after being put down or as a result of minor bumps.

...whether the parent seemed to enjoy the infant most of the time.

...whether the parent responded to the infant's signals of pleasure and how she did this.

...whether the infant's expressions of distress were easy to read.

...whether the infant's crying intensified or diminished when not responded to.

...whether the infant could be soothed easily.

We *listened empathetically* as the parent

...expressed irritation at the infant's crying.

...stated her belief that the infant had to learn to take care of himself.

...talked about not wanting a spoiled child.

We *asked* the parent

...whether she could usually tell why the infant was crying.

...whether she knew when his crying indicated that something was really wrong or that something was bothering him.

...whether the infant let her know what he liked and disliked and how he did this.

We *discussed* with the parent

...how crying was the only way that young infants can let adults know that they need something or that something is bothering them.

...that infants tend to be happier and easier to care for later when their distress is responded to promptly in the early months.

...that responding to a young infant's crying will not spoil him.

...the possible needs the infant might be expressing by crying.

---

[1] It should be noted that the kind of crying referred to here was not excessive. If it had been excessive and if the infant(s) had been difficult to soothe (after 9 months of age), the staff's response would have been different. Prolonged and intense crying after the first 3 months of life may be part of a more extensive pattern of developmental problems or disabilities that require medical attention and diagnosis. Parents of infants who cry incessantly over a period of several months would need the kind of help and support that would make it easier for them to tolerate this stressful situation. None of the infants in the Intervention Program of the UCLA Infant Studies Project exhibited this kind of stressful crying by 10 months of age, the age when the staff began seeing the infants and their parents.

...that by responding to an infant's distress cry the adult helps the infant feel that the world can be trusted and that this trust makes him feel safe later to explore and learn from his environment when he is older.

We *commented positively*

...on the way the infant showed pleasure in being with her.
...on the way in which the parent responded to the infant's expression of pleasure.
...when the parent talked about the infant's likes, dislikes, routine, and rhythm, e.g., "You really are able to read many of his signals and know what to expect from him."
...whenever the parent helped the infant get through situations that might cause him distress, e.g., when she provided a toy when the infant was irritable while she was diapering him or when she held the infant when he showed fear at a stranger's approach.

We *encouraged* the parent

...to respond to the infant's crying by attempting to interpret for her the infant's signals, e.g., "You just want to be close to your Mommy!"

In cases where the infant's crying was difficult to interpret...

We also *discussed* with the parent

...that the cues of some infants are less clear than the cues of others.
...that even though the infant expressed distress only mildly and was therefore easier to ignore, he needed to be responded to just like infants who express distress more vigorously, so that he would continue to express his needs.
...that having his crying responded to would teach him that trying to "tell Mommy something" is worth the effort and that expecting her responses to distress signals (crying) would lead him to develop language because he could then also expect responses to his vocalizations and later to his verbalizations.

We *observed* with the parent

...whether his cues for distress were consistent.
...the subtle cues the infant gave when he appeared to be in distress, e.g., frowning, turning away, or faint intermittent sounds.
...when the infant appeared to give unclear signals of distress, and we talked about what he might be trying to communicate.

We *modeled*

...talking to the infant about what he might be feeling, e.g., "You are tired now, aren't you?" or "You don't want me to come too close," or "You want a change of scenery, you are bored."

...being animated and expressive when interacting with the infant when he was not crying.

...showing the infant how to indicate wants by nodding or shaking his head (12-month-old).

PROBLEM 15:   The parent did not set any limits for the child.

We *listened empathetically* as the parent

...said that she was going to try not to be as "strict" and unreasonable as her parents had been.

...expressed her ambivalent feelings about always giving in to the child.

...described how overwhelmed she was by her child.

...expressed resentment that the child was so unreasonable and demanding.

...related her embarrassment when the child was unmanageable in public.

...talked about how angry she felt about some of the demands the child was making.

...described how the child's behavior often disrupted their family life.

...expressed doubts about whether she was doing the right thing by being so permissive with the child.

We *asked* the parent

...how she thought the child was reacting to not having any limits or restrictions.

...about her expectations for the child in terms of his ability to get along with others in social situations and at school.

...which of the child's demands she thought were not beneficial for the child, were dangerous, or were particularly disruptive to the family.

...which of the child's behaviors were particularly irritating to her.

...in which areas she would like to set limits for the child and which were her highest priorities.

We *discussed* with the parent

...that it may be confusing for children not to be stopped from an activity that they sense is disruptive or upsetting to their parents.

...that when parents allow a child to do things that bother them, they often begin to resent the child, and that this can damage their relationship with him.

...that children who encounter no limits are sometimes frightened of their own power, and, in their own way, ask to be stopped by behaving in a totally unacceptable manner.

...that it is an important learning experience for the child to realize that he cannot always do what he wants and that he has to adapt to a "community of others."

...that a child who never encounters limits forms unrealistic expectations about the world.

...that children who know what their limits are seem to feel safe emotionally and are happier in their interaction with others, and that they adapt to school more easily.

...that reasonable and fairly consistent limits make a child feel secure and free him to pursue his interests within the established boundaries, e.g., knowing that he is not allowed to carry sand into the house, the child gets involved in elaborate sand play in the sandbox.

...that children need to know what is expected of them and what is acceptable to others.

...that a child is likely to feel a sense of self-worth when he is able to meet the parent's reasonable expectations.

...that even though setting some limits at first may be difficult for the parent and for the child, it would improve their relationship in the long run.

...that although it is often wise to distract the young infant from unacceptable activities, distracting the child as he gets older prevents him from learning what is O.K. and what is not O.K. with the parent.

...that most parents find it easier to set limits in one area first and then in another, so that the child can learn to adjust to limits gradually.

...ways of enforcing limits without using punishment or demeaning the child (see Problem 16).

...that she should be clear in her own mind that the limits she is setting are valid ones, because children sense when the parent feels uncertain about the wisdom of setting or enforcing a limit.

We *commented positively*

...when the parent set age-appropriate limits in matters of safety.

...when the parent expressed relief that the child was accepting the limits she was setting.

...when the parent stated that she was enjoying her child more.

We *modeled*

...setting limits with regard to our own person or possessions, e.g., "No, I won't let you have my purse, but you can have this toy," or "No, you can't hit my face, but you can pat my hand."

...setting limits with regard to where certain play materials could be used, e.g., "We can only paint with water outside."

...setting limits in the use of play materials, e.g., "You can build with blocks, but I can't let you throw them," or "Let's use our hands on the tambourine, not this sharp stick."

PROBLEM 16:   The parent had no control over the child (was unsuccessful in enforcing limits).

We *listened empathetically* as the parent

...talked about how the child was "getting into trouble" all the time and nothing she said or did seemed to make any difference.

...expressed frustration that she had so little control over her young child.

...talked about how upset she was when the child broke something she valued.

...expressed worry about what would happen when the child became older if she could not control him while he was so young.

We *asked* the parent

...what usually happened when the child got "into trouble."

...how she had tried to enforce limits.

...whether she had been able to modify any of the child's undesirable behavior and how she had done this where she succeeded.

...whether she thought the child could tell that she disapproved of an activity.

...which of the child's behaviors she was anxious to stop or modify and which limits she considered most essential.

We *discussed* with the parent

...that it was important to convey a clear message to the child and that laughing and saying "no" at the same time might be confusing to him.

...that the adult's tone of voice and demeanor, when setting limits, communicates to the child whether the adult is serious about it or not.

...that high priority limits should be set first, e.g., those essential to the child's safety and that of others, and that other limits should be introduced and enforced gradually because the young child cannot handle too many limits at one time.

...that the young child learns verbal limits when they are combined with actions that clearly define them, e.g., saying, "No, you can't have this knife," while removing it from his hands.

...that the child is more likely to respond to limits if the adult is physically close to him and gets down to his level as she talks to him.

. . . that it may be necessary to enforce the limit calmly and firmly many times before the child learns and internalizes it.

. . . that children need the security of knowing that the parents will follow up on the limits that they set and will enforce them.

. . . that it may help to offer the child an alternative activity when he has been stopped from doing something unacceptable, e.g., "You can't play with this glass, but here are the coasters to play with."

. . . that children will learn faster and adapt to limits more easily if the parents set and enforce reasonable limits fairly consistently.

. . . that being consistent in enforcing limits did not mean that she could not make occasional exceptions when circumstances demanded it.

In cases where the parent's methods of disciplining were inappropriate for the child's developmental level . . .

We also *discussed* with the parent

. . . that some problems can be solved by putting valuable objects out of reach until the infant gets older.

. . . that an infant may react to the tone of "no" and stop what he is doing, but that he does not really understand what is being prohibited and therefore cannot remember the limit at subsequent times.

. . . that usually it is necessary to remove an infant from the situation or take away the object in addition to saying "no."

. . . how with the younger infant, it is especially important to substitute something acceptable when taking the forbidden object away and that when language accompanies the adult act, the infant understands best, e.g., "This stick is too sharp for you, but you can have the spoon."

. . . that isolating a young child as a consequence of violating a limit is more effective if done for a very short period of time (no more than a few minutes) because of his limited concept of time.

. . . that most young children interpret physical punishment as an expression of the parent's anger, but they often will not know or remember the cause of the parent's anger.

. . . that as children grow older and change, it is often necessary to reevaluate limits set for them to make sure that they are still developmentally appropriate.

We *modeled*

. . . setting limits in the use of play materials, e.g., "We can't throw the ball indoors, but we can roll it instead."

. . . getting close to the child and making eye contact with him when setting a limit.

. . . speaking seriously but calmly to the child when setting a limit.

PROBLEM 17:   The parent was punitive in disciplining the child (yelled, threatened, slapped, took toys away).

We *listened empathetically* as the parent

...expressed frustration about living with a small child.

...said that she felt the child was deliberately trying to make her angry.

...told us that no matter how loudly she yelled, the child would not "mind" her.

...said that children need to learn to mind at an early age.

...talked about how she felt a release of tension when she "screamed" at the child.

...said that spanking seemed to clear the air and that it had not harmed her to get spanked when she was a child.

We *asked* the parent

...which situations seemed to result in confrontations between her and the child.

...whether she thought the child always understood what was expected of him.

...how the child reacted when he was punished.

...whether she had found her methods of disciplining effective.

...what alternative methods she had thought of trying.

We *discussed* with the parent

...that many parents experience similar feelings of anger and exasperation when they feel that their children deliberately try to make them angry, but that this intent rarely exists in young children.

...that young children have a strong drive to explore their environment and do not usually do this to provoke their parents, but that exploring things often gets children into situations which are unacceptable.

...how children learn by imitating their parents, and when a parent yells or slaps, the child learns to use the same kind of behavior.

...that many parents find that when they discipline their children often by hitting, they have trouble later when their children frequently hit other children.

...that many parents find it easier to anticipate troublesome situations with their children and try to prevent them rather than react strongly after the children have gotten into trouble.

...some alternative ways of setting limits and enforcing them and which of these she might feel comfortable in trying (see Problems 15 and 16).

...that setting limits requires a great deal of thought and helping the young child learn them takes much adult patience.

...that sometimes a child persists in doing something the parent does not want him to do in order to get her attention.

...that if the child seems to "misbehave" to get attention, it would be important to make sure that the child can count on some "special time" with the parent every day, no matter how short the period has to be.

...that children learn limits faster if the consequence of violating them is logical, e.g., remove food if the child throws it.

...that children learn to accept certain limits better when logical reasons are given for them, e.g., "I cannot let you drink this because it would make you very sick."

We *modeled*

...setting limits non-punitively after providing materials that required that limits be set, e.g., sand, paint, water.

We *encouraged* the parent

...to try alternative methods of setting and enforcing limits and to tell us which felt comfortable to her and which seemed to work best.

In cases where the parent had age-inappropriate expectations for the child's behavior . . .

We also *asked* the parent

...what kinds of behavior she expected of her child.

...whether she thought the child understood what she expected of him.

...what indications the child gave that made her think that he was able to live up to her expectations.

We also *discussed* with the parent

...what kinds of behavior could realistically be expected at the child's stage of development. For example,
1. It is natural for a 6-month-old infant to mouth objects.
2. Few 15-month-old children can eat neatly.
3. It is difficult for a 20-month-old child to be quiet for a long time while the adult is doing something in the same room that requires silence.

..that some parents decide to avoid certain situations where the child's behavior might be particularly irritating to them, e.g., taking him to a restaurant, taking him shopping to a department store.

...how to find opportunities to get together with other parents and their young children.

...what places in the community she could visit to observe other children of similar age and maturity, like the park, a recreation center, or parent-infant or parent-toddler groups.

In cases where the parent seemed to be excessively harsh with the child . . .

We also *listened empathetically* as the parent

. . . talked about how angry she felt when the child expressed negative feelings.

. . . talked about how frustrated she often felt, having to deal with this child 24 hours a day.

. . . talked about how badly she felt after she had punished the child more harshly than she had meant to.

We *asked* the parent

. . . whether she could pinpoint the areas of the child's behavior that made her particularly angry and upset, and then find ways of avoiding situations that evoked these behaviors.

We also *discussed* with the parent

. . . how easy it is to feel frustrated and angry with a young child when one is isolated and has no one to talk to.

. . . that there are groups in the community where parents, who feel isolated and frustrated with their young children, can share their experiences and help each other.

. . . that it is important for parents who tend to punish their children more severely than they mean to, to get help from groups in the community because harsh punishment can inflict injury to the child without the parent being aware of this.

. . . particular resources in her own community where she could get help. (When there is sufficient evidence to suspect child abuse, California law dictates that physicians, nurses, teachers, and other professionals contact Protective Services in the Department of Public Social Services or, in the case of an emergency, the Protective Services division of the local police department.)

We *encouraged* the parent

. . . to call us or a friend when she was faced with a particularly difficult problem with her child, or when she felt especially tense and upset with the child.

. . . to get out of the house with the child occasionally to keep tensions from building up.

. . . to try to find a babysitter so that she could occasionally get away from the child.

. . . to follow up on one or more of the resources provided for her before she loses control over her angry feelings and does something she might regret.

PROBLEM 18:   The parent did not allow the child to make choices or to have control over any aspect of his daily life.

We *listened empathetically* as the parent

...expressed irritation at the many battles she and the child were having over daily routines.

...talked about how she had enjoyed the child more before he started walking, when he was less "willful" and easier to satisfy.

...told us that the child seemed to say "no" to everything she tried to do with and for him.

We *asked* the parent

...how the child indicated his likes and dislikes.

...if she thought her child was giving indications that he wanted to do some things on his own.

...whether there were situations in which battles arose rarely, and what she thought the difference was between those situations and the ones that tended to provoke conflict.

We *discussed* with the parent

...that it was common for pre-verbal children to indicate their likes and dislikes in physical ways, e.g., spitting out food, turning their head away, pushing toys away.

...that most children want to have some control over their bodies and their actions well before they can verbalize these feelings.

...how some of the child's first verbalizations, like *me do it, no,* and *mine,* indicate that the child is beginning to have a sense of self and is ready to make some choices.

...that many parents find it difficult and confusing to go through the transition from the child's total dependence to his wanting to do some things for and by himself.

...that many parents experience that frictions tend to be reduced when the young child who is struggling toward autonomy is allowed to make some decisions about himself that involve simple choices.

...that some children who are allowed to make simple choices when they are ready seem to become independent earlier, e.g., dressing, self-feeding, picking up own toys.

...that parents can prepare their child to make reasonable choices later by acknowledging his likes and dislikes verbally, e.g., "I guess you really like applesauce." or "I can see that you don't like this teddy bear as well as you like this little box."

...that most young children can handle only simple choices between two alternatives, e.g., "Do you want to wear the blue or the red shirt to-day?"

...that she should offer choices only in areas where she is willing to accept the child's choice, e.g., give choice of what to eat or wear but not about bedtime or TV watching.

...that the child will gain confidence and the ability to make choices if the parent is able to acknowledge and respect his choices.

...that giving choices to the young child may be harder in large families because there are so many people to be considered, but that it is important for the child to have a voice in some areas that concern him directly.

...that making choices for himself in the early years may help the child to be more self-reliant and responsible for himself later on.

We *modeled*

...acknowledging and respecting the child's decision, e.g., "I see that you want to look at this book now."

...offering the child a simple choice, e.g., "Do you want the beads or this little truck next?"

PROBLEM 19:   The parent discussed the child's problems, or expressed annoyance about him, in his presence.

We *asked* the parent

...how much she thought the child understood when she talked about him.

...how he would indicate that he did understand the gist of the conversation about him or feelings expressed, e.g., by raising his head when he heard his name, looking at her, quieting and stopping his activity.

We *discussed* with the parent

...that most children understand in their second year the tone if not the exact content of what the parent says, which is much earlier than most people realize.

...that discussing certain problems in areas like toilet training or discipline in front of the child may create additional tension in him and therefore make it more difficult for him to overcome the problem.

...that she should not hesitate to express her feelings directly to the child when he does things that she does not like or approve of. (This point must be carefully handled with parents who are very physical in their negative responses to the child or who are at risk for child abuse.)

...that parents need opportunities to express their annoyance with their children to other adults.

...that it would feel more comfortable talking about the child's problems and the parent's difficulties with him at a time when the child was not present, e.g., over the telephone or at an evening visit.

. . . ways of talking about positive things the child does, in his presence and including him in the conversation, e.g., "Richie is so great about helping me pick up his toys, aren't you, Richie?"

We *modeled*

. . . acknowledging that the child was listening by including him in the conversation, e.g., "You like to hear what Mommy says about you, don't you?"

. . . involving the child with interesting toys when discussion about him in his presence could not be avoided.

. . . cutting short certain discussions of problems in front of the child and planning to talk about certain matters over the phone or arranging for an evening visit when the child would be asleep.

. . . showing awareness of the child's feelings about what was being discussed by changing the subject when he seemed to be listening.

We *commented positively*

. . . when the parent telephoned while the child was asleep to discuss her frustrations about him.

. . . when the parent changed the subject as she noticed that the child was listening to her complaints about him.

. . . when the parent incorporated the child in the conversation as she was saying nice things about him.

PROBLEM 20:   The parent of a child with a handicap or a delay in language and/or motor development was not able to focus or capitalize on his strengths.

Before trying to help the parent focus on the child's strengths. . .

We *listened empathetically* as the parent

. . . talked about her worries regarding the child's development.

. . . talked about her observations of all the things the child could not do or did inappropriately.

. . . expressed her need to do something to help the child overcome his problem.

. . . talked about the frustrations of having to deal with professionals who did not understand the urgency of helping the child.

. . . talked about how upset and depressed she felt at times when she thought about the child's handicap and his future.

We *commented positively*

. . . on the parent's observational skills when she described the child's behaviors—those that concerned her and those she valued.

...on how her knowledge of the child would help professionals to meet the child's needs more effectively.

...on all her efforts to get help for the child.

...on how the parent's activities with the child were helping him, e.g., talking to the child about what was going on around him, giving him interesting toys to motivate him.

We *discussed* with the parent

...the history of the child's problem.

...the progress that the child had made recently.

...that it might help her to note and write down even little changes she observed in the child so that she could see progress over time.

...how children compensate for deficits in one area by developing strengths in other areas, and the importance of supporting and reinforcing the child's strengths.

...how many activities, seemingly unrelated to the child's problems, might work toward positive change in the child's behavior, e.g., playing social games is helpful for language development; offering the child interesting toys encourages him to move.

We *modeled*

...interacting with the child in a variety of ways, responding to his interests, and allowing him to use his skills.

...playing with the child and responding positively to his accomplishments, however minimal.

In order to refocus the parent on the child's strengths...

We *commented positively*

...on developmental changes in areas other than the ones the parent was focused on.

...on some aspects of the child that the parent had not mentioned, e.g., his bright social smile, good looks, interest in cause-and-effect toys, attentiveness to his mother's face when she talked to him.

...on ways in which the child seemed to compensate for his problem, e.g., "It is good to see that he has learned to be very persistent to make up for his difficulty in grasping objects."

...when the parent expressed pleasure in being with the child.

We *discussed* with the parent

...what the child was doing in all areas of development.

...ways in which the child was making progress.

...how important it was for the child to develop skills in his areas of strength so that he could feel successful.

...how she was helping the child by motivating him in his area of greatest strength, e.g., "He is so interested in the toys that you give him that he will develop complex play and, at the same time, practice his fine motor skills."

...how important the child's play was for his cognitive development.

We *modeled*

...playing with the child, emphasizing his strengths.

...responding with strong positive affect to the child's successes.

...playing with the child in a variety of modes, giving him help whenever he needed it to achieve his goals.

We *encouraged* the parent

...to note the child's complex play behavior and not to hesitate assisting him occasionally so that he could achieve some of the goals he was conceptualizing in his mind.

...to acknowledge the child's accomplishments in his play.

PROBLEM 21:   The child avoided eye contact as well as physical contact with parents and other adults.

We *listened empathetically* as the parent

...talked about how frustrated she felt when she tried to talk or play with the infant and he would not look at her.

...expressed her worries regarding the infant's development.

...told us how disappointed she was that the infant was not much fun to be with.

We *commented positively*

...on the parent's patience with a difficult infant.

...on the parent's enjoyment of some of her caregiving interactions with her infant, e.g., giving baths, putting lotion on him, dressing him in attractive clothes.

...when the parent experimented with ways of getting the infant to respond to her.

...on the infant's positive attributes, e.g., his good looks, his ability in the motor area.

...whenever the infant made the slightest social contact with the parent.

...on positive changes in the infant's behavior, however minimal.

We *observed* with the parent

...that the infant was also unresponsive to other adults (to alleviate her feelings of inadequacy).

...to identify subtle cues of the child, indicating when he would tolerate being picked up and held for a short period.

...to identify cues regarding when he might be most likely to respond to efforts to interact with him, e.g., when waking up from a nap or after mealtime.

We *experimented*

...with different activities that might elicit eye contact, e.g., blowing bubbles, waiting for the child to look at the adult's face before blowing, touching and patting the child, presenting interesting objects at the adult's eye level.

...with a variety of social games that might elicit eye contact, e.g., clapping game, putting on hats or glasses and taking them off again while talking animatedly to him, playing peek-a-boo, rolling a ball toward him.

...with alternating between very dramatic and then very quiet social games to discover which the child would respond to.

...with engaging the child in roughhousing to see if he would tolerate this type of contact with the adult.

...with playing active social games with the child while holding him on our lap, e.g., bouncing him while singing to him, moving his body up and down, moving his arms rhythmically.

We *discussed* with the parent

...our successes and our failures in getting social responses from the child.

...how we also felt frustrated (as she did) when we tried hard to get a response and the child just turned his head away.

...that even though the child pushed her away, he might be getting something from the interaction.

...how important it was to continue trying to get the child to respond and interact.

...any changes we or she saw, no matter how minimal, in the child's eye contact and responsiveness.

...activities that she might want to discourage because they prevented the child's involvement with people or constructive involvement with materials, e.g., highly repetitive activity, spinning of objects, long hours of watching TV.

We *modeled*

...gently touching the child's face, hands, and arms.

...prolonging any physical contact initiated by the child by gently touching and holding him briefly and attempting to make or continue eye contact before he wandered off again.

...responding immediately and positively to his eye contact.

...playing games that involved brief physical contact.

...dramatic verbal and facial interaction if he was responsive.

We *encouraged* the parent

...to repeat any of the activities and games that elicited positive responses from the child.

...to incorporate activities that seemed successful in eliciting eye contact and social responses into everyday interactions, e.g., holding toys up to adult's eye level; having child touch her face while she talked to him, while she was changing his diapers, or while she was close to him in any interaction.

...to share with us any new ways she had found to make the child interested in and responsive to her.

...to continue to include the child in some of the family's activities, e.g., meals, outings, even if he did not give a strong outward indication of participation or enjoyment.

...to take some time off for herself, away from the child, who required such effort to be with and who was emotionally draining.

:...to go out occasionally with her husband or with friends and to have time with her husband, away from the child, to renew their emotional energy.

PROBLEM 22: The parent of a child with a visible handicap or deformity avoided taking him to public places.

We *listened empathetically* as the parent

:...talked about how she really enjoyed staying home with the child.

...told us how the child could not handle being taken on outings.

...shared how upset she felt when people stared at the child.

...expressed anger at some of the "stupid" questions she had been asked about the child when she had taken him to the grocery store.

...said how she hated the expression of pity on people's faces when they looked at her child.

...talked about how people are insensitive about a child with a problem.

...talked about how difficult it was for her when the child did not behave like other children when she had taken him out.

We *discussed* with the parent

...that most parents of children with problems find the public's reaction annoying and often upsetting.

...that many parents find it helpful to talk with other parents who are in a similar position in order to share ideas about how best to deal with other people's reactions.

...that parents gradually find ways of dealing comfortably with other people's comments that are at first painful.

...that parents usually feel that it is easier to work this problem through when the child is young than to wait until he is older—that it becomes more difficult the longer one waits.

...that she might find the child happier and more contented if she took him out of the house occasionally.

...that children enjoy seeing new places and people, and that this is a good learning experience for them.

...that many parents enjoy staying home with a small baby, but that they often start feeling "cooped up" when the child gets older.

...that if she or her husband continucs to have difficulty dealing with strangers' reactions to the child and emotionally coping with this experience, they may want to consider seeking professional help in their own community (group or individual counseling; resources are suggested if parent shows interest).

We *asked* the parent (after a lapse of time)

...how the child reacted when she took him to the home of friends.

...if the child had shown interest in children and unfamiliar adults.

...whether people's reactions or questions continued to bother her as before or whether she was beginning to find ways to handle these as well as her own feelings about them.

...what kinds of responses to questions or reactions she had found to be most satisfactory.

We *commented positively*

...on the child's positive attributes and strengths.

...when the parent talked about having friends and children visit.

...when the parent talked about having taken the child with her to visit friends and to go to the grocery store.

...when the parent told us how she had responded to strangers' questions about her child and how proud she felt that she was able to handle it and feel good about it.

PROBLEM 23: The child's deviant, autistic-like behavior was difficult for the parent to tolerate.

We *listened empathetically* as the parent

...told us how difficult it was to live with the child.

...expressed how exhausting it was to be in the same house with this child and to take care of him day in and day out.

We *commented positively*

...on how well she was managing with a very difficult child.
...when the parent found things to do with the child that they could both enjoy, e.g., singing to him for brief times when he would sit on her lap, talking to him softly when they went on walks together.
...on the child's positive attributes and strengths at those times when he was not engaging in autistic-like behavior.
...when the parent experimented with ways to intervene and decrease the child's most annoying behavior.

We *asked* the parent

...whether she detected any pattern as to when the deviant behavior was most intense or continuous.
...what usually preceded an increase or a decrease in deviant behavior.
...whether she had been aware of differences in his behavior when his sugar intake was either high or low.

We *experimented*

...to find activities that helped the child function more normally, e.g., certain kinds of manipulative play, doll play, outdoor climbing equipment.
...to find ways to stop the deviant behavior at least for a while, e.g., change the child's environment by taking him to another room or outside, play soothing music, chant or sing to the child, take him for a short walk.
...to find activities that were incompatible with the child's bouts of screaming or making continuous gutteral sounds, e.g., engage child in playful vocalization, blow bubbles, blow feathers.

We *discussed* with the parent

...possible ways of minimizing conditions or altogether avoiding situations that tended to bring on the child's most intolerable behavior.
...how her efforts to find ways to lengthen periods of more normal behavior were as important for the child as they were for herself because the child isolated himself from opportunities to learn from his environment while he was engaging in these autistic-like behaviors.
...that this behavior that was so difficult to tolerate was likely to diminish at least some as a result of all her efforts, many of which seemed quite effective.

We *encouraged* the parent

...to take some time for herself away from the child on a regular basis.

...to pursue some personal interest of hers at least once or twice a week away from home, so that she could have those times to look forward to during the trying periods with her difficult child.

...to tell us about any changes that she experienced with her child, no matter how minimal they might seem to her.

...to share with us anything new that she might have tried with her child and that seemed to be effective.

PROBLEMS IN THE COGNITIVE-MOTIVATIONAL AREA

1   The parent did not understand the importance of play and did not provide play materials appropriate for the infant's skill level.

2   The parent did not provide adequate play space and did not make play materials easily available for the infant.

3   The parent was not aware of the infant's play needs and individual interests.

4   The parent was not sensitive to the infant's intent or goals in play. Her play interactions with him were non-contingent and controlling.

5   The parent did not know how to deal with the child's slow tempo in play.

6   The infant showed no interest in play with objects.

7   The infant's play was primitive for his age and the parent did not know how to help him raise the level of his play.

8   The child's short attention span interfered with his ability to get satisfaction from his play.

9   The infant did not initiate play with materials and was mostly a passive observer.

10   The child's unusual behavior (perseverative and self-stimulating activity) made it difficult for the parent to provide for his cognitive-motivational needs.

PROBLEM 1: **The parent did not understand the importance of play and did not provide play materials appropriate for the infant's skill level.**

We *asked* the parent

...how the infant occupied himself during the day.
...about changes in the infant's activities over the last few months.
...how the infant played with objects.
...whether the infant seemed interested in exploring objects that he found or that were given to him.

We *observed* with the parent

...how the infant played with available materials.
...the infant's interest in looking at, touching, and exploring objects.
...what skills the infant showed as he played with objects.
...the infant's delight and interest when he was given new objects that he could examine and manipulate.
...how the infant showed different and more advanced skills if given toys with which he could make something happen, e.g., make a noise by banging two cubes together, take rings off a stick.

We *modeled*

...observing the infant as he played with objects.
...showing interest in the child's play by commenting on it to him, e.g., "You took all those beads out of the bowl!"
...experimenting with a variety of play materials to see which were most interesting and challenging to the infant.
...presenting toys in different ways to arouse the infant's interest, e.g., talking about the toy as the infant played with it, demonstrating various ways a particular toy could be used.
...differentiating between toys from which the infant could get satisfaction on his own and toys with which he needed help from the adult.
...using household objects for play purposes (after asking the parent's permission to use some materials around the house).
...bringing and presenting household objects that were slightly modified to make them more challenging to the infant, e.g., cut hole in plastic coffee can lid and give child object that would fit into the hole.

We *discussed* with the parent

...that the infant's way of learning about the world is to explore and play with a variety of materials.
...that play is the infant's and young child's "work," and that it helps him to develop new skills and teaches him important concepts.

. . . how people used to think that children learned only when taught by an adult, but that now we know that children learn a great deal from their own spontaneous, self-directed play.

. . . that an activity may look purposeless to an adult usually is part of a learning sequence for the infant, e.g., infants learn how to put things into containers only after they have taken things out of containers for many weeks, over and over.

. . . how children, no matter how young, like to repeat their successes over and over again, even without reinforcement from adults.

. . . that the infant learns about properties and functions of things by playing with objects, e.g., when he puts his spoon into the cup, he is learning that things make sounds, that they fit into other things, and that they can do different things.

. . . how the infant is learning to set goals for himself and to be persistent when he pursues his goal in play, e.g., he persists in trying to put the lid on the pot until he succeeds.

. . . how much pleasure the infant gets from his successes, and how this pleasure in success reinforces goal-directed behavior that is so important for later school learning.

. . . that by playing with interesting objects, the child learns to concentrate and pay attention to his task: motivational behavior that will be very useful when he gets to school.

. . . that as the infant handles a variety of things, he lays the foundation for understanding concepts like color, shape, quantity, spatial relationships, cause and effect, etc., that will be important to him throughout life.

. . . the kinds of play that her infant seemed to be most interested in and that he attended to longest at the present time, and the kinds of play he would probably be enjoying soon.

. . . that the infant might be more satisfied and therefore easier to take care of if he had access to play materials that interested him and with which he could experience success.

. . . that there were some activities the infant could engage in on his own, whereas he would need adult help to get satisfaction from others, e.g., the infant may be able to pull pop-beads apart, but not yet be able to put them together, or he may get frustrated with toys that have more parts than he can handle.

. . . that infants and young children do not need fancy, expensive toys, but enjoy playing with many household objects, e.g., measuring spoons and cups, pots and pans and lids, coasters, empty boxes and cartons, coffee cans and lids, etc.

. . . that some basic materials which can be used in a variety of ways are particularly interesting to children and encourage more imaginative play than many expensive toys, e.g., blocks and cubes, sand, containers of all sizes.

...that children "grow out of" some toys as their skills increase, and continue to use some toys but in more complex ways, e.g., they outgrow rattles and squeak toys, but continue playing with blocks, boxes, beads, peg toys, containers.

We *commented positively*

...when the infant showed sustained interest in his play.

...when the parent pointed out the new play skills that her infant showed.

...when the parent provided a few appropriate toys or objects at the infant's skill level, which the infant enjoyed.

...when the parent became involved in playing with the infant.

...when the parent described how the infant had used a particular toy.

...when the parent chose a toy from among the ones we brought and explained why she thought the infant would be particularly interested in it.

...when the parent described how she thought the infant's skills and interests were changing.

...when the parent told us how she enjoyed watching the infant's independent play.

We *encouraged* the parent

...to engage in the kind of play with the infant that she particularly enjoyed with him.

...to decide which household objects she would allow the infant to play with, and then to make these easily accessible to him.

...to select from among the toys that we had brought to the home those that she thought the infant would enjoy playing with for a few weeks. (In response to our request that the parents pick out the toys for the infant to keep for a while, many parents would explain why they chose particular toys, and increasingly these explanations were based on the parents' accurate observations of their infants' play skills and interests.)

PROBLEM 2:   The parent did not provide adequate play space and did not make play materials easily available for the infant.

We *listened empathetically* as the parent

...said that she hated the clutter of toys around the house.

...told us that she found it impossible to keep the children's toys separate.

...said that she kept the infant's toys in his room, but that he did not like to play there.

...said that the infant often seemed cranky and bored.

We *asked* the parent

...what kinds of things the infant seemed interested in playing with.

...if the infant was able to play by himself for a while when given a few objects of interest to him.

...whether the infant was able to find his toys when they were mixed in with his older sibling's toys.

...how long the infant would stay in his own room to play.

...if she would like us to bring a shelf or box to store some of the infant's toys or if she had access to these things herself.

We *observed* with the parent

...how the infant explored and manipulated a variety of toys and household objects.

...the infant's goal-directedness and attention span when he played with objects and toys that were challenging to him, while we were talking in the same room.

...that given a limited choice of materials, the infant was able to select toys that kept him involved and interested for quite a while.

We *discussed* with the parent

...that many parents find it difficult to strike a balance between keeping their home neat and attractive and providing space and play materials for the infant in areas where the family spends time, which is where the infant usually wants to play.

...that infants usually want to be close to their parents and therefore do not want to play in their own room if it is away from everyone.

...that the infant might have an easier time learning to play independently with toys when he can be near other family members.

...that she might be able to reduce the clutter by giving the infant a few toys at a time.

...that many parents find the infant to be happier if they provide him with some playthings easily accessible in a box or on a low shelf in the family room or wherever the family spends a lot of time, or in the kitchen.

...that she might find it helpful to sort out toys with many pieces and store them in boxes that could be brought out one at a time and then picked up again easily.

...that infants learn to tolerate distraction and pursue their own goals when they can play on their own but with other people in the room.

...that infants profit by playing with a variety of objects and that they learn different skills by playing with different things, e.g., *pull* plastic beads apart; *manipulate* and *stack* cubes and rings, on or off the stick; *representational play* with household things like pots, pans, spoons, dishes, and dolls.

...that by making play materials available to the infant she was helping him develop goal-directed behavior and problem solving, both important for later school success.

We *commented positively*

...when the parent kept a number of toys easily accessible to the infant in a corner of the family's most used living space.

...when she put away toys that he did not seem to play with, e.g., old rattles and stuffed animals.

...when the infant made good use of the low shelf she had fixed for him and on which she had put a few of his currently favorite toys.

We *encouraged* the parent

...to let us know when a particular toy we had brought would be a nuisance and clutter up the house.

...to experiment with making a few playthings easily available to the infant in a family living space and to see if it worked out for the family, for herself, and for the infant.

...to let us know if problems resulted from making space and toys available for the infant so that we could discuss together how to solve them.

In cases where the parent did not allow the infant to touch or play with any of the objects around the house...

We also *listened empathetically* as the parent

...related that she was teaching the infant not to touch a variety of objects around the house so that he would learn to mind.

...told us how angry it made her that the infant seemed to want to touch and play with everything he saw.

...said how upset she was when the infant damaged or broke objects that she valued.

We *asked* the parent

...whether the infant seemed to understand when she told him not to touch objects, or, if he appeared to understand, whether she thought he would be able to remember.

...which objects seemed to be particularly attractive to the infant and why she thought he liked these so much.

We *discussed* with the parent

... that some parents seem to think that infants are deliberately destruc-
tive and disobedient, but that when they touch objects that they see,
they are simply following their natural inclination to explore and
manipulate what they see.

... that it is natural for infants to want to explore interesting things in
their environment, and that it is this inborn curiosity that helps them
to learn and grow intellectually.

... that it might be helpful and might avoid many unnecessary conflicts if
she removed breakables and objects she did not want the infant to
handle, until he became older and able to handle things more carefully
and to follow directions more reliably.

... that the infant might become afraid of approaching new things if he
were told "no" too often when he explored objects around him.

... that infants do not know the difference between "toys" and other objects and that they will try to play with whatever is in their reach.

... that when infants are discouraged from exploring and manipulating
objects in their environment, it tends to limit their opportunities to
develop intellectually.

PROBLEM 3:   **The parent was not aware of the infant's play needs and
individual interests.**

We *asked* the parent

... how the infant usually let her know what he liked.
... what kinds of toys and activities he seemed to enjoy.
... how he used some of the toys that he especially liked.
... which of the toys we had brought she thought would interest the infant.

We *observed* with the parent

... what the infant was doing with materials that were accessible to him in
his environment.
... the skills the infant showed in his play.
... which toys and household materials seemed to interest the infant but
apparently also frustrated him without adult assistance.
... that the infant seemed to prefer certain kinds of toys, e.g., those that
made sounds, those made of wood rather than plastic, objects he
could use as containers.

...that the infant was more successful in his play when he had only one toy or one part of a toy to deal with at one time.

...that the infant seemed to stay with a toy longer, or show longer attention span with a toy that he could use in a variety of ways, e.g., small boxes with tops, nesting toys, cubes and containers with lids, including pots and pans.

...cues the infant gave that indicated he was bored, overstimulated, frustrated.

...cues the infant gave that indicated pleasure in an activity, involvement, concentration, desire to get adult involved in his play.

...the range of skills or "schemas" that the infant showed in his activities and the most frequent actions he engaged in with the toys.

We *discussed* with the parent

...that while children develop skills in a set developmental sequence, especially in the first 15 months of life, at the same time, they develop different interests, toy preferences, and individual styles of using toys.

...that as the infant grows older, the pattern of his play becomes more individualized because he learns many different ways to use an object.

...that infants develop various play patterns: some like a lot of toys around them and go from one to the other easily and gain satisfaction from each toy, while others get distracted and frustrated by having a number of toys in front of them.

...how some infants like being talked to or having an adult become involved in their play, while others like the parent to be close but want to "do their own thing," but that most infants like to involve an adult in their play part of the time and play independently part of the time.

...that some infants are challenged by toys that have several parts, while others find too many parts confusing and distracting.

...that some infants can handle frustration in play and persist until they reach their goal or eventually turn away from the toy or ask for help when they cannot reach their goal on their own, whereas other infants give up easily and need adult help more often in order to prevent discouragement resulting from frequent frustration.

...that experiencing success in play is as important for the infant as success in work is for the adult, and that when an infant achieves his goals frequently, he gains more pleasure from his activity and develops problem-solving skills, task orientation, and persistence.

...that the infant's motivation in his play and the pleasure he gets from achieving his play goals lead to his motivation to learn in school later and to get pleasure from learning in school.

PROBLEM 4:   The parent was not sensitive to the infant's intent or goals in play. Her play interactions with him were non-contingent and controlling.

We *listened empathetically* as the parent

. . . said that the infant did not play with toys properly.

. . . related that sometimes the infant got upset when she tried to show him how to use a particular toy.

. . . said that sometimes she wondered whether the infant enjoyed playing with her.

We *asked* the parent

. . . what toys seemed to be particularly interesting to the infant.

. . . what happened when the infant was left to play with toys on his own.

. . . what kinds of things she thought the infant liked doing with her.

We *observed* with the parent

. . . what the infant did with his play materials.

. . . whether the infant gained satisfaction from pursuing his own goals in play.

. . . how long an object held his interest if he was allowed to explore it and experiment with it on his own.

. . . the infant's increased interest in his play when the adult followed the infant's lead as she played with him.

. . . how excited and surprised the infant seemed when he discovered by himself a new way to use a toy.

We *modeled*

. . . taking cues from the infant and accepting his use of play materials.

. . . offering the infant a toy that could be used in a variety of ways.

. . . commenting to the infant about the ways in which he used play materials rather than giving him directions, e.g., "You like to put the car in the can and then find it again!"

. . . using a toy in a variety of ways in front of the infant and then letting him do what he wanted with it.

We *discussed* with the parent

. . . that it is frustrating for many parents when an infant will not play with a toy in the way most adults seem to feel it should be used, but that infants perceive objects from the perspective of their experience, and therefore they tend to use materials in their own individual way.

. . . that she might find it enjoyable and less frustrating sometimes to watch the infant play and sometimes to play with the infant but to let him take the lead.

...that by playing alongside the infant occasionally, the adult could give the infant ideas on how materials could be used, but, at the same time, give him the opportunity to choose how he wanted to play with them.

...that some infants find it pleasurable or even amusing when the parent imitates what they do with a toy.

...that illustrations and directions on toy packages are often misleading because they show only one way of using a toy.

...that the infant's use of a toy is largely determined by where he is developmentally as well as by his individual style.

...that the infant may learn most from what *he* decides to do with a toy at a particular time.

...what the infant was learning from using a toy in the way he chose, e.g., "By mouthing the ball he learns what round feels like," or "By dropping the spoon and following it with his eyes, he learns that things are still there when they are out of reach and initially out of sight."

...that sometimes infants can be more imaginative in the use of a toy than either the toy manufacturer or the parent or the infant specialist.

We *commented positively*

...on the many ways in which the infant explored a particular toy.

...when the parent let the infant pursue his own goals, e.g., "He really seems to enjoy it when you let him take the lead in your play with him."

...when the parent expressed delight about the infant's inventive use of objects.

PROBLEM 5:   The parent did not know how to deal with the child's slow tempo in play.

We *listened empathetically* as the parent

...talked about how it "drove her up the wall" when she tried to play with the child and he would take forever to do anything.

...expressed concern about the child's intelligence because he did things so slowly.

...said that if she tried to make the child move faster, he would turn away from her and stop his activity altogether.

We *asked* the parent

...how the child reacted when he was interrupted in his play.

...if the child let her know when he wanted to stay with an activity longer than she had planned.

...whether the child also seemed to do other things slowly, like eating or going to bed at night.

We *observed* with the parent

...how long it took the child to become involved in play when he was given some toys.
...how the child indicated involvement in play.
...that the child showed more skills when he was given plenty of time to explore and experiment with materials.
...how frustrated the child seemed to get when the adult tried to move him too fast from one play activity to the next.
...that the child's play was more complex when he was given time to decide how to use materials in his own way.

We *modeled*

...presenting play materials and waiting for the child to give a signal that he was finished with a toy before giving him another one.
...sitting with the child, watching his play, and commenting in a low voice on what he was doing.

We *discussed* with the parent

...how children, just like adults, vary in how slowly or how fast they do things.
...how difficult it can sometimes be for parents to discover their own child's tempo, especially when it is different from their own.
...that when the parent's tempo is different from the child's tempo, it can be frustrating for both.
...that some children explore toys visually and decide what to do with them before they begin to play actively with them, and that this may look like lack of interest to the adult and may make the adult feel impatient for the child to *do* something.
...that some children need plenty of time with an activity to be able to experience success and feel satisfied.
...that it might help the parent to watch for the child's subtle cues of interest as he approached an activity.
...that she might find the child's play quite interesting if she sat back sometimes and observed what he did when given plenty of time.
...that the child showed considerable complexity in his play when he moved at his own speed.
...that slow tempo in play as well as in doing other things was part of his temperamental style and did not indicate low intelligence.

We *commented positively*

...when the parent allowed the child more time for an activity as she played with him.
...on the parent's enjoyment of playing with the child at *his* tempo.

...on the child's increased satisfaction in play when the parent was in tune with his tempo.

PROBLEM 6:   The infant showed no interest in play with objects.

We *listened empathetically* as the parent

...said that the infant did not seem to like any toys.
...talked about how frustrated she felt when she tried to play with the infant and he paid no attention to anything she did.

We *asked* the parent

...if there were things around the house, not necessarily toys, in which the infant seemed to show interest.
...how the infant usually responded to objects that she showed him or gave to him.
...whether the infant let her know what he liked or did not like in areas other than play, and if so, how he did this.

We *experimented*

...with presenting the infant with various objects around the house to discover some that would interest him and to find out at what skill level he was functioning.
...with various ways of presenting materials to him to enhance his interest, e.g., casually showing him ways of using an object; when a toy had more than two parts, handing him one part at a time; talking to him with dramatic voice and facial expression while showing him a toy; putting an interesting toy in front of him and turning away and talking to the parent.
...with putting the infant into a variety of positions and places to find which were most conducive to his manipulating toys, e.g., in high chair, on parent's or staff's lap, on the floor, using coffee table in standing position, across from adult, next to adult with adult's arm around him.
...with offering the infant toys one at a time or giving him a small number of toys to choose from and removing the ones he did not choose.
...with different toys appealing to different sense modalities, e.g., bright colored toys, musical toys, toys that made loud noises, texturally varied toys, to see which he might prefer.

We *observed* with the parent

...the infant's limited ability to play with objects for any length of time.
...how the infant seemed especially interested in vigorous motor activity or social games—more so than in play with objects.

...how much effort it took to get the infant interested in playing with objects.

We *modeled*

...talking to the infant and verbally reinforcing him during play.

...using his interest in people by engaging him in play with objects as part of a social interaction.

...combining play with things in his environment with vigorous motor play.

...accompanying his play with dramatic facial expressions and comments.

...encouraging him to become more goal-directed in his play by introducing cause-and-effect toys.

...helping him to achieve some success by assisting him in reaching his goal when a goal could be detected. .

...imitating and elaborating on any of the infant's actions with toys, e.g., wave the toy *and* bang it on a surface, take objects out of a container *and* put them back in, etc.

...encouraging the infant to handle a variety of objects even if he would not play with them right away.

...incorporating toys into activities the infant usually engaged in and enjoyed, e.g., put ball or other toy in infant's path of crawling, put chimes on his wrist, play peek-a-boo behind a variety of things such as cloth of different colors and textures, wax paper, brown paper bag, etc.

We *discussed* with the parent

...that some infants need a lot of help to become motivated to play with toys.

...that her infant may need help to start playing with toys, but that eventually he would discover that playing with some toys is fun, and then he would be more likely to play with satisfaction on his own.

...that some infants are so interested in movement or in people that they go through stages of playing little with objects; and that the way to interest them in objects is to try to incorporate these with social or gross motor activity (see modeling above).

...how difficult it was to try to involve an infant in play when he seemed so uninterested.

...that it might help if she picked out things to play with that she would enjoy and that her enjoyment of an activity might become "contagious."

...our successes as well as our failures in trying to motivate the infant to play and to initiate goal-directed behavior.

...that some parents find that infants get more involved in play when they, the parents, sit down near the infant for a few minutes and present toys to him in a playful manner until he becomes "hooked" on one or two of them.

...that many infants are more interested in toys on which they can have a visible or audible effect, e.g., pull a string and make the toy move or drop donut rings on a stick and ring a bell, or in toys with which they can solve a problem at their own skill level, e.g., make a lid fit on a can.

...that some infants need to see the adult do a variety of things with one or more toys before they decide to try something.

...that when the infant does discover things that he can do to a toy that have an effect on it, e.g., make a sound, close a box, pull two beads apart, his play is likely to become more goal directed and he will be more motivated to explore and experiment with new objects he finds.

We *encouraged* the parent

...to share with us what happened when she tried to play with the infant.

...to relate to us her observations of changes in the infant's play behavior, however small.

...to tell us what she observed with regard to the infant's toy preferences.

...to bring the infant to the project Center where she could try out a variety of materials to find what would interest the infant most.

...to observe how her infant used materials when left on his own, and how he used them when an adult was participating in his play.

...to see if she could think of an older child who would enjoy coming occasionally to play with the infant because some infants are especially stimulated in play with children older than themselves.

PROBLEM 7: The infant's play was primitive for his age and the parent did not know how to help him raise the level of his play.

We *listened empathetically* as the parent

...commented that the infant seemed to be doing the same things with toys all the time, e.g., mouthing and waving objects in front of him.

...said that the infant was not interested in playing and was not much fun to play with.

We *asked* the parent

...if the infant played differently when an adult participated in his play.

...what kinds of objects or toys the infant seemed to like.

We *observed* with the parent

. . . the limited skills the infant showed in his play.

. . . the infant's pleasure and increased interest when the parent participated in his play.

. . . that the infant seemed to be able to attend to an activity longer when an adult participated in it.

. . . that the infant was more interested and did more things with toys when an adult looked at him and talked with him about what he was doing.

. . . that the infant became frustrated frequently when he handled toys on his own and that he seemed to deal with his frustration by simply letting go of the toy.

We *experimented*

. . . with play materials to find some which motivated the infant to try different actions or schemas with them, e.g., when given a short wooden spoon, he banged it on the tray, inserted it into a cup, and stroked it with his other hand instead of just mouthing it.

. . . with different activities and toys to find those that the infant enjoyed most, e.g., toys that make sounds, action toys, cause-and-effect toys, etc.

We *modeled*

. . . helping the infant focus on his play by sitting with him and talking about what he was doing.

. . . commenting on the infant's success in play and encouraging him to repeat it.

. . . helping the infant achieve his own goals in play, e.g., steadying the pot as he tried to put the lid on or handing him one peg at a time as he tried to put pegs into holes.

. . . picking up the toy the infant had been using and combining it with another toy, e.g., putting a rattle inside a box or covering the doll with a blanket.

. . . adding to the infant's primitive action with toys by carrying it one step further, e.g., the infant takes one cube out of a container, adult takes another cube out and puts it next to the first one. (This is an example of encouraging sequential play: taking several cubes out of a container is a higher level action than taking one out, which is an isolated act.)

. . . helping the infant experience novelty by showing him how his actions can lead to a new effect, e.g., as the infant bangs a spoon on a tray, put a pot upside down where he is banging so that he will get a different sound.

We *discussed* with the parent

...what skills the infant showed at present and which he would be likely to develop next.

...that the infant experienced some success with challenging toys, but not consistently enough to motivate him to continue playing unless an adult was involved in his play.

...that it appeared that her infant might need more adult help with his play than some other infants, at least for a while until his interest and range of skills increased.

...that her play with the infant was helping him increase goal-directed behavior and lengthen his attention span, and that these behaviors would soon help him get more satisfaction from his independent play.

...that goal-directed behavior and interest in his activity are very important qualities for later school success.

We *commented positively*

...on the infant's increased enjoyment of his activities when the parent participated in his play.

...on increased complexity in the infant's play, such as more sequential play, e.g., taking one cube after another out of a cup.

...when the parent modeled for the infant how a toy could be used in several ways.

...on how the parent was helping the infant develop more intent in play as well as practice of new skills.

We *encouraged* the parent

...to choose materials she would like to borrow to try with her infant.

...to experiment with using these and other materials with him.

...to share with us her observations about what toys and what activities did or did not interest the infant.

...to continue to involve herself in those activities with which the infant still needed help in order to get satisfaction from his play.

In cases where the parent did not take time to sit down and play with the infant...

We also *listened empathetically* as the parent

...talked about her feeling that babies should just "fit in" with whatever is going on in the family and that a lot of special attention would spoil them.

...talked about barely having time to feed and change the infant, much less "play" with him.

We *commented positively*

...on her interaction with the infant that both seemed to enjoy.
...on how much pleasure the infant seemed to get from her company.
...when the parent gave the infant toys to "keep him busy."

We *discussed* with the parent

...that infants usually need opportunities to play by themselves and opportunities to play with an adult.
...that some infants go through a stage when they need some play interaction with an adult in order to develop the ability to play productively by themselves.
...that because her infant's play was somewhat primitive, he needed more adult participation in his play than some other infants might need.
...that she might find her infant happier and easier to care for if she arranged some time during the day when she could sit down and play with him for brief periods.
...that developing increasingly complex play skills is as important for the infant's intellectual development as proper nutrition is for the infant's health.
...that many parents find that they can incorporate some play into caregiving routines, e.g., give the infant different containers at bath time and casually model alternative uses for them.
...ways of including the infant in everyday activities that would give him play experience with the parent, e.g., give him a pot and spoon while the parent is cooking; let him play with a sponge as parent wipes the table; give him a spoon to hold while the parent is feeding him.

PROBLEM 8:   The child's short attention span interfered with his ability to get satisfaction from his play.

We *observed* with the parent

...that the child seldom played with an object long enough to explore its possibilities.
...that the child never seemed to achieve his goals in play because he could not concentrate long enough.
...the child's frequent frustration in his play.
...that the child seemed to concentrate better when an adult participated in his play.

We *asked* the parent

...how long the child usually stayed with a particular activity.
...whether some toys held the child's interest longer than others.

...whether he seemed to be more focused on his activity at certain times of the day.

We *experimented*

...with various seating arrangements to see which would help the child to focus better on his play, e.g., have child sit opposite or next to adult, on adult's lap, in high chair, at small table, etc.

...playing with the child in a variety of locations to see which helped him concentrate on his activity, e.g., quiet corner of living room with mother in kitchen while she was cooking.

...with a variety of materials to find some that were particularly interesting and challenging to the child, e.g., cause-and-effect toys, sound-producing toys, toys that give a sense of completion quickly like peg board with four pegs.

We *modeled*

...sitting at eye level with the child for brief periods and playing with him to help him concentrate.

...talking to the child about his activity when this seemed to help him continue it.

...refocusing the child on his play by handing him a toy or by showing him an interesting way of extending his activity.

...presenting pieces of a toy one at a time to help the child focus on and continue sequential play.

...commenting positively on the child's successes, e.g., "You put the ring on all by yourself, didn't you!"

...commenting positively when the child returned to his play after a brief distraction, e.g., "You remembered that this puzzle needed finishing, didn't you!"

...encouraging the child to finish what he had started, e.g., "Let's see what happens if you put this last ring on the stack."

We *discussed* with the parent

...that a child who has difficulty staying with an activity is less likely to have success in his play and experience satisfaction, and therefore will be less motivated to seek challenges and to play on a more complex level.

...that some children seem to want to explore everything at the same time but end up feeling frustrated because they rarely experience success.

...that some children may need an adult's help in focusing on their play long enough to achieve their own goal.

...that she might be able to encourage the child to stay with an activity by sitting with him and commenting on what he was doing and what might happen next, e.g., "You've put all these people (peg people) on the bus. Two more, one, two, and then the bus will be ready to go. Toot! Toot!''

...that the child seemed to lose interest in an activity quickly unless the adult enriched his play by showing him a number of things he could do with the materials or by dramatizing the activity and, at the same time, trying to extend it (see example in previous item).

...that one possible way to try to get a child involved in an activity long enough for him to experience a sense of completion was to match the toy to his skill level (to avoid frustration), observe what his play goal might be, and assist him if necessary to achieve his goal fairly rapidly.

...that some children play more productively if they have a limited number of toys to choose from at one time.

...that the child might be able to concentrate better if the toys at his skill level had few parts.

...that it might help the child to get satisfaction despite his difficulty in staying with an activity if he could have materials that yielded dramatic effects quickly, e.g., hammer and peg toy, surprise box, etc.

...that achieving success in play with minimal adult help might be so motivating to the child that he would gradually focus for longer periods on his play even when on his own.

We *commented positively*

...when the parent sat down with the child and seemed to enjoy playing with him.

...on the child's increased enjoyment of his play when the parent became involved in his activity and helped him to stay interested long enough to finish it.

...when the parent helped the child over difficult spots to avoid frustration so that he was able to complete an activity, e.g., handed him difficult puzzle pieces and asked him leading questions that helped him find the correct spots, until the puzzle was completed.

...when the parent's genuine expression of pleasure at the child's success made the child express pride in his achievement.

We *encouraged* the parent

...to share her observations with us about what seemed to help the child most to focus on his play.

...to share her observations with us about the particular toys that held the child's attention longest and gave him the greatest pleasure.

In cases where the child was easily distracted by things in the environment...

We also *observed* with the parent

...that once the child was interrupted in his play by something he saw or heard, e.g., person making a loud sound, noise on the TV, motorcycles going by, he rarely was able to return to the activity.

...that the child seemed less distractible when an adult participated in his play.

...that the child seemed to play more productively when there was a minimum of noise and activity near him.

We *asked* the parent

...whether she had noticed what was particularly distracting to him.

...in which situations the child seemed to be able to play longer and get more satisfaction from his play.

We *discussed* with the parent

...that some children have difficulty concentrating on what they are doing because they are easily distracted by many things in the environment.

...that children differ as to how distractible they are and in what is most distracting for them.

...that reducing the noise level in the home, e.g., turning down the radio or turning the TV off when no one is watching, helps some children to concentrate better on their activities and get greater satisfaction from them.

...that it is more difficult for some children than for others to develop new skills or to solve problems in their play if they have to cope with distractions from various sources in their environment.

...that usually children cope with distractions better if they are engaged in an activity that they can easily master.

...that it may help the child to play with challenging toys and to learn new skills if distractions are somewhat reduced in the child's immediate environment.

...that the parent can help the child to learn to return to his play after he has been distracted, by sitting with him and involving herself in his activity until he has achieved his goal and has experienced some measure of success.

...how important it is for the child's later success in school to learn how to return to a task (in this case, a self-chosen play activity) after he has been distracted.

We *commented positively*

...when the parent made adjustments in the environment during part of the day to reduce distractions for the child, e.g., turned off TV, closed windows to noisy street.

...when the child enjoyed his play more as he was able to concentrate more effectively on what he was doing.

...when the parent helped him get back to his activity in a gentle, positive manner, after he had been distracted from it.

We *encouraged* the parent

...to experiment with ways to reduce distractions for the child and to share with us what worked best and what interfered least with the family's ongoing activities.

...to observe and to share her observation with us whether the child seemed less distractible when he had fewer toys available.

PROBLEM 9:   The infant did not initiate play with materials and was mostly a passive observer.

We *listened empathetically* as the parent

...said that the infant seemed happiest when he sat and watched her, her husband, or his older sibling.

...talked about what a "good baby" he was and that he never caused any trouble.

We *asked* the parent

...why she thought the infant was more interested in watching others than in playing himself.

...if the infant showed particular pleasure in any kind of activity.

...at what times of the day the infant seemed most active.

...what happened when someone sat down to play with the infant.

We *observed* with the parent

...how the infant waited to see what the adult would do before he picked up a toy that was put in front of him.

...how little affect the infant showed when he did get involved in some play activity.

...that he kept his hands in his lap and waited until the adult did something with a toy, but if the adult handed the toy to him, he would take it and slowly begin to play with it.

...the infant's limited physical involvement with play materials if left on his own.

...any subtle cues the infant gave that indicated interest in a toy, e.g., looks at it for a long time, makes grasping movements toward the toy.

...that the infant was more likely to play with objects when an adult actively involved him with the toy in a physical way, e.g., put the infant's hands on the ball and helped him roll the ball to the door, handed him a ring and showed him where to put it on the stick.

We *discussed* with the parent

...that the infant's cues indicating interest in play materials were not always easy to read.

...that some parents find they can encourage play by incorporating it into an activity that the infant already enjoys, e.g., give him toys that are fun in the bathtub, give him a spoon and cup at feeding time.

...that less active children sometimes depend on their parent's initiative to get them involved in play.

...that parents of more passive babies usually find them easy to care for, but that their needs are actually harder to meet because they don't ask for what they want and need and their cues are often unclear and ambiguous.

...how easy it is to allow an infant who is not assertive to take a passive stance, especially when there is an older sibling who gets jealous of the parent's attention to the infant.

...that young children need to be actively involved in play at least some of the time to learn skills and concepts, to experience success, and to develop self-esteem.

...that it may help the child to know that the parent values his active play and goal-directed activity.

...that the more passive child may need to hear verbal encouragement and to see the parent's pleasure when he initiates play and remains with an activity until he has achieved some success, e.g., "You started building that building all by yourself and you are making it higher and higher, and so very carefully!"

We *modeled*

...giving the infant lots of time to respond to and reach for a toy.

...talking to the infant about his activity, e.g., "You're putting all the spoons in the bowl!"

...combining object play with social games, e.g., put container on our head and let it fall off, then hand it to him; hide behind a busy box before getting him interested in it; hide blocks and find them.

...encouraging the involvement of the infant's whole body in his play, e.g., roll large ball back and forth with him; help him load a small wagon and then pull it.

We *commented positively*

...when the infant showed more interest in active play and more positive affect as he played for longer periods.
...when the parent was not satisfied when the infant watched his older sibling but tried to involve the infant actively in the activity.
...when the parent told us that she spent some time with each of her children alone as well as with both together to help them enjoy some activities together.

In cases where the child did not initiate play because he had impaired motor ability...

We also *observed* with the parent

...which activities the child seemed interested in and what kind of assistance he needed in order to achieve his play goals.

We *modeled*

...experimenting with a variety of materials at different levels of difficulty, watching closely for the child's subtle cues of interest.
...helping the child manipulate and succeed with materials by gently guiding his hands.
...watching closely for signals indicating that the child wanted to try doing something with less help.
...doing things with materials in front of the child according to his directions, to give him the satisfaction of reaching his mental goal even though he could not use his hands, i.e., acting as the instrument for the child's play ideas (in the case of an intelligent child with severe motor impairment).

We *discussed* with the parent

...that the child was interested in playing with toys even though he was not able to reach for them.
...that it is helpful to observe carefully for the child's cues as to what he *can* do for himself and what he needs a little help with to experience success.
...that children seem to be able to learn from watching others play with materials, and directing others to play with materials according to their ideas, but that they also need to be helped to play with some materials themselves to experience satisfaction and success.

In cases where the child did not initiate play with materials because he was visually impaired . . .

We also *modeled*

. . . physically orienting the child to play materials, e.g., putting objects in close range, near mouth, cheek, or hand; moving child's face and hands toward object, etc.

. . . helping him become aware of the attributes of various objects: texture, sound, size, taste, shape, smell, by isolating them as much as possible from a series of objects and by giving the child verbal labels for the object and the attribute.

. . . motivating the child to reach for objects using sound cues.

We *discussed* with the parent

. . . ways to place materials within reach and in the same location so that the child could count on being able to find them again.

. . . how to check carefully what the child could do alone and what he at first needed help with.

. . . how important it is for the child to gradually increase his independence in playing with objects as he feels increasingly secure in his environment.

. . . how important the mouth is to the child in becoming acquainted with objects and that the mouth in combination with the hands become the eyes of the visually impaired child.

Note: More specialized help is usually available in the community for parents of blind or visually impaired infants. Only a few common-sense suggestions could be made here. An infant suspected of a visual handicap would be referred to resources specially equipped to help the parents and the infant.

PROBLEM 10:   **The child's unusual behavior (perseverative and self-stimulating activity) made it difficult for the parent to provide for his cognitive-motivational needs.**

We *listened empathetically* as the parent

. . . talked about how difficult it was for her to understand why her child did not play more like other children his age.

. . . said that she was at a loss to know what toys or objects to give the child to enable him to play more normally.

. . . expressed worry that the child seemed to get no real enjoyment from his rather intense and repetitive play.

. . . expressed concern that she might have caused his strange play behavior by not directing his activity more when he was younger.

We *asked* the parent

...*when* she first noticed the child's repetitive and unproductive behavior.

...whether the child's unusual play behavior was more in evidence during certain times of the day, e.g., when he seemed tired, hungry, etc.

...what kinds of things he would do when he played more normally.

...whether the kind of play we had seen during the last two visits was pretty typical of his play behavior generally.

We *experimented*

...with a variety of materials to find which ones would tend to motivate the child to play more appropriately, e.g., large blocks, play dough, doll and accessories.

...to see what kinds of skills the child demonstrated when he played more appropriately.

...with ways to prolong the child's normal play activity, e.g., guide his hands, show him new ways of using materials, talk to him about what he is doing.

...with ways to motivate him to engage in appropriate play incompatible with his self-stimulating behavior, e.g., elicit eye contact, remove objects stimulating spinning behavior, guide child in using a toy appropriately so that it will yield satisfaction, talk simply and directly to child while he is playing.

...with activities that might be fun for both parent and child despite the effort it took to get the child to participate, e.g., blowing bubbles, songs, chasing games, pushing and pulling large muscle toys.

We *observed* with the parent

...what was most likely to bring about perseverative or self-stimulating behavior in the child.

...how difficult it was to help the child engage in satisfying play activity.

...how the deviant behavior sometimes interrupted more appropriate play activity.

...instances when the child explored toys appropriately and the circumstances under which he did this for prolonged periods.

...that the child seemed to play more appropriately more of the time when the adult showed him satisfying ways of using materials at his skill level and talked to him simply about his activity.

We *commented positively*

...on the parent's patience in dealing with a very difficult child.

...when the parent was able to help the child engage in appropriate play, however briefly.

...on all the nice things the parent was doing with the child in spite of getting little feedback from him to reward her or guide her.

We *discussed* with the parent

...that her child did have a special need to be guided in some of his play by an adult.

...that she might find it easiest to try to play with the child for brief periods when he was most content and relaxed, e.g., after nap or lunch.

...that she should not feel obliged to sit down and try to play with the child for hours each day, but that even a few minutes of appropriate and satisfying play every day would help the child progress.

...that she would find playing with the child more enjoyable as he became more responsive and expanded the range of his interests and skills.

...that the progress that could be seen in the child's behavior and play, even though it appeared to be minimal, indicated the child's capacity for change in a positive direction.

...that progress occurs in small steps and that it was sometimes difficult for the person closest to the child to see minimal progress.

...that meeting the needs of a child like hers required a great deal of experimenting with materials, different settings, and different patterns of interaction.

...that parenting her child was not easy because he did not let her know what he needed, and he depended on her sensitivity to him and her initiative to expose him to and engage him in a variety of growth-promoting activities.

...that the child's tendency toward this unusual behavior most probably was due to internal neurological causes and that she should not worry about having "caused" this behavior.

...that recent changes, like more eye contact, more smiling, and the beginnings of language, were reassuring signs of change in a positive direction.

...that her tireless efforts to engage him in social and play interactions seemed to be paying off.

...that even though his "different" behavior might have neurological causes, environmental influences, such as what she was doing with him, could continue to have a positive effect.

...that she should explore ways of having some time regularly to herself, away from the child, because her efforts to help him were emotionally draining.

...that it would not hurt him to be taken care of by someone else occasionally, and that a respite for her was as important for her health as it was for her relationship with him.

We *encouraged* the parent

...to share with us her successes and failures in trying to help the child play more appropriately.

...to call us when she felt especially frustrated or discouraged.

...to pursue some personal interests of her own and arrange for someone else to take care of the child on a regular basis.

PROBLEMS IN THE LANGUAGE AREA

1 The parent did not respond to the infant's vocalizations, and she talked very little to the infant.

2 The parent did not recognize or respond to the infant's immature first words.

3 The parent was concerned about how quiet the infant was most of the time.

4 The parent bombarded the infant with language.

5 The infant had stopped vocalizing and the parent showed concern.

6 The infant's infrequent and primitive vocalizations elicited little language from the parent.

PROBLEM 1:   The parent did not respond to the infant's vocalizations, and she talked very little to the infant.

We *asked* the parent

. . . what sounds she had heard the infant make.

. . . in what situations the infant seemed to vocalize most and least.

. . . how the infant made his wants known.

. . . if the infant seemed interested and attentive when she talked directly to him.

We *observed* with the parent

. . . that the infant always looked up when someone said his name or talked to him.

. . . how the infant attended to the face of the person who was talking to him.

. . . how the infant sometimes looked back and forth as adults talked to each other.

. . . that the infant seemed to understand a number of words, e.g., looked at the ball when it was mentioned, touched his nose when it was named, etc.

. . . the infant's apparent enjoyment in vocalizing and how he expressed this enjoyment.

. . . how the infant babbled or jargoned as if he were participating in others' conversation.

We *modeled*

. . . imitating the infant's vocalizations.

. . . playful vocal exchanges with the infant that the infant found pleasurable.

. . . talking about the infant's activity and about the objects he was handling as he was playing.

. . . commenting about noises, events, etc., in the environment.

. . . interpreting the infant's attempts to communicate, e.g., "Yes, that is a doggie," when the infant looked at a dog and vocalized excitedly.

. . . repeating and elaborating on the infant's vocalizations, e.g., "Yes, that is your bottle there on the table."

. . . language games such as matching objects to pictures, rhythmically saying the names of parts of the body, chanting nursery rhymes or finger games.

. . . looking at pictures or books with the infant and talking about the pictures in simple but correct language.

We *commented positively*

. . . on the infant's interest in looking at people's faces when they talked to him.

...on how vocal the infant was.

...when the parent talked to the infant while in physical contact with him, e.g., picking him up, patting him, stroking his cheek, etc.

...when the parent talked to the infant about what was happening in caregiving situations, e.g., feeding, diapering.

...when the parent verbally alerted the infant to what was going to happen next, e.g., "I'm going to give you something to eat in a little while."

...when the parent made "nonsense sounds" to the infant or talked affectionately to him as she looked at him.

...when the parent asked the infant questions without necessarily expecting answers.

We *discussed* with the parent

...that babbling and jargon, even though they didn't sound like adult language, were important steps in learning to talk.

...where the infant was functioning in the sequence of language development.

...that some parents have wondered why they should talk to their infants before the infants can talk back in the same manner, but that the infant listens and learns language from listening, long before he can talk in words we can understand.

...that the infant's vocalizations are his way of experimenting with and imitating the sounds of language that he hears around him.

...that infants enjoy being talked to and that this stimulates them to try to talk sooner themselves.

...that infants enjoy listening to the adult talk to them about things they can see, hear, and touch.

...how the infant's experience with back-and-forth vocalization with the adult (reciprocal communication) gives him the idea that his "language" is part of an enjoyable interaction with the adult.

...that when the parent responds to the infant's vocalization and he, in turn, responds to hers, he feels that he is participating in a two-way communication, and that this experience is an important motivation for learning the adult's language.

...that when the infant begins to sense that sounds, besides being fun to make and experiment with and listen to, are also responded to by others, he gets the idea that sounds he makes are more than "toys" to play with.

...when the infant learns that language is a useful tool with which to communicate his wants, he will be motivated to listen to the adult's language, to learn words, and to produce them (at first accompanied by gestures) when he is ready to do so.

...that it matters little in what form the adult responds to the infant's "language," whether by imitating his vocalizations, making different sounds in response to sounds, or responding to his vocalizations with adult language: a little bit of each may be best.

...that even though infants may not respond immediately when an adult talks to them about their activities or about things in the environment, they are taking it in and learning from listening.

...that infants take in and understand a great deal before they can produce language that is intelligible to the adult.

...that if the adult responds to what she thinks the infant is trying to say, the infant will feel understood or, at least, listened to, and will be motivated to "talk" more.

...that the parent might find the infant most attentive and responsive to her language if she is close to him and looks at him as she is talking.

...that there is usually a time lapse between the adult's language and the infant's response, especially when he gets to the single word stage, e.g., parents' common experience that the infant will say *bye bye* minutes after it has been suggested to him, when the person he is saying *bye bye* to is no longer there.

...that there are times when the infant gives cues that he is "playing" with sounds or words as part of his independent activity, and he does not need or even want the adult to participate.

We *encouraged* the parent

...to observe and listen to the context in which the infant was vocalizing.

...to listen to what kinds of sounds the infant made.

...to share her observations about what the infant appeared to understand.

...to experiment with different activities with the infant that involve language, e.g., looking at books and talking about the pictures and singing simple nursery rhymes to him, and to share with us how he responded to these activities.

...(who was talking to the infant mostly in commands) to talk to him in many different ways, e.g., comment on his actions, ask him questions without expecting answers, sing or chant to him.

PROBLEM 2: The parent did not recognize or respond to the infant's immature first words.

We *asked* the parent

...what sounds the infant made.

...if the infant ever seemed to try to tell her something as he babbled or vocalized.

... if she knew what the infant was trying to say when he made particular sounds.

We *observed* with the parent

... that the infant consistently looked at the same object when making a specific sound, e.g., *baba* for blanket, *ga* for cracker.

... that the infant seemed to try to communicate his wants by using sounds.

... how frustrated the infant appeared to be when he kept making a certain sound and did not get a response.

We *discussed* with the parent

... that the infant was using a symbol or "word" when he made a particular sound only for a particular object or action, even though it did not sound much like the adult word, e.g., *joo* for juice, or *aat* for going outside.

... what an important discovery it was for the infant to realize that a sound can stand for something and that by responding to his new "naming skill," the parent would be letting him know that this was an important way to communicate.

... that sometimes it is difficult for adults to interpret early words of infants because they apply them in such a generalized way, e.g., *dad* for all men, or *gogui* for all animals.

... that infants at this stage of language development cannot respond to requests to say words "properly," but that very gradually they will approximate adults' words more closely.

... that she would help the infant most in his language development if she responded to and interpreted his immature words, e.g., "Yes, you want your bottle," when the infant says *bo*.

In cases where the child was older and the parent tended to correct the child's pronunciation ...

We also *discussed* with the parent

... that some sounds are difficult for toddlers to pronounce but that they will learn to pronounce them as they get older and have better fine motor control of tongue and lips.

... that initial difficulty in saying certain words is not necessarily an indication that the child will have a speech problem.

... that she would help the child most by simply repeating in her language what he was trying to say and give him a model, without correcting his speech.

... that some children react to frequent corrections of what they say by attempting less often to say words and by becoming "quiet children."

We *commented positively*

...on how much the child wanted to communicate and how much he had to say to the parent.

...when the parent responded conversationally to the child's language without correcting it.

PROBLEM 3: The parent was concerned about how quiet the infant was most of the time.

We *listened empathetically* as the parent

...said that she worried about how quiet the infant seemed.

...expressed concern that the infant would never learn to talk.

...wondered how she could get the infant to talk more.

We *asked* the parent

...in which situations and at what times she heard the infant vocalize, e.g., early in the morning in his crib, while riding in the car, when other children were around, when he was playing by himself in the morning, when mother was on the telephone.

...if the infant seemed interested in and responded to sounds and noises he heard around him.

...if the infant seemed to listen when she or other adults talked directly to him.

...whether she thought the infant understood some things that were said to him.

We *observed* with the parent

...the infant's attentiveness when she talked to him while in eye contact with him.

...the infant's behavior when adults were talking, e.g., became animated or quieted and looked at adult who was talking.

We *experimented*

...with language activities that might elicit vocalizations and would be enjoyable for parent and infant, e.g., playing with toy telephone, looking at pictures of family members or of things with which he was familiar, singing simple children's songs with gestures.

...with a variety of play activities that might elicit vocalizations, e.g., bubbles, ball play, doll play, water play, talking to and patting an animal.

We *discussed* with the parent

...that some infants listen to language around them but do not vocalize much before they start to say words.

...that there is great variability in the rate of language development among infants.

...that some infants temporarily lose interest in language during periods when their development is rapid in other areas, e.g., while they are concentrating on learning to creep or walk, or when they are developing more complex play skills.

...that some infants do not vocalize much when they are in new, exciting, or noisy situations or when they are around unfamiliar people, but they may make sounds when playing independently in a quiet room.

...how most parents have found that if they try to pressure their infant to say words, the infants tend to resist and, at the same time, lose their motivation to use words spontaneously for communication or in their play.

...that there is usually a time lapse between an infant's saying a word spontaneously in his play and his being able to use the word functionally, e.g., the infant says "juice" during his independent play, the mother hears this and asks him to say "juice" when he wants juice, but he is not ready to say this "new" word under the pressure of the parent's expectation because the word is not firmly enough established in his repertoire to produce on demand.

...that although talking to the infant is very important, it is also necessary for the adult to leave periods of silence in between so that the infant can "digest" what he has heard and respond to it when he is ready to do so.

...that some infants can attend to language only for short periods at a time and then need to "turn away" physically or mentally when they cannot utilize or tolerate any more stimulation at that time.

...that some infants will vocalize most, in an imitative manner, when there is adult conversation going on that is not directed to them.

(Also see items in this section under Problems 1 and 5.)

PROBLEM 4:   The parent bombarded the infant with language.

We *commented positively*

...on the parent's interest in talking to the infant.

...when the parent used simple, short sentences in speaking to the infant.

...whenever the parent allowed the infant time to respond to her language.

...when the infant attended to and responded to the parent's simple language.

We *observed* with the parent

...that the infant seemed most attentive to language when talked to briefly about his immediate experience.

...that the infant seemed particularly attentive and responsive when words or phrases contingent to his activity were highlighted for him.

...that the infant tended to vocalize most when the adult had watched him quietly for a while.

We *modeled*

...talking to the infant in simple phrases and sentences and pausing to give him an opportunity to respond.

...commenting briefly on the infant's activity as he played.

...talking with a soft, relaxed voice.

...observing the infant's play without talking to him.

...expressing interest in the infant's play by smiling at him when he looked up or by making brief comments, e.g., "You really like that toy!"

We *discussed* with the parent

...how she could help the infant "take in" and learn to respond to what she was saying by making pauses throughout her speech.

...that the infant learns language in a variety of ways: by listening to adults, by experimenting with his own sounds, by hearing his vocalizations responded to briefly and contingently.

...that infants profited from being talked to, but that at times they needed a chance to play quietly, without distraction.

...that the infant would probably listen more attentively to her if she spoke in short sentences, if her language was contingent to the infant's activity, and if there were lots of pauses in her flow of speech.

In cases where the parent seemed to "overtalk" because the infant did not vocalize or respond to her...

We also *discussed* with the parent

...how easy it was to talk a great deal to "fill in" the silences when the infant did not vocalize or respond, but that these silences gave the infant an opportunity to "process" mentally what he heard.

...that some infants are overwhelmed when the adult talks to them continuously and that they sometimes stop listening altogether.

...that it may help the infant if the parent paused longer than usual and gave him a chance to "take in" what he heard before she continued talking.

...that it was important for her to use language intermittently as she socially interacted with the infant, without expecting a response from him.

...how the adult's expectation of a response from the infant might make him a little tense and how this might interfere with his vocalizing or talking.

PROBLEM 5: The infant had stopped vocalizing and the parent showed concern.

We *asked* the parent

...whether the infant had had any recent illness with fever and earache.

...to tell us about any vocalizations that might occur.

...whether there were situations in which the infant occasionally made language sounds.

...whether the infant showed any other behavior that concerned her.

...whether there had been any changes or stressful events in the home recently.

We *observed* with the parent

...that the infant continued to communicate even though he was not using "language."

...that the infant seemed attentive and responsive to language spoken to him and around him.

...the infant's play, social interaction, and expression of feeling to see if any changes had occurred in these areas.

We *discussed* with the parent

...that some infants stop vocalizing when they do not hear well.

...that it might be advisable to have the infant's hearing tested to make sure that a hearing loss was not a factor in his stopping to vocalize.

...that the dropping out of language might be the infant's signal that something was upsetting him.

...that some infants react more sharply to events in their lives than other infants and that this is partly due to differences in temperament.

...some of the things that we could do cooperatively to reduce the infant's tension and to help him use oral language again (see Social-Affective Problem 8 and Language Problem 5).

We *commented positively*

. . . when the parent responded to the infant's non-verbal communication.
. . . on the parent being relaxed with the infant and not pressuring him to talk.

We *encouraged* the parent

. . . to spend some time alone with the infant every day, doing something relaxing that they could enjoy together.
. . . to use simple language or vocalizations in playful interactions with the infant, without expecting a language response from the infant.

PROBLEM 6:   The infant's infrequent and primitive vocalizations elicited little language from the parent.

We *listened empathetically* as the parent

. . . said that the infant did not seem interested in talking or being talked to.
. . . wondered when the infant would start to talk.

We *asked* the parent

. . . what kinds of sounds the infant made and how long he had been making these sounds.
. . . what situations seemed to elicit the infant's vocalizations, e.g., adults talking, parent talking on the phone, presence of other children, quiet room, etc.
. . . what she thought the infant was able to understand.
. . . how the infant let her know when he wanted something.
. . . whether she had noticed any changes in his attention to language or in his vocalizations in the last few days or weeks.
. . . whether she had heard the infant vocalize several minutes after an adult had spoken to him.

We *experimented*

. . . with ways of talking to the infant that might stimulate his interest and elicit vocalizations, e.g., quiet conversation, close physical contact and eye contact while talking softly to him, dramatic use of voice, nonsense sounds, rhetorical questions.
. . . with activities that might elicit vocalizations, e.g., chasing games, playing with bubbles, water play, looking at pictures of familiar objects or people.
. . . with toys of interest to the infant that might encourage vocalizations, e.g., push or pull toys, cars, dolls, cause-and-effect toys, balls.

We *observed* with the parent

...that the infant seemed to vocalize when excited, when the parent was on the telephone, and occasionally when engaged in solitary play.

...the infant's subtle cues indicating some interest in language spoken around him, e.g., looked at speaker when language was not directed to him, looked directly at older child when she spoke to him, interrupted his play and looked up when unfamiliar person spoke, turned so that he could see who was speaking.

We *modeled*

...talking to the infant after making eye contact with him.

...playfully making nonsense sounds, imitating his primitive sounds, alternating whispering with loud talking and then laughing.

...activities with the infant to encourage controlled lip movement, e.g., blowing bubbles, giving a kiss, blowing a feather.

...talking to the infant in an animated or dramatic manner.

...playing and chanting nursery rhymes with the infant, e.g., pat-a-cake, peek-a-boo, this little piggie, etc.

...singing children's songs or simple folk songs accompanied by expressive gestures.

...labeling facial features as the infant touched the adult's face or as the adult touched the infant's face or a doll's face.

...labeling some objects that the infant attended to and played with.

...accompanying the infant's play with interesting sounds, e.g., the sound of a motor, animal sounds, etc.

...talking to the infant about his activity, in short sentences or phrases, leaving "spaces" in between, e.g., "You took the block out of there, didn't you?..."

...playing hiding games with objects, e.g., "Where is the ball?" or "Where did the ball go?" and "Here is the ball!"

...giving the infant simple directions and helping him carry them out, e.g., "Throw the ball," or "Push the car."

...showing the infant pictures of himself and the family members.

...showing the infant pictures of familiar objects.

...matching familiar objects to pictures.

...looking at simple picture books with the infant.

We *discussed* with the parent

...how natural it is for the adult to assume that the infant is not interested in language if he makes only a few sounds.

...that many parents find it difficult to talk to their infant if he responds very little.

... that receptive language (understanding) and expressive language (talking) develop at different rates and that infants understand words long before they begin to say them.

... that infants need to hear adult language to stimulate their vocalizations, to produce new sounds, to imitate sounds, and, eventually, to say words.

... that even though the infant made few sounds, he seemed to show interest in and listen to the adult's language at least some of the time.

... that most infants gradually become more vocal and responsive to language as they continue to hear language around them and directed to them.

... why it was useful to respond to vocalizations the infant made, no matter how primitive, and that the parent, by responding to the infant, communicates to him that she is interested in his "language" and that she is listening to him.

... that most infants enjoy having their sounds imitated by the adult.

We *commented positively*

... on any sounds the infant made, other than crying, whimpering, or whining.

... when the parent responded to the infant's sounds.

... when the parent talked to the infant in simple language and left "spaces" between utterances without necessarily expecting the infant to respond.

... when the parent spontaneously reported the infant's vocalizations between home visits.

... when the parent reported experimenting with language activities with the infant.

In cases where the infant showed little evidence of interest in language...

We also *listened empathetically* as the parent

... said that she felt silly talking to the infant because he never listened or paid attention.

... wondered whether she was interesting enough for him to listen to.

We *asked* the parent

... if she had difficulty getting the infant to look at her with or without talking to him (to find out if a social-affective problem was more basic here).

... if the infant seemed interested and responsive to environmental noises, e.g., doorbell, car horn, telephone ring, trucks going by, airplane noises, animal sounds.

...if the infant responded differently to the voices of different adults or children.

...how the infant reacted when his father or his older sister talked to him.

...what sounds or words the infant responded to most often, if at all.

We *experimented*

...with noises at different levels of intensity and language sounds at different voice pitches to find out what the infant responded to and therefore could probably hear.

...with various ways of getting the infant's attention, like sounds, touching, movement, entering the room, etc.

We *observed* with the parent

...what it took specifically to get the infant to attend to the adult's language or sounds, e.g., clapping hands, talking loudly, using dramatic gestures.

...whether the infant was most likely to attend to language when there was a minimum of environmental noise.

...whether nonsense sounds aroused the infant's interest more than normal language.

We *discussed* with the parent

...the advisability of having the infant's hearing checked to eliminate the possibility of a hearing loss.

...that it can be discouraging to try to talk to an infant who shows so little interest and so rarely responds.

...that some infants show a long delay between being exposed to language, increasing their sounds and vocalizations, and finally, starting to talk.

We *encouraged* the parent

...to experiment with different ways of talking to the infant and to share her observations about when she would get a response and when not.

...to experiment with cutting down on the general noise level in the home at the times when she attempted to get the infant to attend to her language.

We *commented positively*

...on the parent's efforts to get the child interested in language.

...when she reported all the things she tried in order to get the infant to attend to sounds and language.

...when the infant showed more interest in language, especially while she interacted with him.

PROBLEMS IN THE MOTOR AREA

1 The infant moved very little, and the parent was concerned.

2 The infant's poor fine motor coordination prevented him from achieving his goals in play.

3 The parent did not value the gross motor skills of the child that were not common motor milestones like sitting, crawling, and walking.

4 The parent tried to "teach" the child to walk long before he was motorically ready.

5 The parent did not provide the infant with sufficient opportunities for gross motor activity.

PROBLEM 1:   The infant moved very little, and the parent was concerned.

We *listened empathetically* as the parent

. . . said that the infant seemed happy just staying in one place for long periods.

. . . expressed worry that there was something wrong with the infant.

. . . wondered if she did not stimulate the infant sufficiently.

We *asked* the parent

. . . whether there were certain times of the day when the infant was most mobile, e.g., early in the morning, after his morning nap, in the evening after dinner.

. . . in what situations the infant tended to be most active physically, e.g., when father plays with him, when other children are around, outdoors.

. . . what kinds of activities seemed to stimulate the infant to move.

We *experimented*

. . . with a variety of activities to see what would stimulate the infant to be physically active, e.g., rolling or throwing a ball, pushing or pulling toys, rough physical play, singing with gestures and body movement, reaching for bubbles or balloons.

. . . with a variety of toys and materials to find which might motivate him to move.

. . . with things around the house to see which could be used for motor activity enjoyable to the infant, e.g., large pillows, bolsters, boxes, pads from outdoor furniture.

We *modeled*

. . . presenting favorite toys at a slight distance to encourage him to move toward them, and gradually increasing the distance.

. . . hiding objects behind or under physical obstacles, e.g., under or behind pillows, cloths, chairs.

. . . putting favorite objects just out of reach on chairs, tables, etc., so that the infant could see them but had to stretch or pull up on furniture to grasp them.

. . . rewarding the infant with pleasurable social interaction when he was motorically active.

We *discussed* with the parent

... how infants, like adults, differ temperamentally with respect to activity level, and that some infants who are less interested in moving may later be more interested in sedentary activities like reading books or doing puzzles than are more physically active infants.

... that some infants are more placid than others and need the adult's help to become motivated to move.

... that the infant might be more active if he were put in a variety of places around the house and outdoors.

... that changing the infant's position every so often might motivate him to move more, e.g., prone, supine, propped up on couch, in high chair, in infant seat where he can see parent's face.

... that when the infant uses his muscles to reach in order to grasp, turn over, kick, pull up, he is preparing himself to sit, crawl, stand up.

... that it might be fun for both parents to try to engage with the infant in the kinds of activities that they enjoy, e.g., dancing to music, "gymnastics" on a soft pad, "chasing" games.

In cases where the infant preferred lying on his back most of the time ...

We also *modeled*

... putting the infant in a different position and interesting him in objects or social games in the new position.

... acknowledging the infant's mild protest, but expressing confidence that he would soon like the new experience, e.g., "I know it feels strange to be on your tummy, but look at all the things you can see and do this way!"

We *discussed* with the parent

... that sometimes infants become upset when they are put in new positions but that most of them gradually learn to accept and even like the change.

... that some infants adapt more slowly than others to any changes, no matter how small.

... that the infant learns about what his body can do and what it feels like when he is put in a variety of positions.

... that if the infant continues to protest vehemently when put into a particular position, it would be worth mentioning to the pediatrician.

... that the infant is most likely to accept being in a new position while pleasurably interacting with the parent, or if he has something interesting to look at or to do.

PROBLEM 2:   The infant's poor fine motor coordination prevented him from achieving his goals in play.

We *asked* the parent

...what kinds of toys the infant seemed to like.
...what toys seemed to hold the infant's interest longest.
...what activities or toys seemed most frustrating to the infant.
...whether the infant became frustrated when he tried to play with an object and could not achieve what he wanted.

We *observed* with the parent

...that the infant seemed interested in some toys that were difficult.
...how frustrated the infant became when he tried to play with a toy that was difficult for him to manipulate.
...the infant's expression of satisfaction when he was helped just enough to succeed in his activity.

We *experimented*

...with toys that the infant might be able to handle successfully on his own, e.g., bean bags, large pegs, textured balls, sponges of different sizes and shapes, wooden cubes, and wooden spoons.
...with various ways of positioning the infant so that he could use his arms and hands more freely, e.g., put pillow or bolster under trunk or stomach, put in infant seat, in high chair, or at small table.
...with various activities with toys to find out how much help the infant needed in order to experience success.

We *discussed* with the parent

...that infants learn about the world around them by manipulating and experimenting with objects, and that it was important for her infant to have that experience in spite of his problem in the fine motor area.
...that the infant needs to experience success as he plays with objects so that he does not lose the motivation to explore and manipulate things in his environment.
...how the infant's fine motor delay interfered with his experiencing success in his play, and that he needed some help in using some materials.
...that the infant should get the minimal amount of help necessary to allow him to achieve his own goals, e.g., stopping a toy from rolling away when he tried to grasp it, or steadying the pegboard as he tried to insert the peg.
...that the infant might enjoy toys that give dramatic feedback with relatively little effort, e.g., squeaky toys, busy box, musical toys, simple cause-and-effect toys.

. . . ways of adapting toys so the infant could play with them more successfully, e.g., put large handle on end of string of pull toy, put knobs on
puzzle pieces, give him coffee can with large hole in plastic lid instead
of form box.

We *modeled*

. . . giving the infant plenty of time to explore toys.
. . . giving him sufficient help to allow success, e.g., steadying an object so
that he can grasp it, adjusting the can to help him insert the object in
the hole.
. . . facilitating the process of picking up objects by providing a soft textured surface, e.g., flannel-covered board or a small, solid-color rug.
. . . helping the infant with a more severe motor handicap to achieve his
goal by guiding his hands when necessary.
. . . showing pleasure in the infant's achievements and successes, no matter how small.
. . . starting an activity with the infant and letting him complete it by himself, e.g., let him put the last cube in the can, ask him to push the last
and easiest lever on the surprise box.

**PROBLEM 3:   The parent did not value the gross motor skills of the
child that were not the most familiar motor milestones
like sitting, crawling, and walking.**

We *listened empathetically* as the parent

. . . expressed concern that the child would never sit independently, crawl,
stand, or walk.
. . . talked about how little the child had progressed toward sitting and
crawling in the last couple of months.
. . . expressed impatience to see the child crawl or somehow get to where
he wanted to go without having to be carried there.
. . . commented that he was getting pretty heavy to be carried everywhere.
. . . talked about her frustration that the child seemed to be "standing
still" rather than learning new skills.
. . . expressed sadness that the child did not seem to be able to do anything
on his own.
. . . indicated some hope that if she spent sufficient time with the child and
made him practice the skills that she thought were important, he
would progress more rapidly.

We *observed* with the parent

. . . the child's current motor skills.
. . . the child's persistence in repeating newly acquired skills.

...the child's efforts to propel himself forward rather than backward along the floor.

...the child's pleasure when he was successful in achieving his goal, e.g., moving forward and reaching a toy on the floor or propelling himself forward by pulling with his arms in the prone position.

...how the child turned his head away when he was urged to do something for which he was not developmentally ready.

...some signs of motor progress, however small.

We *commented positively*

...on the parent's willingness to help her child make progress.

...on the parent's readiness to spend a lot of time with the child to help him in his development.

...when the parent responded sensitively to the child in helping him achieve his own goal.

We *discussed* with the parent

...that many parents find this slow, step-by-step progress frustrating.

...that it often helps to become a careful observer in order to recognize and appreciate the small steps that mean progress for the child.

...how difficult it was to know exactly what one should expect from the child many months ahead.

...how confusing it can be when different doctors make widely different predictions as to the ultimate skill level the child will be able to achieve in the motor area.

...that motor development tends to be uneven—that there are periods of slow change and, then, more rapid progress.

...how the motor skills the child was exhibiting would lead toward more advanced motor functioning.

...that a motorically delayed child's developmental steps in the motor area tend to be smaller and take more time to become consolidated, but that the sequence tends to be the same in all children.

...the changes that the parent had seen and that we had observed in all areas of the child's development over the last few months.

...that children are likely to reach out, move, and practice their motor skills when they are provided with interesting toys and objects.

...that practice of his most functional motor skills is most likely to occur in the process of interesting play and social games and activities.

...how the young child exercises his muscles most effectively when these movements are an unconscious part of his play, e.g., ball play, going after desired toys on floor or up on a table or chair, maintaining a sitting or standing position while playing with toys on a low surface like a coffee table.

...that the best way to get the child to practice the skills which he needs to master is usually to see to it that the skills are an integral part of interesting activity.

...what skills she might expect next from her child.

We *modeled*

...providing interesting and challenging toys for the child.

...placing different toys just out of reach to encourage the child to move.

...enthusiastically praising the child when he tried to pull himself up to reach an object on the couch, e.g., "You got up there all by yourself!"

...praising the child when he worked hard to reach his goals.

...giving sufficient help so that the child could achieve his goal instead of becoming frustrated and discouraged.

Note: When a parent was too exclusively focused on the child's motor handicap, we tried to refocus her on social, language, and cognitive development (the latter through play), areas in which her efforts would be more rewarding and reinforced by more visible progress. But we learned through our experience that we first had to "stay with her" in the area of her concern and deal with it to her satisfaction before we could help her expand her attention and interest to other areas of development. See also Problem 20 in the Social-Affective category.

PROBLEM 4:   The parent tried to "teach" the child to walk long before he was motorically ready.

We *listened empathetically* as the parent

...talked about her concern that the child was lazy and that this was why he was not yet walking.

...related how she practiced walking with the child every day, even though he resisted it.

...talked about her belief that if the child would only try a little harder, he would be able to walk.

...mentioned that she knew two children in the neighborhood, one slightly younger and the other the same age as her child, and both of them were walking.

We *asked* the parent

...how the child usually moved about.

...whether the child seemed to enjoy moving and crawling to where he wanted to be.

...what she thought were the skills closest to walking that he had mastered.

...whether the child seemed pleased with himself when he achieved something new.

...whether he sometimes remained standing for a short while after he had pulled himself to the standing position.

...whether she had seen him cruise, i.e., walk sideways while holding on to furniture.

We *observed* with the parent

...how persistently the child worked at reaching his goals, e.g., "He really works at trying to turn this box over, even though it is very hard for him."

...the motor skills the child was showing, and we talked about how they fit into the developmental sequence preceding walking.

...the way in which the child practiced an emerging skill over and over again.

...the pleasure the child showed when he had achieved something new.

We *discussed* with the parent

...that many parents get impatient and want to see their child begin to walk.

...how some parents wonder why they awaited the child's walking so impatiently, because they found themselves working much harder to keep the child "out of trouble" once he began walking.

...how children have to master certain motor skills before they can walk safely, e.g., pulling to stand and enjoying the upright position, getting "up and down" easily, cruising.

...that most children have a strong desire to reach new levels of motor skills, to imitate others around them, and to start walking like the other members of the family.

...that children progress motorically at different rates.

...that the rate of motor development, more than other aspects of development (like social, intellectual and language development), is for the most part biologically determined, unless the infant does not have the usual opportunities to move about.

...that except in cases of neurological damage causing specific motor handicaps, the infant who grows up in a home with the usual opportunities to move will reach the motor milestones such as sitting and walking when his body is ready for it.

...that normally developing infants begin to walk anytime between 8 and 20 months of age, and that the specific age at which they begin walking within that range bears no relationship to intellectual development if their other behavior is age-appropriate.

...how the motor skills the child is exhibiting currently fit into the overall motor development sequence.

...that even though some of the child's motor skills don't look like they would lead to walking, they are in fact preparatory to walking, e.g., crawling strengthens the arms, legs, and trunk; pulling up on furniture also strengthens arms and legs and gets him to like the standing position.

...that children usually learn to walk, without adult help, when they are developmentally ready.

...that some parents find that if they pressure the child into trying to walk, the child becomes more hesitant and more resistant to doing it.

...that as long as the child is interested in his environment and enjoys moving about on the floor, he will gradually acquire the necessary skills for walking.

...that most children take their first steps when they are very interested in something or someone and they want to get there quickly, forgetting that they are upright and not holding on to furniture.

...that the most important help toward walking she can give the child is to provide an interesting and safe environment, floor space to "travel," and a minimum of pressure connected with adult expectations.

...how frequent falls, which sometimes occur when a child is urged to walk before he is ready, can undermine his confidence and make him hesitant to walk on his own.

In cases where the child was afraid to walk because his balance was poor...

We also *listened empathetically* as the parent

...talked about her fears that the child would never walk well.

...talked about how upset she was when she saw the child fall and hurt himself.

We *discussed* with the parent

...how she could help the child to develop better balance by playing certain games with him, e.g., bouncing; gentle, playful, reciprocal pushing on a soft, cushioned surface; dancing.

...that some children gain confidence by moving on a well-cushioned surface.

...that some children first learn to move more freely in water.

We *modeled*

...playing gross motor games with the child, e.g., rolling him on a large beach ball, rocking and swaying to music, pushing child gently in sitting position and praising him when he braced himself, and playing games of squatting and getting back to standing position.

...asking the child to take things to his mother or to put them somewhere, so that he would walk without thinking about it.

...providing the child with toys that would support him in walking, e.g., a shopping cart or a weighted down stroller.

...giving the child as much support as he wanted and gradually reducing it, e.g., let him hold on to whole hand, then finger, then string.

PROBLEM 5:   The parent did not provide the infant with sufficient opportunities for gross motor activity.

We *listened empathetically* as the parent

...talked about how exhausting it was to live with a child who seemed to be in constant motion.

...talked about how angry it made her when the child kept climbing all over the furniture and up on the cupboards.

...said that the child rarely was able to play quietly on the floor or in his high chair like other young children.

We *asked* the parent

...how the child reacted when he was taken outdoors.

...if the child behaved differently indoors after he had been outdoors.

...whether there were any parks or playgrounds in her neighborhood.

...if there was an area in the home where the child could engage in physical activity without endangering himself or damaging furniture.

We *discussed* with the parent

...that because some children are naturally much more physically active than others, they need more opportunity for vigorous play.

...that most children need to alternate quiet play with physically active play.

...that the child might be easier to live with if he had regular times every day when he could be physically active.

...that sometimes even a walk around the block might help him to expend some of his excess energy.

...that children practice their gross motor skills over and over before they meet with success.

...that new gross motor skills can emerge only if the child has plenty of opportunities to move about and experiment with the use of his body.

...that gross motor play is also important for learning spatial concepts.

...that active physical play could be kept manageable indoors by designating one or two areas of the house for this type of play and by providing suitable equipment and materials, e.g., boxes for climbing, large pillow for tumbling, a mattress, indoor toddler slide, etc.

We *modeled*

...adapting available household materials for gross motor play, e.g., cardboard boxes for hiding and building; heavier boxes for climbing; old crib mattress for tumbling; laundry baskets for filling and emptying or hiding, etc.

...physical games and exercises to do with children indoors, e.g., throwing beanbags in bucket, dancing to music, pretending to be different kinds of animals and moving like them.

We *encouraged* the parent

...to give the child opportunities to be outdoors frequently.

...to explore parks and playgrounds in the neighborhood or within easy reach by bus.

PROBLEMS IN PARENTING-CAREGIVING

1 The parent who stayed home with her young child or children felt depressed and isolated.

2 The parent felt ambivalent about "mothering" as a full-time job.

3 The parent lacked confidence in her parenting skills.

4 The parent worried about spoiling the infant.

5 The parent did not know what to expect from her child because of her limited knowledge about and experience with young children.

6 The parent was unaware of potential dangers for the child in the home environment.

7 Feeding became a struggle for the parent when the child began wanting to participate in the process.

8 The parent was unresponsive to the child's cues regarding food preference and quantity because she was concerned that he was not eating enough.

9 The parent was concerned about the child's frequent demands for food.

10 The parent was not realistic about the process of toilet training nor aware of signs of the child's readiness.

11 The parent found it difficult to get the child to go to sleep at night.

12 The parent was distressed about the child's night waking.

13 The working parent found it difficult to spend the necessary time and energy to maintain a positive relationship with her child.

14 The working parent had difficulty coping emotionally with the child after returning home from work.

15 The parent was not aware of the importance of quality child care.

16 The parent of an infant with a traumatic birth was overprotective and limited the infant's experience.

17 The parent had anxiety regarding the normalcy of the child due to his traumatic birth and difficulties in the neonatal period.

18 The parent was so involved with the infant that she tended to neglect the needs of other family members and her own needs.

19 The parent was concerned about sibling rivalry and was uncertain about how to deal with it.

PROBLEM 1:   The parent who stayed home with her young child or children felt depressed and isolated.

We *listened empathetically* as the parent

. . . discussed her feelings and concerns, whether these were related to the child or not.

. . . related how difficult it was to be a parent and how discouraged she was at times.

. . . told us how lonely and isolated she felt being at home all day with young children.

. . . expressed regret that she had no time or opportunity to pursue her personal interests and abilities.

We *asked* the parent

. . . if she occasionally got out of the house with her infant.

. . . whether she could get a babysitter occasionally so that she could have a few hours to herself.

. . . if she knew other parents with young children in the neighborhood.

. . . if she could explore some cooperative babysitting arrangements with other parents of young children in her neighborhood.

We *discussed* with the parent

. . . that mothers of young children frequently express similar feelings.

. . . that many parents miss daily contact with other adults.

. . . that staying home with a baby, especially after having worked for several years, is a big change, and that the adjustment can sometimes be difficult.

. . . that it usually helps to try to find friends who are in a similar situation.

´ . . . that it takes time to make new friends.

We *encouraged* the parent

. . . to get out of the house, sometimes by herself, and sometimes with her young children.

. . . to explore parks, libraries, and other facilities in the community that might offer classes and groups for parents and young children.

. . . to talk to other parents with young children in her neighborhood about a babysitting cooperative arrangement and the possibiity of developing a neighborhood playgroup if there was not one already.

. . . to find some time for herself on a regular basis and to explore ways of pursuing her personal interests.

. . . to seek information about resources and activities available in her community where she could meet others who shared her interests.

. . . to seek support in the extended family, church, or community groups.

...to consider seeking professional counseling help if she continued to feel depressed.

(This is particularly applicable if the parent is seriously depressed and not able to act on any of the other suggested measures. The staff's policy was to motivate the parent to get the kind of support for herself that she needed. If her state was such that she needed more direct assistance in seeking such support, this assistance was given.)

PROBLEM 2: The parent felt ambivalent about "mothering" as a full-time job.

We *listened empathetically* as the parent

...wondered about whether she would have a better relationship with her children if she worked outside the home.

...discussed her feeling that she had to "love" her children at all times in order to be a good parent.

...talked about how she just was not capable of feeling warmly toward her children all the time.

...talked about her feeling that her main responsibility in life at the present time was to take care of her young children the best possible way so as to give them a "good start" in life.

...expressed guilt about getting angry at her children so frequently.

...described her loneliness, frustration, and lack of fulfillment as a person because parenting seemed to take so much time and energy.

...talked about how she missed regular adult contact and that although she usually enjoyed her children's company, it was not enough for her.

...talked about feeling guilty about staying home and not contributing to the family income.

We *asked* the parent

...what aspects of being a full-time mother she enjoyed.

...what aspects of being a full-time mother she found most difficult.

...what had made her decide to be a full-time mother.

...if she had anyone to turn to and talk to at the times she felt frustrated and upset.

...whether she was able to take time for herself on a regular basis.

We *discussed* with the parent

...what a significant role change it is to switch from working outside the home to full-time childrearing.

...that it is very common for parents to have some negative feelings about childrearing and even toward their own children at times.

. . . that many parents have expressed similar feelings.

. . . that there is hardly a parent who doesn't get angry and frustrated with her children at times.

. . . that being a full-time parent unfortunately does not have the same social status and monetary rewards as pursuing a career outside the home, but that more people are beginning to value it as a full-time occupation for those who want to do it and who enjoy it.

. . . the need to talk with other adults after having been home with young children.

. . . the increasing number of parent-infant, parent-toddler, and parent-child groups in the community that give parents with the same age children an opportunity to get together to share their problems and joys and to learn from each other and from the group leader.

. . . ways of finding out about such groups in her community.

. . . alternatives to full-time mothering, e.g., part-time work, full-time work with adequate child care, recreational activities for herself, going to school a couple of times per week, etc.

. . . the lack of research evidence that children are hurt by being away from their parents for a few hours a day as long as the substitute care provided is of good quality.

. . . ways to find "respite" babysitting so that she could have a few hours for herself on a regular basis.

We *encouraged* the parent

. . . to think about the possible options and to sit down with her husband (or friends) to decide what was right for her and her children at the present time.

. . . to seek out other mothers with young children, who were likely to have experiences and feelings similar to hers about staying home with their young children.

. . . to look for some opportunities for activities for herself that would give her satisfaction so that she could feel more fulfilled as a person.

. . . (if she decided to continue as a full-time parent) to discuss her feelings with her husband and to explore how he might help her pursue some outside activity by taking care of the children on a regular basis.

PROBLEM 3:   The parent lacked confidence in her parenting skills.

We *listened empathetically* as the parent

. . . expressed her anxiety about being a parent.

. . . confided that she really did not know anything about young children and had not had much experience with children of any age.

...said that she had not expected parenting to be this difficult.

...blamed herself for her child's negative behaviors and put herself down as a parent.

...related how embarrassed her child's behavior made her feel in front of her friends.

...stated that other people could sometimes handle her child better than she could.

...explained how helpless she felt in trying to meet the child's needs, and always being uncertain whether she was doing the "right" thing.

...talked about her feeling that her mother was right when she criticized her caregiving practices.

...talked about not knowing whom to listen to and that so many people seemed ready to give her advice on childrearing.

We *asked* the parent

...what aspects of being a parent she enjoyed.

...what she and her child enjoyed doing together.

...what kinds of things she did feel good about as a parent of her child.

We *commented positively*

...on the parent's natural style of interacting with her child, e.g., her way of talking, her expressive face when interacting with him, etc., and we talked about how the different things she did were beneficial to her child's development.

...on the excellent way in which she had handled a particular situation with her child.

...on her child's positive responses to her most of the time.

...on the fun they seemed to have together.

...on the parent's sensitivity and skill in handling a delicate situation with the child in front of the grandmother (who tended to be critical of the parent).

...on her openness in sharing her feelings of inadequacy with us and mentioned how common these feelings are among parents.

We *discussed* with the parent

...that learning how to be a parent is a process we all go through, that it can be painful and difficult, and that we are not taught how to be parents.

...that each parent gradually has to find out what feels right and comfortable for both herself and her child.

...that each child is different and that therefore we have to learn to be good observers, to be sensitive to the child's cues, and to find things that we can enjoy doing with the child.

...some of the difficulties that the staff person has had as a parent, and how unsure of herself she was with her first child.

...how impossible it is to achieve the unrealistic model of a "good parent" as it is portrayed in the media.

...that she was experiencing problems in the same areas in which many other parents frequently have problems.

...that there is no one right way to be a "good parent," that there are many ways for many different parents and many different children.

...that her overall positive relationship with her child was more important than any specific way of handling a particular incident with him.

...that early childhood is a difficult period for parent and child, but that some day she would look back on that period and see that things really went comparatively well for her and her child.

We *encouraged* the parent

...to assert herself with members of her family regarding her ideas about childrearing.

...to tell her babysitter how she wanted her child to be cared for, and to provide information about the child that would help the babysitter to meet his needs in the ways the parent felt were important.

PROBLEM 4:   The parent worried about spoiling the infant.

We *listened empathetically* as the parent

...expressed doubt about whether she should respond to the infant whenever he asked for attention.

...talked about the infant being cranky and wondered whether this was a sign of being spoiled.

...indicated concern that her responsiveness to the infant's crying would result in excessive demands for attention.

...said that her husband thought she was spoiling the infant.

...told us how much she enjoyed playing with the infant but wondered whether playing with him would prevent him from learning to play by himself.

...related that her relatives were telling her that she was spoiling her infant.

We *commented positively*

...when the parent responded to the infant's distress.

...when the parent and infant seemed to enjoy each other's company.

...when the infant played happily by himself.

...when the parent set limits calmly and firmly (at age 14 months or older).

...on the infant's friendly social behavior with others.

We *asked* the parent

...how the infant behaved with others in and outside the home.

...in what ways her husband thought she was spoiling the infant.

...what she thought a spoiled child was like.

...whether *she* thought the child acted spoiled, and if so, in what way.

We *discussed* with the parent

...how responding to the infant's needs and giving him attention are not spoiling him.

...that infants and young children need their parents' attention and how interaction with their parents enhances their development.

...that when an infant can rely on the parents' responsiveness, he learns to trust and explore the world around him and tends to become independent earlier.

...that one cannot usually spoil an infant under about 1 year of age, but how after that age, demands may not always express needs.

...that when an infant asks for attention, it is sometimes difficult to know what he needs; at times he may need only to be launched on an interesting activity.

...that it is important for the infant to have opportunities to play by himself with satisfying play materials as well as with his parents and others.

...that most parents can trust their own perceptions of when the child needs them and what the child needs: after all, the parent knows her child best.

...that differences between need and demand grow more complex in the child's second year of life.

...that it is possible to "spoil" a child after the first year of life by always giving in to unreasonable demands and by not setting clear limits and enforcing them consistently (within reason): this can make the child uncertain, manipulative and, indeed, difficult to live with.

...that it is important for her to know what reasonable limits are for her child at his level of development, what limits she wants to set, and how to enforce them (also see Problems 15 and 16 in the Social-Affective section).

...that some people perceive a child as "spoiled" when they expect behavior from him that is beyond his developmental level.

...that relatives or friends may label the child as spoiled when he is unsure of himself with unfamiliar people or when he is in a new environment and needs the parent's support and reassurance.

PROBLEM 5: **The parent did not know what to expect from her child because of her limited knowledge about and experience with young children.**

We *asked* the parent

...what she especially appreciated about her child and what behavior she found particularly difficult to deal with.
...what kinds of activities and what kinds of toys seemed to interest him.
...what activities she and the child enjoyed doing together.
...whether she could usually predict how the child would react to someone or something new.
...how the child had changed in the last few weeks.

We *observed* with the parent

...what kind of play held his attention longest.
...the degree of persistence he showed in pursuing a goal in play.
...his general tempo when eating, playing, changing from one activity to another, and how his compared with her own tempo.
...the specific skills the child exhibited.
...his responsiveness to language and his own language communications.
...how he expressed his likes and dislikes.
...his characteristic approach to new things and new people.

We *discussed* with the parent

...in what way the child's behavior fit into his stage of development.
...the particular strengths of the child.
...what the child seemed to enjoy most at this stage and how she could provide opportunities for these activities.
...the areas of behavior in which the child might need special attention or encouragement from the parent.
...how children go through developmental stages during which they exhibit behavior that is difficult to deal with although it is perfectly normal, e.g., being dependent and at the same time wanting to do everything on his own.
...the developmental meaning of those toddler behaviors which are often particularly hard for parents to cope with, e.g., toddlers saying *no, me do it* and having physical tantrums when they get frustrated: these are the ways in which a child tries to establish control over his own body and activities and they are a necessary part of becoming an independent person with self-esteem.
...what kinds of behavior she might expect next from her child.

We *encouraged* the parent

...to observe the child and to share with us her observations of his play, language, and social interactions.

...to observe other children in order to become acquainted with the ways in which children at about the same age are similar and different.

...to let us know if she was interested in reading about the development of children. If so, we said that we would be glad to recommend books and pamphlets to her.

...to explore programs in her community for parents and young children where she could observe her child with other children and adults and where the child could enjoy the company of other young children.

PROBLEM 6:   The parent was unaware of potential dangers for the child in the home environment.

We *asked* the parent

...whether her child seemed to be getting around and "into" things now that he was so mobile.

...if there were things that the child could reach that she would not want him to have.

...how she kept him out of cupboards with dangerous substances in them.

...how she stopped the child when he was about to do something dangerous.

We *discussed* with the parent

...that many parents find that their children get into things much sooner than they had anticipated.

...that young children do not know what is dangerous for them and will play with or eat anything within reach.

...that young children do not understand or remember mere verbal prohibitions about dangerous situations and that punishment is also not effective in keeping the child away from something dangerous; that making dangerous substances inaccessible and eliminating potentially dangerous situations are the only sure ways of protecting the child.

...what kinds of things the child might "get into" next, e.g., climbing out of the crib, opening the door to the outside, poking things into electrical outlets, climbing to reach high shelves or cupboards.

...that parents have found that the only way of assuring the child's safety from swallowing toxic substances was to keep medicine and household chemicals totally out of the child's reach.

... the necessity of setting clear and simple limits in matters of safety, and also the need for enforcing these limits repeatedly until the child can be trusted to have learned them thoroughly (usually not until the fifth year of life).

... how limits have to include verbal prohibitions and physical follow-up, e.g., removing child from the situation, removing object and putting it out of reach.

... our personal experiences as parents in finding ways to keep children out of dangerous situations.

... that it is sometimes difficult to anticipate all the dangerous things a child might do.

... that "child-proofing" the house is often not very convenient for the adults, but that it is a necessity at some periods in the child's development.

... that most parents find their jobs easier if they child proof the house than if they constantly have to say "no" and chase after the child.

... some of the child's interests and skills that necessitated making things safe for him.

... different ways of making the home environment safe, as the parent and staff person walked through the house or apartment and discussed what might be dangerous to the child at the time, e.g., padding coffee table with sharp corners, plugging electrical outlets, taping loose electric cords along walls, putting detergents and medicines out of reach, putting locks on cabinets containing breakables and household chemicals, keeping front and back door locked while the child is in the house, etc.

... that some activities that the child enjoys are only safe in the presence of an adult, e.g., playing in the bathtub.

We *modeled*

... setting clear and simple limits in matters of safety when appropriate, e.g., "Come and hold my hand while we walk across the parking lot," or "I'll put you over here to play, away from the heater," or "I will have to stop the car if you climb out of your car seat."

... removing a toy that was dangerous for the child, e.g., a rattle that the child kept hitting himself with, a puzzle with very small pieces that he tried to put in his mouth.

... giving the child an alternative after he had been stopped from doing something dangerous, e.g., "I cannot let you have this sharp pencil, but why don't you try this crayon," or "Here is a sturdy box to climb on rather than the window ledge."

... providing equipment for the child's safety if the parent did not have it or did not have the means of getting it, e.g., car seat, high chair with safety straps, locks for cabinets, safety plugs for electrical outlets.

...anticipating the child's changing safety needs, e.g., saying at the project Center, "I think we will put him in a child-sized chair now; he is so big and heavy that he might topple over in the high chair."

In cases where the parent's failure to provide for the child's safety bordered on neglect...

We also *discussed* with the parent

...that it is the adult's responsibility to protect the child from himself at an age when he does not understand danger and has a strong drive to explore.

...our concern about the situation in the home, and we emphasized that the child needed to be protected from dangerous situations at all times.

...how badly she would feel if her child was hurt accidentally.

...that while her child might seem very smart and independent, he still was not yet able to recognize danger or understand the consequences of his actions.

...our willingness to extend our home visit long enough so that we could help her right then to child-proof the home, if she felt that she wanted that kind of help.

PROBLEM 7:   Feeding became a struggle for the parent when the child began wanting to participate in the process.

We *listened empathetically* as the parent

...talked about her concern that the child would not be adequately nourished if she allowed him to feed himself.

...said that it would take "forever" if she let the child feed himself.

...talked about how much she had enjoyed feeding her child in the past, and how disappointed she was that he did not enjoy mealtimes anymore.

...expressed her need to have a clean kitchen and her "disgust" at children who play with their food and "make a mess."

...talked about the waste of food that was inevitable if the child were allowed to feed himself.

We *observed* with the parent

...the child's cues that indicated he wanted to feed himself, e.g., grabbing spoon or cup, reaching for food on his or other people's plates.

...the child's attempts to imitate the parent's behavior, including eating and feeding.

...the child's purposefulness and dexterity in handling manipulative materials, and we noted how this seemed to indicate his readiness to begin self-feeding.

...how the child seemed to eat more eagerly when he was allowed to feed himself at least part of a meal.

We *discussed* with the parent

...that many parents of preterm or "at risk" children are especially concerned about their children's food intake.

...that some parents particularly enjoy the stage when the infant is fully dependent on the adult and find it difficult to accept the child's increasing demands for independence.

...how she might find mealtimes more pleasant and less of a battle if she allowed the child first to hold a spoon while she was feeding him and then if she allowed him to feed himself part of a meal.

...that often the child's resistance to feeding at this stage is not directed at the food but at being fed.

...that children at her child's age usually want to begin to feed themselves, even if they need practice to do so neatly.

...that the child might enjoy being offered some things at each meal that he can handle himself without too much "mess."

...the foods that are finger foods and that would be less messy than foods that require a spoon, e.g., small chucks of cheese, chicken or cooked vegetables, crackers, and dry cereal.

...the possibility of allowing the child to practice with a spoon at the end of a meal when there is just a little bit of food left.

...that at this stage, most children cannot handle a full bowl of food at one time, but that they will self-feed themselves better if they find a very small quantity in the bowl.

...that the mess children make when feeding themselves is more manageable when they sit in a high chair with a tray rather than in the parent's lap.

...that it is usually a good learning experience for the child if the parent calmly takes the food away when the child begins to throw it on the floor.

...that if the child first eats well and with concentration and then begins to "mess" and throw food, it usually means that he is not hungry any more.

...that the play activity of dropping things off the high chair tray is something that young children go through and that this activity can be very upsetting to parents, especially when it is interpreted, falsely, as being done intentionally to upset the parent.

...that some parents find it helpful to put newspapers around the high chair during the child's mealtime.

We *commented positively*

...when the parent reported that she had experimented with foods that the child could eat by himself.

...when the parent reported that she had allowed the child to "play" with his spoon during mealtime so that he could learn to handle it.

...when the parent talked about how serious and intent the child seemed about feeding himself some foods.

...when the parent expressed some enjoyment at watching the child develop skills of feeding himself with the spoon.

In cases where the child had a motor impairment that made self-feeding particularly difficult...

We *listened empathetically* as the parent

...talked about her fear that the child would gag or choke on food if he fed himself.

...anticipated that the child would get so exhausted from unsuccessful attempts to feed himself that he would then refuse to be fed and would not get sufficient nourishment.

...talked about how painful it would be for her to watch him struggle with self-feeding and how long feeding sessions would take.

We *observed* with the parent

...the level of his manipulative skills.

...the size and shape of objects that he was able to handle most easily.

...what kind of help he seemed to need in order to handle some objects successfully.

We *experimented*[2]

...to find utensils that would make self-feeding easier for the child, e.g., different-sized cups, feeding dish stabilized by suction cup, weighted bowls, special infant cups, spoons with thick handles.

...with offering a variety of finger foods to find some that the child could manipulate, chew, and swallow without difficulty.

...with ways of adjusting the child's posture in the high chair to give him maximum freedom to use his hands, arms, fingers.

We *discussed* with the parent

...the sense of achievement that the child would get when he learned to handle some foods on his own.

...whether it might be a good idea to include the child in family mealtimes by giving him a few bits of food that he could handle by himself.

---

[2]We would try things with the child in cases where the parent was discouraged, but we would encourage the parent to experiment when she seemed motivated to do so.

PROBLEM 8:   The parent was unresponsive to the child's cues regarding food preference and quantity because she was concerned that he was not eating enough.

We *listened empathetically* as the parent

... described her attempts to prepare well-balanced meals and her feelings of rejection and frustration when the child would not eat them.

... expressed her fears that the child would be undernourished if she let him determine how much he would eat.

... talked about her concern that the child still did not weigh as much as other children his age.

... expressed her belief that the child would not eat regularly if she fed him only at those times when he indicated he was hungry.

... talked about her dislike of "finicky" eaters.

... expressed strong feelings about wanting to teach the child not to waste food.

We *observed* with the parent

... several feeding situations so as to better understand the problem.

... what indications the child gave that he was hungry or satiated.

... how the child showed that he enjoyed, tolerated, or disliked particular foods.

... which textures of food the child seemed to prefer; whether he liked warm or cold foods; which flavors, smells, and colors he seemed to like especially.

... what aspects of the feeding situation the child seemed to enjoy most, e.g., the parent's attention, being at eye level with parent while he was in the high chair, the parent talking to him, his playing with his spoon.

We *discussed* with the parent

... that many parents express concerns similar to hers.

... that she might feel better if she shared her concerns about adequate weight gain and food intake with her pediatrician.

... that adequate nutritional intake is a very individual matter based on many factors such as metabolism, height, amount of motor activity, etc.

... that many parents report that their children's appetites fluctuate and their food preferences change over time.

... that some children tend to be hungrier at certain times of the day than at other times.

... that concern about food intake can sometimes be overcome when the parent writes down what the child eats over a period of several days. (Some parents find that their child eats more than they had thought.)

...that many young children seem to enjoy a very simple diet with a few foods repeated over and over, while others like a great diversity of flavors and textures.

...that she may find it easiest to introduce new foods at the time when the child is likely to be hungriest.

...that new foods are most easily accepted when introduced in very small quantities and along with foods the child already likes.

...that children go through states of eating more and then eating less, and that the typical pattern of decreasing appetite, along with a slower rate of physical growth, is usually found in the second year of life.

We *commented positively*

...when the parent accurately responded to the child's cues in any area of interaction, e.g., "You really picked up on what he was telling you."

...when the parent described how much the child seemed to enjoy having her all to himself during mealtimes.

...as the parent talked about her child's individual food habits and preferences that were different from others in the family.

...when the parent talked about allowing the child to have some control over what he ate during what she considered the "least important meal of the day."

...when the parent shared her recent observation that the child seemed to eat more readily when she was not forcing or urging him to eat.

...when the parent reported that she allowed the child to have small portions of the food he reached for at the family dinner table.

PROBLEM 9: The parent was concerned about the child's frequent demands for food.

We *listened empathetically* as the parent

...said she was tired of her child's incessant demands for food.

...described her frustration in trying to keep the child out of the cupboard and refrigerator.

...expressed worry that the child might become overweight.

...said that she prepared and fed the child adequate and nutritious foods at mealtimes, and that she could not understand the child's almost constant desire for food.

...expressed her feeling that children needed to learn to eat when everyone else in the family ate.

...wondered whether she might be wrong about what was the right food for children of this age.

...expressed concern that there might be something "wrong" with the child.

We *asked* the parent

...to describe the child's eating pattern during the day.

...if there were certain situations or times that seemed to trigger the child's excessive demands for food.

...how frequently the child saw the adults in the family eat.

...if the child ate what was given him at mealtime.

...if she thought the child was truly hungry or was mainly asking for attention.

...whether the child showed any other problems at the present time.

...whether she had any reason to believe that the child was under particular stress.

We *discussed* with the parent

...her ideas about food, nutrition, and mealtime.

...that it might be helpful to record the child's actual food intake over several days as well as to observe the child for any signs of stress before deciding on how to deal with the eating situation.

...that many young children do get hungry more often than adults and may need mid-morning and mid-afternoon snacks.

...that children as well as adults differ in the quantity of food they feel comfortable eating at any one meal and in how often they want to eat.

...that young children go through stages when they eat more, and then, between ages 2 and 3, they often eat less than before.

...that nutritional needs vary according to metabolism, activity level, rate of growth, and other factors.

...that when some young children see others eating, they want to eat too.

...the alternative of giving the child several scheduled small meals a day if she was not comfortable with irregular snacks.

...foods that most children like and that require very little preparation, e.g., leftover meats, vegetables, cereal, juices.

...various kinds of nutritious snacks, e.g., fruit, vegetables, certain kinds of crackers, chunks of cheese.

...that children, like adults, often ask for food when they are under stress, are tired, or are bored.

...that some parents find that young children are more satisfied with their food when they eat some of their meals with the family and when mealtime becomes a social time.

...that some parents have reported that if they offer the child food to comfort him or to keep him busy, he will come to expect food whenever he is upset or bored.

...that sometimes a child will forget about wanting food if he is given total attention for a short while.

In cases where the child was overweight . . .

We also *listened empathetically* as the parent

. . . expressed her desire to have a physically attractive child and not one who was overweight.

. . . expressed worry about whether the child was going to be an obese adult.

. . . questioned whether the child had an organic problem.

We *asked* the parent

. . . whether she had discussed her concerns with the child's physician.

. . . to describe the kinds of meals and snacks the child usually had over the period of a day.

We *discussed* with the parent

. . . that some parents find that letting the child have some control over his food intake but only offering him low calorie foods allows the child to regulate his own calorie intake and, as a result, he might have less of an urge to eat.

. . . various publications and guides that give both the nutritional value and calorie content of common foods.

. . . the kinds and quantities of food that other people in the family consume.

. . . that often children learn to like what the other family members like and that this applies to foods as well as to other things.

. . . the notion of not buying or having on hand non-nutritive or empty calorie foods, e.g., soda pop, potato chips, junk foods of all kinds, because if the food is not available, the child cannot eat it.

. . . what kinds of low calorie foods she thought her child might like, e.g., celery, carrots, green beans, oranges, cottage cheese, yogurt, hard-boiled eggs, tomatoes, whole wheat crackers or small quantities of whole wheat bread, raisins instead of candy, etc.

. . . that young children do not have the ability to delay immediate gratification and that they have to rely on adults to establish limits for them.

. . . whether she thought she could tell her child that she recognized he wanted more food but that this was all he was getting for now.

. . . that it might help to think about planning a regular, special "fun time" for the child and parent right after mealtime, that the child could anticipate and look forward to.

PROBLEM 10:   **The parent was not realistic about the process of toilet training nor aware of signs of the child's readiness.**

We *listened empathetically* as the parent

...expressed how much she disliked changing diapers, especially in the last few months.

...talked about how eager she was for the child to be trained before the new baby arrived so that she would not have two children in diapers.

...expressed frustration and anger at her futile attempts to train the child.

...described the pressure she felt from both relatives and friends to toilet train the child quickly.

...talked about a friend's child who was younger than her child but already toilet trained.

...expressed concern that he would not be trained in time to start nursery school in the fall.

...said that she did not want to give the child a "complex" by pressuring him too much.

We *asked* the parent

...about any behaviors which she thought indicated that the child was ready to be trained, e.g., comes to parent to be changed, is interested in watching others in the bathroom, likes to imitate others, dislikes being wet.

...when toilet training was expected to take place in her extended family.

...how her efforts at toilet training had gone so far.

We *discussed* with the parent

...common signs that indicate the child's readiness for toilet training, e.g., the behaviors listed above and also: stays dry for long periods, has a word for elimination, shows some regularity in bowel and bladder function, is uncomfortable when soiled.

...that children differ greatly in their rates of development in all areas, including readiness for toilet training and speed with which they can be trained: some learn early and some later, but all learn eventually.

...that mores as to when to begin toilet training and how to go about it vary greatly among cultures and have changed in the United States over the last 30 years, as reflected in the childrearing literature.

...that when an infant is toilet trained very early, it usually means that the parent has learned to "catch" him rather than that the infant has the control himself.

...that bowel control usually comes before bladder control, and that daytime control is usually achieved before control during the night.

...that toilet training usually takes at least a few weeks and sometimes a few months, and that success should not be expected overnight.

...that problems can usually be avoided when the parent is relaxed and anticipates that it might take some time until success is achieved.

...that for toilet training to be successful, the child has to be ready and the parent has to feel certain that she is ready to put the effort and time into it that is required.

...that it may take longer for the child to understand what is expected of him if the parent sometimes puts him in diapers because it is more convenient (for outings) and at other times expects him to use the potty.

...that gaining control over his body is an important developmental achievement for the young child, and that he needs parental support and patience to succeed at it.

...methods that other parents have found helpful:

1. Chart the time of day when the child has a bowel movement, and put the child on the potty chair about that time.
2. Make "potty time" comfortable for him and no longer than seems reasonable, regardless of results.
3. Make the potty chair easily accessible.
4. Praise the child's successes, no matter how small.
5. If the child is interested, let him watch other children (or adults, if that feels comfortable) go to the toilet.
6. Let the child wear training pants.
7. Keep the child in clothing that he can easily pull off himself.
8. Give the child a baby doll with which to play "potty."
9. Continue to say to the child that some day soon he will be able to "go potty" like his mother and father. (This is reassuring to the child as well as to the parent.)
10. Allow the child to flush the toilet.

...that it helps the child to have accidents treated matter-of-factly and not to be shamed for them, e.g., "I guess you had a BM in your pants this time; let's go and clean up. Pretty soon you'll be able to make it into the potty all the time."

...that many children regress in toilet training when they have to cope with stress, like a new sibling or the parent's or his own hospitalization.

...that most parents find that it is easier not to initiate toilet training at a time when the child is going through a stage of intense negativism.

...that a partially trained child often learns very quickly when he is exposed to other children his age or slightly older (such as in a nursery school or play group) who are toilet trained.

PROBLEM 11:   The parent found it difficult to get the child to go to sleep at night.

We *listened empathetically* as the parent

... told us how frustrated and drained she felt when the child would not fall asleep at night.

... talked about how irritated she would become when the child would not fall asleep and spoiled the evening for herself and her husband.

... described the child's earlier sleep problems and expressed worry that she might not have handled these well.

... expressed concern that something was wrong with the child because he had such difficulty in falling asleep at night.

... talked about how she had hoped that if she were understanding and reassuring, the child would outgrow his difficulty in going to sleep, but that this had not happened.

... wondered about whether she should simply let the child scream himself to sleep.

... related her husband's feelings that the child was manipulating her and needed stronger discipline.

We *commented positively*

... about the appropriate techniques the parent was already using in order to help the child to go to sleep.

... on the parent's desire to work through the problem in a manner that would help the child.

... when the parent reported trying out a new routine for bedtime even though it took more time.

... when the parent talked about having read child development materials on the issue and that this had helped her to think about it in a little different way; that she realized now that this problem was not so uncommon.

... when the parent indicated that she was going to do what was comfortable for her and the child, whether the experts agreed or not.

We *asked* the parent

... to describe the sequence of events at bedtime in detail.

... how the child went to sleep for his daytime nap.

... whether she thought the child was tired enough at bedtime to go to sleep easily.

... how long the child usually slept during the day.

... whether she saw any relationship between length of daytime nap and difficulty in falling asleep at night.

... about the routine she had established at bedtime and which parts of it she and the child particularly enjoyed.

We *discussed* with the parent

...that many parents describe similar problems with children at this stage of development.

...that problems over bedtime can be particularly frustrating and irritating because the parent herself is tired at that time of the day.

...that it was easy to understand why she was anxious not to have to spend hours trying to get the child to go to sleep as she had done when he was an infant.

...that some parents find that it helps to set aside some special time to devote exclusively to the child just before bedtime.

...that some children get very excited and stimulated by having active physical play shortly before bedtime and find it difficult to go to sleep afterwards.

...the possibility that the mother or father conclude the day with the child with a quiet activity, e.g., looking at books or lying on the floor and listening to soft music.

...that most parents find that a brief, pleasant, and calming bedtime routine gives children the security of knowing when they are expected to go to bed and to sleep.

...that it may help some children to incorporate into the bedtime routine some physically relaxing activities, e.g., warm bath, backrub, soft music, quiet time with books, warm milk before going to sleep.

...that some parents find that if they describe each step of the bedtime routine as they are going through it, the child learns to accept the sequence more easily and that there is less resistance at the end.

...that parents as well as children need to know that there will be an "end" to the going-to-bed process.

...that it was important to say "good-night" with conviction and a tone of finality once the bedtime routine had been completed.

...that many children are helped to go to sleep if they can have a night light in their room, have the door ajar, and have a favorite stuffed animal or soft doll in their bed as they go to sleep.

...that if problems over going to sleep arise because the child may not be tired enough, it might be worth experimenting with a later bedtime or an earlier or shorter nap.

...that if she finds that she needs to try out new methods, it is important to expect a new routine to take some time to yield success.

...that if new methods are tried, the aspects of the "old" routine that seemed to be helpful and enjoyable for parent and child should be continued.

...that sometimes children react to stress by having trouble falling asleep at night, e.g., weaning, toilet training, new caregiver, new baby in family, etc., or by waking up during the night (see Problem 12).

PROBLEM 12:   The parent was distressed about the child's night waking.

We *listened empathetically* as the parent

. : . told us how tired and irritable she felt after being awakened several times during the night.
. . . talked about how disruptive the child's night waking was to her husband and other children.
. . . described her unsuccessful attempts to get the child to go back to sleep.
. . . expressed how angry she felt when the child woke up during the night without apparent reason.
. . . talked about how worried she was that she had spoiled the child by going to him whenever he cried at night.
. . . told us how difficult it was to strike the balance between reassuring the child and telling him firmly that he needed to go back to sleep.

We *asked* the parent

. . . how often the child usually woke up during the night.
. . . how the child acted when he woke up, e.g., screaming, whimpering on and off, calling.
. . . whether the child usually went to sleep by himself at bedtime or whether he needed rocking, patting, or some other kind of help from the parent.
. . . what the usual routine was before bedtime.
. . . how long the child napped during the day.
. . . what methods she had tried in dealing with the child's night waking and which seemed to have been most effective.
. . . whether she had noticed any change in the child's behavior during the daytime since the night waking began.
. . . whether she had noticed any signs of physical discomfort such as teething, earache, cold, general fussiness during the day.
. . . whether there had been any changes in the home or in the child's routine recently.

We *discussed* with the parent

. . . that many infants who have slept through the night for several months begin to wake up during the night (frequently between 8 and 10 months of age).
. . . that most parents are relieved to learn that this is a passing stage and that it does not mean that their child is "disturbed" or will always have sleeping problems.
. . . that children who sleep less soundly than others or who have irregular sleep patterns are more likely to wake during the night.

...that it can be frustrating when the child cannot tell the parent what is waking him.

...that minor discomforts that the child can ignore while he is active during the day can make him irritable and wakeful during the night.

...that the young infant tends to wake up hungry or when experiencing physical discomfort, while the toddler may be awakened by nightmares or fears.

...that night waking because of fear indicates the growing cognitive ability of the child to use his imagination in dreams or fear fantasies.

...the child's need for extra reassurance at night at this stage, and that he will outgrow this stage as he learns to cope with nightmares and fears on his own.

...that many children wake at night after upsetting events, changes in routines, or overstimulation during the day or over several days.

...that some children seem to feel more secure when they can have a night light on, a door open, or when they sleep with a favorite soft toy or blanket.

...the diminishing need for daytime sleep as the child grows older, and the possibility of reducing daytime naps if the night waking appears as "just not being sleepy."

...that children, like adults, do not wake up deliberately and that some children can go back to sleep on their own while others need a little help.

...how waiting a few minutes before going to the child may give him time to learn to comfort himself (unless the child's cries have a frantic quality that expresses distress or fear).

...that most toddlers like the security of a bedtime routine, and that repeating the last part of that routine after night waking may comfort the child and help him go back to sleep, e.g., a "bear hug," "tucking him in," a kiss, a verbal "good night" with a tone of finality, the way it is done at bedtime.

...that some parents let the child sleep in their bed during the period of frequent night waking, but that although this may make it temporarily easier on the parents, it may create other problems and make it more difficult to get the child used to sleeping in his own bed again.

...that comforting the child in his own room and bed may take a lot more effort and interruption of the parent's sleep, but that there may be less of a problem in the long run to get the child to sleep by himself.

...that offering food or playing with the child when he wakes up during the night tends to create expectations of "fun" at those times, and this may help to create a habit of waking up as well as making it more difficult for him to learn to go back to sleep.

...the importance of accepting the child's feelings but also the need to let him know that it is time to go back to sleep, e.g., "I know you don't want to stay in your bed because you are afraid, but Mommy is right here and can't let you climb out of bed; it's nighttime and sleep time.''

PROBLEM 13:   The working parent found it difficult to spend the necessary time and energy to maintain a positive relationship with her child.

We *listened empathetically* as the parent

...described her feelings of guilt about being away from her child so much.

...expressed worry about being "responsible" if her child should develop problems.

...talked about her fear that the child would begin to like the daycare provider better than her and wondered if that person was more competent than she was.

...talked about how demanding and exhausting it was to raise children, have a full-time job, and run the household.

...expressed resentment about never having time for herself.

...described how tense she was much of the time when she had to attend to many different household responsibilities and felt that she should also be spending time with the child.

...described losing her patience too often with the child after a long day.

...wondered if she could ever find satisfaction in either her job or in parenting while she was trying to do both.

We *asked* the parent

...how she spent the time she did have with the child before and after work and on weekends.

...which times seemed enjoyable for both of them and which were rushed and tense.

...what activities the child seemed to enjoy particularly.

...what she enjoyed doing with the child.

We *discussed* with the parent

...how difficult most parents find it to be with young children when both parent and child are tired.

...that many parents have expressed concerns similar to hers.

...that interactions during caregiving routines such as feeding and bathing can be enjoyable for parent and infant.

...that young children find almost any activity with a parent enjoyable if they are involved in a meaningful way, e.g., playing with pots and pans while the parent is in the kitchen, pretending to peel a carrot, "helping" to load and unload the washing machine.

...that the quality rather than the sheer quantity of time spent with children is the important factor in the development of a good relationship with them.

...ways in which she could best use the limited time that they had together, e.g., talking to him while dressing him.

...the importance of letting the child know the parent is aware of him even while she is busy, e.g., talking with him while she is working in the kitchen.

...that older children can learn to wait for "their time" with the parent if they know they can count on it, e.g., "I need to unwind right now, but I will play ball with you after we eat."

...how some parents find that spending a small amount of time when they give their full attention to their child seems to bring more satisfaction to both than large amounts of time when the child has to compete with other people and things for the parent's attention.

...that many parents feel that if they meet some of their own needs and take time to enjoy something special for themselves occasionally, they willingly give more of themselves to the child.

...ways in which the child showed how important the parent was to him.

...how her efforts to ensure the continuity of quality daycare for her child while she worked gave evidence of her being a concerned and good parent.

We *commented positively*

...when the parent was affectionate with her child.

...when the parent responded to the child's bids for attention.

...when the child indicated pleasure in being with his parent.

...when the parent reported that she and the child were having a much better time together.

...when the parent talked about trying to find ways to do more things with the child.

...when the parent talked about taking some time for herself.

...when the parent told us how happy she was with the daycare provider.

...when the parent related how good her communication was with the daycare provider.

PROBLEM 14:   The working parent had difficulty coping emotionally with the child after returning home from work.

We *listened empathetically* as the parent

...described how depressing it was to have her child cry when she came to pick him up in the daycare home.

...said that at the end of a hard day, the responsibility of caring for a cranky child was just too much.

...said that the child was very demanding at the end of the day and that she, the parent, had no patience with him.

...described the awful temper tantrums the child had when they got home.

...talked about how upset she got when the child was so fussy at bedtime.

...said that after a bad evening with the child, she was so exhausted that she could not sleep.

...expressed doubt about herself as a parent because she was sometimes unable to calm the child when he cried.

We *asked* the parent

...how the child reacted to her when she picked him up at the daycare home.

...about the usual sequence of events when she picked up the child after work.

...whether there was an adult or older child in the home that could take charge of the child to allow her to have a few minutes to herself and then to get dinner ready.

...how she was dealing with him when he cried and fussed in the evening.

...how she managed to help the child become relaxed at times other than the end of the day.

We *discussed* with the parent

...whether she could try to use the same method of calming the child in the evening that worked for her during the weekend (follow-up from previous item).

...that she might want to experiment to see if the child would be less fussy if she sat down with him for a few minutes after work and talked and played with him, before doing her chores.

...that it might save her time and emotional energy in the long run if she spent a few minutes longer getting him relaxed before bedtime (also see items under Problem 12).

...practical ideas for occupying the child so that he would not get upset about waiting for his dinner, e.g., bringing a snack for the ride home, giving him a favorite toy while she is fixing dinner.

...how crying upon reunion could be an indication of the child's sense of relief upon seeing her again and, at the same time, remembering how he felt when she left him in the morning.

...that young children like the reassurance of a physical greeting after being separated from their parents, e.g., a hug, being picked up, etc.

...that his "falling apart" a little in the evening did not mean that he had been "bad" or unhappy all day in the daycare home.

...that some parents get upset when their children give them a difficult time at night after having heard how "delightful" the child had been in the daycare home.

...that the way in which the child felt free to express his frustrations and negative feelings to her was an indication of how secure he felt with her.

We *commented positively*

...when the parent reported that she felt a little more relaxed in the evening.

...when the parent expressed greater confidence in her ability to deal with the child when they were both tired.

...when she talked about asking a 12-year-old neighbor over to play with the child while she was fixing dinner.

...when the parent talked about experimenting with changes in her routine to make things easier for herself and the child at night.

PROBLEM 15:   The parent was not aware of the importance of quality childcare.

We *listened empathetically* as the parent

...talked about problems in finding someone to care for her child.

...expressed concern about the cost and location of available childcare.

We *asked* the parent

...how she had found the current daycare provider.

...whether she was satisfied with how the infant was cared for.

...whether the infant seemed happy in the daycare situation.

...whether she and the daycare provider had a chance to talk about the infant regularly.

We *discussed* with the parent

...that small children need adult attention beyond just having their physical needs met.

...that inadequate adult attention for the child during the day might result in problem behavior at home.

...that most children who are cared for adequately get used to the new caregiver and environment and feel secure enough to play and socialize with new people.

...that the child is likely to be happier upon the parent's return if he had good care during the day.

...that some daycare situations that may be adequate for very young infants may not be so appropriate for toddlers, e.g., someone who meets physical needs and likes young babies may not meet the toddler's social and play needs.

...the child's particular developmental needs that should be met in a daycare situation, e.g., toddlers need to explore their environment, need some adult attention, and need some chance for large motor activity.

...that it may be easier for the child to get used to a caregiver if there is some consistency in childrearing practices between home and daycare.

...the importance of choosing caregivers who enjoy children, who know children's developmental needs, and who respect the parent's ideas and values in childrearing.

...how to evaluate the quality of childcare situations by observing: how many young children are being taken care of by one adult; how much space is available to the children; whether there is indoor and outdoor space for the children; whether the environment is safe and reasonably clean and orderly; whether there are places for comfortable eating, napping, and toileting; whether the caregiver seems warm and affectionate with the children; whether the children in the situation seem to turn to the adult trustingly; whether the children interact with the caregiver and each other happily; how the caregiver handles children's distress; whether the caregiver responds to children's vocalizations or language.

...different types of daycare that might be available to the parent, e.g., family daycare, daycare centers, cooperative babysitting arrangements.

...the possibility of our visiting the daycare situation occasionally in addition to seeing the parent and her child in the home.

...whether she would like us to visit and help her evaluate various daycare situations.

We *encouraged* the parent

...to clarify in her own mind and to the daycare provider what was important to her in the care of her child.

...to communicate regularly with the daycare provider about what her child was doing and how he was changing at home.

...to provide the child with some of his favorite toys to play with at the daycare home.

...to choose toys from those we brought that she would like the child to take with him to the daycare home.

...to seek a new childcare arrangement if the parent felt dissatisfied with the current one.

In cases where the working parent was not aware of the importance of having a consistent caregiver for her young child...

We also *discussed* with the parent

...that even very young infants know the difference between a familiar and an unfamiliar person.

...that this awareness increases as the infant grows older and that infants between 8 months and 2 years of age may be particularly upset by frequent changes in caregivers.

...that children who have frequent changes in caregivers may get confused and show signs of stress such as night waking, excessive fear of separation, frequent crying, etc. (Also see Problems 13 and 14.)

PROBLEM 16: **The parent of an infant with a traumatic birth was overprotective and limited the infant's experience.**

We *listened empathetically* as the parent

...talked about how difficult the infant's first few weeks of life had been for her, when she did not know whether he would survive.

...expressed her lingering fears that the infant might have suffered brain damage, which would soon show up in the form of some abnormality.

...told us how it scared her when the infant bumped or bruised himself.

...told us that she felt it was not safe for the infant to move about freely as he might injure himself.

...said that the infant was too young to have to cope with pain or frustration that she could prevent.

...expressed concern that the infant might "catch" an illness if she took him where he would be with other children, and that he might become more dangerously ill than other children.

We *asked* the parent

...whether the infant had had any problems since his traumatic birth.

...whether the physician had told her to take special precautions with the infant because of his difficulties at birth and during the neonatal period.

...how the infant reacted when he encountered frustration or when he hurt himself.

...whether the infant seemed to want to move about and explore on his own.

We *observed* with the parent

...the infant's behavior in the different developmental areas: his play, social behavior, language, and motor activities.
...how mildly the infant reacted to frustrations.
...the determination with which the infant seemed to pursue his activities and goals in play, even when he encountered some obstacles.
...the infant's interest in social interaction with other adults and children.

We *discussed* with the parent

...how many parents find it difficult to see their infant cry because of discomfort, pain, or frustration, but that neither pain nor frustration can or should be prevented all the time because both are a natural part of life.
...that the infant takes cues from the adult as to how to react to minor bumps and bruises and that he may become fearful of exploring his environment (so necessary for learning) and of trying out new motor skills if he sees the adult react sharply.
...that she might feel more confident about letting the infant explore his environment if she made special provisions for his safety, e.g., padding the floor well, moving furniture with corners out of the way or padding the corners.
...that children often have a greater sense of mastery if they are able to overcome obstacles on their own, e.g., "It really was hard for him to pull himself up on the sofa, and he whimpered as he worked at it over and over again, but look at him now! He knows he has done it all on his own and his face is beaming!"
...how children need and enjoy exposure to new people and new surroundings.
...that she might feel better about taking the infant to friends' homes if she assured herself ahead of time that nobody in the home was ill.
...that it would be a good experience for the infant to get to know and trust another adult who could care for him occasionally.
...that children who had some exposure to colds and other mild illnesses while they were young seemed to have more resistance to illness when they entered group situations.

We *encouraged* the parent

...to go on outings with the infant so that both of them could enjoy a change in environment.
...to explore the possibility of participating with the infant in a parent-infant group in the community so that she could have the opportunity

to talk with other parents and observe her infant interact with other infants and toddlers of approximately the same age.

In cases where the child was handicapped or delayed...

We also *listened empathetically* as the parent

...talked about how she felt the child should not have to cope with any more frustrations than his handicap was creating for him.

...expressed how terrible she felt when she saw her child struggle and struggle to accomplish what would be so easy for other children his age.

...talked about her feeling that it was part of being a good parent to a handicapped child to protect him from falls and bumps and bruises.

...said that nobody understood her child's needs as well as she did and that she could not leave him in anybody else's care for that reason.

We *discussed* with the parent

...that all children need to have the experience of doing something *on their own,* no matter how hard this might be for them.

...that children must be able to experience the sense of mastery that comes from accomplishing their own goals.

...that if the child were not given the opportunity to achieve something on his own, he would have not have the chance to develop a feeling of self-esteem that is so necessary to a healthy personality.

...that she could help the child develop the courage to try by expressing confidence that he could cope with little frustrations and overcome obstacles to his goal.

...that she might help the child achieve his goals by dividing tasks into small steps so that he could experience success after minimal frustration, e.g., hold a toy stable, but slightly out of reach, so that the child has to move toward it but will not knock it further out of reach when he grasps for it.

...that in many situations during the day she could figure out what minimal help he might profit from in order to accomplish a task he set for himself or, in some cases, that the parent set for him.

...that her child, like all children, needed to learn that not all his wishes could be satisfied immediately and at all times.

...that she should try to get away and do something for herself occasionally and that this might be difficult at first, but that it would help her and her relationship with her child in the long run.

PROBLEM 17:   The parent had anxiety regarding the normalcy of the child due to his traumatic birth and difficulties in the neonatal period.

We *listened empathetically* as the parent

. . . described the difficulties experienced during the early weeks of the child's life.

. . . talked about how she still feared that he might have suffered some brain damage at that time (as one doctor had told them might have occurred).

. . . expressed concern that her child did not always seem to act like other children his age.

. . . talked about how she kept expecting some problems to show up as the child grew older.

We *commented positively*

. . . on her child's special strengths and skills.

. . . on the parent's observational skills.

. . . on how she and the child seemed to enjoy each other's company.

We *discussed* with the parent

. . . that it is natural to have lingering concerns and that many parents feel anxious after their child has gone through early traumas.

. . . that most children are pretty resilient and often recover from early traumas without any lingering problems.

. . . that the child's play and language behavior were just what one would expect from a child his age.

. . . the vast differences in children's behavior within the normal range.

. . . how her child had been moving along a normal developmental sequence and was doing well.

We *encouraged* the parent

. . . to continue enjoying her child and not to let her worry overshadow her enjoyment of him.

. . . to try to see the child as he was at the present time rather than to focus on his earlier problems.

. . . to continue sharing her concerns with us.

In cases where the staff suspected that the child might be delayed . . .

We also *discussed* with the parent

. . . that we saw the behaviors that she was seeing and that worried her and that we shared her concern.

...that it is necessary to observe a child in all areas of development over a long period of time and in different situations in order to find out what the child's problem might be.

...what we saw as the areas of the child's strengths and how we could help him build on these strengths and, at the same time, strengthen his skills in his areas of weakness.

...how useful her observations of the child were in our working cooperatively to find activities that would foster the child's development of skills in various areas.

...that it might be helpful for her to see a developmental pediatrician if her concerns persisted.

PROBLEM 18: **The parent was so involved with the infant that she tended to neglect the needs of other family members and her own needs.**

We *listened empathetically* as the parent

...talked about her anxiety regarding the infant because he seemed so vulnerable.

...talked about how much time and attention the infant required.

...mentioned that there was little time left for her to do anything other than take care of the infant.

We *asked* the parent

...how the sibling was reacting to the infant and all the attention that he was getting.

...whether she and her husband had any time together away from the children.

We *listened empathetically* again, as the parent

...described how the sibling sometimes acted like a baby and how irritating she found this.

...talked about how the sibling seemed to get into trouble whenever she was busy with the infant.

...talked about how she had thought the sibling would help her take care of the infant but that, instead, she had become more demanding.

...talked about her concern that other family members might feel resentful toward the infant because he took up so much of her time.

...told us about the tension that was developing between her and her husband because she had so little time for him.

...said that her husband had been asking her to go out with him for an evening, but that she did not feel she could leave the infant.

...talked about how little time she had for herself and how exhausted she felt by the end of the day.

...talked about how much her life had changed since this infant was born.

We *observed* with the parent

...ways in which the infant indicated that he was ready for some independence, e.g., playing by himself or sitting on the floor on his own.

...ways in which the sibling indicated that she needed her parent.

...the infant's interest in other people.

We *commented positively*

...when the parent was affectionate with the sibling.

...when the parent recognized the sibling's need by providing special toys and activities for her while the parent was busy with the infant.

...when the parent talked about spending some time with the sibling while the infant slept or was happy playing on his own.

...when the parent talked about going out occasionally with her husband.

We *discussed* with the parent

...that many parents whose infants had difficulties in the first weeks of life feel anxious about their infant and think that he continues to need special care.

...that children are remarkably resilient (with some exceptions) and that they usually develop perfectly normally after a difficult start.

...that it was often difficult for a parent to realize that an infant who was vulnerable at first may not need special care any more.

...that the sibling needed attention even though she seemed quite grown up to the parent.

...that parents often overestimate the maturity of the first-born once he has become the "older" child.

...that young children cannot be expected to "help" consistently with their younger siblings.

...that she might find the sibling easier to get along with if she could regularly arrange to have "special times" with her.

...that it helps to verbalize to the older child all the things she can do that the baby cannot do.

...that the older child may appreciate special outings with relatives and friends because she is the "older one."

...that many parents find it difficult to strike a balance in meeting the needs of everyone in the family.

...that most children between 1 and 6 or 7 years of age are expected to regress when a younger sibling is born, that this is difficult for the parent to bear, but that it is usually only a passing stage.

...that many parents find that they need to spend some time away from the infant in order to maintain their positive relationship with each other and with their other children.

We *modeled*

...recognizing the sibling's needs by talking and playing with her and by bringing along special toys for her.

...involving the sibling in play with the infant in a manner that was pleasurable for the sibling.

...accepting the sibling's feelings when she did not want to play with the infant.

In cases where the child was handicapped...

We also *listened empathetically* as the parent

...talked about how the child needed her and her special care.

...said that the other healthy children in the family could take care of themselves.

...expressed the belief that if she only spent enough time and effort with the child, he would get better.

...talked about her efforts to find the best possible medical care for the child.

...expressed sadness that her husband did not seem to "understand" the child.

...talked about how special this child was to her.

We *discussed* with the parent

...that most parents find that the responsibility of taking care of a handicapped child takes a lot of physical and emotional energy.

...that many families find that having a handicapped child puts a strain on all the relationships among the family members.

...that individual family members have to work through, in their own way, their acceptance of and relationship with the handicapped child.

...that young children do not understand the nature of a handicap and often develop scary fantasies about their sibling's handicap.

...that siblings need emotional support from their parents as they adjust to life with a handicapped sibling in the family.

...that it is important for the siblings to continue to be involved in their own activities that are meaningful to them.

. . . that she might find taking care of the child less draining if she would get away occasionally and do things that were of real interest and enjoyable to her.

. . . that couples with handicapped children have found that in order to be supportive of each other through trying times, they need to be together occasionally, away from home and from their everyday worries.

PROBLEM 19:   The parent was concerned about sibling rivalry and was uncertain about how to deal with it.

We *listened empathetically* as the parent

. . . talked about how much she hated it when her children did not get along with each other.

. . . told us how angry it made her when she saw the older child tease the younger one.

. . . said that she had expected her children to be able to be friends and to play together.

. . . talked about how she felt she had to protect the younger child from his older sibling.

. . . related how shocked she was when the sibling tried to hurt the younger child.

We *observed* with the parent

. . . what the children enjoyed doing together, e.g., older one clowning for the younger one to make him laugh, younger one being pulled in the wagon by the older one.

. . . ways in which the younger child interfered in the older one's more elaborate play.

. . . how the older one teased the younger child, apparently in order to get the parent's attention.

We *asked* the parent

. . . what situations tended to precipitate conflict between the children.

. . . how she had tried to handle fights and what she had found particularly effective.

. . . what she thought would happen if she did not attempt to resolve every conflict between the children but intervened only when she thought one might hurt the other.

We *discussed* with the parent

. . . that some sibling rivalry was unavoidable.

. . . that the children's age difference and different levels of social and cognitive functioning made it difficult for them to spend long periods with each other without conflicts, but that when they were both a little older, it might become easier for them to play together.

...that although the sibling was older, he was still a young child who might feel that he had to compete with the younger one for the parent's attention.

...that preschool age children often do not understand how toddlers are different from them and that much conflict arises because they expect the toddler to be able to play the same way they do.

...that some parents find that they can reduce the fighting and jealousy by making sure that their time alone with the older sibling is carefully protected.

...how frustrating it can be for the older sibling to have his play disrupted by the younger child.

...that sometimes it helps to try to establish a special area for each child where each can play without disturbances from the other.

...some multi-age activities that the preschool child and the toddler would enjoy together, e.g., bubbles, finger games, water play, sand play.

...that even young children often can work out ways of getting along with each other if trusted to solve some of their less explosive conflicts on their own.

...that, although it is important to comfort a child who is very upset or hurt in an altercation with a sibling or other child, constant parental intervention may increase the tension between children.

...that parents are sometimes able to reduce the jealousy of the older sibling by pointing out to him some of the privileges that only he has because he is the older one.

...the jealousy that the older child (especially if he is still a preschool-age child when the second child is born) often feels toward the younger one because, all of a sudden, he has to share the mother with the "intruder."

...that the older child may need the parent's help in learning how to deal with the younger one more gently, e.g., "Instead of pushing him away so that he falls, when he grabs your toys why don't you try telling him that it's your toy and offer him a different toy."

...that young children learn from watching adults deal verbally with conflict situations.

We *commented positively*

...when the parent got the sibling involved in an interesting activity to divert him from teasing the younger child.

...when the older sibling played with the younger one in a positive manner.

. . . when the younger one indicated affection for and interest in the older one.

. . . when the parent talked about each child's individual skills and strengths.

: . . when the parent did not intervene immediately in the impending conflict between the two children but waited to see if they could resolve it by themselves.

. . . when the parent protected the older sibling's play from the younger child's intrusion and interference.

. . . when the parent reported spending time alone with each child.

We *modeled*

. . . talking to the sibling about his skills.

. . . commenting on the sibling's mature way of playing with the younger child.

. . . presenting multi-age activities and involving both children.

. . . paying attention to the older sibling so that he would not feel left out by bringing special toys for him and playing with him for a while.

. . . finding ways to involve the sibling, at least for a little while, in the play with the younger child, e.g., taking turns with younger child in putting pegs in holes.

PART V

SUMMARIZING THE INTERVENTION EXPERIENCE

In Chapter 9, some factors that were found to influence the effectiveness of intervention are summarized. Some observations and thoughts about working with parents of handicapped infants, which have not been presented in other parts of the book, are also included. The chapter concludes with some generalizations that have been derived from the experience gained in the Intervention Program, which is described in earlier chapters of the book.

Chapter 9
Reflections upon the Intervention Experience

INFLUENCES ON INTERVENTION EFFECTIVENESS

Two factors seem to have been critical with regard to intervention effectiveness. Intervention was generally effective when the infant was a high priority in the life of the parent who functioned as primary caregiver, and when there was some parental concern regarding the infant's current and future development. When the parents were aware that the infant had problems and when they saw the program as a potential source of assistance for themselves in coping with the infant, the parents were motivated to participate fully in the program.

Although there is a relationship between the concerns parents have about their infant and the priority the infant occupies in their lives, there is also the possibility that serious and pressing problems unrelated to the infant might distract the parents' attention away from the infant, sometimes temporarily, sometimes for extended periods. In some families who were under considerable internal and external stress that was unrelated to the infant, the infant understandably did not play a prominent role in the lives of the parents. Before these parents could think about and attend to their infants, they had to begin to cope with some of their other problems. For some cases, the most useful intervention might have been a coordinated network of community services with the potential of meeting the families' economic, legal, housing, social, and psychological problems.

It is conventional wisdom that the effectiveness of intervention is also affected by the quality of rapport between the staff and the families. Since no systematic assessment or analysis of the interaction between parents and staff was made, comment can be made only on certain impressions of the influence that rapport had on intervention effectiveness. The establishment of good rapport was one of the important goals in the initial phase of intervention with every family. An effort was made to maintain staff continuity with the families. In most cases this effort was successful because from the outset there were two staff members assigned to each case. When one staff member had to leave the program, the other one was usually able to remain on the case until it was terminated. The relative ages of staff members and parents may have had some bearing on the ease with which rapport was established and maintained. In cases with mothers in their late thirties or older, a trusting relationship usually developed more readily with the older of the two team members. On the other hand, there seemed to be more variation among the teen-age mothers and among parents in their early twenties as to the age of the person in whom they had the greatest trust. Some young mothers related more easily to the team member closest to their own age; others seemed to prefer the older team member.

Considerable thought has been given to the relationship between the staff's attitude and emotional reaction to parent, infant, and home and the effectiveness of intervention. There were a great number of highly positive and enthusiastic reactions to parents and infants and a few negative reactions to particular parents or to aspects of the home situation. The staff's emotional reactions to the infant ranged from very positive ones to relatively neutral ones, like "Not a very 'interesting' baby," or "I find it difficult to become involved with that infant." There appeared to be a surprisingly strong relationship between positive feelings of staff toward parents and effective intervention. There is no doubt that the relationship between parental responsiveness to intervention and staff reaction to parents was a reciprocal one, and that the staff's positive reaction to the parent was both an antecedent to and consequence of parental responsiveness to the staff and to their intervention efforts. It is less clear whether a relationship existed between staff reaction to the infant and effectiveness of intervention. One could hypothesize that infant behavior that has a negative effect on the adult, like unresponsiveness, may be viewed by staff as a challenge to their intervention skills. On the other hand, similar behavior on the part of the parent, like unresponsiveness of the parent to intervention, may be more threatening to staff self-esteem.

WORKING WITH PARENTS OF
HANDICAPPED INFANTS: CLINICAL OBSERVATIONS

Although this book is intended for those who work with parents and infants regardless of the specific characteristics of the population, there are some issues that are of particular concern to individuals who work with parents of infants with identifiable handicaps. It seems important to address some of these particular issues within the framework of the interaction approach.

Professionals who work in programs for handicapped infants often witness what parents go through as they attempt to cope with the difficult reality of having a handicapped child. It is important for the infant specialist, who usually is in continuous contact with parent and infant, to be aware of the emotional upheaval that parents experience. This awareness can help the infant specialist to decide the kind of help and support a parent might need at a particular time.

Many parents of handicapped infants may first go through a period of denying that there is anything wrong with their child. Or, they may believe that the child will outgrow what appears to be only a temporary problem. This denial is at times followed by feelings of guilt and anger and a period of mourning for the normal child that the parents had expected but did not get. In some cases the parents may become seriously depressed. When a parent emerges from this most difficult phase, a serious attempt is usually made to face the task of meeting the child's general and special needs. When the mother is the primary caregiver who spends long hours daily with the infant, she tends to move through this emotional turmoil more rapidly than does the infant's father, who may have had less intense daily contact and less continuous deep emotional involvement with the infant from the start. It sometimes happens that by the time the father becomes depressed, the mother may already have reached the next stage, that of confronting the child's problem and attempting to cope with the care of the child. If each parent can be helped to understand what the other is going through at a particular time, additional stress on the marital relationship can sometimes be averted (the event of a handicapped child often places considerable strain on a marriage). Therefore, it may be important that the father and mother, as well as other family members, have opportunities for contact with individual members of the medical and intervention staff and, of course, with the social worker if one is available. When the parents can share these experiences with each other, it may lessen the temporal gap in their emotional states.[1]

Parents' perceptions of their handicapped infants change as their emotional state changes. Their perceptions of the child at a particular time largely determine the priority of their concerns. It is always important to "tune in" to a parent's perception of the child so that, if necessary, one can help the parent gradually to expand that perception. In working with the parent of a handicapped child, the staff found it essential to know and understand how the parent perceives the child at a particular time. How the parent sees her handicapped infant is often colored by her continuing ambivalent feelings as well as by contradictory and confusing messages that she may receive from professionals of various disciplines. However, these perceptions are the parent's current reality with regard to her child, and therefore they must serve as the starting point for working with the parent in an intervention program.

---

[1]Many but certainly *not all* parents go through these states. Some parents show neither denial nor depression. The reference to "*many* parents" is deliberate; it should *not* be taken to signify "*most* parents."

Focus on Strengths

Unfortunately, a large number of parents of handicapped infants are at first so preoccupied with the handicapping condition or deficit that they cannot discern the *child* "behind the handicap." When one accepts the parent's perception of the child as a starting point for intervention, and if that parent is almost exclusively focused on what the child *cannot* do, the challenge to the intervention staff is to begin with the parent's focus on the child's deficits and gradually help her to see those deficits in relation to the "whole child" and in the context of how the child functions in every area of behavior. But first, the staff must acknowledge the parent's concerns, offer help with those problems which lie within the staff's expertise, and refer the parent and child to other appropriate resources and professionals as needed. If the staff tries to move the parent too rapidly away from her concerns and toward the infant's strengths (which the parent may have difficulty seeing at first), the parent may lose trust in the staff and turn elsewhere for help that is focused only on the child's handicap. While offering the kind of help the parent is seeking (directly or indirectly), the staff at the same time can help the parent see the things the child *can* do. Gradually, the parent is likely to understand the importance of helping the child to develop optimally in areas in which he functions normally or in which he functions at least more efficiently than he does in the areas of his most severe deficits. The parent can gradually be helped to appreciate and, at times, support the child's natural propensity to compensate for his deficits.

Through joint staff-parent observations and discussions, the parent will be able to become more aware of the infant's strengths and to recognize and learn about the many ways in which she can help the child build on these strengths so that he can function optimally within the constraints imposed by his handicap. For example, if the child is hemiplegic and therefore has normal use of one hand and one leg, it is important for the parent to learn to recognize how much the child *can* do with the "good" hand. The parent can be helped to be sensitive to the child's interest in activity with the normally functioning parts of his body so that she will provide opportunities for him to engage in spontaneous play, to increase his skills, and to experience pleasure in success, all of which are vital to his self-esteem. As the child increasingly shows pleasure in his activities and as the parent begins to value his pleasure and his successes, the positive interaction between parent and child will tend to perpetuate the parent's responsiveness to the child. The staff can also model for the parent that focusing on the child's strengths in interactions with him often motivates the child to attempt new things in the area of his deficit, e.g., giving the hemiplegic child an interesting toy that requires the use of both hands will motivate the child, who enjoys spontaneous play, to use both hands (one hand for steadying the object) without being prodded by the adult to use the "tight" hand. The staff's repeated comments on what the child is doing and their interpreting to the parent why he is doing it will eventually help the parent to acknowledge and appreciate some of the child's accomplishments.

Another helpful avenue toward expanding the parent's focus is to stress the interrelatedness of various developmental areas. Activities that are seemingly unrelated to the child's problem can be explained in terms of their benefits for the child's handicap, e.g., "Playing social games will help him develop language; he focuses on you and listens to the rhythm of the language," or "We are showing him a variety of interesting toys—often children will move toward a toy if it intrigues them." While at first the parent may see these activities only as a means to accomplish something in the problem area, she will gradually come to appreciate her child's abilities and strengths on their own merit. As she learns to recognize the child's strengths, the parent is more likely to be able to enjoy her child. Too often parents of handicapped children are so overwhelmed by the situation and so intent on finding ways of ameliorating the "problem" that they cannot enjoy being with their child. The staff can try to find and model activities that fit into the parent's style and that are enjoyable to both parent and child.

Importance of Self-Confidence in Parenting

Parents of handicapped children often lack confidence in themselves as parents. They have had to relinquish the responsibility for decision making about the child to the medical profession, and they have come to feel that only experts know how to deal with the child properly. In addition, the handicapped child often gives unclear cues about his needs. Consequently, the parents find it difficult to decide what their child's needs are, and they do not trust their intuitions. As a result, parents of handicapped children are particularly likely to want to turn to the staff as experts who have the answers to their questions and the solutions to their problems.[2] The staff has to work toward helping the parent see that she is the one who knows her child best, and the staff can point out to the parent the ways in which she is helping her child. The parent needs to gain confidence in her own decision-making power in the face of much professional advice. She is the one closest to the child and she has the greatest impact on his life and behavior. Once the parent feels confident in her role as parent and is able

---

[2]This tendency to look to professional staff for "expert" advice is also common among parents of newborn high risk infants after the infants are discharged from long hospitalizations. The "professionals" have cared for the infant for so long that the parent does not at first trust herself as a caregiver.

to enjoy her child, a good foundation is laid, regardless of the child's problem.

Not only must the parent be helped to recognize what she is doing well, but she must also be helped to appraise realistically the difficulties that her child presents. Many parents feel that their child's difficulties stem from their ineptness as parents—that the child would be better off if the parents had only tried harder or had done the "right" things from the start. Often, the most effective way to boost a parent's confidence and to relieve her of the burden of guilt is to have the staff share with her that they, too, find the child difficult to deal with in many ways. By talking about the patience that is required to work with the child and the many attempts at new activities that are necessary before one is successful, the staff can free the parent to talk about her own failures with the child—failures that may be causing her guilt feelings. The parent may gradually understand that her failures are not the result of her "incompetence," but are the result of her having a difficult child. With the staff's support she is encouraged to continue interacting with the child despite the difficulties. Just knowing that somebody understands and even experiences, in part, what she has to contend with helps the parent to continue her efforts with the child until he becomes more rewarding to be with. After that, the parent-child interactions will be reciprocally reinforcing. Intervention will have accomplished much when the parent is able to perceive her child as an individual with both strengths and problems rather than as a child who is hopelessly limited by his handicap.

Coping with the Reality of a Handicap

Many parents look long and hard for someone who can help them with their child before they settle into a program. When the parents begin to trust the staff and when they feel that both the child and they themselves are accepted, a kind of euphoria sometimes sets in temporarily. Finding a satisfactory program for their child is a tremendously important event for the parents. In addition to feeling a sense of relief at having found the program, parents sometimes fantasize that the program and its knowledgeable staff of specialists might make the child well again or "cure" him. A well-meaning physical or occupational therapist or other specialist may inadvertently reinforce this fantasy about the child becoming cured when they emphasize the importance of having their directions followed regarding exercises and "physical therapy" to be administered by the parent to the child in the home. When staff members become aware of the parent's euphoria regarding the child, they often begin to worry and feel that the parent should be faced with "the truth" about the child. At a time like this it would help the staff to recall that, after denying the handicap, mourning the loss of the "normal" child, feeling guilty, angry, and depressed, and seeking diagnoses and help, the parent may need a reprieve from these draining experiences and debilitating emotions. A mild and temporary euphoria under these circumstances may accompany the parent's positive feelings about having found help and being accepted. Unrealistic perceptions should not, of course, be "reinforced" by professionals under any circumstances, but there is a difference between listening without agreeing with the parent and confronting her with the "objective reality." If the parent's fantasies about the child's recovery extend over a long period and if the parent's perception of her child seems to be moving progressively away from the "reality" about the child, one then needs to be concerned about the parent's emotional state. At that point the parent may well need a psychological referral.

A related issue that frequently arises in programs for handicapped children is whether, when, and how to communicate to the parents of a moderately or severely handicapped child the present reality of the child's functioning. An even more controversial issue is how to discuss with parents or answer their questions regarding what the future may hold in store for their child. First, the accuracy of predictions by medical and related specialists, based on "clinical facts" and behavior in infancy, appears to be quite limited in relation to all but extreme cases of certain clearly diagnosable conditions like profound blindness, deafness, and severe retardation. For the remainder of the population of handicapped infants and young children, it seems to be difficult at best to make accurate predictions about potential capabilities when the child is under 3. Second, it is acknowledged in psychological and psychiatric literature that a person will only be able to profit from and accept those "facts" with which he or she can deal without "falling apart." Considering these circumstances, perhaps the greatest service an intervention staff can render a handicapped child through his parents is to do the following:

1. Support the parent's gradual progress toward coping with the idea of having a handicapped child and with the reality of caring for and living with this child
2. Help the parent see the child as he is currently, with his strengths and his deficits, and help the parent accept him for what he is and to understand what this means in terms of parenting the child
3. Enable the parent to acquire a variety of skills that will assist her both in coping with the child and in helping the child develop optimally within the limits of his potential

Parents' Perceptions as a Guide to Staff

An intervention staff is usually most helpful to the parents and to the child when they tune in to the parents' current perceptions and help them gradually to expand their perspective. Carefully guided observations and sensitive responses to the parents' questions can lead the parents toward becoming increasingly realistic about the child's strengths as well as his deficits. For example, when the parent of a child who is not likely to function beyond the trainable retarded level asks a staff member whether the child will be able to do well in a regular school setting without special help, the staff member might throw the question back to the parent, to check what her current perceptions are. If the parent says, "No, I think he will need special schooling," the staff can agree with the parent and then they can together observe and discuss the child's present behavior that seems to indicate his need of special help both now and, probably, later on. If the parent should answer affirmatively, that the child will be able to do fine in a regular classroom, the staff might not want to continue the conversation at this point, letting the parent's answer stand for the time being, but without agreeing with it. If the parent does not demand a response to her statement, it may be that she is not ready to cope at this time with the reality about her child. The staff can, however, make a mental note to observe the child with the parent and to ask her some questions about his language, his self-help and play skills at home, and his interactions with other children, thus giving the parent opportunities to see her child more realistically as she becomes ready to do so. If, however, the parent requests a response to her assertion that the child will function normally, the professional must respond honestly that she believes the child may well need special help later, just as he does now. Whether the parent is ready to discuss this issue further at that particular time will be indicated by her reaction to the statement by the professional.

The author believes that it is a disservice to give parents false hope about their child's current functioning or potential, as much as it is a disservice to tell them that there is no hope for their child. Erik Erikson has stated that often in the human condition it is only hope that makes human existence tolerable. But giving or actively supporting false hope is a deception. Most parents who have an infant who is likely to continue throughout his life to function at a very low developmental level will gradually come to realize this when they are ready to deal with it emotionally, provided that they have not been given false reassurances or forced into a "confrontation with the facts" before they were ready to deal with "objective reality." In this emotionally gruelling process, the parents will need all the help and support they can get, including that of a social worker who knows what the realistic alternatives are.

Parents need to be given time to face and cope with the day-to-day problems of living with their handicapped child. They may need help in this painful process. Prognoses, given early in the child's life, that are either overly pessimistic or unrealistically optimistic can be confusing and upsetting to the parents and often disruptive to the important process of coping and adaptation. This is an important lesson that has been learned from parents who have successfully moved through the early stages of emotional adjustment to the reality of having a handicapped child.

The integration of a few non-handicapped infants in a center-based intervention program will allow parents, while in a protective setting, gradually to gain a greater sense of reality about their child. The staff can help most effectively by being supportive as the parents begin to face the differences as well as to observe the similarities between their children and the non-handicapped children. In this kind of setting, where everything is there for them to see, the parents will usually "take in" what they can deal with—the part of "objective reality" that is useful to them at any particular time.[3]

SOME GENERALIZATIONS DERIVED
FROM INTERVENTION EXPERIENCE

A few clinical observations were sufficiently similar in a number of cases to justify the generalizations that are stated and discussed below. Although some of the content presented here is discussed in other parts of the book, its importance justifies its inclusion in concise form in this chapter.

1. Parents' Delayed Expressions of Concern

Some parents do not express their feelings of anxiety or concern about their infant until after the condition that caused the concern has lessened or disappeared and after they have come to terms with these feelings on their own. These delays in expressions of early concerns can occur even though the staff and the parents have formed a close and trusting relationship. When an infant is very sick during the neonatal period, the attending medical staff is usually aware of the parents' anxiety related to the infant's survival or their fear of permanent brain damage. Such information, or even the awareness that such fears might have existed, can help to make the intervention staff sensitive to the possible effects of these fears on parent-infant interactions. Many parents have revealed the powerful effect on them of the first medical opinion or prognosis that they receive after the birth of the baby. At that time, parents are anxious and eager for information from a reliable source, and whatever they *hear* the doctor say initially about their infant seems to be difficult to erase from their minds, regardless of what happens subsequently.

---

[3]The above observations and reflections on working with parents of handicapped infants are based on experience with parents and infants not only in the UCLA Infant Studies Project, but in other programs as well.

2. Differences between Concerns of Parents and Staff

In some cases the parents' and the staff's concerns about the infant can be quite different. For example, a parent may be worried about the timing of her infant's achievement of motor milestones, whereas the staff may be much more worried about the infant's general passivity and lack of interest in his surroundings. Therefore, the staff might want to direct the parent's efforts toward finding activities and engaging in interactions that are motivating to the infant in play and in language, as well as in movement. The awareness that the parent's efforts in the area of play would lead more quickly to observable changes and would therefore be more rewarding to the parent might reinforce the staff's wish to redirect the parent. However, it appears that a parent is not able to utilize modeling or suggestions in areas of behavior that are not of concern or interest to her. When the staff insists on working with infant and parent in such areas and fails to respond to the parent's concern, there is a danger that the parent will lose trust in the staff. Moreover, the staff may become increasingly frustrated in fruitless efforts to change the parent's focus of concern. The challenge for the staff is to find ways to be responsive to the parent's concern and, at the same time, to try to help her become more aware and interested in other areas of the infant's behavior.

3. Common Problems Related to Normal Development

Issues of concern to parents and to staff seem to arise in a fairly predictable sequence, in line with developmental changes of the infant. Following are some examples of difficulties related to the changing behavior of the infant.

At around 15 months developmental age, many parents feel at a loss in dealing with the infant's assertive and negative behavior.

In some homes, the physical safety of the infant becomes a concern of the staff when the infant begins to be mobile and especially when he starts walking. Some parents are unaware that a 15- or an 18-month-old infant does not yet have the cognitive ability to make complex judgments about what is safe for him and what is not, even if the parent tells him repeatedly to "stay out of trouble." The more obvious fact that the infant does not have the experience on which to base such a judgment is also frequently ignored.

Around the same time, when safety precautions are important, mothers' feelings of isolation tend to increase. Some mothers feel "cooped up" with the child (or children) who "gets into everything!" Helping the mothers find places in their own communities where they can take their children, such as parks, playgrounds, or mother-toddler programs, often relieves their tension.

It is desirable to help parents anticipate some of the child's behaviors that are likely to cause difficulties for them. It is often difficult, however, to help them prepare to deal with behaviors that have not yet emerged. Parents will be most likely to discuss and think about their interactions with the infant at a future stage of development in a group situation with other parents. As the parents of older children are facing problems and talk about them in the group, the parents with younger children are introduced dramatically to what might be ahead for them.

4. Play Undervalued in Infant Development

Many parents are unaware of the role and the significance of play in the infant's development. Some mothers will not allow play behavior that is age-appropriate for the infant, e.g., the child mouthing objects at 6 months or the child playing with kitchen utensils and other materials found in homes, like coasters, boxes, cartons, coffee cans with lids, etc., at 1 year of age and beyond. Intervention should help parents to focus on the importance of play as the mode in which the young child learns and develops intellectually and spontaneously discovers the pleasure of success. This valuing of play as a spontaneous activity for which most infants are naturally motivated and through which they develop cognitively is quite different from the notion that the infant has to be "taught" the skills that are listed on an infant development scale.

5. Receptive Language Undervalued in Infant Development

Most parents seem to be unaware that the infant's receptive language, that is, his understanding of language, is usually much ahead of his expressive language (speech). The notion that helping the infant to increase his understanding is at least as important as, and often more important than, developing his expressive language is difficult for some parents to accept. When parents are encouraged to report the words, phrases, and sentences that the infant responds to, without being prompted by gestures, they are usually surprised and pleased about how much the infant understands even though he is not yet talking.

6. Changing Parents' Language Patterns with Infants

Many infants who show problems or delays in any developmental area also tend to have a delay in language development. Parents usually do not become aware of language delays until their child is about 18 months of age, when the contrast between their child's language and that of other children of similar age becomes more apparent to them. Parents who fail to perceive their infant's low level of language development as a problem appear to be resistant to changing the language patterns that they use with their infants. Some parents do not talk spontaneously to their infants about things and events in the infant's immediate experience. One parent's statement reflects an attitude that prevails among some parents: "Why should I talk to him before he can talk to me?" Some parents are more likely to increase their language interaction with their child when they notice how responsive the child is as staff members talk to him while maintaining eye contact. The parents observe how much the child seems to enjoy being talked to. With sufficient modeling of pleasurable language interaction, parents will sometimes talk more with their infants or respond to the infant's vocalizations.

In contrast to the parent who talks little to her infant is the highly verbal parent who does not leave "time" or "space" for her infant to talk back. Such a parent must be helped to become aware that language develops as a reciprocal process of communication. "Bombarding the child with language," a phrase that is sometimes heard in programs for handicapped children, can be very misleading to parents.

7. Staff's Reward Is Parent's Independence

If the sharing of observations and information and the cooperative solving of problems are processes that have predominated in the interaction between staff and parent in an intervention program, the result is likely to be a parent who is growing in self-confidence, independence, and competence in parenting; who enjoys being with her child; who recognizes and is pleased by changes that signify growth; and who knows how to seek the resources that she needs for her infant, for herself, and for the family.

If, after a period of participation in a program, a parent says to the staff, "I think I am doing a pretty good job as a parent," or "I'm really getting more confident," or "I didn't know I had it in me to enjoy my child so much," or "It's been great having you to help me realize that I was really doing O.K.," the staff has reaped the rewards of the kind of intervention program that is presented in this book. If, however, the parent becomes increasingly dependent and tells the staff repeatedly that she doesn't know what she would do without their help, it may be time for the staff to re-examine the process of intervention to assess what has been done to increase rather than decrease the parent's dependence. It is certainly true that most parents who need help badly—and who are aware of this need—will go through a stage of being quite dependent on the help the program provides. However, the staff should grow concerned if the temporary dependence does not gradually change into the parent's gaining better observational skills, more resourcefulness, and, consequently, a growing self-confidence and independence.

In sum, parent-infant intervention as described in this book builds on the strengths of the parents with the expectation that parents, in turn, will build on the strengths of their children. It is intervention that enhances mutually pleasurable parent-child interaction crucial to the child's growth. It is intervention that helps parents to gain self-confidence, to become sensitive observers of their children, and to achieve increased satisfaction in their parenting role.

APPENDICES

The following pages contain Forms 1 and 2 of the Parent Behavior Progression (PBP). Form 1, applicable to parents of infants between birth and 9 months developmental age, was adapted from the original version of the PBP. Form 2, applicable to parents of children between 9 and 36 months developmental age, is an expanded version of the original instrument used in the Intervention Program described in the book. For the sake of brevity, examples for individual behaviors have been excerpted from the PBP Manual for Form 1 only.*

The levels are the same on the two forms; the differences in specific *behaviors* are greatest for levels IV through VI. It should also be noted that, even on Form 1, only a portion of the behaviors apply to parents of infants in the first few weeks of life; moreover, very few of the behaviors in levels IV through VI on Form 1 are applicable to parents of infants functioning under 5 to 6 months of age. These and other characteristics of the PBP in its present state pose problems for its use as an instrument to evaluate program effectiveness. Efforts are under way to further refine and revise this instrument, with the help of programs that are currently using it.

DIRECTIONS FOR USING THE PBP†

The PBP should be used by educational or clinical staff working with families in an ongoing program and *not* by independent evaluators from outside the program. In order to utilize this instrument in an appropriate manner, the information needed has to come from observations and conversations in the context of an ongoing relationship between parent and staff. The statements describing behaviors in the PBP should not be used as a basis for questions in a formal interview or parent conference.

The following procedures are recommended for the use of both Form 1 and Form 2 of the PBP. The staff assigned to a particular family should:

1. Carefully read the descriptions of the behaviors contained in the form of the PBP to be used.

---

*The Manual, which includes examples for both forms, and Forms 1 and 2, each with its own checklist, can be obtained by writing to the author.

†Excerpted from the PBP Manual.

2. Make several contacts with the parent and infant for the purpose of building rapport with the family, observing spontaneous parent-infant interaction, and talking informally with the parent.
3. Try to check the behaviors on the PBP for which staff members have evidence. (In contrast to other evaluation tools, the PBP is *not* intended to be filled out in the parent's presence.)

The evidence for checking a behavior on the PBP can come from what the parent says in her conversation with the staff (R or report) or from direct observations of the parent with her infant (O or observation). An O, R, or O-R after each behavior item indicates the possible source for evidence of the behavior.

There are no guidelines in the PBP that indicate the amount of evidence or the quality sufficient to give a check for a particular behavior. These judgments must be left to the staff of particular programs. Doubt as to whether behavior is clearly not part of the parent's repertoire or whether it simply has not been observed can be indicated by a question mark. A small check with slash ($\checkmark$/) can be used to alert the staff to behaviors that are only minimally present and may need to be given further support by the staff in order to improve the frequency and quality of a behavior.

The problem of obtaining accurate evidence about parenting behavior is one faced by most programs. We found we could obtain the most reliable evidence after the staff had established rapport with the family. It must be kept in mind that the PBP is the product of an intervention program based on the principles that staff must establish a relationship of mutual trust and respect with the parent, and that the staff must respect the parent's need for privacy as well as the parent's need to be in control in her own home.

Appendix A
Parent Behavior Progression (PBP) Form 1
For Parents of Infants from Birth to 9 Months Developmental Age (With Examples from the PBP Manual)

Developed by: Rose M. Bromwich, Ellen Khokha, L. Suzanne Fust, Eleanor Baxter, Dorli Burge, and E. Wallie Kass

PARENT BEHAVIORS

I. **Level i:** **The parent enjoys her infant.**

    A.   PLEASURE IN WATCHING INFANT

        1.   Parent shows or reports pleasure in watching the infant at least some of the time. (O-R)
Example: "Sometimes I like to sneak in and watch her lying in her crib."

        2.   Parent shows or reports pleasure in infant's physical appearance. (O-R)
Examples: "It tickles me that he looks so much like his grandfather," *or,* even though the mother is very much aware of the deviance of her child's physical appearance, she enjoys dressing her up.

3. Parent shows pride in the infant by ascribing to him qualities that the parent values. (R)

Examples: "She's a tough little girl. I think she's going to be somebody in this world," *or,* "Look at how he smiles at the girls already. He's going to be a real ladies' man."

4. Parent spontaneously talks about the things the infant does that please her. (R)

Examples: "She looks up when I come in the room. I think she knows me!" *or,* "It feels so good when he snuggles in my lap and lets me rock him."

5. Parent shows or reports pleasure in watching the infant respond pleasurably to other adults or children. (O-R)[1]

Examples: "He gets so excited when his Daddy comes home," *or,* "It's so funny when she crawls right over to her brother and tries to get into his activity."

6. Parent shows or reports pleasure in watching infant play. (O-R)

Example: "I notice that she can really kick her mobile to get it to move now. That's really exciting."

7. Parent shows or reports pleasure in infant's *enjoyment of his own activities.* (O-R)

Examples: Mother smiles when she hears baby squeal with joy, *or,* "I love when he gets all excited and happy in his bathtub!"

B. PLEASURE IN PROXIMITY—INCLUDING PHYSICAL CONTACT

8. Parent gives evidence of enjoying the presence of her infant—having the infant near her. (O-R)

Example: Mother says she puts the infant in his seat on the counter while she does the dishes because she likes to have him with her, *or,* Mother brings baby from his crib so he can play in the room where she is conversing with the visitor—she smiles at baby frequently.

9. Parent reports that she looks forward to doing something with her infant (not necessarily alone with infant—others may be present also). (R)

Examples: "I really enjoy taking him to my mom's where everybody fusses over him," *or,* "I get impatient for her to wake up from her nap so we can take a walk together."

---

[1]Behaviors 5, 6, and 7 should not be expected to appear until the baby begins to smile or show pleasure in some manner.

10. Parent gives evidence that she enjoys physical contact with infant (without necessarily playing with him). (O-R)
Examples: Mother smiles as she reaches over and touches her baby who is lying next to her on the couch, *or,* Mother spontaneously picks up her baby, hugs him and holds him on her lap for a few minutes.

11. Parent gives evidence that she enjoys some aspects of the physical care of the infant. (O-R)
Examples: Mother gazes contentedly at baby while she is feeding him, *or,* "It's fun bathing him even though he is so floppy and I have to hold his head up."

C. PLEASURE IN INTERACTION

12. Parent seeks eye contact with her infant much of the time when she is attending to him. (O)
Example: While changing infant's diapers, mother looks into his face as she softly talks to him.

13. Parent gives evidence that she enjoys engaging in some type of play or playful interaction with her infant, even if only on her terms—physically, vocally, or with toys. (O-R)
Examples: After her infant wakes up, mother plays peek-a-boo with him through the bars of the crib before picking him up, *or,* Mother smiles at her baby, tickles him lightly even though this delayed baby responds with a quizzical look (unclear cue).

II. **Level ii: The parent is a sensitive observer of her infant, reads his behavioral cues accurately, and is responsive to them.**[2]

A. READING BIOLOGICAL CUES

1. Parent is able to read the infant's signals of distress (crying, whimpering, fussing). (O-R)
Examples: "That's his 'Hurry up, I'm starving' cry," *or,* Mother reports she's beginning to distinguish when her baby is hungry and when he's just fussy because he's tired.

2. Parent gives evidence of knowing the infant's biological rhythms with respect to sleeping, eating, elimination. (R)
Examples: "I can always count on his having a BM right after his morning nap," *or,* "I can't plan her feed-

---

[2]If a behavior is checked in section D, a corresponding behavior should be checked in section A, B, or C. The reason for this is that a *response* to a cue (D) signifies the prior *reading* of that cue (A, B, or C).

ing schedule too tightly because she doesn't always get
hungry at the same time every day.''

3. Parent recognizes signs indicating whether the infant is
safe and comfortable (satiated but not too full, physically
secure, comfortably warm). (O-R)
Examples: Father reports his baby seems happier when
he holds him snugly, *or*, ''Very often she'll stop sucking
and look all around, but I know she'll come back for
more in a few minutes.''

B.   READING INFANT'S SOCIAL-AFFECTIVE
AND TEMPERAMENTAL CUES

4. Parent reports on the infant's responses to herself and to
others. (R)
Example: ''She always seems to quiet down when
someone talks to her.''

5. Parent makes reference to infant's temperamental and
behavioral characteristics, i.e., attentiveness, physical
vigor, intensity, reaction to change, etc. (R)
Examples: ''She really stares at that new mobile I put
up over her crib'' (attentiveness); *or*, ''When she laughs,
I can hear it in the next room!'' (intensity); *or*, ''Every
time I give her a new food, she spits it out'' (reaction to
change); *or*, ''Unlike his sister who is always in motion,
he enjoys sitting in one spot exploring a toy'' (activity
level).

C.   READING INFANT'S RESPONSE TO ENVIRONMENTAL STIMULATION

6. Parent reports details of the infant's response to his physical environment. (R)
Examples: ''The baby likes going for a ride—he stops
crying the minute the car starts moving,'' *or*, ''She sleeps
anywhere as long as she has her blanket.''

7. Parent talks about the amount of stimulation the infant
can handle and profit from. (R)
Examples: ''She gets fussy when the TV is on and there
is a lot of commotion around,'' *or*, ''My first baby just
loved when his father used to 'roughhouse' with him, but
this one doesn't like it at all—she starts crying,'' *or*, ''I
have to try to remember to go in and play with him occasionally because he hardly ever asks for attention. It
would be so easy to let him lie in his crib all day but I feel
he needs *some* stimulation.''

D. RESPONDING TO INFANT'S NEEDS AND CUES

8. Parent adapts caretaking practices in response to infant's cues related to his biological needs. (O-R)
Examples: "I put her down a little early because she seemed sleepy," or, "He seems quite happy playing past his usual lunchtime—so I've been feeding him a little later," or, "The medication they prescribed for my baby makes him sleepy so I try to give it to him when it won't interfere with his interest in eating."

9. Parent is responsive to infant's changes in state or mood. (Exception: When an infant has unusual difficulty in inhibiting crying, the parent would not be expected to show sensitivity to his crying behavior.) (O-R)
Examples: When the baby begins to fuss, the mother goes to him, changes his position, and talks to him soothingly, or, When the baby makes little noises and moves around in his crib after waking up, the father takes him out of the crib.

10. Parent adapts the amount and intensity of stimulation to what the infant can handle and profit from. (O-R)
Examples: When the baby gets restless in the same room as siblings watching a loud TV program, mother puts baby in a quieter part of the house and calms him, or, Mother puts her passive, motorically delayed baby in the middle of the living room where she enjoys being "part of the action."

11. Parent takes into account infant's level of development and behavior in providing for his safety. (O-R)
Examples: Parent removes fork from baby's reach and substitutes a short wooden spoon, or, When baby is able to turn over, mother takes him off the bed and puts him on the floor while she goes to answer the phone, or, Mother reports that when the baby began to crawl, she covered the electrical outlets and kept household chemicals out of reach.

III. **Level iii: The parent engages in a quality and quantity of interaction with her infant that is *mutually* satisfying and that provides opportunity for the development of attachment.**

A. PARENT OR STABLE CAREGIVER TIME WITH INFANT.

1. Parent provides situation with some stability of caregiving where the same adult(s) cares for the infant during his wakeful periods of the day. (O-R)

2. Parent plans her day or the infant's day so that she can spend time with him giving some attention to him during his waking hours (not necessarily in interaction or alone with him). (O-R)

    Examples: "I try to do some of my housework while the baby is asleep so that I can spend more time with him while he's awake," *or,* "My baby doesn't seem to mind that I wake him up a little earlier in the morning so that I can spend some time with him before I go to work."

B.   MUTUALITY OF ENJOYMENT IN INTERACTION[3]

3. Parent and infant enjoy spending time in each other's company (not necessarily engaged in an activity with each other). (R)

    Example: "I really get a feeling that she enjoys watching me, and I enjoy having her in the same room with me."

4. Parent and infant interact pleasurably during some caretaking routine. (O-R)

    Example: "When I diaper her she stares at me with those big eyes and I make little sounds. Pretty soon she starts smiling and that really makes my day!"

5. Some non-caretaking interactions between parent and infant give pleasure to both. (O-R)

    Example: "I love to kiss his tummy and I know he loves it too because he laughs out loud."

6. Some *pleasurable interactions* are initiated by parent, some by infant. (Exception: In cases where infant is very unresponsive socially, sometimes to the point of deviance, parent learns to initiate interaction, does it steadily, and is credited with this item.) (O-R)

7. Sequences or chains of pleasurable interactions between parent and infant suggest mutuality in the relationship. (O-R)

    Examples: Baby coos, mother nuzzles baby, baby coos back, etc. . ., *or,* Mother moves her head to side, baby follows visually and smiles, mother moves head to other side, etc. . . .

---

[3]The seven behaviors listed under section B are not usually expected to appear until the infant is approximately 4 months developmentally. By that time, most infants will have behaviors such as smiling, cooing, and babbling to show pleasure.

IV. **Level iv: Parent demonstrates an awareness of materials, activities, and experiences suitable for her infant's current stage of development.**

A.   PROVIDING AND STRUCTURING ENVIRONMENT
FOR SATISFYING EXPERIENCES

1.   Parent provides environment in which infant can engage safely in motor activity at his skill level. (O-R)
Example: Mother lets her infant climb up and down the doorstep while she watches him.

2.   Parent positions infant to allow wide range of vision and movement (young or handicapped infant). (O-R)
Examples: Parent puts wide-awake young infant, who cannot lift his head, on his back so that he can follow visually and move his limbs, *or,* Mother props up infant with delayed motor development against pillows in a sitting position in corner of couch to enable him to move his arms freely and have a wide field of vision.

3.   Parent provides for some variety in the infant's physical and social environment. (O-R)
Examples: Parent puts infant outdoors where he can watch his father do the gardening, *or,* "I take him to the park quite often where he likes to watch the children play."

4.   Parent provides the kind of space for the infant that he needs for his level of play. (O-R)
Examples: "I put an old bedspread on the floor in the corner and she loves playing there with her things," *or,* Parent seats 8-month-old motorically handicapped infant comfortably in a high chair (thus providing a play platform) to allow him to use his hands freely with safe objects.

5.   Parent provides materials (not necessarily toys) at infant's skill level for adaptive play. (O)
Examples: Mother gives baby an object that he can mouth, hold, bang, or shake, *or,* Mother gives 8-month-old baby cereal and finger foods he can practice picking up.

6.   Parent allows infant to mouth, touch, or play with a variety of things he discovers around him. (O)
Example: Mother allows baby to crumple pages in an old magazine that he finds on a low shelf.

7. Parent gives infant access to sufficient play materials to lead to profitable play and removes materials not of interest to him. (O-R)
    Examples: Mother of 6-month-old hangs a plastic mirror on side of playpen and removes some of the stuffed animals, *or,* Mother of a blind infant consistently places some favorite materials where her baby plays so he can count on finding them in the same spot.

B.   INTERACTING WITH INFANT TO ENHANCE HIS PLAY

8. Parent is aware of infant's tempo in play and paces appropriately. (O)
    Examples: Mother allows infant time to play with object in which he shows interest before giving him another one, *or,* Mother of a passive, slow baby is animated and vigorous in her play with him, without being overwhelming.
9. Parent facilitates the infant's play with objects. (O)
    Examples: When baby drops rattle, mother puts it within reach, *or,* When mother realizes baby is unable to grasp a toy that he wants, she helps him hold it.

C.   PROVIDING FOR LANGUAGE EXPERIENCE

10. Parent responds to infant's sounds. (O-R)
    Examples: Mother smiles at baby when he babbles, *or,* Mother imitates baby's sounds.
11. Parent talks, sings, or hums to infant even if he does not give a vocal response. (O-R)
    Example: Parent of deaf child makes certain to have face-to-face contact while talking and signing to him.

D.   ENCOURAGING SOCIAL-EMOTIONAL GROWTH

12. Parent deals with infant in an affirmative manner the majority of the time. (O)
13. Parent accepts attachment and separation behaviors and responds to them appropriately. (O-R)
    Examples: Seven-month-old infant whimpers when mother steps out of his sight—mother talks to him in a reassuring manner; *or,* Mother explains that her baby seems to warm up faster to a visitor when she can sit on mother's lap for a while; *or,* "I know Grandpa doesn't like it when Tammy won't go to him right away, but that's just the way she is right now"; *or,* Mother places

her visually handicapped infant so he can easily have physical contact with her in an unfamiliar situation.

V. **Level v: The parent initiates new play activities and experiences based on principles that she has internalized from her own experience, or on the same principles as activities suggested to or modeled for her.**

A.   PROVIDING MORE EFFECTIVELY FOR COGNITIVE (PLAY), LANGUAGE, AND SOCIAL LEARNING

1. Parent provides infant with a variety of developmentally appropriate materials for different sense modalities and which encourage different schemas, e.g., holding, shaking, exploring visually, banging. (O-R)
Examples: Mother makes texture ball out of different cloths for baby to feel, *or*, Mother puts bell on a favorite stuffed animal.

2. Parent enhances the quality of play and the infant's satisfaction from it by introducing alternative ways of using materials. (O-R)
Example: Parent of infant who only mouths objects puts her hand around his and helps him shake his rattle.

3. Parent finds ways of increasing the infant's interest level by the way she organizes play materials or situations. (O-R)
Examples: For baby that seems distracted by lots of stimulation, mother removes other toys before presenting new ones; *or*, Infant is intrigued when mother places an old toy in a pot with a lid.

4. Parent modifies her style of verbal communication with infant as she observes his differential responses to different kinds of language. (O-R)
Examples: Mother observes that infant calms down when grandmother talks to him with her soft and slow voice. Mother uses this kind of speech later when she puts him to bed; *or*, Mother shifts her baby's position so that he can see her face when she notices this increases his interest in her language; *or*, Mother experiments with ways to get her handicapped baby with a language delay to vocalize.

5. Parent begins to differentiate between those infant behaviors that she should try to modify and those she should adapt to as she looks for a comfortable modus

vivendi for herself with the baby. She experiments with ways of making some of the infant's behavior more tolerable for her without restricting him unnecessarily. (O-R) Example: Mother can't tolerate baby's banging toys on metal high chair tray; she covers tray with a piece of cloth. When baby removes the cloth, mother replaces hard toy with a softer one (one that will still make some noise, so that the infant gets some satisfaction from banging it).

VI. **Level vi: The parent independently generates a wide range of developmentally appropriate activities and experiences, interesting to the infant, in familiar and in new situations and at new levels of the infant's development.**

A. ANTICIPATING NEXT STEPS IN DEVELOPMENT

1. Parent keeps pace with her infant's changing skills and interests and plans activities that will continue to challenge him. (O-R)
   Examples: "She's been kicking pretty hard while lying on her back; I'll attach a cradle gym to her crib and soon she will be able to touch it with her feet and make things move," *or,* Mother observes infant's attention to consequence of his banging an object and gets him a cause-effect toy.

2. Parent anticipates infant's changing responses to people and places, and plans ahead to try to meet his emerging needs. (O-R)[4]
   Examples: "It is getting harder for him to sleep just anywhere, so I will take along his blanket and other familiar things when we go places," *or,* "I know he'll enjoy going over to my sister's again when he gets over this 'clingy stage,' but in the meantime, I'm not going to leave him there without me."

B. CONSIDERING THE INFANT IN CONTEXT OF FAMILY

3. Parent recognizes infant's interest in watching family social interactions and finds ways to include him more and more in family activities; she encourages other family members to do the same. (O-R)
   Examples: Mother allows 4-year-old sibling to help feed the baby even though it takes a little longer, *or,*

---

[4]Not applicable to parent of infant before 6 months developmental age.

Mother pulls baby's high chair to table while the rest of the family eats.

4. Parent tries to respond in a balanced manner to the infant's needs as well as her own and those of the rest of the family. (O-R)

    Examples: Mother does not allow infant to chew on sibling's favorite toy; *or,* Mother contacts nearby community college to find someone capable of taking care of her young infant so she can get some time for herself and with her husband on a regular basis; *or,* "It's very difficult for me to leave my handicapped baby with a sitter because he cries so hard—but I feel I have to get him to feel comfortable with someone other than myself"; *or,* Infant begins dropping his food on the floor. Mother can't change his behavior so she spreads newspaper under and around his chair when he eats; *or,* Mother allows infant a few minutes to find his fingers to suck before going in to comfort him at night; *or,* Mother finds she can shorten the time it takes for baby to relax and fall asleep if she bathes him just before putting him down.

5. Parent exercises her own judgment before following suggestions of other "experts" (pediatricians, relatives, peer group, books for parents, etc.). (R)

    Examples: "My mother-in-law can't understand why I let him make such a mess but I enjoy watching him try to feed himself"; *or,* "All my friends think I'm crazy not to have gone back to work yet, but I want to take the time to find a really good sitter for her"; *or,* Grandmother advises mother to begin feeding the baby cereal at 6 weeks, but mother senses that he is quite satisfied with breast milk, and so postpones solids until baby is a little older.

Form 1

BEHAVIOR CHECKLIST
PBP-Form 1

Caregiver _____   Checked by _____
Date _____

Level i	Level ii	Level iii

A. Pleasure in Watching Infant

$\overline{1}$ $\overline{2}$ $\overline{3}$ $\overline{4}$ $\overline{5}$ $\overline{6}$ $\overline{7}$

B. Pleasure in Proximity

$\overline{8}$ $\overline{9}$ $\overline{10}$ $\overline{11}$

C. Pleasure in Interaction

$\overline{12}$ $\overline{13}$

A. Reading Biological Cues

$\overline{1}$ $\overline{2}$ $\overline{3}$

B. Reading Social-Affective and
Temperamental Cues

$\overline{4}$ $\overline{5}$

C. Reading Responses to Environmental Stimulation

$\overline{6}$ $\overline{7}$

D. Responding to Cues

$\overline{8}$ $\overline{9}$ $\overline{10}$ $\overline{11}$

A. Parent or Stable Caregiver Time
with Infant

$\overline{1}$ $\overline{2}$

B. Mutuality of Enjoyment in Interaction

$\overline{3}$ $\overline{4}$ $\overline{5}$ $\overline{6}$ $\overline{7}$

Level iv	Level v	Level vi

A. Providing and Structuring Environment for Satisfying Experiences

$\overline{1}$ $\overline{2}$ $\overline{3}$ $\overline{4}$ $\overline{5}$ $\overline{6}$ $\overline{7}$

B. Interacting with Infant to Enhance
his Play

$\overline{8}$ $\overline{9}$

C. Providing for Language Experience

$\overline{10}$ $\overline{11}$

D. Encouraging Social-
Emotional Growth

$\overline{12}$ $\overline{13}$

A. Providing more Effectively for
Cognitive (Play), Language
and Social Learning

$\overline{1}$ $\overline{2}$ $\overline{3}$ $\overline{4}$ $\overline{5}$

A. Anticipating Next Steps in
Development

$\overline{1}$ $\overline{2}$

B. Considering the Infant in
Context of Family

$\overline{3}$ $\overline{4}$ $\overline{5}$

Appendix **B**

Parent Behavior Progression (PBP) Form 2

For Parents of Infants between 9 and 36 Months Developmental Age

Developed by: Rose M. Bromwich, E. Wallie Kass, Ellen Khokha, Eleanor Baxter, Dorli Burge, and L. Suzanne Fust

PARENT BEHAVIORS

I. **Level I: The parent enjoys her infant.**

    A. PLEASURE IN WATCHING INFANT

       1. Parent shows or reports pleasure in watching infant at least some of the time. (O-R)

       2. Parent shows or reports pleasure in infant's physical appearance or attributes. (O-R)

       3. Parent shows pride in the infant in connection with some area of his behavior; ascribes qualities to him that parent values. (O-R)

       4. Parent spontaneously talks about the things her infant does that please her. (R)

       5. Parent shows or reports pleasure in watching infant play with other caregiver or other adults. (O-R)

       6. Parent shows or reports pleasure in watching infant play by himself or with other infants or children. (O-R)

       7. Parent shows or reports pleasure in infant's *enjoyment of his own activities.* (O-R)

B. PLEASURE IN PROXIMITY—INCLUDING PHYSICAL CONTACT

8. Parent gives evidence of enjoying presence of infant —having infant near her. (O-R)

9. Parent reports that she looks forward to and enjoys doing something with her infant (not necessarily only with infant—others may be present). (R)

10. Parent gives evidence that she enjoys physical contact with infant (without necessarily "playing" with him). (O-R)

11. Parent gives evidence that she enjoys some aspects of the physical care of the infant. (O-R)

C. PLEASURE IN PLAYFUL OR PLAY INTERACTION

12. Parent gives evidence that she enjoys engaging in some type of play or playful interaction with her infant, even if only on her terms—physically, vocally, or with toys. (O-R)

II. **Level II: The parent is a sensitive observer of her infant, reads his behavioral cues accurately, and is responsive to them.**[1]

A. READING BIOLOGICAL CUES

1. Parent is able to read or interpret the infant's signals of distress (crying, whimpering, fussing). (O-R)

2. Parent gives evidence of knowing the infant's biological rhythms with respect to sleeping, eating, elimination. (O-R)

3. Parent recognizes signs indicating whether the infant is safe, comfortable, and feeling well. (O-R)

B. READING SOCIAL-AFFECTIVE AND TEMPERAMENTAL CUES

4. Parent reports on infant's responses to herself and to others. (R)

5. Parent is sensitive to infant's changes in mood and feelings. (O-R)

6. Parent makes reference to infant's temperamental and behavioral characteristics, i.e., vigor, attention span, reaction to changes, speed of response, etc. (R)

---

[1] If a behavior is checked in section D, a corresponding behavior should be checked in section A, B, or C. The reason for this is that a *response* to a cue (D) signifies the prior *reading* of that cue (A, B, or C).

C.   READING INFANT'S RESPONSE TO ENVIRONMENTAL STIMULATION

7.   Parent reports details in infant's response to his physical environment. (R)
8.   Parent shows awareness of the amount of stimulation infant can handle and profit from. (O-R)

D.   RESPONDING TO INFANT'S NEEDS AND CUES

9.   Parent adapts caretaking practices in response to infant's cues related to his biological needs. (O-R)
10.   Parent is responsive to infant's current interest in being with particular members of the household. (O-R)
11.   Parent is responsive to infant's changes in mood and feelings. (O-R)
12.   Parent adapts the kind, amount, and intensity of stimulation to what the infant can handle and profit from. (O-R)
13.   Parent takes into account the infant's level of development and behavior in providing for his safety. (O-R)

III.   **Level III: The parent engages in a quality and quantity of interaction with her infant that is *mutually* satisfying and that provides opportunity for the development of attachment.**

A.   PARENT OR STABLE CAREGIVER TIME WITH INFANT

1.   Parent provides stable situation where the same adult(s) cares for the infant during his wakeful periods of the day. (O-R)
2.   Parent plans her day so that she can spend time with the infant, giving some of her attention to him during his waking hours (not necessarily in interaction or alone with him). (O-R)
3.   Parent finds some "special time" during the day that she spends just with the infant (in addition to caretaking). (R)

B.   MUTUALITY OF ENJOYMENT IN INTERACTION

4.   Parent and infant enjoy spending time in each other's company (not necessarily engaged in an activity with each other). (R)
5.   Parent and infant interact pleasurably during some caretaking routine. (O-R)
6.   Some non-caretaking interactions between parent and infant give pleasure to both. (O-R)
7.   Parent selects things for her and the infant to do together that both enjoy. (O-R)

8. Some *pleasurable interactions* are initiated by parent, some by infant. (Exception: In cases where the infant is very unresponsive socially, sometimes to the point of deviance, parent learns to initiate interaction, does it steadily, and is credited with this item.) (O-R)

9. Sequences or chains of pleasurable interactions between parent and infant suggest mutuality in the relationship. (O-R)

IV. Level IV: Parent demonstrates an awareness of materials, activities, and experiences suitable for her infant's current stage of development.

A. PROVIDING AND STRUCTURING ENVIRONMENT FOR SATISFYING PLAY

1. Parent provides environment in which infant can engage safely in gross motor activity at his skill level. (O-R)
2. Parent provides materials (not necessarily toys) at infant's skill level for adaptive play. (O)
3. Parent provides for some variety in the infant's physical and social environment. (O-R)
4. Parent provides the kind of space for the infant that he needs for his level of play. (O-R)
5. Parent allows infant to touch or play with a variety of things he discovers around him. (O-R)
6. Parent assures infant's access to play materials in a way that makes his selection manageable and leads to profitable play experience: allows physical access, keeps parts together, excludes materials not currently of interest. (O)
7. Parent takes into account the infant's particular interests in selecting materials, activities, and experiences for him. (O-R)

B. INTERACTING WITH INFANT TO ENHANCE HIS PLAY

8. Parent is aware of infant's tempo in play and paces appropriately. (O)
9. Parent breaks down elements of task to facilitate infant's success (in play). (O)
10. Parent encourages, helps, or redirects infant when he has difficulty achieving his goal in play. (O)
11. Parent redirects unacceptable play activity predominantly in a positive manner. (O-R)

C.   PROVIDING FOR LANGUAGE EXPERIENCE

12. Parent responds to infant's language (includes vocalizations and verbalizations). (O)

13. Parent talks to infant about what he sees, hears, feels, or does (helps him connect language with what he is experiencing). (O-R)

14. Parent makes pictures and books part of infant's experience. (O)

D.   ENCOURAGING POSITIVE SOCIAL BEHAVIOR/INTERACTION

15. Parent provides opportunities for infant to develop self-help skills. (O-R)

16. Parent sets reasonable and age-appropriate limits that encourage behavior which elicits positive feedback from others. (O-R)

17. Parent deals with infant in an affirmative manner the majority of the time. (O)

18. Parent accepts attachment and separation behaviors and responds to them appropriately. (O-R)

V.   **Level V: The parent initiates new play activities and experiences based on principles that she has internalized from her own experience, or on the same principles as activities suggested to or modeled for her.**

A.   BROADENING EXPERIENCES—INCLUDING PLAY AND LANGUAGE

1. Parent provides infant with a variety of developmentally appropriate materials for different sense modalities and requiring different skills. (O-R)

2. Parent enhances the quality of play and the infant's satisfaction from it by introducing alternative and more complex ways of using materials. (O)

3. Parent finds ways of increasing the infant's interest level by the way she introduces or organizes play materials or situations. (O-R)

4. Parent now differentiates between activities that lend themselves to autonomous play and those that are more satisfying in an interactive situation with an adult. (O-R)

5. Parent adapts her language to the infant's increased complexity of receptive and expressive language. (O)

6. Parent begins to explore new situations and tries different activities to expand the infant's experience. (O-R)

B. PROVIDING MORE EFFECTIVELY FOR SOCIAL-AFFECTIVE NEEDS

7. Parent experiments with ways of dealing more effectively with infant's undesirable behavior. (O-R)
8. Parent provides opportunities for a greater variety of social experiences. (O-R)
9. Parent accepts the infant's feelings and helps him to cope with these feelings. (O-R)

VI. **Level VI: The parent independently generates a wide range of developmentally appropriate activities and experiences, interesting to the infant, in familiar and in new situations and at new levels of the infant's development.**

A. RECOGNIZING INFANT'S ABILITIES TO PROFIT FROM MORE COMPLEX EXPERIENCES

1. Parent makes everyday family activities and tasks meaningful for the infant. (O-R)
2. Parent allows infant to make choices in a variety of daily situations according to his ability to handle them. (O-R)
3. Parent keeps pace with the infant's changing play skills and interests by providing activities that are challenging to him. (O-R)

B. AIDING SOCIAL-EMOTIONAL GROWTH

4. Parent anticipates infant's responses to changes in his environment, and plans to help the infant anticipate and cope with these changes. (R)
5. Parent gives infant support *as needed* in his social encounters. (O-R)
6. Parent independently adapts her limit-setting methods of discipline to the infant's changing level of understanding and degree of self-control. (O-R)
7. Parent tries to respond in a balanced manner to the infant's needs as well as her own and those of the rest of the family. (R)

C. UTILIZING RESOURCES

8. Parent considers community resources as she anticipates the infant's social, intellectual, and physical needs. (R)
9. Parent exercises her own judgment before following suggestions of other "experts" (pediatricians, relatives, peer group, books for parents, etc.). (R)

Form 2

BEHAVIOR CHECKLIST
PBP-Form 2

Caregiver_____   Checked by_____
Date_____

Level I	Level II	Level III

A. Pleasure in Watching Infant

‾ ‾ ‾ ‾ ‾ ‾ ‾
1 2 3 4 5 6 7

B. Pleasure in Proximity

‾ ‾ ‾ ‾
8 9 10 11

C. Pleasure In Interaction

‾
12

A. Reading Biological Cues

‾ ‾ ‾
1 2 3

B. Reading Social-Affective and
Temperamental Cues

‾ ‾ ‾
4 5 6

C. Reading Response to Environmental Stimulation

‾ ‾
7 8

D. Responding to Cues

‾ ‾ ‾ ‾ ‾
9 10 11 12 13

A. Parent or Stable Caregiver Time
with Infant

‾ ‾ ‾
1 2 3

B. Mutuality of Enjoyment in Interaction

‾ ‾ ‾ ‾ ‾ ‾
4 5 6 7 8 9

Level IV	Level V	Level VI

A. Providing and Structuring Environment for Satisfying Play

‾ ‾ ‾ ‾ ‾ ‾ ‾
1 2 3 4 5 6 7

B. Interacting with Infant to Enhance
His Play

‾ ‾ ‾ ‾
8 9 10 11

C. Providing for Language Experience

‾ ‾ ‾
12 13 14

D. Encouraging Positive Social
Behavior/Interaction

‾ ‾ ‾ ‾
15 16 17 18

A. Broadening Experiences—Including Play and Language

‾ ‾ ‾ ‾ ‾ ‾
1 2 3 4 5 6

B. Providing More Effectively for
Social-Affective Needs

‾ ‾ ‾
7 8 9

A. Recognizing Infant's Abilities to
Profit from More Complex Experience

‾ ‾ ‾
1 2 3

B. Aiding Social-Emotional Growth

‾ ‾ ‾ ‾
4 5 6 7

C. Utilizing Resources

‾ ‾
8 9

LITERATURE CITED

Ainsworth, M. D. S., and Bell, S. M. 1974. Mother-infant interaction and the development of competence. In: K. Connolly and J. Bruner (eds.), The Growth of Competence. Academic Press, New York.

Ainsworth, M. D. S. 1973. The development of infant-mother attachment. In: B. M. Caldwell and H. N. Ricciuti (eds.), Review of Child Development Research, Vol. 3. University of Chicago Press, Chicago.

Beckwith, L. 1976. Caregiver-infant interaction and the development of the high risk infant. In T. Tjossem (ed.), Intervention Strategies for High Risk Infants and Young Children. University Park Press, Baltimore.

Beckwith, L., Cohen, S. E., Kopp, C. B., Parmelee, A. H., and Marcy, T. G. 1976. Caregiver-infant interaction and early cognitive development in preterm infants. Child Dev. 47:579-587.

Bell, R. Q. 1974. Contributions of human infants to caregiving and social interaction. In M. L. Lewis and L. A. Rosenblum (eds.), The Effect of the Infant on Its Caregiver. John Wiley and Sons, New York.

Bell, R. Q. 1971. Stimulus control of parent or caretaker behavior by offspring. Developmental Psychology 4:63-72.

Bloom, B. S., Hastings, J. T., and Madaus, G. F. 1971. Handbook on Formative and Summative Evaluation of Student Learning. McGraw-Hill Book Co., New York.

Brazelton, T. B., Koslowski, B., and Main, M. 1974. The origins of reciprocity. In: M. L. Lewis and L. A. Rosenblum (eds.), The Effect of the Infant on its Caregiver. John Wiley and Sons, New York.

Bromwich, R. M. 1976. Focus on maternal behavior in infant intervention. Am. J. Orthopsychiatry 46:439-446.

Bromwich, R. M. 1977. Stimulation in the first year of life? A perspective on infant development. Young Child. 32:71-82.

Bromwich, R. M., and Parmelee, A. H. 1979. In: T. M. Field, A. M. Sostek, S. Goldberg, and H. H. Shuman (eds.), Infants Born at Risk. Spectrum Publications, New York.

Bronfenbrenner, U. 1974. Is Early Intervention Effective? Department of Health, Education, and Welfare, Office of Child Development, Publication No. (OHD) 74-25, Washington, D.C.

Brown, B. (ed.). 1978. Found: Long Term Gains from Early Intervention. Westview Press, Boulder, Colorado.

Clarke-Stewart, K. A. 1977. Child Care in the Family. Academic Press, New York.

Clarke-Stewart, K. A. 1973. Interactions between mothers and their young children: characteristics and consequences. Monographs of the Society for Research on Child Development 38: no. 6 and 7. (Serial no. 153).

Fraiberg, S. 1974. Blind infants and their mothers: an examination of the sign system. In: M. Lewis and L. A. Rosenblum (eds.), The Effect of the Infant on its Caregiver. John Wiley and Sons, New York.

Gesell, A. L., and Amatruda, C. S. 1954. Developmental Diagnosis. Hoeber, New York.

Goldberg, S. 1977. Social competence in infancy: a model of parent-infant interaction. Merrill-Palmer Q. 23:163–178.

Gordon, I. J., Hanes, M., Lamme, L., Schlenker, P., and Barnett, H. 1975. Research Report of Parent Oriented Home-Based Early Childhood Education Programs. Institute for Development of Human Resources, College of Education, University of Florida, Gainesville.

Kass, E. R., Sigman, M., Bromwich, R. M., and Parmelee, A. H. 1976. Educational intervention with high risk infants. In: T. Tjossem (ed.), Intervention Strategies for High Risk Infants and Young Children. University Park Press, Baltimore.

Korner, A. F. 1974. The effect of the infant's state, level of arousal, sex and ontogenetic stage on the caregiver. In: M. Lewis and L. A. Rosenblum (eds.), The Effect of the Infant on Its Caregiver. John Wiley and Sons, New York.

Lasater, T. M., Malone, P., Ferguson, C. J., and Weisberg, P. 1976. The Birmingham Parent Child Development Center Model: Five Year Summative Report. 1970–1976. Administration for Children, Youth, and Family, Department of Health, Education, and Welfare, Washington, D.C.

Levenstein, P. 1970. Cognitive growth in preschoolers through verbal interaction with mothers. Am. J. Orthopsychiatry 40:426–432.

Matas, L., Arend, R. A., and Sroufe, L. A. 1978. Continuity of adaptation in the second year: the relationship between quality of attachment and later competence. Child Dev. 49:547–556.

Meier, J. H. 1978. Introduction. In: B. Brown (ed.), Found: Long Term Gains from Early Intervention. Westview Press, Boulder, Colorado.

Radin, N. 1972. Three degrees of maternal involvement in a preschool program: impact on mothers and children. Child Dev. 43:1355–1364.

Rutter, M. 1979. Maternal deprivation, 1972–1978: new findings, new concepts, new approaches. Child Dev. 50:283–305.

Rutter, M. 1972. Maternal Deprivation Reassessed. Penguin, Harmondsworth, Middlesex.

Rubinstein, J. L. 1967. Maternal attentiveness and subsequent exploratory behavior. Child Dev. 38:1089–1100.

Sameroff, A. J., and Chandler, M. J. 1975. Reproductive risk and the continuum of caretaking casualty. In: F. D. Horowitz, M. Hetherington, S. Scarr-Salapatek, and G. Siegels (eds.), Review of Child Development Research, Vol. 4. University Chicago Press, Chicago.

Sigman, M., and Parmelee, A. H. 1979. Longitudinal evaluation of the preterm infant. In: T. M. Field, A. M. Sostek, S. Goldberg, and H. H. Shuman (eds.), Infants Born at Risk. Spectrum Publications, New York.

Sroufe, L. A., and Waters, E. 1977. Attachment as an organizational construct. Child Dev. 48:1184–1199.

Stern, D. N. 1974. Mother and infant at play: the dyadic interaction involving facial, vocal, and gaze behaviors. In: M. L. Lewis and L. A. Rosenblum (eds.), The Effect of the Infant on Its Caregiver. John Wiley and Sons, New York.

Stevenson, M. B., and Lamb, M. E. 1979. Effects of infant sociability and the caretaking environment on infant cognitive performance. Child Dev. 50:340–349.

Thomas, A., Chess, S., and Birch, H. G. 1963. Behavioral Individuality in Early Childhood. New York University Press, New York.

Thomas, A., Chess, S., and Birch, H. G. 1968. Temperament and Behavior Disorders in Children. New York University Press, New York.

Thomas, A., and Chess, S. 1977. Temperament and Development. Brunner/Mazel, New York.

Yarrow, L. J. 1972. Attachment and dependency: a developmental perspective. In: J. L. Gewirtz (ed.), Attachment and Dependency. Winston, Washington, D.C.

Yarrow, L. J., Klein, R. P., Lomonaco, S., and Morgan, G. A. 1975. Cognitive and motivational development in early childhood. In: B. Z. Friedlander, G. M. Sterritt, and G. E. Kirk (eds.), Exceptional Infant, Vol. 3. Brunner/Mazel, New York.

Yarrow, L. J., and Pedersen, F. A. 1976. The interplay between cognition and motivation in infancy. In: M. Lewis (ed.), Origins of Intelligence. Plenum Press, New York.

Yarrow, L. J., Rubenstein, J. L., and Pedersen, F. A. 1975. Infant and Environment. John Wiley and Sons, New York.

Index